THAT AMERICAN RAG

"That American Rag"

THAT
American
RaG

The Story of Ragtime from Coast to Coast

DAVID A. JASEN

GENE JONES

SCHIRMER BOOKS

NEW YORK

Schirmer Books
An Imprint of Macmillan Library Reference USA
1633 Broadway
New York, NY 10019

Library of Congress Catalog Card Number: 99-31803

Printed in the United States of America

Printing Number 1 2 3 4 5 6 7 8 9 10

Library of Congress Cataloging-in-Publication Data
Jasen, David A.
   That American rag : the story of ragtime from coast to coast / David A. Jasen and Gene Jones.
       p. cm.
   Includes bibliographical references (p.   ) and index.
   ISBN 0-02-864743-2
   1. Ragtime music—History and criticism. I. Jones, Gene (Gordon Gene) II. Title.
ML3530.J38   1999
781.64'5—dc21   99-31803
                                                                                    CIP

This paper meets the requirements of ANSI/NISO Z.39.48-1992
(Permanence of Paper)

To my mother Gertrude Jasen, my wife Susan,
and our son Raymond

To Annie, Julie, and Christopher

and

To Robert Russell "Ragtime Bob" Darch, the world's best saloon entertainer and a tireless promoter of ragtime. For more than forty years, Bob has taken his enthusiasm for this music to all of the cities and most of the towns mentioned in this book. He digs up ragtime lore everywhere he goes, and he puts it where it will do the most good. In addition to his barroom seminars, he has made the case for ragtime at city council meetings, at chamber of commerce breakfasts, and at literally hundreds of public schools. If a town or a city has any ragtime connection at all, people know what it is after Bob has been there. Because of him, the music of many long-forgotten local composers, players, and publishers has been kept alive. He knows what time the bars close everywhere, but he will stay longer if you want to hear some more.

Other Books By

DAVID A. JASEN
Recorded Ragtime, 1897–1958
Tin Pan Alley

DAVID A. JASEN AND GENE JONES
Spreadin' Rhythm Around: Black Popular Songwriters, 1880–1930

DAVID A. JASEN AND TREBOR JAY TICHENOR
Rags and Ragtime: A Musical History

GENE JONES
Tom Turpin: His Life and Music
The Original Dixieland Jass Band

Contents

Illustrations

Acknowledgments

To begin at the beginning, we had the idea of writing about ragtime from a geographical perspective about five years ago. We are music collectors, and we have long been fascinated with the breadth of ragtime's reach across America. In our collections was ample evidence that in almost every city and in hundreds of small towns ragtime was written and published. Other books (and some theatre projects) came along, and we worked at those, with the ragtime geography idea, shapeless but still tantalizing, in the back of our minds. Then, through the help of Ann Steele, the book became possible. Ann created a complex data base in which to store publication information about ragtime. She went the extra mile—and the extra months—by entering tens of thousands of pieces of data. Suddenly, the book was doable. We could see hundreds of rags arranged in any way we wanted to see them: by town, by publisher, by composer, by date. Patterns emerged, geographical and chronological shapes presented themselves, careers could be traced at a glance. Thank you, Ann, for letting us see ragtime in literally a new way and for steering our manuscript through to completion.

The task then became to learn as much as we could about rags, composers, and publishers we'd never paid much attention to before. We needed help and lots of it, and we were fortunate to get it, from friends of ragtime as well as just plain friends. Many ragtime experts shared research with us, and some of them did new research on our behalf. The music's fans and friends set upon county and city historical societies and newspaper morgues, looking for any scraps of information about long-dead composers and long-shut presses.

Often, all we knew about a composer was the name on a piece of sheet music that had been published ninety years ago. When and where was this near-anonymous composer born? If the composer was credited by initials instead of a first name, was the composer male or female? Did the composer really live in the town where the rag was published, or was he/she just passing through? Was the publisher a piano dealer, a stationer, or a music professional? With such blanks to fill in and only shreds to go on, many of our helpers had surprising success. They sent us xeroxed obituaries and pages from city directories, pieces of locally published music, family photos, articles, and official records. Our indefatigable searchers have contributed much to ragtime lore, and we are pleased to present their findings in this book.

Trebor Tichenor, one of our greatest friends in ragtime, has generously shared his thoughts and artifacts with us. From his home base in St. Louis, he has led a true and complete ragtime life, and it has been a pleasure and inspiration to be part of it.

Another longtime ragtime friend is Dick Zimmerman. Through his *Rag Times*, first issued from Los Angeles and now from Grass Valley, he has given unswerving support to all ragtime endeavors for more than thirty years. The facts and photographs that Dick has dug up are nothing less than incredible, and his publication is the most-cited source in our bibliography.

The specialty of our friend Soloman Goodman has been crucial to our research. Sol's knack for cutting through dozens of kinds of bureaucracy has provided us with death certificates of ragtime composers and publishers from thirty states. His persistence in getting these hard-to-get documents has provided us with the most vital of vital statistics and, in the cases of many composers, the only data it is possible to gather about them, decades after they lived.

Several devoted researchers worked for us in more than one geographic area, and to them we are especially grateful. Our thanks to those who crossed state lines to help us: Galen Wilkes, Dan Grinstead, Nan Bostick, and Clifton and Jackie Tarver. Three New York actor friends, John Tillotson, Paul Blankenship, and Lanny Flaherty, had our question lists with them when show business took them out of town. David Reffkin and Stephen Kent Goodman shared their vast knowledge of band and orchestra ragtime.

T. Cat Ford saved our collective sanity by coordinating the final push in our research effort in New York. Valerie Ballard patiently gave of her time to help us format our manuscript.

Three books, all of them standard works on ragtime, were especially helpful. Each is cited in our bibliography, but we must give special thanks for the care and diligence that went into Edward A. Berlin's *King of Ragtime*, Terry Waldo's *This Is Ragtime*, and the Old Testament,

Rudi Blesh and Harriet Janis's *They All Played Ragtime*. Like all classics, they get better with every reading.

Many of our helpers were our friends, but even more of them were people who had never met us. Most of the names below are of people who simply got a letter from two strangers named Jasen and Jones, asking them to do some digging into local composers' and publishers' lives. Something—politeness, civic pride, love of music—impelled them to give hours of their time to our questions, and we will always be grateful to them. Here is our honor roll, arranged by state:

CALIFORNIA
Eric Bernhoft-San Francisco

CANADA
John Arpin-Toronto
Audrey J. Whipps Field-Vancouver

CONNECTICUT
Merrie London-Farmington

FLORIDA
Russell R. (Ray) Boyd-Atlantic Beach
Leo C. DeRuntz-Inverness

GEORGIA
Karalyn Kavanaugh-Atlanta

IDAHO
Judith C. Odmark-Boise

ILLINOIS
Dick and Doris Balzer-Moline
Mark Barnett-Evanston Historical Society
Betty Bates-Evanston

Alexis Berry-Auburn
Collins Burgener-Mowequa
Lawrence Gushee-Urbana
Martin H. Leon-Moline
Tom Riis-Chicago
Kathleen Saybee-Prairie City
Mike Schwimmer-Lake Bluff

INDIANA
George Bennett-Indianapolis
Rhoda H. Buss-West Lafayette
Maggie Jackson-Indianapolis
Bob and Sally Murphy-Indianapolis
Terry Parrish-Indianapolis
Harley W. Rhodehamel-Indianapolis

IOWA
Jim Boston-Sioux City
Roger Natte-Ft. Dodge

KANSAS
Gene DeGruson-Curator of Special Collections, Leonard H. Axe Library, Pittsburg State University
Dennis Pash-Lawrence

KENTUCKY

Ron Day-Assistant Librarian, Bell County Public Library, Pineville Branch

Anne MacFie-Stanton

Patrick and Pat Madden-Lexington

LOUISIANA

Deena S. Bedigan-Registrar, Louisiana State Museum, New Orleans

Ralph and Penny Gossard-Baton Rouge

Herman Vincent-Lake Charles

MASSACHUSETTS

Joan E. Barney-Reference Department, New Bedford Public Library

Tina V. Furtado-Archivist, Special Collections, Buttonwood Community Library, New Bedford

Mrs. Barbara Meehan-New Bedford

Phil Milstein-Boston

MICHIGAN

Martha Bloehm-Grand Rapids Public Library

Robert Bloenk-Bay City

Willard Burkhardt-Grand Rapids

Bob Milne-Lapeer

Claire O'Laughlin-Bay City Historical Society

Randall Stehle-Kalamazoo

MINNESOTA

Sarah Elizabeth Giola-Minneapolis

MISSOURI

Robert Ault-Florence

Dr. Leslie Irene Coger-Springfield

Lowell Fleenor-Springfield

Steve Hinson-St. Louis

Fred and Trudie Homan-Blue Springs

Duane and Gwen Hunt-Webb City

Janet and Tom Keller-St. Louis

Sharol Higgins Neely-Local History Associate, Springfield-Greene County Library

Jeanene Wright-Sedalia

NEBRASKA

Mrs. Janice Cleary-Omaha

NEW JERSEY

Chris Fuson-Colonia

NEW YORK

Doris Soladay-Brewerton

NORTH DAKOTA

Yvonne McDonald-Jamestown

OHIO

Ronald Crutcher-Cleveland

Ted Piskur-Lorain

Susan Talton-Berea

David M. Van Doren-Lodi

OKLAHOMA

Mitch S. Meador-Lawton

C.I. Stewart-Tulsa

PENNSYLVANIA

Jane Glogower-Pittsburgh

SOUTH DAKOTA

Helen Montgomery-Mitchell

Mary Ann O'Neill-Fulton

Mary Soladay Wipf-Mitchell

TENNESSEE

Carol Kaplan-Librarian, Nashville Room, Ben West Library

TEXAS

Bobby Alexander-Dallas

John Dawson-Dallas

John and Dixie Scogin-Sachse

WISCONSIN

James L. Hansen-Reference Librarian, State Historical Society of Wisconsin, Madison

Timothy Sandor-Superior

Judith Simonsen-Milwaukee County Historical Society

Ruby O. Thomas–Superior

Finally, a deep bow to our keen-eyed and sympathetic editor, Richard Carlin.

DAVID A. JASEN
GENE JONES

Sheet music store stock room in 1899

Introduction

Ragtime will always be popular—anywhere,
everywhere—except, perhaps, at a funeral.

AXEL CHRISTENSEN, 1914

Of all the kinds of American music from a hundred years ago, ragtime
alone continues to intrigue us on purely musical terms. Most theatre
and pop songs of this time seem only quaint artifacts now, enjoyed
more for the nostalgia they evoke than for their musical value. Only two
or three of the once-popular marches remain in our concert and media
programming. Cakewalks, "coon songs," art songs, ethnic "characteristics," "light classics," and intermezzos have all been blown away by the
winds of musical and social change. Not ragtime. It remains fresh and
exciting to modern ears, still delivering satisfaction wherever it is
heard—in a concert hall, a living room, or a bar. It doesn't need updat-
ing to make it palatable for us; it was so progressive that it is *still* progressive.

For many years, historians of popular music thought of ragtime
(when they considered it at all) as merely one of several precursors to
jazz. But the sheer musicality of ragtime has weathered all the slander
and misunderstanding and changing tastes that have followed it
through the century. Ragtime has not only endured, it has prevailed, not
as an old-timey way station to another form but as a living music.

Ragtime remains the quintessential American music: vigorous,
restless, and optimistic. It sounds like the adolescent country that produced it, a nation rushing headlong toward a new century. The distinctive sound of ragtime is, in fact, the sound of anticipation: the
syncopated leap forward, the melodic thrust that takes the ear to unex-
pected places while the foot moves to a methodical beat.

Ragtime, like every other enduring popular music, was at first considered a fad. But it was not a novelty ahead of its time: it was a novelty
in perfect sync with its time, a great invention in an era that embraced

inventions. The 1890s began an unending parade of improvements to living—electric trolleys, electric sewing machines, zippers, automobiles, ice cream cones, telephones, canned soup, the rural free delivery system (and the consequent rise of mail-order houses), subways, safety razors, moving pictures—and ragtime was the music that accompanied the parade. There were still trusts to be busted, suffrage battles to be fought, lynchings to be stopped, diseases to be checked, but at the dawn of the twentieth century, America was healthier, happier, smarter, and more confident than it had ever been. Ragtime is the expression of that confidence. In it you can hear the smile and swagger of a promised land that seemed to grow more promising every day.

Ragtime and democracy fed each other. The music drew its strength and complexity from the mix of peoples in the American stewpot, and our nation became more "American" because of its love for ragtime. The music's appeal jumped all the fences of race, class, and sex, defying the demographics that clung to every other musical expression of its day. The clichés held generally true: highbrows liked opera; lowbrows liked tearjerkers; men liked marches; women liked parlor songs; Swedes liked polkas; Latin Americans liked tangos—but, whatever his background or the height of his brow, anybody with a wide-awake musical mind could find something to enjoy in ragtime. In an age of social and cultural exclusion, ragtime said, "Come on in." It was open, friendly, inclusive.

Not only did all sorts of people want to play and listen to this good-natured music, they wanted to write it. About half of the 2,000 or so published rags were written by nonprofessionals. Housewives, clerks, druggists, photographers, lawyers, railroad men—Americans of every economic class and ethnic stripe, amateurs who had not a march or a waltz or a love song in them, were impelled to write and publish rags and to play any ragtime they came across, never mind who wrote it. Black saloon players played rags written by white middle-class shopgirls and vice versa. Syncopated America was America at its most democratic.

There were several kinds of syncopated music popular between 1897 (the year of the first published rag) and 1917 (the year of the first jazz recording), but it is *piano* ragtime that has held its appeal continuously through the ensuing decades. There were a hundred or so rags written solely for bands during the "classic rag" era, which, in comparison to those written for piano, is not many. Most of the rags played by community and professional bands were arrangements of successful—and previously published—piano rags. Likewise, banjo clubs and mandolin societies sent away to Remick, Witmark, and other publishers for string arrangements of currently popular piano rags and raggy songs. The earliest recordings of rags featured bands and banjos primarily because recording engineers of the time didn't think the sound of the piano reproduced well.

Given the wide popularity of town bands and the early band recordings of ragtime, it is obvious that string and brass ensembles played a great role in the dissemination of early rags. But in the hundreds of ragtime concerts and radio shows and the scores of ragtime festivals produced since 1960, the piano has almost always been the centerpiece of programming. Bands and banjos are often featured for their period flavor or for a change of pace, but it is the piano rag that puts the people in their seats. So this book is about ragtime written and published for the piano, the music that is the foundation of the ragtime revival that began in mid-century and that continues to this day.

THE MAIN INGREDIENT

The word that usually comes to mind at the mention of ragtime is *syncopation*, and syncopation is indeed ragtime's hallmark. But ragtime was one among several genres of syncopated music published in the late 1890s. Much of this music was tame and shallow, and some of the syncopated songs were offensive; however, because syncopation was the common thread, there was early confusion about what was truly original in ragtime. Essayists and preachers of the day, along with the "serious music" establishment, usually classified ragtime with its inferior musical kin and decried it. Only the most perceptive observers saw ragtime for the innovation that it was. It was derided variously as "whorehouse music," as simpleminded, as low-class, or as rinky-tink accompaniment to immorality of all kinds. While ragtime has long outlived its guilt by association with scandalous behavior, there is some-times still the problem of mistaken musical identity, of seeing it plain, apart from other kinds of syncopated music that have gone into and out of fashion during ragtime's first hundred years.

Syncopation is an ancient musical device, a trick that tickles the ear by putting a stress where we don't expect to hear it. In its baldest form, it is simply a rhythmic jump toward what would ordinarily be a "weak" beat in a bar of music. When we sing the first two words of the chorus of "Oh! Susanna," we are syncopating. The melody notes for the first two syllables fall exactly on the beat, aligning themselves precisely with the rhythm, where we expect to hear them fall. So does the third note. But the fourth note surprises us by breaking the pattern—"Oh, Su-san-NA"—and the surprise is syncopation. The stress is early, not where the preceding three beats have led us to expect it would be. The "rhythmic jump" is the oldest kind of syncopation in Western music, and it may be heard in Bach's Fugue in C, in Handel's "How Vain Is Man," in Beethoven's sonatas, and in Stephen Foster's songs, among many other pre-ragtime works.

In this primitive form, syncopation had been a common feature of popular music since the 1840s, used by bands and banjoists in a thou-sand minstrel shows to put the "characteristic" ethnic kick into planta-tion songs and walkarounds. When the young hustlers running Tin Pan Alley's publishing houses realized that syncopation could put a kick into anything, they began to buy and issue music full of mild jolts of misplaced meter. Syncopation, the distinctive sound of good-time songs for fifty years, became an all-purpose aural synonym for fun. Beginning in the mid-1890s, America went crazy over it.

Before we look at the various kinds of syncopation and see how rag-time uses them, let us consider what happens in a situation when rhythm really matters to us: when we are at a party or in a ballroom and are about to dance. As we move onto the floor, we quickly and instinc-tively judge the music we hear. We consider Dick Clark's perennial questions: Does it have a good beat? and Can we dance to it? The rea-son we can move to a tune we have never heard before is that we sense a regular, predictable rhythmic pattern. On hearing a few measures, we find the pattern and know what to expect—and therefore, what to do—throughout the number.

A piece can have a two-beat feel (as does a Charleston), a three-beat feel (a waltz), a four-beat feel (a blues or a ballad or, when the four beats come faster, a jitterbug number), and so on. The "strong"/regular beats are the first beat of each measure (the recurrence of which establishes the general rhythmic pattern in the listener's mind) and often—as in a blues or a fox-trot—the third beat of a four-beat measure ("Got the SAINT Louis BLUES, just as BLUE as *I* can be"). When dancing, we need rhythmic predictability, and we want no surprises. Syncopation can give the feeling of swing to dance music, but it must be simple and obvious, as predictable as the rhythm itself. It may add to our fun, but it is not what we are dancing to.

To boost the sales of rags, publishers often gave them subtitles suggesting that they were dance tunes (calling them cakewalks, two-steps, trots, and glides). Because rags have a "regular" rhythm, they can be danced to, especially if their syncopated kinks are smoothed out, in the way that most salon orchestras presented them. But ragtime was generally and primarily written for listening, not for dancing, and predictability was not its object.

Ragtime is about surprise. Its aim is to exhilarate us with a constant, teasing interplay between a steady beat and a mischievous melody. The innovation of ragtime lay in the degree and complexity of its syncopations. While earlier composers used syncopation occasionally and sparingly, ragtime writers took it as their primary ingredient. By conceiving melodies sophisticated enough to use various types of syncopation in many combinations, they created an entirely new kind of music, one that was all syncopation, all the time. Ragtime melodies dart, leap, and tease. Rags have a fluid, restless quality unlike any other music, and their restlessness comes from ceaseless syncopation.

Cakewalks are syncopated, too, but without the flow and ease of ragtime. They have a brittle sound, which comes from the fact that they are built on the "rhythmic jump" alone. There is only one syncopated trick up their sleeve, so they offer the same surprise over and over. Ragtime plays a more sophisticated game with the listener, offering a variety of syncopated effects, woven into pleasing melodic forms. The banjolike melody "jump" was part of ragtime thinking, but ragtime composers had subtler ways to syncopate as well, and they mixed them all in unending hide-and-seek with the beat.

One of ragtime's other syncopations is also simple: the iambic, dotted-eighth-and-sixteenth syncopation, which mimics the ordinary lilt of English speech ("NOTH-ing COULD be FIN-er THAN to BE in CAR-o-LI-na") and which is the most common syncopation in popular songs. There is also a three-over-four pattern of syncopation (heard in "Twelfth Street Rag" and "In the Mood"), in which the repetition of a three-note melody figure over a four-beat rhythm gives a continual shifting of accents to the melody. A fourth way to syncopate is by prolonging an unexpectedly stressed melody note, holding it longer than the listener expects to hear it (and throwing the melody-rhythm relationship further askew, thereby setting the scene for more syncopation to come). The first few measures of Joplin's "The Entertainer" contain all four types of syncopation, but no single device overrides the others.

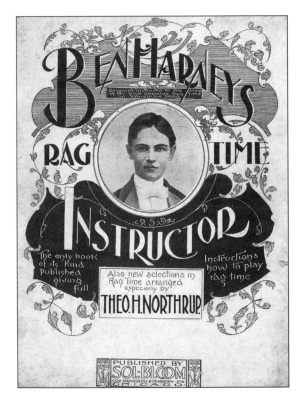

Ben Harney's Ragtime Instructor

They blend to make a satisfying melodic line, and the blend shows masterful ragtime thinking and writing.

There was "ragging" before there was ragtime. It doesn't take much more than a playful impulse to improvise a syncopated lick while playing a hymn or pop song, and pianists have long known the fun of doing so. When ragtime compositions first began to be heard, the reaction of many pianists must have been, "Why, I've been playing ragtime for years." The first ragtime method book, *Ben Harney's Rag Time Instructor*, published in Chicago in 1897, confirmed the mistaken idea that anything syncopated is ragtime. Harney, a vaudeville pianist-singer who claimed to be the "Inventor of Ragtime," maintained that ragtime was only "a way of playing," and the arranger Theodore H. Northrup provided exercises to support Harney's notion. There is not an original Harney rag in the nine-page "book" (he never wrote one), and the "instruction" consists of ways to spice up hymns and pop songs with syncopation.

However, there is a big difference in the musical mind required to goose "Annie Laurie" and that required to compose "Maple Leaf Rag." For Harney, ragtime *was* merely a way of playing, but for Scott Joplin, Joseph Lamb, and Eubie Blake, it was a way of thinking and, consequently, a way of writing. But because ragtime was built of common clay, many players and listeners during the first ragtime era did not appreciate the intricacies of its architecture.

WHAT THEY USED TO CALL "RAGTIME"

In tempo and form, the rag's nearest musical kin is the 2/4 (not the 6/8) march, but ragtime has been most often confused with its half-wit cousin, the cakewalk. The confusion comes from a historical coincidence: the cakewalk, also a highly syncopated music, was at the peak of its popularity as accompaniment for social dancing during the years 1899 to 1901, precisely when America was first becoming aware of ragtime. The June 10, 1900, edition of *The San Francisco Call* ran a feature story about the John Philip Sousa Band's recent triumph in France, under the headline PARIS HAS GONE RAG TIME WILD. The story says that the "principal conversation all along the boulevards" is Sousa's "'Le Temp du Chiffon,' commonly known in this country as 'rag time.'" The concert number that "seems to have caught the populace is the characteristic cake walk march, 'Bunch o' Blackberries,'" and "many of the most blaze [sic] Parisians are practicing the delicate steps" of this dance. If the first piece of syncopated music that you heard was the cakewalk and the world's most famous conductor told you that it was ragtime, you would no doubt believe him, even if you were "blaze."

Cakewalks preceded ragtime into print by five years (the first being "Opelika Cakewalk" in 1892), and their vogue lasted until about 1903. They were originally written as accompaniments to the traditional dance finale of minstrel shows, the high-kicking strut known as the walkaround. The comedy team of Bert Williams and George Walker so captivated audiences with their cakewalking specialty in the mid-nineties that a tamer version of the stage dance soon found its way into ballrooms.

Cakewalks were written for the set of specific and well-known steps of this dance (as waltzes, tangos, and polkas had their own tempos and musical forms), and when partygoers heard a cakewalk, they knew exactly what to do (as they knew how to waltz, tango, and polka). When a dance ensemble played a rag, there was no set of specific steps, no particular "rag dance," that came to mind. Some dance arrangements of rags evoked the one-step, others suggested the two-step, some appealed to fox-trotters; the slower rags prompted the generic "businessman's bounce," the simple walking to music on a dance floor. Ragtime could be (and is) danced to, but other kinds of music are more dancer-friendly. A fox-trot is better than a rag for fox-trotting, and a two-step is better for two-stepping.

This leads us to a distinction of purpose between cakewalks and ragtime: ragtime was not written specifically for dancing. There was no strong connection between early ragtime and social dance, and the whirlwind tempos and rhythmic spikes of novelty and stride ragtime, beginning in the early 1920s, precluded their use as dance music at all. Although cakewalks are fun, it is easy to see why they were supplanted by ragtime. Ragtime is simply more interesting to play and hear. Cakewalks are songlike instrumentals, easily whistled and hummed.

The one-note melody is their essence, but a single-note melody line is not a fair representation of what is in a rag. Humming a rag's melody will not capture its melodic or rhythmic juice. Cakewalk syncopation incessantly imitates the rhythmic jump of the banjo, and cakewalk composers rarely bothered to harmonize their tunes. This plainness makes them sound thin compared to ragtime, and, given their similarly constructed strains, repetitive in ways that ragtime is not. In many of the best rags, especially those by Joplin and Lamb, there is a harmonic richness which gives them a hint of melancholy that is without counterpart in the cakewalk. The cakewalk was neither designed for introspection nor capable of it. It offers liveliness and nothing else.

As ragtime's popularity grew (and as the cakewalk was fading), publishers appended the word *rag* to the titles and subtitles of many of their cakewalk numbers to get them out of the store. But the difference is easy to hear, and the difference is always in ragtime's favor. When contemporary critics knocked ragtime for its musical shallowness, it was usually the cakewalk they had in mind.

The first use of the word *rag* on a published musical composition did not occur on an instrumental but on a song, and therein lay another source of confusion about what is ragtime. The word was used to describe the accompaniment to the chorus of Ernest Hogan's "All Coons Look Alike to Me," issued in August 1896. Hogan's number was the first smash hit coon song, the kickoff of another syncopated fad of the mid-nineties. The linking of coon songs and ragtime was the main source of ragtime's scurrilous reputation in its early years. Coon songs were racist jokes rhymed and set to music, and there was no more lowbrow genre of musical expression. But they were shot through with syncopation, and their vogue was white-hot just as ragtime began to appear in music stores. Publishers tried to cash in on two fads at once by issuing rags that looked like coon songs and coon songs that looked like rags. The grinning "darkey" cartoon emblazoned the covers of both. The marketing scheme worked to such a degree that, by 1898, the two were synonymous in the public mind. In that year the editor of *Etude* defined ragtime as "a term applied to the peculiar, broken, rhythmic features of the popular 'coon song.'"

Like the tear-jerking commercial ballads of the day, coon songs were short stories in song. The simpleminded tearjerkers were sad stories, and the simpleminded coon songs were funny stories. And like tearjerkers, coon songs stood on the strength of their lyrics. They inspired no great melody writing, because melody was not the point. The tune was there only to float the joke. Coon songs were highly syncopated, but, like cakewalks, they relied on only one basic type of syncopation. They told their slangy stories in the most natural and economic way, in the conversational syncopation of everyday speech, marked in music as the dotted eighth and sixteenth. The verse of George M. Cohan's 1897 song "The Warmest Baby in the Bunch" is rhythmically typical:

> You're well acquainted with the "highborn lady,"
> You might have heard of Hot Tamale Sal,
> But there's a wench that makes them all look shady,
> You've got to take your hat off to dis gal.
> You'll all be dazzled when you see dis member,
> You'll think that you've been drinking nigger punch,
> The steam comes from her shoes in cold December,
> For she's the warmest baby in the bunch.

It would be sung in exactly the meter in which it would be said.

Coon song lyrics were usually couched in minstrel-show dialect, and they dealt solely in black stereotypical character and situations: the eating of watermelon and possum, domestic fights, sexual boasting, and shenanigans in church. They celebrated the use of the razor in settling quarrels, and they rhapsodized over the taste of chicken and the joys of crapshooting. The sheet music covers of coon songs (as well as those on many rags and cakewalks) depicted the subjects of such stories, as well as riotous doings in fictional "Coontowns" and "Blackvilles." Because many professional ragtime performers wrote and sang this syncopated slander, the coon song's lowlife aura clung to ragtime long after the coon song fad died of exhaustion (around 1905). Throughout the ragtime era, a grinning darkey's likeness on a piece of music promised the buyer that, whatever kind of number it was, a good time lay therein.

Slightly more respectable than the coon song, the rag songs of the early century also offered syncopation to be played and sung. But, like the coon song, the rag song pales in musical comparison to instrumental ragtime. In form, the rag songs of the era owe nothing to the three- or four-themed rags. They are constructed exactly like other popular songs of their time: in two sections (verse and chorus) of sixteen or thirty-two bars each. When publishers tried to recycle their best-selling instrumental rags by putting words to them, usually only two of the three or four original strains were kept, and the jagged melody lines were ironed out to accommodate the lyric. Rag song lyrics are generally vapid, assuring the listener that it will be great fun to learn a new (and often nonexistent) dance: We will go on a jag when we hear that rag, each new wiggle will make us giggle, etc. The rag songs offered no adventurous syncopations, and only a few examples of good melody writing. The use of the word *rag* in their titles was another mark against ragtime. The rag songs made *ragtime* and *triviality* seem synonymous.

As for the hodgepodge of (sometimes syncopated) ethnic "characteristic" pieces of the first ragtime era, they are mostly collections of musical clichés strung together to suggest whichever "ethnic" is in the title. If you bought "Sonora: A Spanish Novelette," "In Chinatown: A Characteristic Dance," "Sayonara," or "Cairo," the title told you precisely what you were getting. Steady pounding of eighth notes in the bass as Indian tom-toms, fourths in the treble clef to sound "Chinese," quotations and paraphrases of folk songs—of such stuff were the "characteristics" made.

The piano "patrols" of the day even had a set scenario that was played out in their dynamics: they were written to describe the sound of a marching band first heard at a distance, then getting louder as it approaches, then fading away as the "parade" passes the listener. The "intermezzos" of the time are a bit more complex, but, again, their titles say it all. Intermezzos were most often written to "illustrate" aurally a setting in nature: "Falling Water," "Moonlight," "Dance of the Honeybees," and so on. While the characteristics and intermezzos were often laced with syncopation, syncopation is not their core.

Ragtime is not program music. It was written to create moods, not pictures, and the titles of rags rarely indicate what's coming. The titles of "The Lily Rag," "Aeroplane Rag," "Pork and Beans," and "On the Rural Route" could be shuffled interchangeably without affecting what we hear in them. Ragtime is often witty, but it rarely depends on sound effects or titles for its jokes.

Adding to the uncertainty about what ragtime was in its early years was the fact that no professional composer ever wrote rags exclusively. Brand-name rag writers experimented in many other musical genres, and they often studded their experiments with syncopation. Scott Joplin's catalog includes "Solace: A Mexican Serenade," marches, two-steps, and rag waltzes. There are coon songs and Indian intermezzos by Charles L. Johnson, rag songs by Joseph Lamb, jazzy symphonic works by James P. Johnson and Luckey Roberts, and rag-based jazz pieces by Jelly Roll Morton. Syncopation floated through it all, and the titles and subtitles of pieces were not trustworthy guides to what might be heard in the music. W. H. Krell's "Mississippi Rag," sometimes called the first published rag, is actually a cakewalk. Scott Joplin and Arthur Marshall's "Swipesy Cake Walk" is not a cakewalk—it is a rag; Irwin Leclere's "Triangle Jazz Blues" is neither a jazz number nor a blues—it is a rag. The most common subtitle for rags was "March and Two-Step," but customers shopping for ragtime were also confronted with such labels as "Cake Walk-Two-Step," "Novelty Rag or Fox Trot," "Novelty One-Step and Trot (Maxixe)," "Rag Time Intermezzo," "Rag Time March," and "Slow Drag." Given the blizzard of syncopated product in the stores, it is no wonder that the music fan of the early century did not bother to dissect and classify it all. The inclination must have been to say, "To hell with what they call it. I know what I like."

But we don't have to sort out what is ragtime, because the passing years have done the job for us. Whatever ephemera may have been called ragtime, we needn't call "ragtime" anymore. The musical fads and oddities of the early century may help us conjure that lost era and may add to our understanding of it, but that era is gone. What is left is the music that John Stark, Axel Christensen, and a few others in the mid-teens called "real ragtime." If a piece sounds good enough for modern audiences to want to hear it over and over, year after year, chances are that it's the real thing.

HOW RAGTIME GOT AROUND

Only about two dozen instrumental rags approached "hit" status in sheet music sales, and only a handful—"Maple Leaf Rag," "Dill Pickles," "Black and White Rag," "Twelfth Street Rag," and a few others—surpassed the million-selling mark. The promotion of piano ragtime by its publishers was erratic at best. Aside from printing the music, listing it in ads on the back of other music, and providing the occasional orchestration for professional use, most publishers were usually content to let ragtime make its own way.

There was rarely any concentrated "plugging" effort on ragtime's behalf, as there was for comic songs and ballads. The very short list of recorded ragtime in the cylinder and early disc era shows that the most obvious plugging medium for rags was seldom used. Indeed, except for John Stark, no major publisher specialized in ragtime. It was an incidental product to everyone else. Publishers knew that songs were better bets to take to market for amateur players. A parlor pianist could toss off "Bill Bailey" or "On the Banks of the Wabash" after one or two attempts, but "Maple Leaf Rag" took some practice. Despite the fact that song fads (jungle songs, Hawaiian songs, Indian songs, etc.) usually lasted for five years or so—and despite the fact that ragtime outlived them all—publishers were never quite convinced that the home player was up to the effort of playing ragtime for pleasure.

So how did ragtime, which was more sophisticated and difficult than any American music that had preceded it, survive the music industry's neglect to outlive the simpler forms that grew up at the same time? Why did ragtime not disappear after "Maple Leaf Rag" had thwarted several hundred of its first few thousand buyers? The answer must be that the exhilaration of ragtime made it worth the trouble of learning it. Someone who had played a rag well had *done* something. The professional's payoff was the customers who kept drinking (and tipping) until closing time because they liked the music. The amateur's payoff was the smiling faces and tapping feet of the family in the parlor. The satisfactions offered by ragtime ran deep.

Before we examine the dissemination of ragtime, which emanated from local music printers and piano stores, as well as from the biggest music publishers of Tin Pan Alley, let us look at some events and trends that led to ragtime's acceptance.

Throughout the first half of the nineteenth century, most Americans lived in small towns and in small cities, and they were generally too busy with the basics of staying alive and making a living to have much time for "culture." Except for the eagerly anticipated annual visit of the minstrel show or a third-rate circus ("mud shows," they were called), recreation was homemade. In many towns, generations lived their lives without ever seeing a professional entertainer of any kind. So the cheap and convenient "parlor entertainment" became a staple of family life. This diversion was first centered on the written word. Family members read aloud to each other, from newspapers, novels, poetry, classical orations, the Bible, religious tracts, whatever was available to them. Only the grandest of homes could boast a piano, as the cost of the instrument was far beyond the reach of ordinary incomes.

But in the 1860s and 1870s, as the prices for most products rose, piano prices actually dropped, due to more efficient manufacturing methods. Assembly line production of action, soundboard, and case (along with less expensive materials) meant that pianos could be made faster and sold cheaper than ever before. American companies turned out 2,500 pianos in 1829; 21,000 in 1860; and 370,000 in 1910. Wheezy harmoniums and the older, square pianos were displaced by sleek new uprights. The 1902 Sears, Roebuck catalog offered the company's house brand, the American Home piano, for $98.50. (Shipping was extra, of course, but the upright "parlor grand" came with a twenty-five-year guarantee.) Thus, the family "recital" by the resident piano student(s), almost always female, became a prominent feature of the family's after-dinner ritual. With varying degrees of patience, mothers, fathers, and siblings listened as little sister ran her repertoire of hymns, "autumn idylls," and "evening reveries."

By 1875 most American cities of any size had, if not a piano manufacturing company, at least a retail piano store, selling all types and sizes of keyboard instruments, as well as sheet music. Several of these regional piano companies played major roles in the publishing and promulgation of ragtime. It was only natural: the buyers of all those pianos needed "software"—printed music to play on them. By the late 1890s, America had become a nation of amateur piano players, and most of them had already had a generation of practice. The ragtime seed fell into fertile soil.

Another spur to the acceptance of ragtime on the grassroots level was the rise of town bands. The American tradition of community bands began with the brass-and-drum groups sponsored by local militia organizations in the late eighteenth century. The first nationally known bandmaster was Patrick S. Gilmore, who formed his first band in 1859. During the Civil War, Gilmore was appointed Bandmaster of the Union Forces, and the unit under his personal direction toured extensively during and after the conflict. When the military bandsmen of both sides returned home after the war, many of them organized town bands, in imitation of Gilmore's. As the bands of John Philip Sousa and Arthur Pryor began to include cakewalks and ragtime in their concerts (around the turn of the century), small-town bands wanted to follow suit. Seeing a new market for their music, publishers began to issue cakewalks and rags arranged for various combinations of instruments, and syncopation began to ring out from the local band shell. The earliest recordings of syncopated music are those of military bands, predating the first piano recording (a cakewalk, "Creole Belles," in 1901) by four years.

Other venues for the amateur musician were the banjo and mandolin clubs that arose in the 1880s and 1890s. Although the banjo had an image problem by this time, being associated with minstrel buffoonery, the instrument was taken up by thousands of (mostly male) college students. The Ivy League led the way, with banjo and/or mandolin clubs at MIT, Georgetown, Amherst, Barnard, and Wesleyan. Eager to disassociate their instrument from its backwoods origins, young banjoists ventured everything from the published banjo arrangement of Mendelssohn's Violin Concerto to the *William Tell* overture. But the hugely successful banjo recordings of Vess L. Ossman and Fred Van

Eps, two early soloists who specialized in cakewalks and rags, kept syncopation alive even in the most "elevated" banjo repertoires. The dazzling novelty rags written and performed by the banjoist Harry Reser held the interest of collegians throughout the 1920s.

During this period of widespread amateur music making, a sea change was occurring in professional entertainment, which would help ragtime make its way into every corner of America. The minstrel show, the nation's favorite entertainment for fifty years (and most Americans' first exposure to syncopated songs), was losing its audience to vaudeville. While minstrel characters (such as Jim Crow, Zip Coon, Uncle Tom, Mammy, and Topsy) continued as mainstays in advertising, with their cartoony pictures adorning everything from menus to matchbooks to Currier and Ives prints, the trappings and format of the minstrel show itself were beginning to look tatty and old-fashioned.

The impresario who dethroned the minstrel show from its eminence and changed the national taste in entertainment was Tony Pastor. Pastor, who began his career as a blackfaced singer, had managed theatres in New York and New Jersey for about fifteen years before he hit upon his revolutionary idea. The idea was simple but economically profound: he would open a showplace for variety entertainment in a house clean enough (and with acts clean enough) to attract the patronage of women and children, as well as the men who had been variety's audience in the rowdy music saloons. The Tony Pastor Music Hall, on East Fourteenth Street at Union Square, opened on October 24, 1881, and it was immediately the talk of New York. Pastor's kaleidoscope of acts included something for everybody: acrobats, dramatic sketches, singers, contortionists, male and female impersonators, and instrumentalists of all types. This never-ending stream of talents made the frozen format of the minstrel show seem narrow and trite to Pastor's New York patrons. The cozy predictability of the minstrel evening (overture, two-man jokes, sentimental songs, stump speech, burlesque sketch, and walkaround finale) that had once seemed charming now seemed just predictable. When compared to the novelties of variety, the annual visit of Mose and Rastus was a bit of a bore. Variety was also cheaper to produce than minstrel shows. Many acts needed no sets at all, and those performers who relied on sets and special equipment were themselves responsible for building, painting, and transporting whatever their acts required.

Other showmen began to imitate Pastor's programming ideas, and in 1885 B. F. Keith and E. F. Albee expanded upon them. They opened their Bijou Theatre in Boston, offering a "continuous entertainment" policy from 10:00 A.M. until 10:00 P.M., admission ten cents. They called their variety "vaudeville," and the Bijou became the flagship of the Keith-Albee chain that, by 1914, numbered nearly 400 theatres in the East and Midwest. The Orpheum Circuit (headquartered in the Orpheum Theatre in San Francisco) dominated vaudeville in the Western states. The "small-time" Sun Circuit covered 200 towns in Ohio and Pennsylvania by 1909. The Pantages chain reigned in about thirty theatres in the Midwest, with a few in the far West.

Vaudeville blanketed America as the cumbersome minstrel shows never had, reaching into towns large and small, and the czars of the circuits sent their talent everywhere. America could claim nearly half of the railroad mileage in the world by 1900, and it was the vast network of railroads that made vaudeville's booking system work. A town might get a minstrel show once or twice a year, but there was a new vaudeville show every Monday.

Music publishers were quick to capitalize on the fact that thousands of acts, almost every one of them requiring some kind of music, were barnstorming the nation. Here was a chance to plug everything in the store, from comedy songs to instrumentals to love ballads. Among the kinds of music that received national exposure in vaudeville was ragtime. And, in a happy concurrence with the coming of vaudeville, publishers found a new answer to their oldest problem: distribution. The rise of the dime-store chains, with a music department in each store, ensured that the latest in ragtime would be available while it was hot. Any town large enough to have a vaudeville theatre probably had a Woolworth's, so vaudeville fans could get the newest songs and rags at a price everyone could afford.

Ragtime was the mainstay of variety performers like Ben Harney, Joe Jordan, Les Copeland, and Louis Chauvin. They were followed by Mike Bernard and Zez Confrey, as well as many lesser known ragtimers, such as Cora Salisbury, Jay Roberts, Tom Brown, and Harry

Cook. Often ragtime was the specialty of a piano act, and sometimes it was merely the accompaniment for jugglers or clowns; but the music got around, and audiences attuned their ears to it. The last fad that the minstrel show had to offer was the cakewalk, which was quickly co-opted by the variety stage and, soon after, by the ballroom. The popularity of the dance couldn't save the medium that it sprang from. By 1900 there were only a few minstrel troupes left on the road. Vaudeville, with its hearty quotient of ragtime, would dominate American entertainment for the next thirty years.

The ragtime traffic traveled both ways: into and out of the small towns of America. Professionals used ragtime in their acts, and they often published their compositions along the road, in towns where

Les Copeland

vaudeville bookings had taken them. Amateurs—especially women, who would never have gone into a saloon—heard ragtime on the vaudeville stage and were inspired to write their own rags. Many of these homegrown rags, sometimes composed to impress friends, were published by their composers, who paid local stationers or music stores to print them. Or a local music publisher might buy the rag outright (no royalties) for $25 or so to see what he could do with it. A hundred copies was the average run, and these were gamely issued and offered for sale in the music shop or dime store. There was rarely any thought of distributing them beyond the city limits or of printing a second edition. When the hundred copies disappeared from the music shop window, the local composer's day in the sun was over. Tin Pan Alley publishers, who are sometimes cast as villains in the ragtime story, saved many of these local rags from oblivion by republishing them and giving them national distribution.

We hope that our geographic look at ragtime will remind people everywhere of this important piece of our heritage. Nowhere else in the world did ragtime flourish and develop as it did in America, and every section of our country has its own composers and publishers to be proud of. We would like to see an awakened interest in finding and playing the regional ragtime that fed and reflected the national craze for the music. Celebrate the rags that were written and published in your town, your county, and your state. Add the rags of local writers and publishers to your piano and band concerts. Some of these rags that never left home are works of genius, and all, including the very least of them, are full of sass and fun. They are valentines, composed by clerks, piano teachers, and housewives, as well as by professional musicians, all of whom were smitten with syncopation.

THE ORGANIZATION OF THIS BOOK

To the authors, a rag is a syncopated composition for the piano, written in duple time (2/4 or 4/4), made of three or four melodic sections of sixteen or thirty-two measures each. Our ragtime lists and examples do not include songs, rag waltzes, or numbers based on one or two simple syncopations. The pieces we are interested in are those that use complex syncopations and use them in a pianistic way. If your definition is broader than ours, think of our selections as hard-core ragtime.

We will deal only with commercially published ragtime, that is, those rags that were issued for sale in stores between 1897 and 1980. Since 1980 the dissemination of ragtime has largely been through the medium of recordings, not printed music. Contemporary rags available only as photocopied manuscripts or in computer-generated printouts are not "on the market" as were the rags that could be bought in a local music shop or from stationers.

Our ragtime map is divided into six major regions. Because publishers were somewhat stationary and writers were not, our focus will be centered on the publishers of each region. We are identifying as "major" publishers those who issued the most rags and/or who had ongoing professional relationships with ragtime composers. In a few instances, in the narrative sections only, we will standardize our use of a publishing company's name, ignoring brief partnerships and name/initial variants that appear on the company's sheet music. In the cases of the two major publishers of ragtime, John Stark and Jerome H. Remick, we have chosen not to break up their stories by telling them in two places. We will treat Stark in St. Louis (folding his five years in New York into his Missouri story) and Remick in New York City (although Remick's roots were in Detroit).

Appendix A lists ragtime composers by birthplace. It is hoped that local and regional historians will be able to contribute birth/death dates/places of other composers for future editions of this book.

Appendix D is an alphabetical checklist of 2,002 published rags. The spelling and punctuation of titles are those given in the copyright files or on the sheet music covers (not the title pages). When the date, month, and year of copyright are known, they are given. When a rag was not copyrighted or the copyright date is unknown, only the year of publication is given.

To simplify our bibliographic listings, we have listed general references (those that were used as source material for more than one region) in a "Select Bibliography." The books and articles that apply to one chapter only are cited as "Chapter Sources." Many of these chapter sources were provided to us by friends and ragtime fans throughout the country, who have made invaluable contributions to our ragtime geography. The passion of its fans has always kept ragtime alive, and we are grateful to those who put their passion to work to help us.

"Maple Leaf Rag," St. Louis edition

Missouri Ragtime

Throughout the first decade of published ragtime, Missouri grew rags like Kansas grew wheat. There were more rags—and more good rags—from Missouri than anywhere else. Along with the output of two nationally known publishers, John Stark, in St. Louis, and J. W. Jenkins' Sons, in Kansas City, Missouri could also boast more small-town rags than any other state. Missourians were quick to embrace this new music, and their rags multiplied and thrived.

The question for a ragtime geographer is simply, Why Missouri? Why didn't a similar harvest of ragtime occur in Ohio, Illinois, Louisiana, or New York? The answer is that many Missourians—white and black; piano players, saloon keepers, publishers, music store owners, composers, and fans—believed in ragtime and wanted it to happen there. The music had its champions—both professional and amateur—in other parts of the country, but in Missouri many of those who loved it were in a position to help it along. Some of them were in Missouri by chance, some by choice, and others had generations of Missouri ancestors. However they got there, they made the perfect set of godparents for ragtime.

The U.S. map is the place to begin. If, as fast-food merchandisers believe, location is everything, Missouri was destined by its location to be an area of commercial, social, and cultural change. Since the early eighteenth century, St. Louis has served as midpoint and stopover for north-south traffic on our largest river, and when going west was a national imperative, the city was the "Gateway to the West." The accommodation of travelers has always been a St. Louis specialty, and in the late nineteenth century, other Missouri towns also began to offer amenities to visitors. Wayside inns evolved into hotels, and country bar-

1

rooms grew into taverns, offering menus and selling whiskey that did not come from barrels. When towns became large enough to keep secrets, red-light districts arose. As Missouri gentrified, it became a state where a piano player could make a good living.

St. Louis, at the confluence of the Mississippi and Missouri rivers, was founded as a French trading post in 1764, and in 1822, when its population was 5,000, it was chartered as a city. As they always had, trappers, traders, and boatmen walked its riverfront day and night looking for food, lodging, and fun. Charles Dickens, visiting St. Louis in 1842, stayed at the Planter's Hotel. He called it "an excellent house," in which "the proprietors have most bountiful notions of providing the creature comforts." Among the innovations in hospitality that began in St. Louis were the highball, Southern Comfort, and Planter's Punch.

In 1857 the railroad came, and the city's real boom began. By 1870 St. Louis was the third largest city in the United States, after New York and Philadelphia. Around 1890 a huge sporting district began to grow westward from the Mississippi (beginning where the Gateway Arch now stands), along Chestnut and Market streets, in the very center of the city. Entertaining out-of-towners became big business; saloons, hotels, whorehouses, wine rooms, gambling dens, theatres, and cafes sprang up. The district drew itinerant pianists from all over the South and Midwest to compete for jobs there. St. Louis led in the accommodation industry, and smaller cities soon followed. In the 1890s, as prosperity took hold across the state, sporting districts grew in Kansas City, St. Joseph, Joplin, and Sedalia. Many of the small-town saloons were rough-hewn and dangerous places, but there were usually enough free-spending locals and visiting businessmen to keep the piano player's tips coming. There was no systematic booking of musicians; they literally roamed, picking up when the spirit moved them—going from town to town, bar to bar, house to house—never more than a half-day's train ride from a row of joints that had pianos in them.

These opportunities for piano players brought to Missouri the main characters in our story, those pianists who wanted to write down and publish their compositions. The writing and publishing of ragtime was an incidental activity to most of the pianists, because their real money came from playing. The salary at whorehouses and saloons was not much, a dollar or two a night, but a good night might bring anywhere from $15 to $40 in tips. The hours spent writing down a rag—which a publisher almost always bought outright (with no royalty agreement) for $25 to $50—could be more profitably spent playing and singing dirty songs in a bar. So most of the pianists did not (and some could not) write. It took real commitment even to get the music on paper, and even more dedication to peddle it. In Missouri there were twenty or so such committed souls, and they produced the best rags of the music's first generation.

The composers of ragtime in Missouri were fortunate to have more than a dozen publishers who were willing to take a chance on it. The most important was John Stark, owner of a music store in Sedalia, who published his first rag at age fifty-eight. He had had no hands-on musical

John Stark

experience since he laid down his bugle at the end of the Civil War, and, up until he issued ragtime's first hit (Joplin's "Maple Leaf Rag," which was also Stark's first ragtime publication), he was a typical small-town publisher. But Stark eventually became a fanatic about ragtime, and for thirty years, he offered a catalog of rags unmatched in their quality. Although he had the commercial acumen of a country storekeeper and his ads seemed to have been written by Baron Munchausen, he was the best friend ragtime ever had. He was the first publisher to see the musical worth of ragtime, and he stayed with it longer than anyone else.

In Kansas City, J. W. Jenkins' Sons, a firm old enough to be stable yet young enough to be hungry, was also keen on ragtime, and it marketed its music in a more professional way than did Stark. Charles L. Johnson, of Kansas City, who issued his own rags as well as those of others, was the savviest of the regional publishers. After their local publication, Johnson sold many of his rags and songs to Tin Pan Alley firms, which gave them wide distribution and reaped hits as a result. Several St. Louis piano stores, to keep their customers happily playing the piano, published rags for them. A. W. Perry & Sons, Stark's competition in Sedalia, issued rags, as did Dumars Music Company in Carthage and Allen Music Company in Columbia. Rags popped up in Missouri like mushrooms after a spring rain. Locals were proud of their composers, and there were even some piano teachers who were not too snobbish to encourage their students to play these homegrown rags.

Other places had similar elements of a ragtime environment, but none had the collection of talents—and the respect for them—that came together in Missouri. Chicago had a larger sporting district than St. Louis had, but in Chicago's Levee (as it was known) there was no haven for pianists like Tom Turpin's Rosebud Bar. New York had scores of publishers, but none as dedicated to ragtime as Stark, Jenkins, and Johnson. Many places had good rag players and composers, but no place had a collection of ragtime giants to compare with those gathered in Missouri in the early 1900s: Tom Turpin, Scott Joplin, James Scott, Arthur Marshall, Scott Hayden, Louis Chauvin, Charles L. Johnson, and Charles Hunter.

And this was just the varsity. A few sketches of early players will show the degree to which ragtime was in the Missouri air. Young and old, white and black, educated and illiterate, internationally famous and unknown—these people, who were alike in no other way, loved ragtime and demonstrated their devotion to it. As the ragtime virus spread, they all caught it and gladly became its carriers.

~~~

Six Profiles in Missouri Ragtime

BRUN CAMPBELL

Sanford Brunson Campbell, born into a poor white family in Oberlin, Kansas, in 1884, spent his early teens in St. Joseph, Missouri, and Arkansas City, Kansas, trying to teach himself to play "hot" piano. He wasn't very good, but he was good enough to work where there was a scarcity of piano players—in the plank-board saloons of western Kansas and Oklahoma (then still Indian Territory). When he was bumming around Oklahoma City at age fourteen, he came upon a crowd gathered at the Armstrong-Byrd Music Store listening to a light-skinned black man play a rag. The boy was transfixed by the music, and when it was over, he introduced himself to the pianist. The player's name was Otis Saunders, and he told Campbell that the piece that had so thrilled him was called "Maple Leaf Rag" and that it had been written by Saunders's friend, Scott Joplin, who was living in Sedalia, Missouri.

A light switched on in Campbell's soul, and he saw his calling. He had to meet the man who could create such music, learn from him, and carry his music everywhere. Campbell hoboed his way to Sedalia and found Scott Joplin. The composer had had only one rag published at that time ("Original Rags," recently issued by Carl Hoffman Music in Kansas City), but he had written several others. The boy worked up four of them under Joplin's coaching. The master dubbed him "The Ragtime Kid," gave him a fifty-cent piece for good luck, and sent him out to spread the gospel.

For ten years Campbell pounded out ragtime in prairie saloons and gilded hostels. He had a long residence as pianist at the Kerfoot Hotel in El Reno, Oklahoma, where he played for guests such as Pawnee Bill, Teddy Roosevelt, Frank James, Bat Masterson, and showmen George Evans and Lew Dockstader. Campbell married in 1908, and with his marriage came an ultimatum: give up the saloon life and learn a trade. He chose barbering, as had his father, and he ran his own shop in Venice, California, until his death in 1952.

Campbell never published a rag, and he didn't play professionally after 1908. But the flame that Joplin lit in him never went out. He lived long enough to see the beginnings of the ragtime revival, and he became something of a totem to the interviewers who sought him out for his reminiscences. He made a few boisterous recordings near the end of his life. There are quirks and mistakes in them, but they convey the fun of having been a "Ragtime Kid"—which is what every piano-playing kid of his day wanted to be.

CLARENCE WOODS

Clarence Woods was born in Blue Earth, Ohio, in 1888, and his family settled in Carthage, Missouri, a small town in the southwestern part of the state, in the mid-1890s. One of Clarence's friends in Carthage was James Scott, a black boy who was three years older. Clarence and James studied at the Calhoun School of Music with the same piano teacher, Miss Emma Johns, and James was already becoming a local musical star. At Lakeside Park, just west of Carthage, Clarence got his first musical thrill, that of listening to the Carthage Light Guard Band. The band's director (and Scott's employer) was Charles Dumars, owner of Dumars Music Company.

Scott was beginning to compose music, and in March 1903 Dumars published his first work, a rag called "A Summer Breeze." Four months later, Dumars issued his second rag, "The Fascinator." Possibly inspired by seeing Scott's music in the Dumars window, Clarence Woods decided to write his own. He took his first effort, a 6/8 march called "The Meteor" (dedicated to the Frisco System, a railroad line), to Dumars, who published it in 1904. Carthage was small, but it offered enough encouragement to both of its teenage composers to confirm them in their choice of musical careers. Neither of them would waver from the path he had chosen.

Woods was the traveler of the two. Not long after "The Meteor" appeared, he left town as accompanist for the thundering melodramas of the Bleeding Hearts Stock Company, and he never looked back. Around 1907 his wanderings took him to Ft. Worth, Texas, where he worked for ten years as a bandleader and touring pianist, billed as "The Ragtime Wonder of the South." Woods published only two rags ("Slippery Elm" in 1912 and "Sleepy Hollow" in 1918), each with a bluesy, small-town flavor.

Woods was a theatre organist in Tulsa throughout most of the 1920s and a local radio entertainer in the 1930s. In 1949 he began a four-year stint as organist/arranger/composer for the Barnum & Bailey Circus. In 1953 he retired to Dallas, and he died while visiting his son in Davenport, Iowa, in 1956.

CALVIN LEE WOOLSEY

Across the professional spectrum from the nomadic Campbell and Woods was Calvin Lee Woolsey, who was born near Tinney's Point (Ray County), Missouri, in 1884. His family moved to Braymer, Missouri, when he was a child, and it was there, in this little town about forty miles northeast of Kansas City, that ragtime somehow seeped into his staid, middle-class life. Calvin was a bright student and was obvi-

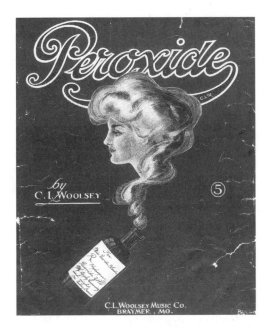

"Peroxide Rag"

ously headed for education beyond Braymer. After high school, he enrolled at St. Louis School of Medicine, and he interned at State Hospital in St. Joseph after his graduation. He began postgraduate studies at Harvard University Medical School but dropped out to return home when his mother became seriously ill. We don't know when he learned to play the piano, or who taught him, but during his college years, he became more than a connoisseur of ragtime, he became a composer.

While at Harvard, Woolsey managed to place two of his rags with Jerome H. Remick & Company, New York's leading ragtime publisher. His "Funny Bones" was the first to see print, in July 1909, and "Medic Rag" followed nine months later. Woolsey was back in Braymer by the spring of 1910, and he self-published his "Poison Rag" and "Peroxide Rag" there, both in May of that year. In 1911 he published his "Mashed Potatoes" in Braymer, and in 1914, he issued his last rag, "Lover's Lane Glide," from St. Joseph. He also self-published a few of his songs and other instrumental pieces.

After service in World War I, Woolsey returned to Braymer, where he was the town's physician until his death in 1946. The thought of playing professionally probably never entered his mind, but the doctor had ragtime in him. And since his home was Missouri, publishing his rags at home was not an eccentricity at all.

BLIND BOONE

The first concert pianist to feature spirituals and syncopated music in his programs was the black Missourian John William ("Blind") Boone. Boone, the illegitimate son of a cook who worked for the Seventh Militia, was born at the militia camp near Miami, Missouri (a bluff town overlooking the Missouri River, about twenty miles north of Marshall), in 1864. At the age of six months, he contracted what a local doctor called "brain fever," and his eyeballs were removed as a life-saving measure.

When he was eight years old, his mother, Rachel, married a man named Harrison Hendrix, and they moved into a one-room cabin on a small farm near Warrensburg, in west central Missouri, about forty miles from the Kansas line. In 1873, through a community fund-raising effort, Boone was sent to the St. Louis School for the Blind. Henry

Robyn, a music teacher there, had recently codified a system of braille musical notation, and it was with the help of Robyn and his system that Boone learned to play the piano.

After a year of Robyn's instruction, Boone far outstripped his teacher. He had great technical facility, and he could replicate any piece played for him after a single hearing. The boy already had professional ambitions, and he acted on them in the only way that was open to him: by sneaking out at night to play in the whorehouses of Chestnut Valley. He was expelled from the school for this activity, and he returned to Warrensburg, where he played at socials and in saloons.

In 1877 Boone played a Christmas concert in Columbia, Missouri, and a few days later, he was taken by John Lange, Jr., the black community leader who had hired him, to a concert given by the *savant* Blind Tom Bethune. The event was a life-changing experience for the thirteen-year-old Boone. He heard a black man, blind, as he was, playing the piano on the concert stage, and Boone realized that he could aspire to more than his whistle-stop, pass-the-hat evenings in central Missouri. Lange offered to act as his manager and began to look for bookings. Their first was a concert at the courthouse in Columbia, where they took in seven dollars. Next came a string of performances at county fairs, picnics, and small-town theatres, any place that would have them.

Boone was a dazzling player, but because of his color and his disability, his concerts had a tinge of the freak show about them. Like Blind Tom before him, Boone leaned heavily on his uncanny ability to play anything that he had just heard. Pianists were invited up from the audience to challenge him. In turn, they played their most difficult numbers, and Boone played them back flawlessly. It was a marvelous stunt, but it was only a stunt. To be taken seriously as a pianist, he needed some serious music in his repertoire.

A year or so after Boone began his concert career in earnest, he was stalled, between bookings, in Corydon, Iowa. B. T. Raisor, an instructor at Iowa State Teacher's College, offered to coach him until more concerts materialized, and Boone soon had twenty-five classical numbers in his mind and fingers. (About ten years later he would study again, this time with Anna Heurmann, who was in the music department of William Woods College, at Fulton, Missouri.) In 1880 Boone composed "The Marshfield Tornado," a pianistic description of the ferocious storm that devastated the small south-central Missouri town in April of that year. His classical pieces—which included Liszt's *Hungarian Rhapsody No. 6* and Gottschalk's *The Last Hope*—and his topical showstopper put him in the first rank of regional concert players, and the sixteen-year-old Boone put $18,000 in a Columbia bank at the end of his 1880 tour.

Boone expanded his repertoire further during the next decade by adding concert arrangements of spirituals to his programs. He married his manager's sister, Eugenia, in 1888, and they bought a two-story brick house in Columbia. His popularity brought him major tours of the United States and Canada with his Blind Boone Concert Company throughout the 1890s. He made two European tours, and played concerts at Yale and Harvard universities. As Missouri began to take pride in its ragtime, Boone began to use syncopated pieces as encores after his classical numbers. His standard introduction to these was, "We are going to put the cookies on the lower shelf now, where everybody can get at them."

Boone never wrote a rag, but in 1908 and 1909 Allen Music Company, in Columbia, issued his "Southern Rag Medley No. 1: (Strains from the Alleys)" and "Southern Rag Medley No. 2: (Strains from the Flat Branch)," two pieces that stand as the strongest evidence of the link between black folk song and ragtime. Also in 1908, Allen published his "Geo'gia Melon," a plain, four-square song with a raggy eight-bar dance section appended as a coda.

In 1912 Boone made six hand-played piano rolls for the QRS company, and taken together, they suggest Boone's concert mix of classical playing, syncopation, and folk song. The rolls of "Woodland Murmurs" and "Sparkling Spring" are busy but ordinary intermezzos, full of bird trills and burbling water. A pop song, "When You and I Were Young, Maggie," is given an epic, arpeggio-laden treatment. But there is a spirituals medley called "Camp Meeting Melodies" that is wildly rhythmic, and a "Southern Rag Medley No. 2" that is downright polyphonic. The "Rag Medley" has a rough, eerie sound, and it seems to be rhythmically erratic and full of wrong notes until it is realized that Boone is playing in 5/4 with one hand and in 4/4 with the other. Trebor Tichenor, who owns all of the Boone rolls, thinks the two medleys sound "like what ragtime must have been at first"—which is to say, unlike any piano playing that had ever been heard before.

Boone's fortunes declined after the death of his manager in 1916, but he continued to perform into the 1920s. His May 31, 1927, concert in Virden, Illinois, was his last, and he died in Warrensburg the following October. Boone knew more about ragtime than he published or played in concerts, but the hints that he left us about its origins indicate some tricky piano playing going on in small-town Missouri long before the ragtime era.

PERCY WENRICH

Percy Wenrich, one of the most successful songwriters of the teens, was born in 1880 in Joplin, Missouri, a town as well known for its gambling as for its mining of lead and zinc. All five members of his family played the piano, and his father, a postmaster, wrote campaign songs for local Republican office seekers. As a teenager, Percy joined an amateur

Percy Wenrich

minstrel group, in which he learned and performed coon songs and cakewalks. Late in his life he would recall his days as "a typical hick-town pianist," and like most of this breed at this time, he made no distinction among the various kinds of syncopated numbers he enjoyed. He tossed off "At a Georgia Camp Meeting" and "My Coal Black Lady" with as much vigor as he put into Tom Turpin's "Harlem Rag."

Percy knew good playing when he heard it, though, and he heard it all over Joplin. J. Frank Walker, a music store owner, often shoved a piano or two near the front door of his shop to encourage any passing pianists (including Percy and his friend Rube Stone) to step inside and play. Percy was most impressed by the playing of the "colored fellows" in Joplin's sporting district. He told Rudi Blesh where he heard them:

> The north end of Main Street was as wide open as the barn door. When you left the hotel, there was just a barber shop and then you were right in there at the House of Lords Saloon [one of the forty or so saloons in 1890s Joplin]—bar on the first floor, gambling on the second, and sporting house on the third. . . . Lionel (Babe) LaTour, a gambler from Sedalia, knew all the colored players. He used to take me around when I could have been hung for even being there.

When Wenrich was seventeen, he sent his piano composition "L'Inconnu" (which he called "a two-step with a fancy title") to Sol Bloom, a Chicago publisher, and paid to have it printed in a thousand copies. This vanity publication, which he peddled door to door in Joplin and in Galena, Kansas, was the beginning of Wenrich's career as a composer. He moved to Chicago in 1901, to make his way in the music business there.

Wenrich is not considered a major composer of rags (although he wrote twenty-one of them, beginning with "Ashy Africa" in 1903), but his adolescent love of all things syncopated colored his songwriting throughout his career. His most popular tunes, "Put on Your Old Gray Bonnet," "Moonlight Bay," and "When You Wore a Tulip and I Wore a Big Red Rose," are so rhythmic that they demand a ragtime treatment. And three of his songs—"The Skeleton Rag," "Alamo Rag," and "The Red Rose Rag"—are especially fine, unlike most of their kind in that they are truly raggy.

In 1951 his hometown honored Wenrich with a citywide festival centered on the release of *On Moonlight Bay*, a Doris Day film that featured his songs. Wenrich was too ill to attend (he died in New York the following year), but he sent a long telegram expressing his gratitude and saying that he was there in spirit. He was always there in spirit, and his songs prove it.

JAMES SCOTT

Perhaps the surest indication of ragtime's good health in the state of Missouri is the fact that one of its most gifted composers and players, James Scott, could stay home and have a solid—and lifelong—career in music. Scott was seventeen years younger than his idol, Scott Joplin, and the seventeen years made all the difference in the musical climate and in the opportunities available to him. The itinerant pianist's life was certainly still an option when James Scott was a teenager, but he did not choose it, nor did he have to. So far as it is known, Scott never played in a saloon or a whorehouse. Except for the year or so he spent in Ottawa, Kansas, as a child and the move he made in 1920, to Kansas City, Kansas, he probably never traveled outside the borders of his home state. (After his move, he commuted back across the state line to his teaching and theatre work in Kansas City, Missouri.)

When Scott Joplin began his musical career in the mid-1880s, there were no vaudeville houses that needed pianists, no silent movies to accompany, no music stores that needed demonstrators, and few publishers issuing piano compositions by black writers. There was nothing for a black pianist to do except hit the road and try to piece out a living. By the time James Scott was sure that he wanted to be a musician, at about age eighteen, his adopted town, Carthage, Missouri, could offer him all of the things that Joplin didn't have. And because of Joplin's "Maple Leaf Rag," Carthaginians knew what ragtime was, and they were supportive of anyone, black or white, who wanted to write and publish it.

Compared to other Missouri towns, Carthage was relatively saloon-free (it had three in 1903, compared to Joplin's fifty-five), but saloons were never the source of Scott's income. Because fate put him down in Carthage at just the right time, it was possible for James Scott to be one of the first professional musicians to combine ragtime with respectability.

James Sylvester Scott, Jr., was born in Neosho, Missouri, in 1885. The Scotts enjoyed music, but since James Sr. was a laborer with six children to feed, there was no money for a family piano. Their neighbors had one, however, and Jimmy couldn't keep his hands off it. He had perfect pitch, and he quickly progressed from one-finger melodies to experimenting with chords. His precocity was brought to the attention of a black pianist, John Coleman, who agreed to teach the child without pay. Through Coleman, Jimmy got a solid foundation in the classical repertoire, technique, reading, and notation. His family moved to Ottawa, Kansas, when Jimmy was thirteen, and the disruption of his studies with Coleman was eased somewhat when relatives in Ottawa gave the Scotts a small parlor organ for him to practice on.

After a little over a year in Ottawa, the Scotts resettled in Neosho in 1901. They moved again in 1902, this time about twenty-five miles north, to Carthage. James Jr. was seventeen—shy, good-natured, and handsome—and he could play the piano like a demon. His charm and talent took the onus off of being the new boy in town. Carthage was a segregated community, of course, but as in many segregated towns, music could often suspend the social rules. Carthage was home to many amateur musical groups, black and white, and the pavilion at Lakeside Park was the place where everybody could hear them. Choral groups, church choirs, military bands, and dance orchestras presented programs there, and in the summers, Chautauqua lectures, professional concerts, and silent films (with piano accompaniment) were added to Lakeside's cultural fare. James had not been in town very long before he was asked to perform on the park's giant steam calliope. It was the first public display of Scott's ability, and Carthage was enthusiastic in its response. (Reminiscences of his contemporaries suggest that Scott may have been the best player among the Missouri masters.)

One of Carthage's leading musicians was Charles Dumars, director of the Carthage Light Guard Band and owner of Dumars Music Company, at 109 South Main Street. Besides carrying a wide stock of instruments and sheet music, the store specialized in picture framing, and Dumars hired James Scott as janitor and apprentice framer. Before long, Scott left his broom and tackhammer to become Dumars's chief clerk and demonstrator. People who had no intention of buying pianos or sheet music gathered at the store every day to hear him play.

In March 1903 Dumars Music fed Scott's local fame by publishing his first composition, a rag called "A Summer Breeze." A Carthage *Evening Press* story called Scott "a musical prodigy" and said that his composition was "original and catchy." In September Dumars issued his second rag, "The Fascinator," and in April 1904 Scott's "On the Pike," a ragtime salute to the St. Louis World's Fair, appeared in the Dumars window. In July, Charles Dumars honored his clerk by making a band arrangement of "On the Pike" to perform at a Light Guard concert at Lakeside Park. The following month James Scott shared a program with Blind Boone at a Chautauqua evening given by the Missouri State Negro Improvement Association. While Boone was in town, he came by to see Scott at the music store. The two had some fun playing four-handed piano accompaniment to a recording by the Sousa band. The local press wrote up their prank, calling Scott "Our Local Mozart."

The melodies and structure of Scott's earliest rags show him completely in the thrall of Scott Joplin. Like Brun Campbell before him, James Scott craved to meet his hero. In 1906, the opportunity came. Scott heard that Joplin was back in St. Louis after some time in Chicago, and he made the trip across the state on the chance of seeing him. Joplin was approachable, as he always was to young talents, and he thought highly enough of Scott's work to get it to his publisher, John Stark. Scott had mailed rags to Stark for several years without success, but now, at Joplin's urging, Stark bought "Frog Legs Rag" and issued it in December 1906. "Frog Legs" became Stark's second-best seller (after "Maple Leaf"), and its publication began a sixteen-year professional relationship between Scott and Stark, during which Stark would issue twenty-four Scott rags.

When he returned to Carthage from his successful foray into St. Louis, James Scott found himself the pride of the town, and opportunity lay all around him. He played at the graduation exercises for Lincoln High School, and seats were set aside for the whites who had no other reason to attend ceremonies at the black school except to hear him. He organized a chorus of twenty-five male voices, which he called the Carthage Jubilee Singers, and presented them in concert. He played regularly at the Delphus Theatre, a silent movie house on East Fourth

Street. He was solidly employed at the Dumars store, and he had just placed a composition with ragtime's leading publisher. In March 1906, he bought a house on Sixth Street for $425. A few months later—with property, employment, and prospects in order—he married Nora Johnson, from Springfield.

Scott was in his mid-twenties and happy with his life. Fine rags poured out of him, all except one published by Stark: "Kansas City Rag" (1907); "Great Scott Rag" (published by Allen Music, in Columbia in 1909), "The Ragtime Betty," "Grace and Beauty" (his masterpiece), and "Sunburst Rag," all from 1909; 1910's "Ophelia Rag" and "Hilarity Rag"; and "Quality," "Ragtime Oriole," and "Princess Rag" from 1911. Dumars published two of his songs in 1909, and Stark issued a waltz by Scott in 1909 and another in 1910.

Scott's writing would slow a bit in the teens, but Stark would continue to issue one or two of his rags a year. His late rags are denser than

"Grace & Beauty"—Scott's perfect rag

those of his youth, but they still sound like the work of a composer in high spirits. Scott knew that ragtime was in a standoff against jazz, and his last rags hurl defiance at what he considered a sloppy and unschooled musical form.

In the mid-teens, Scott organized a black military/dance band in Carthage, while he continued to mail his rags to Stark for publication. Around 1918, obviously seeking greener pastures, Scott and his wife, Nora, moved to Kansas City. He was not the star in the larger city that he had been in Carthage, and most of his income during his first few years there came from his giving piano lessons. He eventually became organist and arranger for the Panama Theatre, a small silent movie house on East Twelfth Street, and thus began the occupation that he would hold for the rest of his life. He occasionally accompanied his cousin, the blues singer Ada Brown, in performances at Liberty Park.

Scott and Nora had taken rooms at 402 Nebraska Avenue, and he headquartered his teaching activities there. But in 1920, probably feeling an economic pinch, they moved across the river to Kansas City, Kansas. Scott joined Kansas City, Missouri's black musicians' local in 1924, the same year he became the pianist in the seven-piece orchestra (led by Harry Dillard) that accompanied vaudeville acts at the Lincoln Theatre.

During his time at the Lincoln, Scott established himself as one of the top musicians in the city. In 1926 he began a stint with the orchestra in residence at the Eblon Theatre, a silent movie house that advertised itself as "The Only Theatre Owned by a Negro in Greater Kansas City." In 1928 the Eblon fell on hard times, and its orchestra was replaced by a pipe organ. But Scott, a fine organist as well as a pianist, kept a job there. He stayed at the Eblon until 1930, when the popularity of sound films finally drove it out of business. As the city's territory jazz roared around him, Scott took no part in it as player or listener.

Nora Scott died in 1930, and Scott's own decline began soon after her death. The closing of the Eblon left him with little income, and he had to retrench. Shortly before the end of his life, taking his dog and his grand piano, he moved into the home of a cousin, Ruth Callahan, at 1926 Springfield Street, in Kansas City, Kansas. He still gave piano lessons, and he played occasionally, but his health was fading. Scott succumbed to kidney failure in August 1938.

Although he died relatively young, he was not burned out or killed by the ragtime life. The vogue for ragtime died a natural death, and Scott did, too. (His brother Douglas, who was a typically rootless saloon player, died at age twenty-six in 1918.) His home state nurtured his talent, encouraged his efforts, and applauded his successes. Scott's rags are marked by the sounds of optimism and contentment. It was over when it was over, but his career had a long time in the Missouri sun.

ST. LOUIS BEFORE RAGTIME
Music with a German Accent

The original settlers of St. Louis were French, but it was a great wave of German immigration, beginning in the 1830s, that gave the city its musical character. To the French, music was a commonplace activity, a natural and useful part of everyday living. Theirs was an oral tradition, through which one heard, picked up, and passed on the ballads, party songs, and dance tunes that leavened the hardships of pioneer life. The German settlers thought of music as something that was good for you, something so valuable that it deserved study. Music brought pleasure, of course, but, even more important, it forged community bonds. The right kind of music set a high moral and social tone for those who heard it and those who made it.

A music teacher, A. C. van Hirtem, "late from Amsterdam, Organ Factor and Professor of Music on the piano-forte," advertised for students in St. Louis as early as 1818, and by 1821 there were two persons listed as professional musicians in the city's directory. Many of the German settlers brought their music libraries with them, and they began to organize upscale amateur music groups, such as the St. Louis Sacred Music Society, the St. Louis Brass Band, and the St. Louis Musical Society Polyhymnia. There had been symphonic groups in the city for fifty years before the St. Louis Symphony Orchestra was founded in 1880. There were enough of these community groups to justify the opening of a music store, J. C. Dinnies Company, by 1839.

In the summer of 1848 two German immigrants, Charles Balmer and Carl Heinrich Weber (who were brothers-in-law), opened a music store at 141 Market Street. They poured out reprints of classical pieces, as well as compositions by Balmer, the partners' families, and friends. Balmer & Weber was successful from the start, and it soon absorbed the catalogs of its smaller competitors. The company issued teaching pieces for all levels of ability and, beginning in the 1880s, published dance tunes—waltzes, polkas, mazurkas, and galops—in great numbers. (Balmer & Weber would issue only one rag, in 1902, a decade after the founders' deaths.)

Balmer & Weber held preeminence during the second half of the nineteenth century, but as St. Louis continued its growth, other piano store-publishers arose to compete with the local giant. Adam Shattinger left his job at Kunkel Brothers music company to found his own firm in 1876. (In December 1897 Shattinger Music would publish the first rag issued in St. Louis, Walter Starck's "Darktown Capers," which beat Tom Turpin's "Harlem Rag" into the marketplace by only a few days.) Thiebes-Sterlin had joined the game by 1895. Joseph Placht & Son (whose 1904 rag, "One o' Them Things," by James Chapman and Leroy Smith, contained the first published twelve-bar blues strain), Hunleth Music (Joe Jordan's first publisher), and Val A. Reis (publisher of two Joplin rags) were all issuing locally composed numbers before 1905. In the late 1890s St. Louis's old musical culture, rooted in European traditions, met a newer culture, and the meeting ground was ragtime.

The New Ingredient

The new music had traditions, too, but they weren't European and they weren't written down. After the Civil War, when African-Americans were finally free to choose their professions, some of them chose to be musicians. It was a brave choice, because there was no musical establishment, black or white, to support it.

There was only one form of organized show business for black musicians to consider—the black minstrel company—and many made careers in minstrel bands. African-Americans who wanted to be pianists found even the minstrel door closed to them. The show day parade, which used bandsmen as living advertisements, was as important as the show itself, and most companies had no need of a musician who, because of his choice of instrument, could do only half of his job. The chances of employment were even slimmer in the world of classical music. Blind Tom and Blind Boone had concert careers because their managers knew that their disabilities were more interesting to the public than their abilities were. Each of these prodigies finally earned respect for his talent, but only after years of promotion as a sideshow attraction in evening dress.

Despite near-hopeless prospects in the 1870s and 1880s, a few dozen black pianists dared to hope for musical careers. They were the sons of slaves, some of them no more than a generation away from the polyrhythmic drumming and ring-shouts of African ritual. Some of these piano players were musically literate, most were not. A few had studied with teachers, most were self-taught. They did not come to music-making from the European piano tradition. Indeed, they carried no piano tradition at all. They were individualists, inventing and reinventing performance techniques for themselves, each making up his own way of playing the piano.

With their slam-bang attacks and rhythmic teasing, they reconceived piano performance. They became the first pop virtuosi, aggrandizing schottisches and minstrel ditties with noisy and extravagant effects. Their common belief was that every kind of music—marches, hymns, Stephen Foster songs—needed a good shaking up. Spurred by necessity and unfettered by notions of what couldn't—or shouldn't—be done, they created a new kind of piano playing.

The East had long been set in its cultural ways, so it would not harbor such audacious musical thinking. The pioneer pianists needed listeners as adventurous as they were, and the great westward expansion of the late nineteenth century provided them. As Americans scrambled to discover and to exploit their country's bounties—gold, oil, lead, timber, the land itself—rawboned communities sprang up in every place where the prospects seemed good. Roads intersected to form crossroads, tentacles of rails groped toward the Pacific, steel-trussed bridges spanned even the widest rivers—and every link made among roads, rails, and water turned a settlement into a town.

Most towns quickly threw up facades of respectability, but the piano players knew that, even in Victorian America, every respectable town had its underside, with at least a bar or two, a house, or a club that needed good-time music. The far-flung saloons and whorehouses of the Midwest and South became their marketplace. Because their professional world was small, they found themselves in cutthroat competition with each other. Whoever was flashiest got the job, and he held it until someone flashier came along. These itinerants were not in the network of show business, so most of them never published anything. But although there are relatively few published rags by black composers, the best early rags are theirs.

TOM TURPIN

From Savannah to St. Louis

By the mid-1880s St. Louis had become the hub of the pianists' wheel, a crossroads for vice as well as for rolling stock. The city's sporting district, known as Chestnut Valley, was crawling westward from the river along Chestnut and Market streets, sprouting new places to play as it claimed each block in its progress. One of the new businessmen in this area was a black man named John L. Turpin, who had moved to St. Louis in 1887—with his wife, Lulu, his teenage sons, Charles and Tom, and two younger daughters, Eleanora and Nannie—from Savannah, Georgia. Turpin opened a saloon called the Silver Dollar at 425 South Twelfth Street. This rough neighborhood bar was the beginning of a family empire in Chestnut Valley, the first of many places in which the Turpin men catered to revelers for nearly fifty years.

The Turpin sons did not stay in St. Louis to help their father with his new business very long. Wanderlust took them to the West, and they spent several years there, mining for gold in Searchlight, Nevada, then moving on to speculate in land and jewelry, not making a fortune but not losing one, either. The St. Louis city directory shows that they were back home by 1892, living with their family. Tom had learned (or had taught himself) to play the piano during his wandering years, and his first job on returning to St. Louis was as pianist at "the Castle," a three-story white brick whorehouse at 210 South Sixth Street, run by Madam "Babe" Connors. The 1896 directory listed Tom as a bartender, and we can see by the 1897 directory that the young man had been saving his money. He was still living at home with his parents that year, but he had opened his own saloon at 9 Targee Street.

As important as Tom's saloon might have been to the Turpin family finances, another of his achievements had implications far beyond St. Louis. In December 1897 a piece of music appeared with his name on it: "Harlem Rag," the first piece of published ragtime by a black composer. There were only a handful of previously published rags (all from 1897), and none as good as "Harlem." Turpin's first work stands as the defining piece of early ragtime, the one that is solid in style and structure, the first in which it is plain to hear what ragtime will be.

"Harlem Rag" was published by Robert DeYong, who was not a professional publisher but a prominent (white) lawyer and civic leader. Whatever tie there was between Turpin and DeYong is lost in the mists of time, and their unlikely association continues to baffle us. Because the Turpin family was influential in Chestnut Valley, perhaps Tom's publications were political payoffs of some sort. Perhaps DeYong, like John Stark and Jack Mills, published rags simply because he liked them. In any case, DeYong published a landmark. "Harlem Rag" announced St. Louis as a ragtime city, and it introduced the music's first important composer.

Turpin's second rag, "Bowery Buck," was issued by DeYong in 1899, and his "Ragtime Nightmare" appeared a year later. DeYong is named as publisher on a handful of songs issued between 1897 and 1900, but Turpin is the only composer he published more than once, and the Turpin pieces are his only rags. The first three Turpin rags were arranged by D. S. DeLisle (who would later make orchestrations for John Stark), and it is believed that the printing and distribution of them were handled by the Hunleth Music Company. These early rags were printed in small quantities, and were sold only in and around St. Louis, so neither Turpin nor his publisher got rich from them. (DeYong real-

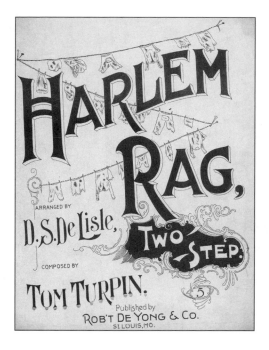

"Harlem Rag"

ized more from the rags than Turpin did, by selling the copyrights to larger publishers. The Joseph Stern Company, of New York, bought "Harlem," and the succeeding two were purchased by Will Rossiter, of Chicago.)

In 1900, around the time that his "Ragtime Nightmare" appeared, Tom Turpin closed his Targee Street saloon and opened a rambling entertainment complex at 2220–2222 Market Street. He called his new place the Rosebud Bar, and for the next six years it would be the den for the young lions of ragtime.

The Rosebud was a full-service pleasure establishment. There were two barrooms (for men only), a large gambling room, a room designated as "The Hunting and Shooting Club," a poolroom, private dining areas, and a "hotel" upstairs. Turpin held court in the wine room (where women were welcome), pounding away on a piano raised on blocks about a foot high so that he could play standing up. (He was a big man and a powerful player, and no piano stool or bench could

Newspaper ad for Turpin's Rosebud Bar

withstand the bouncing of his 350-pound frame.) Turpin was not the wine room's sole player for very long. Young black pianists were drawn to the Rosebud as pilgrims to Mecca. Even those who could not read music were impressed by Turpin's three published rags, and the man who, as far as they were concerned, had invented ragtime was on hand day and night, demonstrating his boisterous art. The kids who soaked up ragtime at the Rosebud knew that any vacant piano in the place was up for grabs, and no piano went unoccupied for long. They played for customers and for each other, for drinks and tips, and, no doubt, for Turpin's approval.

Two of the earliest Turpin disciples were Joe Jordan and Louis Chauvin, both gifted players in their late teens who were smitten with the fat man's music even before he opened the Rosebud. Jordan was the more industrious of the two, and he learned to read music at Turpin's urging. There was a quick payoff for Jordan's new skill: the first of his six published rags ("Double Fudge," issued by Hunleth in 1902) and a brief job as arranger for the acts in Turpin's short-lived vaudeville company in 1903. In 1904 Jordan left St. Louis to take a job as music director for the New Pekin Theatre in Chicago. By 1910, he was in New York, well on his way to what would be a long career as composer and arranger of theatre music. When Jordan was over sixty, he joined the faculty of the Modern Institute of Music, in Tacoma, Washington, where he continued to use, and pass on, the knowledge that Turpin had insisted he acquire.

Turpin's other "pupil," Louis Chauvin, was a brilliant wastrel who was so proficient at the piano that he never learned to read music because he saw no need to. He was a thunder-and-lightning player whose awesome technique and unique harmonic sense won him prize after prize in the Rosebud's piano contests. He warmed up with a rhapsodic treatment of a Sousa march, then tore into ragtime, producing a sound that burned in the brains of his listeners for decades after his death. Chauvin was a stalwart of local vaudeville, as dancer, singer, and accompanist for anyone in any key. But along with his great gifts, he harbored insatiable appetites: for women, alcohol, and opium. There is only one rag that bears Chauvin's name ("Heliotrope Bouquet," co-composed with Scott Joplin in Chicago), and, when Stark issued it in December 1907, Chauvin had three months left to live. His lurid living took its toll two weeks after his twenty-seventh birthday.

In late 1900 Scott Joplin moved to St. Louis, and his arrival made the city's reputation as ragtime capital of the world. Unlike the others who were gathering at Turpin's bar, Joplin was not a kid. He was thirty-two years old, and the fame of his published rags preceded him. With Joplin's arrival, the St. Louis triumvirate was complete: the city was home to ragtime's first patron (Turpin), its first major publisher (John Stark), and its first composer to be considered a genius.

SCOTT JOPLIN

From Sedalia to St. Louis

Scott Joplin was born to a dirt-poor family in Bowie County, Texas, in 1868. The little musical training that he had was given to him by Julius Weiss, a German immigrant who was tutoring a wealthy landowner's children in Texarkana, Arkansas, where the Joplins moved around 1880. With Weiss's instruction in the classics as his only musical education, and playing at churches and picnics as his only experience, Joplin left Texarkana in his late teens to become a musician. Like most black pianists of the time, Joplin roved from saloon to saloon, taking what jobs he could get and moving on when he lost them or when other prospects beckoned him. He headquartered in St. Louis, at "Honest John" Turpin's Silver Dollar, in the late 1880s; when he returned there from the Chicago World's Fair in 1893, he met the Turpin sons, Charlie and Tom.

After nearly fifteen years on the road, Joplin wanted a more substantial life, and in 1894 he relocated to Sedalia, Missouri, to find it. Sedalia was a saloon town, so there would be opportunities for work, but what seems to have drawn him there was the recent opening of George R. Smith College, established by the Methodist church for the "moral and intellectual culture of the colored people of the west." Before he could commit to the $1.50 per month tuition and the $2.50 per month fee for music instruction, there was a living to make, and Joplin made his in various ways. He played in saloons, of course, and for dances and parties. He gave piano lessons to several students, including Arthur Marshall, the teenage son of the family with whom he was boarding at 135 West Henry Street. He was a member of the Queen City Cornet Band for a while, but he left this band to form his own orchestra to hire out for dances. He got up an eight-member vocal group called the Texas Medley Quartette, and took them out for concert bookings. It was while touring with the Quartette that Joplin began to publish. His first two publications (both songs) were issued in Syracuse, New York, in 1895, and his next three (two marches and a waltz) were issued in Temple, Texas, the following year.

After his touring, Joplin returned to Sedalia, where he began to do some heavy thinking about music and about his place in it. Unlike most black pianists of his day, he knew there was music beyond the kind generally pumped out in saloons. He had sampled the classics with Professor Weiss and also, it is believed, at George R. Smith College. (The college records were lost in a fire, so we do not know if or when Joplin attended Smith.) He had organized vocal groups and played with bands and touring shows. He had published a bit and had been a teacher. His experience was richer than that of his contemporaries, but his future was no brighter because of it. Art was calling to him, but saloons were still his main source of income.

During a three-year period in which he published nothing, Joplin clarified a goal in his mind: if he could not make "respectable" music popular in the places he was given to play, he could try to make popular music respectable. Had he lived in another time or place, other kinds of music might have won him, but in Sedalia, Missouri, in the late 1890s, he chose ragtime as his metier. His decision was not a compromise nor was it made by default. He would not subvert the form by writing arty rags; he would honor it by writing rags of the highest order.

By late 1898 Joplin had written several rags, and he began to seek a publisher. He took them first to A. W. Perry & Sons, a music store-publisher that had been in business at 306 West Broadway in Sedalia since 1870. Perry turned them down, so Joplin went farther afield, to Kansas City. At the urging of his sheet music clerk, Charles N. Daniels, Carl Hoffman took a chance on one called "Original Rags," and thus became the first publisher to issue a Joplin rag. "Original Rags" appeared in the spring of 1899 (with Daniels named as arranger), and it announced the arrival of a master, not a talented beginner.

Joplin continued his professional double life. He was still a respected teacher (with Arthur Marshall's young friend Scott Hayden now among his pupils), and he still played in Sedalia saloons. In December 1898 he was among the charter members of a new social organization for black Sedalians, the Maple Leaf Club, and he was named on the club's business card as "the entertainer." During its thirteen-month existence, the Maple Leaf occupied a second-story room at 121 East Main Street.

"Original Rags"

About five blocks away, at 114 East Fifth Street, was the company that would send the club's name around the world: the music store of John Stark & Son. Stark would publish Joplin's "Maple Leaf Rag" in September 1899, and this peerless rag would transform American music. It was perfectly conceived and perfectly realized, the one rag that players and listeners could not get out of their heads—ever. Its journey around the world began with a single step, when, in the year after its issue, its publisher and its composer left Sedalia for St. Louis.

JOHN STARK

From Kentucky to St. Louis

The "Son" of John Stark & Son was William P. Stark, and he loved to recall the summer day in 1899 when Scott Joplin came into the store to try to interest his father in publishing one of his compositions. Joplin held a manuscript in one hand and the hand of a little boy in the other. He sat down at the piano to demonstrate the piece, and the boy began to dance. The elder Stark liked what he heard but thought it would be too hard for amateurs to play. Will Stark was so taken with the dancing boy (and with the composer's ingenuity in bringing him along) that he urged his father to buy the number anyway. A contract signed on August 10 gave John Stark & Son exclusive right to publish "Maple Leaf Rag." Joplin received no money in advance, but because a clause in the contract offered the (unusual) provision of a one cent per copy royalty, the publication of this, his second rag, would change his life.

John Stark's life would be irrevocably altered, too, but Stark was never shaken by change. For most of his fifty-eight years, he had gone from one profession to another totally dissimilar to it. He was born in Spencer County, Kentucky, in 1841, and his childhood was bleak. He was the youngest of eleven surviving siblings; his mother died bearing a twelfth child when John was three. The Stark children wore homemade clothes and rode horses to a log cabin school. The clan lived on the vegetables they could grow and the game they could shoot.

At twenty-two, John Stark enlisted in an Indiana artillery regiment and served as its bugler. His unit was one of those occupying New Orleans in the last year of the Civil War, and while on garrison duty there, Stark met and married a thirteen-year-old girl named Sarah Casey. After the war, with a soldier's pension as his only steady income, he and his child bride tried farming, first on his brother's place in Indiana, later as homesteaders near Maysville, Missouri.

In the early 1870s, Stark sold his farm and moved his family (now including three children) to Cameron, Missouri, to set himself up in the ice cream business. He roamed the countryside of northwestern Missouri selling ice cream out of a Conestoga wagon, and, amazingly, he prospered. He moved his growing enterprise to Chillicothe, where a salesman for the Jesse French Piano Company convinced him to carry pianos and reed organs with him as he made his rounds peddling ice cream. The unlikely combination of merchandise was a success. Stark was so good at talking farmers into buying keyboard instruments that he inspired himself. He began to look around for a town that needed a music store, and his eye fell on Sedalia. The town had only two music stores, A. W. Perry & Sons and J. W. Truxel, and one of them was ailing. In 1886 Stark bought out Truxel and moved his family to Sedalia.

Music became the center of the Stark family's life, and two of the three children seemed set on musical vocations. Eleanor, the youngest, was a promising pianist, and Etilmon, the oldest, was acquiring great skill on the violin. (Eleanor would study in Germany from 1895 to 1897 and would have a career as a concert artist as well as a teacher. Etilmon would teach music at various institutions and would become the Stark company's chief arranger.) The middle child, Will, who showed no talent as a performer, was bound to music in another way when John Stark chose him as a business partner. Stark had always liked music, and now that he was a proper bourgeois, he immersed himself in it. He grew to love the classics, and he presented Eleanor and her friends at musicales and recitals in his store.

Along with the store stock acquired from Truxel were seven copyrights, on music that Truxel had published in Sedalia, and Stark was intrigued by them. More as a hobby than a business venture, he began to dabble in publishing himself, issuing a handful of waltzes and schottisches to add to their number. He may not have known what ragtime was when he heard Joplin demonstrate the "Maple Leaf," but the sound of it moved him. Whatever it was, it was good music, and, against his commercial judgment, Stark decided to publish it. He chose as a cover illustration a drawing of two cakewalking couples from an American Tobacco Company ad, and he sent an order to the Westover Printing Company in St. Louis for 400 copies. By mid-September 1899 "Maple Leaf Rag" was on the counter at John Stark & Son.

It took a year for the 400 copies to sell, and during that year something stirred in John Stark. At fifty-nine, when he had already lived longer than insurance company actuaries thought he should, he was moved to roll the dice again, to walk away from his hard-won security in Sedalia, to go someplace bigger and do something more. These feelings did not come on him because of a sudden fanaticism for ragtime. "Maple Leaf" was difficult to play, as Stark had said it was, and it sold slowly, as he knew it would. He did not leave Sedalia to become a ragtime tycoon, but Joplin's rag was the catalyst for his leaving. When

"Maple Leaf Rag," Sedalia edition—Joplin's perfect rag

Stark tried to reorder copies from Westover, he was told that the press was busy with bigger and more important projects. It was the last time that John Stark would be told no by a printer. In the summer of 1900, he bought the Westover company and moved his family and his music business to St. Louis.

Joplin followed Stark to St. Louis a few months later, bringing with him his new bride, Belle Hayden, the widowed sister-in-law of his pupil Scott Hayden. The couple shared the second floor of a two-story house at 2658A Morgan Street (now Delmar Boulevard) with Scott Hayden and his wife, Nora. Joplin's name was not nationally known yet, but it was gold in the St. Louis underworld. He had written the rag that everybody there wanted to hear and that every pianist needed to know. Miraculously, it had gone into a second edition, issued by Stark in 1900 with a drawing of a maple leaf and Joplin's photograph on the cover. For the first time, a piece of ragtime had a face on it—and the face was black. Tom Turpin and the boys at the Rosebud gave Joplin a hero's welcome on his return to St. Louis.

THE FLOWERING OF ST. LOUIS RAGTIME
1900—1905

Stark's first St. Louis publication was another Joplin rag, "Swipesy," written in collaboration with Arthur Marshall, issued in July 1900. With only three published rags to his credit, Joplin began to draw the attention of the St. Louis musical establishment and of the white press. A February 1901 article in the St. Louis *Globe-Democrat* said that Alfred Ernst, director of the St. Louis Choral Symphony, was an admirer of Joplin's work and that he planned to take copies of Joplin's rags with him on his next trip to Germany as examples of good American music. About a month after his mention in the *Globe-Democrat*, Joplin's "Peacherine" and "Sunflower Slow Drag" (a collaboration with Scott Hayden) were issued under the Stark imprint.

That summer Stark and Joplin had a falling-out over Stark's refusal to publish Joplin's lengthy, balletlike "Ragtime Dance." Perhaps to declare his independence from Stark, Joplin self-published his "Easy Winners" in October 1901. Perhaps to intimidate Joplin, Stark issued his first non-Joplin rag (Fred Brownold's "Manhattan Rag") two months later.

In April 1902 the composer and his publisher reached a compromise regarding the troublesome "Ragtime Dance" when Stark published a simplified song version of the piece (with lyrics by Joplin). Joplin warily returned to the Stark fold, and Stark issued all four of his 1902 rags. A shadow of the rift hung over their relationship, however, and Joplin began to seek other publishers. A song version of "Maple Leaf Rag" (with lyrics by Sydney Brown, a clerk in Stark's store) was the only Stark-Joplin publication of 1903. Two of the three new Joplin rags of that year were published by Val A. Reis, and the third was issued by Victor Kremer in Chicago. Joplin's big project of 1903 was the touring production of his opera, *A Guest of Honor*, another experiment that John Stark had no intention of publishing.

St. Louis continued to attract ragtime talents. Among the new arrivals was the blind composer Charles Hunter, who came to St. Louis in 1902 to work as a tuner for the local branch of the Jesse French Piano

Company (headquartered in Nashville). Hunter seems not to have crossed the color line by visiting or playing at the Rosebud, and none of the survivors of that era mentioned him in their recollections. Joplin's Sedalia protégé, Arthur Marshall, stopped touring with McCabe's Minstrels to relocate in St. Louis in 1903 and quickly became a Rosebud regular and a fierce competitor in the club's piano contests.

The golden year in this golden age of St. Louis ragtime was 1904, when the city played host to the twenty million visitors who came to see the wonders at the Louisiana Purchase Exposition, known to St. Louisians and visitors alike as the World's Fair. (The Democratic party's national convention was also held in St. Louis that summer, as were the third Olympic Games of the modern era.) From April 30 until December 1, forty-three nations occupied separate exhibit buildings in Forest Park, and forty-five states and territories displayed artifacts of their culture and commerce in pavilions. For a fifty-cent admission fee, one could stroll the 1,275-acre fairgrounds and behold wondrous things: the world's largest pipe organ; a reenactment of a Boer War battle; a recreation of the Holy City; a reproduction of the Grand Trianon at Versailles. Aboriginal villages dotted the shores of Arrowhead Lake, where tattooed headhunters from the Philippines squatted around open fires. A giant Ferris wheel, 264 feet high, carried thirty-six cars, each seating sixty people. The Pike, an elegant mile-long midway at the northern edge of the grounds, was lined with concessionaires, offering snacks of all nations.

Even before the exposition opened, Chestnut Valley was in a festive mood. Tom Turpin held his third annual Rosebud Ball and piano contest on February 22 at New Douglass Hall, at the corner of Beaumont and Lawton streets. Louis Chauvin won the gold medal as piano champion, and Joe Jordan and Charlie Warfield tied for second place. In March the Arthur Pryor Band made the first recording of a Turpin composition, his "St. Louis Rag," for Victor, and provided another occasion to celebrate.

The John Philip Sousa band played at the fair for the entire month of May. Although ragtime was not to Sousa's personal taste, he was showman enough to program some syncopated numbers in deference to the city's musical rage. (His favorite was "At a Georgia Camp Meeting," an 1897 Kerry Mills cakewalk that he recorded nine times.) He told the

Globe-Democrat, "Good ragtime delights the heart and is characteristic of the American people." This pronouncement from the world's most famous bandmaster reassured St. Louis that its popular music was not so sinful and trashy after all. After listening to Sousa's cakewalks, fair-goers could go to the Spanish Cafe (where Arthur Marshall was playing) or to Old St. Louis (a beer hall where Louis Chauvin and Sam Patterson held forth) and hear the real thing.

Several rag composers offered syncopated impressions of the fair. Tom Turpin's "St. Louis Rag," published in November 1903 in anticipation of the fun, became popular through the timely Arthur Pryor recording of 1904. Scott Joplin's "Cascades" described the fair's ornate watercourse of fountains and lagoons. James Scott published his jaunty "On the Pike" in Carthage. Theron C. Bennett's "St. Louis Tickle" was issued in Chicago, as was W. C. Polla's "Funny Folks" (which depicts silhouettes of various ethnic types at the World's Fair on its cover).

Tom Turpin marked the end of the splendid year with his biggest party. A December 24 article in the *Palladium* offered the invitation:

> ... Mr. Tom Turpin, proprietor of the "Rosebud Bar," who, in addition to the new fixtures (which have recently been installed), has decided to remember his many friends and customers by placing an electric "Christmas tree" in his saloon, at No. 2220 and 2222 Market Street, upon which he will place presents for all. ...
>
> Appreciating the fact that providence has not dealt unkindly with him, and desiring to, in a measure, share his prosperity with his friends and customers, Mr. Turpin will expend upwards of $250 or $300 for presents, and the list embraces everything from a miniature bottle of Applegate's Famous Rosebud Whiskey (which has been made especially for the Rosebud Bar) to a diamond stud. The tree is beautifully illuminated by scores of electric lights in all colors. ...
>
> At a time like Christmas, when there are so many calls upon one's purse, a gift such as will be given on this occasion should be more than highly appreciated, and Mr. Turpin should be highly commended for his extreme largeness of heart.

One of the most pleasing events of the evening is that everybody in attendance Sunday, December 25, (Christmas night) will receive a present.

THIS MEANS YOU.

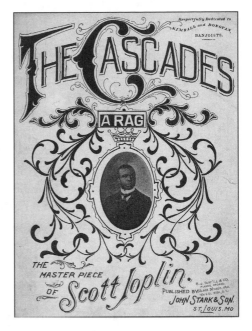

The Cascades

Neither John Stark nor Scott Joplin capitalized on the good will for ragtime that was generated by the fair. Stark moved his business (for the fourth time in his four years in St. Louis) to 210 Olive Street, and his firm published only three rags that year, including Joplin's "Cascades." Joplin was sidetracked by personal and financial woes. His marriage to Belle had always been stressful, and the death of their infant daughter broke them apart. Belle left him, it is believed, early in 1903, around the time that he became consumed with the preparation of his opera, *A Guest of Honor*. Joplin struggled valiantly to mount a production of this work and to keep it on the road, but the opera could sustain only an erratic six-week swing through small towns in the Midwest in the early fall.

The opera's failure saddled him with debt. Joplin set aside his goals as teacher and composer; he needed playing jobs again. He remarried in the summer of 1904, and took his new bride to Sedalia; she died of pneumonia about ten weeks after their wedding. Joplin's string of misfortunes seemed endless, and it unmoored him. Cutting his ties to Sedalia and St. Louis, the places that had nurtured his professional and artistic growth, Joplin became an itinerant once more.

For thirty months Joplin lived nowhere and did nothing in particular. He shuttled between St. Louis and Chicago, staying with friends in each city while he halfheartedly peddled his work. He wrote only one rag in 1905 ("Leola") and one in 1906 ("Eugenia"). He is credited as composer of two songs and as arranger of two others during this time, all of them tame and all of them probably done for hire.

The Rosebud boys began to move, too, but, unlike Joplin, they knew where they were going. Traveling men had tempted them with stories of Chicago. They said that city's sporting life, centered in the district known as the Levee, was grander than anything Chestnut Valley had to offer—with bigger houses, bigger saloons, bigger spenders. Every place was elegant there, and every place needed a piano player. One by one, the corps of St. Louis ragtimers answered Chicago's siren call: Scott Hayden first, then Joe Jordan, Arthur Marshall, and finally Louis Chauvin. In the summer of 1906, after they had all gone, Tom Turpin shut the Rosebud Bar.

INTERLUDE

John Stark in New York, 1905—1910

Although "Maple Leaf Rag" was by far the most successful Stark publication (selling 3,000 copies per month by 1905, according to the company ledgers), Stark did not yet see himself as a ragtime publisher. He thought of ragtime as one of many kinds of good music, and he was pleased to say that he published all kinds. In January 1905 Stark began issuing a monthly magazine, *The Intermezzo*, edited by himself and reflecting his own taste. There was a biography of a featured classical composer every month, along with tidbits of music history, jokes, and tips for piano teachers.

In the very first *Intermezzo*, Stark spelled out his catholic credo:

> This paper will have no hobbies in kind or class of music—we enjoy the works of the old masters. . . . [W]e also like the better class of simple home songs and easy instrumental pieces. . . . [W]e have seen even in the much discussed and cussed ragtime some real strokes of genius. The young player will do well to lay aside any prejudice and try all things holding fast to what is good.

But also in that first issue were hints of the direction Stark's passion would take. He reprinted another magazine's article defending ragtime and citing classical antecedents in syncopation. Then he added his own comments:

> What is ragtime? Let those who are sure they do not like it think up an answer. In the meantime, let us say that it is a rhythmic treatment of a melody, or score, and consists in tying an unaccented note to an accented one. It also intensifies the accent. Why is it bad? Echo answers why? The energetic fight against it by those who cannot play it gets funny when we consider that those syncopations have nothing whatever to do with the genius of melody or the scholarship of its harmonic treatment. . . . The good rag will live and the poor rag will die. It is not a sign of low taste to like ragtime of the better class.

Feeling his oats as publisher, editor, and tastemaker, the sixty-four-year-old Stark was ready for another bold move. In August 1905—one month after he declared in *The Intermezzo,* "And we will say again that we are no ragtime specialist"—he changed the name of his firm to Stark Music Company, and he moved its headquarters to New York City. He and Sarah took a house at 2321 Old Broadway, in upper Manhattan, and they set up an office and music store at 127 East Twenty-third Street. The shop was literally and figuratively outside the mainstream of commercial music, the enclave of publishers on West Twenty-eighth Street collectively known as Tin Pan Alley.

Because Stark refused to do business the way business was done, he would remain an outsider in New York. He joined no professional organizations, nor did he seek recordings of his numbers. He disdained the usual methods of music promotion, such as vaudeville plugging, star endorsements, and price wars. Except for writing cranky letters to trade journals, he did little to call attention to his presence. The only way that prospective buyers could know about his publications was to visit his music store.

American Musician and Art Journal, a trade paper of the time, often ran photographs of the movers and shakers in the music business. In the January 8, 1909, issue there is a portrait photo of the publisher F. B. Haviland and one of a Remick manager, Fred Belcher. Haviland and

John Stark's New York office

Belcher look like what the newspapers used to call "captains of industry," keen-eyed, square-jawed, and prosperous. In the same issue there is a photograph of Stark, taken in his Twenty-third Street office, that lets us see him as his competition—the Remicks, Havilands, and Sterns— must have seen him. He is coatless, goateed, and bespectacled, sitting in a rocking chair examining some papers spread before him on a cluttered rolltop desk, which sits across the room from an ancient typewriter. There is a fire ax hanging on the wall behind him. He looks like a Chillicothe grain merchant catching up on his accounts.

For all his shortcomings in marketing, Stark was at least beginning to understand what his product was. In the August 1905 *Intermezzo*, he took a poke at Walter Damrosch, New York's leading music critic. Damrosch had written that he was "not exactly in love with ragtime as exemplified in the coon song and the cake walk." Stark excused his poor taste as ignorance:

> His whole article, like most Eastern writers who attempt to enlighten
> us on the evils of ragtime, fails to touch the *fact* of the St. Louis arti
> cle . . . a distinctive . . . twentieth century creation. None have arisen
> above the coon song or the cakewalk and seem to mistake this for *the*
> *real thing*.

Stark's source for "the real thing" was Missouri, and the majority of Stark's twenty-three New York rags were by writers he had cultivated in his home state: James Scott, Arthur Marshall, and Scott Joplin.

In the spring of 1907 Scott Joplin moved to New York. The passing of time had exorcised his demons, and he was ready to start afresh, to capitalize on his reputation as composer of the most popular rag ever written. There had been three recordings of "Maple Leaf" so far (one by the U.S. Marine Band and two by the banjoist Vess Ossman), and Stark was shipping several thousand copies a month. Joplin's name could open doors now, so he began to visit publishers. The first to issue his work that year were Joseph W. Stern & Company ("Searchlight Rag" and "Gladiolus Rag") and Boston's Joseph M. Daly Company ("Rose Leaf Rag"). And of course, he had to call on John Stark. Stark took his "Heliotrope Bouquet" (his recent collaboration with the dying Louis Chauvin in Chicago) and "The Nonpareil," both of which Stark published late in 1907.

In the autumn of 1907 a young man named Joseph Lamb came to browse in the Stark store. When he remarked to Mrs. Stark how much he admired the rags of Scott Joplin, she asked if he would like to meet Joplin. Lamb said that he would like nothing more, so she led him to the back of the store, where her husband and Joplin were chatting. They all talked a while, then Joplin and Lamb left together, still caught up in a conversation about music. Lamb mentioned that he had composed some rags himself and that Stark had turned them down. Joplin offered to hear them. A few days later, Lamb went to Joplin's boardinghouse to play for his idol. When he played "Sensation," the white New Jerseyan got the supreme compliment from one of the black boarders, who pronounced it "a genuine Negro rag."

As he had done for James Scott, Joplin interceded for Lamb with his publisher. In 1908 Stark issued Lamb's "Sensation" (with Joplin named as its arranger), and another important and exclusive writer-publisher partnership was born. Stark would eventually publish twelve Lamb rags, and Lamb's work would come to be considered on a par with Joplin's and Scott's. The addition of Lamb's name to his catalog gave Stark all three of the most important composers in ragtime. He began to call his offerings "high-class rags" and to refer to his company as "the classic rag house," and his boasting was justified.

Not all of Tin Pan Alley's lessons were lost on Stark, and the practice that he adopted in 1908 cost him his prize composer. Almost alone

"The Top Liner Rag"—Lamb's perfect rag

among ragtime publishers, Stark had for years shown the foresight and fairness to offer his writers royalties on their work. His buying price was low, but his penny-a-copy terms ensured some profit to the composer over the life of a publication. In 1960 Arthur Marshall told Bob Darch, "That's one thing about old man Stark. He was pretty fair with us people that he bought rags from. He'd give 'em a royalty on it—and that's the only way it should be."

But in 1908 Stark began to offer flat fees, and the occasional "tip" later, as payment for compositions. Joe Lamb received $25 for "Sensation," along with a promise of $25 more if a thousand copies were sold. Lamb got the second $25 in four weeks but nothing further. In 1909 J. Russel Robinson sent Stark his "Sapho Rag" from Macon, Georgia, where he was working as a silent movie pianist. Stark sent Robinson $25 and said that he could also have some copies of his work. Robinson wrote asking for 1,000 copies, and Stark, probably prodded by guilt at having nicked the young composer, sent them. Robinson sold his free copies, making much more than Stark had paid him for the composition.

Such penny-ante payment was agreeable to first-time composers like Lamb and Robinson, but Joplin would have none of it. His "Fig Leaf Rag," published by Stark in February 1908, marked the end of their association. It is not known on what terms "Fig Leaf" was sold to Stark, but whatever the terms were, Joplin didn't like them. After a three-year dry spell, he was thinking in ragtime again. He was coming into a productive period, and he knew it. He could not set the precedent of selling good rags to John Stark for peanuts, plus copies. There were other publishers and better deals.

In April 1908, Seminary Music issued "Sugar Cane," the first of six Joplin rags published by that firm. Joseph Stern and Joplin himself published the three remaining Joplin rags issued before his death in 1917. Stark would issue three "new" Joplin rags after 1908, but they were all purchased previously, before the matter of royalties clouded their relationship.

J. Russel Robinson

Stark's ledger for 1909 shows that "Maple Leaf Rag" had sold a half million copies by then, and "Frog Legs" and a few others were also doing well. Stark was not without his successes, but the New York competition exasperated him. He wrote in a trade circular that Leo Feist had "filled up the Woolworth 5 and 10 ct. stores with music on sale" and that "New York Music Company (Albert Von Tilzer) actually sends a man to these 10 ct. stores to sing and push their pieces." Price-cutting and plugging, the most ordinary of Tin Pan Alley practices, appalled him. He saw it all as a ruthless game, and he refused to play. Early in 1910 he issued one last New York imprint (Harry Ellman and S. Lew Schwab's "Sand Paper Rag") before he closed his Twenty-third Street office. He went back to St. Louis, where they knew chalk from cheese.

ST. LOUIS

Stark and Turpin Play It Out, 1910—1922

As John Stark retrenched in his new headquarters at 3818 Laclede Avenue, the Turpin brothers began new professional ventures. In 1910 Tom opened the Eureka Club at 2208 Chestnut Street, and he hired Arthur Marshall, recently back from Chicago, as his house man. Charles Turpin ran for, and won, the office of district constable, becoming the first African-American elected to public office in St. Louis. Together, the Turpins went into show business that year, opening the Booker T. Washington Airdome, a tent theatre, at 2323 Market Street. The Airdome presented vaudeville revues with local talent in "theme" shows (African, cowboy, Egyptian, etc.) that changed every week. Charlie did the booking and ran the business, while Tom was in charge of the music. The responsibility of arranging and composing to suit new performers and themes each week required that Tom take on an assistant at the Airdome. The young man that he hired for the job was Artie Matthews, the last of the St. Louis ragtimers to have Turpin as his mentor.

Artie Matthews was born in Braidwood, Illinois, in 1888, and he settled in St. Louis when he was twenty years old. He made the typical ragtime pilgrim's progress: beginning as an ear player, hymn-centered studying with his mother, taking some pianistic tricks from other players, working in saloons, finally teaching himself to read and write music. In addition to his job at the Airdome, Matthews played at Barrett's Theatorium, a combination vaudeville-silent movie house. He published a pop song with Thiebes-Stierlin in 1908, and in 1912 his name appeared as arranger of two songs by the black vaudevillian Baby Seals ("Baby Seals Blues" and "Well, If I Do, Don't You Let It Get Out," both published locally by Seals and Fisher). Matthews was learning by doing, and within a few years, he would be the city's most important composer and arranger of ragtime.

In 1912 Matthews made his first arrangement for John Stark, a work that brought Stark the closest he would ever come to having a hit song. The Stark publication that became nationally famous in the

Stark Music Company building in St. Louis

spring and summer of that year was a faux-hillbilly number called "They Gotta Quit Kickin' My Dawg Aroun'," written by Stark's daughter-in-law, Carrie Bruggeman Stark (Will's wife), using the hickish pseudonym "Cy Perkins." The song was devised for Representative Champ Clark, a Missourian who was Speaker of the House as well as the underdog in a nip-and-tuck battle with Woodrow Wilson for the presidential nomination of the Democratic party. The pugnacious ditty was

"The Lily Rag"

played at Clark rallies around the country, and it garnered enough notoriety to catch the attention of M. Witmark & Sons in New York. Witmark made an offer of $10,000 for it, and the amazed Stark accepted. Witmark quickly reissued the song (using Stark's cover, with a drawing of a forlorn dog labeled "Jim"). On July 1, at the Democratic convention in Baltimore, Wilson wrested the nomination from Clark on the forty-sixth ballot, and the song's vogue ended in a stroke, along with the presidential hopes of Missouri's favorite son.

With "Maple Leaf Rag" on its way to the million-copy mark, "Frog Legs" selling steadily, and the big sale of a song to a New York publisher, John Stark became energized again. He had always enjoyed ragtime, and now he became monomaniacal about it. He had amassed fifty rags by 1912, a list unique in its scope and its quality. Any ten of them were better than any ten in anyone else's catalog. Stark, now over seventy, decided to commit wholeheartedly to his rags, to add to their number, and to plead their case before a tin-eared public. There would be no more new rags from Joplin or Marshall, but James Scott was at the height of his productivity, and Joseph Lamb was coming along. J. Russel Robinson, still an itinerant silent movie accompanist in the South, sent three rags to Stark in 1911.

Stark had pulled the plug on *The Intermezzo* a few years earlier, and now he stopped proselytizing for classical music altogether. Anyone could reprint the works of the old masters, but nobody had what Stark had. It was time to exploit the treasures that were his alone. He began by issuing an orchestra folio called *Standard High Class Rags*, which contained fifteen of his gems in new arrangements made by his son Etilmon and D. S. DeLisle. Seven of the fifteen rags were by Scott Joplin. If the public wanted to think that the king of ragtime was Stark's house composer, so be it. The publication of this 1912 collection, which became known to musicians as "The Red Back Book," was the kickoff to Stark's most active years as publisher and promoter of ragtime, 1913 to 1919.

Also in 1912 Stark created a second publishing imprint, Syndicate Music Company. Carrie Stark recalled that the purpose of Syndicate was to issue rags that "were not quite up to the Stark standard." Syndicate would issue only eight rags in its eight-year life (beginning with Charles Humfeld's "That Left-Hand Rag," published in December 1912), while Stark Music would issue forty-three during the same period. Stark's top drawer was fuller than the drawer below it. (The only Syndicate rag that was misread by Stark as a second-class work was Charles Thompson's 1914 masterpiece, "The Lily Rag," one of the most original conceptions in all of ragtime literature.)

As Stark expanded his enterprise in the early teens, so did Tom Turpin, and both men leaned heavily on the arranging and composing talents of Artie Matthews. In 1913 the Turpins' Booker T. Washington moved its shows indoors, into a large permanent theatre building, and dropped the "Airdome" from its name. Black vaudeville was becoming big business, and Charles Turpin joined its major cartel, the Theatre Owners' Booking Association. The T.O.B.A. circuit, called "Toby time" by its performers, had grown from a motley string of tent shows in the South and Midwest into a chain of first-class houses. The Turpins' affiliation with the T.O.B.A. signified their evolution from producers of semi-professional and amateur talent to presenters of the biggest names in black entertainment. Artie Matthews and Tom Turpin weren't cob-bling together music for local acts anymore; they were working with stars. The Booker T. Washington Theatre was the most successful and longest-lived of the Turpin businesses, hosting Bessie Smith, Butterbeans and Susie, Ethel Waters, and Ida Cox throughout the 1920s and enduring into the early 1930s, outliving white vaudeville in St. Louis by several years.

In 1913 the obvious dawned on John Stark: if Artie Matthews could compose and arrange to order every week for the Booker T. Washington, he could likely write some rags. Stark made Matthews the uncharacteristically generous offer of $50 apiece for any rags accepted for publication, and before long, Matthews brought in the first in a set he called the "Pastimes." Stark issued "Pastime Rag No. 1" and "Pastime Rag No. 2" that year. ("No. 3" would appear in 1916, "No. 5" in 1918, and "No. 4" in 1920.) Taken together, Matthews' five "Pastimes" are the apogee of teens ragtime, made in the classic form but full of advanced and highly theatrical ideas, suggesting the parade of variety acts that passed through the Booker T. Washington. There is a lot of chromatic action in them, much of it using chord clusters to produce restless and unusual harmonies. All of the "Pastimes" were issued with the same cover, which labeled each of them "A Slow Drag," but they contain a kaleidoscope of rhythms, from shimmering tangos to crisp stop-time to *misterioso* sections in which the melody moves to the bass, winding underneath relentless sixteenth notes in the right hand. Stark got a lot of music for his money when he bought the "Pastimes."

Matthews came into his own as an arranger in 1914. As a Stark employee, he worked on Thompson's "Lily Rag" that year, as well as Robert Hampton's "Cataract Rag." The following year he arranged Hampton's "Agitation Rag" and Lucian Gibson's "Jinx Rag." ("Jinx" had been self-published in 1911 by Gibson, and Matthews's reworking improved it greatly.) The Hampton and Gibson rags are marked by Matthews's distinctive chromatics and dense chording. Also in 1915 Stark issued Matthews's instrumental "Weary Blues," containing two twelve-bar melodies and a middle section with a walking boogie bass line. Stark was still paying on the "flat fee plus" system: he bought "Weary Blues" outright for $50, but he threw in another $27 so that Matthews could buy a suit of clothes. Probably at Matthews's suggestion, Syndicate Music published the black vaudevillian Willie Too Sweet's song "I'm So Glad My Mamma Don't Know Where I'm At" in 1915, another work that bears Matthews's harmonic touches, although his name is not on it.

In 1914 Stark added another star, the Indiana-born Paul Pratt, to his impressive roster of ragtime composers. Stark had previously published a handful of Pratt's songs, including "That Gosh Darn Hiram Tune," a vaudeville favorite of 1912, but none of Pratt's rags. Pratt sent "Hot House Rag" to Stark in January 1914, and Stark thought it too hard for the amateur player. He replied in a February 3 letter: "The rag you sent is a tough proposition . . . there is not many millions of the guileless denizens of this great country who can interpret it. This class is not a swift seller with us but is steady and permanent. What is your idea of compensation for the manuscript?" Pratt's idea of compensation must have been somewhere around $25 plus copies, because "Hot House" was issued by Stark in July. The five piano roll versions of "Hot House" issued in 1914 indicate that it attained some degree of popularity. In 1916 Stark published his second Pratt instrumental, "Spring-Time Rag," which syncopates Mendelssohn's "Spring Song." In 1917 Pratt's "On the Rural Route" appeared under the Stark imprint.

John Stark had much to crow about in the mid-teens, and his crowing, in the form of blurbs on his music and advertising circulars, was shrill, sarcastic, and pompous all at once. Under the headline OUR RAG TIME IS DIFFERENT, he wrote:

> Positively if you have never heard "Maple Leaf Rag," "Sunflower Slow Drag" or the other RAGS OF OUR LIST, then you have never heard RAG TIME—the simon pure, the REAL THING.
>
> If we simply say to you, that they are fine above all others—then you have heard language as strong from others and the music was weak. If we tell you that these "RAGS" are really startling and thrilling—why, this is a bromide, rank, and may not even attract your attention. What shall we say then? Shall we sound the hew gag, blow our trumpet inside-out and smash the big bass drum?
>
> It may be that you have heard all the great operas, perhaps have been to Coney and have shot the Chutes and bumped the bumps.

Possibly have visited the art centers of many nations and have blown yourself for all the treasures and pleasures that came in your way; but, if you have never heard these syncopes played with artistic precision and effect, then you are poor indeed, and life's joys have been but meager. No words can describe them. If one falls in a new place it sets the woods on fire. If played by request or as an encore at a concert, it smashes the programme and must be repeated to the end of the show. They have actually been known to stop the conversation at a church social. Seriously, they are both classic and popular, profound and simple. They please at once the untutored and the cultured.

Everybody likes them the first time they hear them played, and they like them still better when they have heard them one hundred times or more. "Age cannot wither nor custom stale their infinite variety." No musician can outgrow them. They will add luster to any repertoire.

They are played by the country fiddler and are turned loose on the circumambient by the greatest bands and orchestras, in all cases reducing competitive imitations to the cube root of a vacuum.

In thus describing them we are surprised at our own moderation. The half has not been told. If you have heard Maple Leaf, then know that we have many others as good. Send for free catalogue. You cannot do without the entire set.

STARK MUSIC CO.

Other publishers sold "slush," "filthy songs," and "Molly crawl-bottom stuff posing under rag names," Stark said, while he offered "the perfection of type," "classics that line up ragtime with the Masters of all time." His rags contained "more genius and psychic advance than a Chopin nocturne or a Bach fugue." His company was "the fountain head," the "one classic rag house." Lamb's "Contentment" was "an inspiration that will live forever." Scott's "Sunburst" was "profound as Beethoven and thrilling as a country fiddler." "Hilarity" was as "furious as a cat fight." In writing "Cataract," Robert Hampton "left foot prints on the sands of time." In 1914 a Stark ad announced that "Maple Leaf Rag" had sold a million copies, and that "there will be a temporary stop to its sale when every family in the civilized world has a copy."

There is a lot of P. T. Barnum in Stark's ads, but there is a bit of the mad Lear, too. While he was haranguing about classic ragtime, a new generation of pianists was emerging, and these players saw Stark's rags only as precursors to other, more dazzling kinds of music. The influence of these players was even beginning to seep into the agon of ragtime, Tom Turpin's annual piano contest. Turpin held his last big competition over a four-week period in 1916, when sixty-eight players vied for the gold medal and the $175 offered as prizes. The winner, who clinched his victory in a playoff with Turpin himself, was Charles Thompson. Thompson had recently returned from the East, where he had acquired some new weapons for his pianistic arsenal: the speedball tricks of James P. Johnson. Thompson didn't play stride in 1916, but he didn't win the contest by playing "Peacherine" at a lope, either. In Chicago, Charley Straight, musical director of the Imperial Player Roll Company, was evolving a style of playing that would replicate the magic of the player piano itself. W. C. Handy's blues began to sweep America in the mid-teens, and the predictable patterns of blues chords made confident improvisers out of pianists who weren't even good players. In 1917 the first jazz recording was released, and it was a smash. The cacophony of jazz was the death knell of classic ragtime.

Many of the Stark rags were marked with admonitions to the player: "Do not play this piece fast" and/or "Do not fake." The kids who were practicing Charley Straight's "Hot Hands" wanted nothing more than to play fast, and those taking up blues and jazz knew that faking was de rigeur. The craft of the classic rag seemed to them as stodgy as the craft of tatting.

Stark hung on in a dwindling ragtime market, but most of his pioneer contemporaries did not. The first to give up was Scott Hayden, who had been the first of the Rosebud gang to go to Chicago. After a couple of years of getting nowhere as a pianist in the Levee, Hayden took a job as an elevator operator at Cook County Hospital. He rode the hospital's elevator for twelve years, until his death in 1915. Late in 1916 Arthur Marshall finished his stint at St. Louis's Moonshine Gardens, then retired from active composing and playing. In New York, Joseph Lamb tried the music business for a while, as plugger and arranger for the J. Fred Helf Music Publishing Company, but he didn't like it. In 1914 he went to work for a financial firm specializing in import and customs business, and he would hold this job until his retirement in 1957. He sent rags to Stark through the mid-teens, and Stark published his last Lamb rag, "Bohemia," in February 1919. Artie Matthews had had enough of the ragtime life by 1915, the year he left St. Louis to become the organist at Berea Presbyterian Church in Chicago. Tom Turpin wrote his final rag ("Pan Am Rag") in 1914, but it went unpublished. He spent his last years as manager of his brother Charlie's Jazzland Dance Hall at 2216 Market Street. The godfather of St. Louis ragtime also resided at Jazzland for a while, at 2216A. He was employed as a deputy constable when he died in 1922.

Even Joplin, the best and best known of all ragtimers, was moving away from the music that his work had defined. He turned out some top-notch rags in his first three years in New York ("Pine Apple Rag," "Wall Street Rag," "Fig Leaf Rag," and "Stoptime Rag"), and late in 1910 he completed the writing of what he believed to be his masterwork, not a rag but an opera, *Treemonisha*. He self-published the piano-vocal score in May 1911, confident that he would soon get a production. A black vaudeville producer named Thomas Johnson assembled a cast of fifty-one and scheduled a premiere in Atlantic City for November 1911. While the company was in rehearsals, Johnson disappeared and the premiere was canceled. Joplin tried to salvage something from the debacle by presenting a script-in-hand performance as a backers' audition in a Harlem rehearsal hall. The audience numbered fewer than twenty, none of them backers.

"*Fig Leaf Rag*"

Treemonisha became Joplin's obsession. After Joseph Stern's publication of "Scott Joplin's New Rag" in 1912, Joplin would have no more to do with mainstream publishers and little to do with ragtime. He wrote "Magnetic

Rag," which he self-published in 1914, and he plucked three numbers from the *Treemonisha* score to issue under his own imprint. As his Tin Pan Alley contacts fell away, so did his writing and teaching. In 1915 he placed an ad in the Indianapolis *Freeman*, offering to send any six of his compositions on receipt of a one-dollar money order. It was around this time that he began to exhibit symptoms of the syphilis that would destroy his mind and then take his life. He died on Sunday, April 1, 1917, in the mental ward of Manhattan State Hospital. In December of that year, John Stark issued "Reflection Rag," the last Joplin work to bear the Stark name.

The world was going jazz-crazy, and there were only two players left in the classic rag game: John Stark and the "local Mozart," James Scott. The Scott-Stark publications of the late teens were the last gasp of Missouri ragtime. In September 1921 the two diehards took a shot at the enemy with a Scott number entitled "Don't Jazz Me—Rag (I'm Music)," but the enemy was making too much noise to notice. By 1922 it was time to go. In January of that year Stark issued Scott's "Broadway Rag," the composer's last piece of ragtime and the publisher's last ragtime publication.

The corpse of Stark Music Company twitched a few times in the 1920s. In an undated letter obviously written after he had stopped buying new work, Stark introduces himself (fifteen years too late) to the Edison Phonograph Company. He reminds Edison that he has a line of rags "known in all countries where people wear clothes," and he implores the company to "use one of our best late rags and put one of the older ones (before 1909) on the opposite side. We assure you that it will be the best instrumental record that you have made. Should not be Jazzed, there are notes enough and they are in exactly the right place." The "to whom it may concern" letter did not prompt Edison to record any Stark rags. In 1925 Stark sold the orchestrations and the mechanical rights to "The Red Back Book" folio to Melrose Brothers Music of Chicago.

Stark left for the office every morning at six throughout the mid-1920s, but there was little to do there except handle orders for reprints, many of them for "Maple Leaf Rag." Lottie Joplin renewed the copyright on "Maple Leaf" and reassigned the publishing rights to the old man who had had his doubts about it in the Sedalia music store twenty-eight years earlier. John Stark died on November 20, 1927, at age eighty-six. His company sputtered along for a few years until his family decided to turn the publishing plant back into a commercial shop. The ragtime factory became a printing press again.

KANSAS CITY
The First Frontier

Like St. Louis, Kansas City began as a trading post. At the juncture of two rivers, the Missouri and the Kansas, the first white settlement was established in the spring of 1821 by François Chouteau, a representative of the American Fur Company. In 1825 the town of Independence (named for the steamboat that proved the Missouri River to be navigable in 1819) arose about ten miles east of Choteau's outpost. In 1832 a merchant named John Calvin McCoy set up shop about four miles south of Choteau and proclaimed his store the terminus of the Santa Fe Trail. The following year, McCoy platted his toehold on the trail and named it Westport. This clump of three rawboned communities, with a few dozen families each, provided the jumping-off point for those going west from the central United States. Trappers were the first to stop for supplies, and they were soon followed by traders and homesteaders outfitting themselves with horses, wagons, and provisions for their treks to the Promised Land.

Because Westport's storekeepers received their merchandise from the riverboats that docked at Choteau's settlement, this site became known as Westport Landing. The auxiliary to Westport grew into an active trading center, independent of Westport itself, and in 1838 the Landing was platted and renamed the Town of Kansas, a belated nod to the Kansas Indians, the original settlers of the area, who had been uprooted by the coming of the white man.

The dirt streets of the three neighboring (and rival) towns bustled with oxcarts and mule-drawn wagons laden with supplies for pioneers: groceries, cotton, notions, and lots of whiskey. Francis Parkman passed through Westport in 1846, and his description of it could have set the scene for a dime novel:

> Westport is full of Indians, whose little shaggy ponies were tied by dozens along the houses and fences. Sacs and Foxes with shaved heads and painted faces; Shawnee and Delawares fluttering in calico frocks and turbans; Wyandottes dressed like white men, and a few wretched Kansas wrapped in old blankets, were strolling about the streets. Whiskey circulates more freely in Westport than is altogether safe in a place where every man carries a loaded pistol in his pocket.

In 1853 the Town of Kansas was incorporated as the City of Kansas. After some stormy years preceding and during the Civil War, when the city was a hotbed of marauding Southern sympathizers, it became a place with growth and industry on its mind. The Missouri Pacific railroad came in 1865; the first stockyards were built in 1870; and in 1877 a huge grain exchange building was erected, turning Kansas City into a center for storage and milling. In 1897 Kansas City annexed Westport. Within a quarter of a century of its incorporation, the wild town tamed itself.

J. W. JENKINS' SONS

The music business in Kansas City seems to have taken its tone from the shopkeepers who were the city's founding fathers. The St. Louis music scene had nearly a hundred-year head start, but Kansas City's had more commercial hustle. Despite a smaller population and fewer publishers, and without a clutch of composer-geniuses in residence, more hit songs and rags originated in Kansas City than in St. Louis. No local publisher had long-term relationships with "star" writers; indeed, except for Charles L. Johnson, the city had no writer whose name alone would sell a rag. There was not much local publishing of classical reprints or choir music. The music stores, and presumably their customers, were mainly interested in band pieces and pop numbers.

Although its reputation was that of a rough-and-tumble cow town, Kansas City fostered a surprising amount of musical activity in the late nineteenth century. Mrs. Mary Donahue brought the first piano to the village in 1850 and began giving lessons in her studio at Pearl and Market streets. In 1859–1860, when Kansas City's population was about 5,000, the city directory listed its first music store proprietor, Robert T. Wilson, who was "on Main Street opposite the Court House." By 1871 there were five music stores, including that of Kansas City's first music publisher, Abram Kimmell, who stayed in business for thirty years. In 1878, fifty-one-year-old John Wesley Jenkins, the publisher who would grow the largest and outlast them all, opened his first music shop, in the back room of A. C. Moffat's combination wallpaper-and-piano store at 615 Main Street.

At the time of his reach into Kansas City, John Jenkins was a traveling salesman for the music store owned by Henry M. Hoffman and his brother Carl Hoffman in Leavenworth, Kansas. (Carl Hoffman would later become Jenkins's main music store rival in Kansas City. Hoffman and Jenkins would vie for the same composers, arrangers, and demonstrators in the local talent pool, and at various times, each bested the other for their services. There were fewer than six degrees of separation among those in Kansas City's ragtime scene.) Jenkins commuted the thirty miles between his job with the Hoffmans and his one-room store for a year before he decided that Kansas City was the place to bet on and moved there. In 1880 he bought out Moffat and began to build a musical empire. He had his own line of guitars and mandolins manufactured under the Harwood label, and he added these to the Moffat stock of pianos and organs. This heavy investment in instruments led Jenkins to create an instrument repair division of his company. He began publishing in the early 1880s, issuing music for mandolin and guitar. Elmer Grant Ege was placed in charge of Jenkins's publishing division, a position he would hold for more than forty years.

The Jenkins family provided the staff. The "Sons" were John and Frederick (both clerks) and Clifford (the bookkeeper). Jenkins's daughter Florence handled sales in the store and gave on-site piano lessons.

E. Grant Ege

Each division of his enterprise flourished from the beginning and kept on flourishing. At the time of the founder's death in 1890, J. W. Jenkins' Sons was the preeminent music store in the central Midwest. After the founder died, the Sons moved their inherited company to larger quarters at 921 Main Street.

The company's continuing growth inspired Elmer Ege to change its publishing line. Jenkins opened a branch in St. Joseph, Missouri, and another in Hutchinson, Kansas (the first links in a chain that would eventually number sixteen stores in the Midwest and South). By 1900 the time was right to expand the music catalog, which had primarily offered method books and parlor pieces, no better or worse (and no more attractive) than those of other local publishers. Now that Jenkins stores could sell Jenkins imprints in three cities, it made sense to exploit this broad customer base with some popular music. This meant acquiring snappier songs and instrumentals and giving them covers that caught the eye with color and design rather than with typography. Any turn-of-the-century publisher who was going commercial had to have some syncopated numbers. Jenkins's first regional hit was a cakewalk, written by the company's star demonstrator, Charles L. Johnson.

Charles Johnson had previously published a few waltzes, marches, and songs with Jenkins, but nothing caused a stir like his first syncopated piece, issued in 1899. It was "Doc Brown's Cakewalk," named for Doctor William Henry Joseph Cutter Brown, a local character who cakewalked through life. Brown was not a professional dancer (he worked as a cook's helper in a boardinghouse), but he was Kansas City's Terpsichore. He was small, slender, and, as one of his admirers put it, "black as the inside of a cow." And he was the struttingest man in town. Dressed in a stovepipe hat and black morning coat, he took the prize at every local dance contest; he was a one-man unit in minstrel show parades; he danced at the opening of the new Convention Hall in 1899. If there were no occasion to cakewalk, he created his own. He cakewalked through the streets as he did errands for his employers; children wishing to see him do the grapevine twist had only to stop him on the sidewalk and ask him. He eschewed the streetcar, preferring to prance his way to wherever he was going.

Because of its beloved subject, "Doc Brown's Cakewalk" was assured of local success. Jenkins issued the number early in 1899 (with a photo of Doc Brown on the inside front cover), and on the piano solo edition were listed fourteen other versions arranged for various combinations of instruments. "Doc Brown's Cakewalk" got the supreme plug when the Sousa band performed it at a Heim Park concert shortly after its release.

In May 1899 Jenkins published Johnson's first rag, "Scandalous Thompson," with the composer's photo on the cover. The publication of two syncopated numbers did not turn Johnson into a ragtime writer nor Jenkins into a ragtime publisher, but they opened the door a little wider for ragtime in Kansas City. In November 1899 Jenkins issued Frank X. McFadden's "Rags to Burn," a medley of folk themes. Charles Johnson left Jenkins in 1901 to work for Carl Hoffman, and Jenkins published no more rags until 1902, the year that the company moved its headquarters to a six-story building at 1013–1015 Walnut Street. In a tit for tat after losing Johnson to Hoffman, Jenkins lured away Hoffman's star plugger, E. Harry Kelly, in 1903. (Kelly was once sent home to change his clothes after he appeared at work wearing a bright red vest. His employment with Jenkins did not last long.)

Johnson had his greatest influence on the Jenkins company after he left his job there. In 1907 Johnson's "Dill Pickles" (originally published by Carl Hoffman in 1906) was bought by Charles N. Daniels for reissue by Remick in New York, and it became a huge hit. Seeing Johnson's local rag attain national prominence spurred Jenkins to its most intensive years of ragtime publishing, 1907–1911. During this time Jenkins published and republished the rags of local composers such as Charles Johnson, Harry Kelly, Ed Kuhn, Lucien Denni, Irene Cozad, and Mamie Williams.

Kansas City was slightly more amenable to women composers than St. Louis was. No female composer published more than one rag in St. Louis, but several Kansas City women found a publisher for a second one. The most prominent female ragtime composer in St. Louis was Irene Giblin, who was a music demonstrator at the Stix, Baer & Fuller department store, but none of her nine rags were published there. Except for Joplin's "Original Rags" (1899) and James Scott's "Dixie Dimples" (published by Will Livernash in 1918), there were no Kansas City rag publications by black writers.

In June 1914 the famous bandmaster, Missouri-born Arthur Pryor, brought his band to Kansas City for a series of concerts. He gave an interview to the *Star* congratulating the city on the maturation of its musical taste:

> Kansas City is home to me, and for that reason I am proud of the fact that out of scores of requests for special numbers since we have been playing here, there has not been one for ragtime music. America seems to have been cured of that disease. . . . This has been very pleasing to me, but I fully expected it. Kansas City was always musical.

Around the time of Pryor's pronouncement, a Texas composer named Euday Bowman was putting the finishing touches on the rag that would become Jenkins's biggest hit. If the country had been cured of ragtime, it had a relapse when it heard "Twelfth Street Rag."

Bowman ran away from his Ft. Worth home to be a pianist in 1897, when he was eleven years old. He made his way to Kansas City, where he soaked up the sights and sounds of night life around Twelfth Street and Main. The atmosphere inspired him to devise a jumpy, three-note melody, which he called "Twelfth Street Rag." He took it back to Texas, and his mother set it down on paper for him. Over the next fifteen years he played it in restaurants, saloons, and shoeshine parlors, embellishing it and adding to it as his proficiency increased. He copyrighted two manuscript versions of it in 1914. Finally, in January 1915, he self-published it and waited for the money to roll in. Of course, he had no way to distribute his music, so he realized almost nothing from it. He remembered Kansas City's big music store and saw a way to cut his losses. He sent Jenkins two of his blues songs and the printing plates for "Twelfth Street" and offered to sell all rights to all three numbers for $300. Elmer Ege, the hit-seeking missile, pounced on them. Late in 1915 Jenkins issued "Twelfth Street Rag" and began to plug it.

Elmer Ege wrote to a friend in 1937, "I suppose there was not at any time as much money put into the popularization of a number as we put into 'Twelfth Street Rag.'" The push paid off, giving Jenkins the biggest-selling, fastest-selling, most-recorded rag of all time. A spate of piano rolls appeared, and Earl Fuller's Orchestra was the first to record it, in June 1917. In 1919, because of the unceasing demand for the tune, Jenkins issued a song version, with lyrics by James E. Sumner, the company's professional manager. Black composer Billy Heagney's "Twelfth Street Blues" appeared under the Jenkins imprint in 1924. This song spinoff liberally quotes two of the "Twelfth Street Rag" melodies as filler after its phrases. "Twelfth Street Rag" received dozens of recordings in the 1920s, and in 1929 it was used in the Buddy Rogers–Nancy Carroll musical film *Close Harmony*. The movie plug was an occasion to issue another song version, this time with new lyrics by Spencer Williams.

Jenkins issued two other Bowman rags ("Petticoat Lane" in 1915 and "Shamrock Rag" in 1916) and several of his blues, but nothing approached the popularity of "Twelfth Street." Meanwhile back in Texas, Bowman was publishing his own numbers again, losing his shirt, and going mad with resentment at Jenkins for making a fortune on his syncopated phenomenon and sharing none of it with him. He played occasionally in Ft. Worth bars, more often for drinks and tips than for a salary. He had lost a leg to a train wheel during his youthful hoboing, so he could not do manual labor, and because his music was not supporting him, he became a junk dealer. Bowman smoldered for the remainder of the twenty-eight-year wait required by the copyright law, then in 1942 he reclaimed his rights to "Twelfth Street Rag" and immediately resold it to Shapiro-Bernstein, with a royalty provision in his contract. The rag's third owner fitted it with another new lyric (this one by Andy Razaf) and kept it in print. In 1948 Bowman got a taste of vindication when Pee Wee Hunt recorded "Twelfth Street Rag," and the record began its climb to sales of three million copies. The composer did not have long to enjoy his royalties or his revenge; Euday Bowman died in May 1949.

Bowman's rags were the last published by Jenkins. As the nation turned its attention to blues and pop songs in the late teens, Kansas City's preeminent publisher did, too. The chain of Jenkins stores served as a launching pad for several songs that became nationally known in the 1920s: Billy Smythe and Art Gillham's "Mean Blues" (1923), Lucien Denni's "You're Just a Flower from an Old Bouquet" (1924), and Phil Baxter's "Piccolo Pete" (1929). The Missouri-born Willard Robison published a few songs with Jenkins in the mid-twenties ("Deep Elm," "Peaceful Valley," "Rhythm Rag," and "Page Mr. Handy"). The company's most promising writer of blues was a young woman named Billie Brown, who was a demonstrator in the main Jenkins store. Her "Dangerous Blues" was issued in 1921, and her "Lonesome Mama Blues" appeared in 1922. Before her second publication with Jenkins, Billie Brown died of smallpox, in December 1921 at the age of eighteen.

Jenkins published its last number in 1930, and in 1932, after thirty years at 1013–1015 Walnut Street, the company moved to an eight-story building two blocks away, at 1217–1223 Walnut. Jenkins sold its song catalog to Lou Levy's Leeds Music in 1943 and sold its chain of stores to David Richardson of Rich Music in 1973.

CHARLES L. JOHNSON & COMPANY/JOHNSON PUBLISHING COMPANY

With more than 200 publications credited to him, Charles Johnson was the most prolific and most successful Kansas City composer. Four of his rags sold over a million copies each during his lifetime, an achievement unmatched by any other ragtime writer. He also had hits with an Indian intermezzo ("Iola"), a waltz ("Dream Days"), and a song ("Sweet and Low"). Only nine of his thirty-two rags were self-published; his work was more likely to appear under the imprints of Remick, Witmark, or Forster than under his own.

Johnson worked the high and low ends of the ladder. During the years when his compositions were being issued by the giants of Tin Pan Alley, Johnson hired out to the rankest amateurs in the Midwest, setting "song poems" to music for local versifiers to publish themselves. He wrote a campaign song for Herbert Hoover in 1928 and one for Franklin Roosevelt in 1936. He wrote a march in honor of a music store in Oklahoma City and a waltz called "French Auto Cylinder Oil" at the request of a petroleum company in Marshalltown, Iowa. He saw his opportunities and he took them, big and small. Except for the two years that he worked as a song plugger, he never left Kansas City.

Charles Leslie Johnson was born December 3, 1876, in Kansas City, Kansas. He began piano lessons at age six, and he became proficient on violin, banjo, guitar, and mandolin in his teens. Charlie was more interested in popular music than in the classics, and when his piano teacher forbade him to play ragtime, he stopped going for lessons. He joined several guitar and mandolin clubs and began to compose for these groups. His first publication, a set of marches written for the Walton Mandolin Club, was issued in 1895 by J. R. Bell, of Kansas City, Missouri. His string club contacts brought him occasional playing jobs in theatres and restaurants. When he was about twenty, Johnson went to work for J. W. Jenkins' Sons as a demonstrator.

In 1898 Jenkins began to publish Johnson's piano pieces, and in 1899 the company had regional hits with his "Doc Brown's Cakewalk"

Charles L. Johnson

and his first rag, "Scandalous Thompson" (which was "Dedicated to my rag-time friend Mr. Harry Kelly"). In 1901 Johnson left the Jenkins company to take a job with Carl Hoffman, who also employed E. Harry Kelly. One of Johnson's first assignments in his new position was to make an arrangement of Kelly's "Peaceful Henry." In 1902 Hoffman published Johnson's second rag, "A Black Smoke."

Johnson married Sylvia Hoskins in 1901, and upon the arrival of their daughter Frances, he began to look around for ways to make extra income. He ran an ad in a 1904 *Etude* headlined COMPOSERS SEND YOUR MANUSCRIPTS, offering to "correct, rearrange, and reconstruct musical manuscripts . . . making them suitable to any publisher" and to "set music to suitable words." His composing and arranging songs for amateurs was a sideline, but he continued to do it, even after he was making big money. Also in 1904 Johnson, still an employee of Carl Hoffman, started his first publishing firm, Central Music Publishing Company. This was a short-lived venture, but it survived long enough to produce Johnson's first nationally known composition.

To get in on a current pop vogue, Johnson wrote an "Indian inter-mezzo" called "Iola" in 1904, and Central Music issued it as an instrumental and as a song (with lyrics by Karl Knappen). Whitney-Warner's manager, Charles N. Daniels, the Kansas Citian who had started the vogue with his song "Hiawatha," bought "Iola" for his Detroit employer in 1906. Daniels hired James O'Dea to write a new lyric, reissued "Iola" in song and instrumental editions, and plugged them heavily. The perky "Iola" sold more than a million copies in two years. It was the first hit to bear Johnson's name, but he would soon have a bigger one.

Jenkins hadn't done much with Johnson's first rag, nor had Hoffman done much with his second, but he continued to publish songs and instrumentals with both companies. In 1906 Johnson wrote a third rag, "Dill Pickles," and Hoffman issued it. "Dill Pickles" was a departure from his funkier, folk-based "Scandalous Thompson" and "Black Smoke." It is a bright, jangling number, with its first melody built on the three-over-four pattern and with a trombonelike bass figure introducing each phrase of its second strain. Unlike the four-strain Joplin rags, "Dill Pickles" has only three sections, and its harmonies are so thin as to be skeletal. There is an empty-headed gaiety in "Dill Pickles," and it is irresistibly catchy. "Dill Pickles" blithely ignores the classic architecture of the St. Louis rags and rushes headlong into modernity.

Charles Daniels, now the Detroit manager of Remick and flush with the success of "Iola," bought "Dill Pickles" for Remick in 1907. It became Remick's first million-selling rag, and it set Charles Johnson firmly on the ragtime path. Shortly before the sale of "Dill Pickles," he left Carl Hoffman to establish Charles L. Johnson & Company, head-quartered in the Braley Building in the heart of Kansas City's business district. The first rag issued by his new firm, "Lovey-Dovey," was snapped up by Remick and reissued as "Southern Beauties" a few months later.

Charles L. Johnson & Company was a one-man operation, but its owner didn't want it to seem so. In 1908 Johnson published three of his rags written under the pseudonym "Raymond Birch." ("Raymond Birch" would be credited with four more Johnson rags; "Ethel Earnist" and "Fannie B. Woods," two other Johnson aliases, would be used on one rag each.) The first non-Johnson rag to be published by Charles L. Johnson was Frances Cox's "The Tickler," setting his pattern of publishing only women composers' rags (by Cox, Maude Gilmore, and Lucy B. Phillips) besides his own. Johnson's company didn't have national distribution (or even regional distribution, as Jenkins had), so he kept up his contacts with national firms and sent his rags to them, in manuscript and in commercial copies. None of the six rags written by Johnson in 1909 were published by his own firm.

Johnson had hits with his 1908 "Powder Rag" (published by himself and reissued by Harold Rossiter in Chicago, his second best-seller) and his 1909 "Porcupine Rag" (first issued by Witmark in New York). "Dill Pickles" was still going strong, and he was beginning to get recordings of his work by Charles Prince's Band and by Arthur Pryor. The small company with no distribution attracted the attention of Harold Rossiter, and in August 1910 the Chicago publisher bought Johnson's catalog. Johnson was on a roll as composer and publisher, and unfazed by the fact that he had not a copyright to his name, he simply started over. In January 1911 he created Johnson Publishing Company and issued the first rag under his new imprint, his own "Cloud Kisser."

In 1912 Johnson went to work as a plugger for a Chicago company, F. J. A. Forster. He spent about two years traveling the Midwest and South for Forster, ducking into Kansas City whenever possible to oversee his own company. One of his last assignments was to push the "Missouri Waltz," which Forster acquired in 1914. Johnson pitched it hard to regional bandleaders, but he couldn't generate much interest in the song. He went back to Chicago to tell Forster that the "Missouri Waltz" was "a flivver," and he retired from plugging.

Whatever his failures at plugging, Johnson's relationship with Forster served him well throughout the teens. Beginning with "Sweetness" (issued in June 1912), Forster would be the exclusive publisher of Johnson's rags and would also issue many of his songs and instrumental pieces. Johnson's own company stayed in business until 1940, issuing his songs occasionally (most of them vanity publications written with amateurs), but he preferred to leave the publishing of his best work to a firm with national distribution. The decision to channel his compositions through Forster was wise. In 1913 Forster had a million-seller with Johnson's "Crazy Bone Rag" and another with his waltz "Dream Days." Two more Johnson rags, "Blue Goose Rag" and "Teasing the Cat," became popular in 1916. In 1918 Forster issued Johnson's last rag, the exquisite "Snookums." In 1919 Forster published Johnson's waltz-song "Sweet and Low," which earned its composer $30,000 in royalties.

Charles Johnson did not go on to write in the novelty idiom that his breezy rags had foreshadowed. Novelty rags, like all musical fads, were a young man's game, and Johnson was over forty now. He could live comfortably on his royalties and the occasional lyrics sent to him that needed tunes. He became an arranger for hotel orchestras and was musical director of the annual "Nit Wits" revue at the local University Club. An article on Johnson ran in the Kansas City *Star* on September 27, 1924, in which he observed that hits seemed to "wear out" more quickly than they used to. "The public is the judge," he said, "and a peculiar one." In 1940 he won a copyright infringement suit against the songwriter Saxie Dowell, whose recent hit, "Playmates," was lifted from the chorus of "Iola." Charles Johnson died three days after Christmas 1950 at his home on Tracy Avenue.

CARL HOFFMAN MUSIC COMPANY

Although Carl Hoffman published only six rags, three of them are of such musical and historical importance that he must be included among Kansas City's major publishers of ragtime. The successes of his big three did not prompt him to seek out more ragtime for publication. Hoffman began as a publisher who issued a little bit of everything, and he proudly remained so. If he had no ear for ragtime, he at least had an

Carl Hoffman

eye for talent. Charles N. Daniels, who worked as a clerk for Hoffman, would pilot his employer's trio of hits to national fame.

Carl Hoffman was born in Brensbach, Hesse Province, Darmstad, Germany, in 1847. He was educated in the public schools of his home city, and he took advanced music studies at the University of Giessen. When he was twenty, he emigrated to the United States. He taught piano and organ privately in Pittsburgh, Pennsylvania, and for one year he was on the music faculty at a women's college there. He moved to Leavenworth, Kansas, in 1868 to open a music store with his brother Henry at 422 Delaware Street. He opened a second store in Kansas

City, Missouri, in partnership with Vincent R. Andrus, in 1887, but this operation lasted only a year. As the Leavenworth store continued to prosper, Carl Hoffman put aside money for another foray into Kansas City. By 1894 he was able to do it right. He bought a five-story building—enough room for offices, sales floors, warehouse, repair shop, and teaching studios—at 1012–1014 Walnut Street. The Carl Hoffman Music Company arrived full-grown.

Hoffman had published a bit in Leavenworth, and he stepped up his publishing effort in Kansas City, issuing church music and teaching pieces, some of them his own compositions. One of his first ventures into syncopation was an 1896 coon song, "Mistah Police, Don't 'Rest Me," by N. C. Smith.

In 1897 Charles N. Daniels was hired by Hoffman as a clerk and song demonstrator. Daniels was born in Leavenworth in 1878 (his family was probably acquainted with the Hoffmans), and he had

Charles N. Daniels

recently graduated from high school in Kansas City, Kansas. Still a teenager, he had already clerked in two local music stores, and he was obviously headed for a career in the music business. In 1898 Hoffman offered a $25 prize for the best two-step by a local composer and, risking charges of nepotism, he declared Daniels the winner for his composition "Margery." John Philip Sousa was in town with his band at the Coates Opera House, and when he heard about the contest, he offered to perform the winning work. Sousa's endorsement of "Margery" gave Carl Hoffman his first regional hit. The piece would eventually sell over a quarter of a million copies, but Daniels saw nothing from its sales, as Hoffman's $25 prize money bought him the copyright. (The Sousa connection would later prove to be very important to Daniels, however.) Perhaps it was the profitless hit that led Daniels to form his own publishing firm, Western Music Publishing Company, in October 1899. He wasn't ready to publish anything yet, but he was obviously making plans that did not include working for Carl Hoffman.

In December 1898 Daniels introduced Scott Joplin to his employer, and Hoffman made the momentous decision to buy Scott Joplin's "Original Rags," which he issued in March 1899. "Original Rags" was Joplin's first ragtime publication as well as the first piece of ragtime published in Kansas City. Daniels also chose a Blind Boone song, "Dat Mornin' in de Sky," and his own "Poster Girl March" for publication by Hoffman that year.

In late 1899 Daniels left Hoffman to manage the sheet music department of the Barr Dry Goods Company in St. Louis, and he took his nearly nonexistent publishing company with him. Western Music was renamed Daniels, Russell & Boone (to include Daniels's two new partners). In St. Louis DR&B issued the first Daniels composition that would be nationally known, a waltz song called "You Tell Me Your Dream, I'll Tell You Mine," with lyrics by Seymour Rice, a Kansas City minstrel show director.

In 1901 Daniels's firm published his "Hiawatha," an Indian intermezzo, which Daniels prevailed upon John Philip Sousa to include in his concert programs. The Sousa plug was the making of "Hiawatha" and of Daniels. In 1902 Jerome Remick offered Daniels $10,000 for his publishing company so that Remick could own "Hiawatha." He also gave Daniels a job as general manager of Whitney-Warner, a newly acquired Remick company in Detroit. Daniels would be invaluable to Remick over the next ten years, partly because he remembered where ragtime came from.

The irreplaceable Daniels had to be replaced, and in 1901 Carl Hoffman hired two bright young men for the job. First he wooed Charles L. Johnson away from J. W. Jenkins' Sons to be his chief demonstrator and arranger, then he took on E. Harry Kelly to assist Johnson. Hoffman issued Kelly's "Peaceful Henry," a sturdy folk-rag named for the company's janitor and "Dedicated to Chas. L. Johnson," in 1901. Johnson's rag "A Black Smoke" appeared in 1902, the year that the Hoffman company was incorporated, with its founder as president and $60,000 in capital stock.

In 1903 Charles Daniels, still riding high on "Hiawatha," decided to expand the Whitney-Warner catalog to include ragtime, and he knew where to get it. He bought "Original Rags" and "Peaceful Henry" from Carl Hoffman and began to plug them. He got a recording of "Peaceful Henry" by the banjoist Vess Ossman in October, and Kelly's work became the first nationally known rag from Kansas City. To cover all his bases, Daniels also bought Hoffman's song version of "Peaceful Henry," with lyrics by Seymour Rice. Harry Kelly drifted away to work for Jenkins that year, but Johnson stayed with Hoffman until 1906. "Dill Pickles," a rag that he wrote on company time, would be his biggest hit.

"Dill Pickles" was good for everybody involved in its publication. Carl Hoffman had a regional hit with it in his 1906 edition; Charles Daniels's purchase of it for Remick in 1907 gave that company its first million-selling rag; and Charles Johnson was firmly established as the composer of the first rag to "break," to become instantly popular with its first national exposure. A big factor in the rag's success was the virtuoso recording made in July 1908 by Chris Chapman, who played a glass xylophone. (Chapman's performance would remain in the Victor catalog for nearly twenty years.) The profits from the sale of "Dill Pickles" must have figured into the reorganization of Carl Hoffman Music in 1908. Louis Rosenfield was taken in as a partner (and as acting manager of the company, now at 1108–1110 Grand Avenue), and the capital stock stood at $130,000.

Carl Hoffman remained as president of the newly reorganized firm, and it was he who made the decision to cut back on publishing and to concentrate more on sales of music and instruments. Hoffman officially retired in 1915, but he continued to supervise the operations of his store until his death in 1921. His widow, Ida, and his son John ran the Leavenworth store for another ten years.

"Louisiana Rag"—the first published rag

CHAPTER TWO

Ragtime in Mid-America

*Illinois, Indiana, Iowa, Kansas, Michigan,
Minnesota, Nebraska, Ohio, Wisconsin*

Ragtime was not just a fad in the Midwest, it was a staple of the region's cultural life for more than thirty years. As the waves of rag-time came—from the cakewalkish early rags, into the classic era, through the pop rags of the teens and the novelty rags of the twenties—Midwesterners enjoyed them in turn.

During this long love affair with ragtime, religious revivalists—who questioned the morality of ragtime music—came in waves, too. But on the home turf of Dwight L. Moody, Billy Sunday, and Gipsy Smith, reform was more a fad than ragtime was. Ragtime was too close to home to think of giving it up. It was in the living room, serving as "prac-tice music" for two generations of girls and delighting the older folks after supper. Besides being more fun than the Czerny and Hanon stud-ies, it developed agile fingering and it engendered a keener sense of rhythm. Surely the reformers were wrong about this lively and useful music. Ragtime's core audience didn't know much about the under-world or sporting districts, but it knew what it liked. Prior to World War I, more than half of all published ragtime came from the Midwest.

Midwesterners approved of ragtime in whatever medium they heard it, and thanks to a generation of Midwestern bandmasters, they often heard it blazing forth at the city park and at the circus. The first "star" band directors, Patrick S. Gilmore and John Philip Sousa, were from the East, and they shared the Easterners' wariness of syncopation.

71

Gilmore was stiff as starch, and he eschewed even the simplest minstrel show rhythms. For most of his career, Sousa's rhythmic ventures went no further than the cakewalk. But, to a man, the second-generation bandmasters were all bred in the Midwest, and they all laced their music with syncopated surprises. They valued precision, as did their predecessors, but they put precision at the service of amusement. Most of them wrote at least a few rags for band, and they all had raggy arrangements in their band books. In theatres, in band shells, and in circus tents, they set their brass sections to playing tag with one another and delivered syncopation to delighted crowds.

Detroit was the first city to have a major "pops" orchestra in residence, and for nearly four decades it was under the direction of Theodore Finney, a black violinist. Finney was born in Columbus, Ohio, in 1837, and he moved to Detroit when he was twenty. He ran a saloon for a couple of years, and around 1860 he and a friend, John Bailey, organized the Bailey and Finney Orchestra, which they co-led until Bailey's death in 1870. Finney took over the group, recruited the finest black musicians in the city, and turned Finney's Orchestra into a source of local pride. They played every venue in Detroit: in cafes, in concert halls, on excursion boats, and in street parades. Because he was a stickler for discipline and a fanatic about the importance of reading, his musicians began calling their leader "Old Man" Finney before he was forty.

Around 1890, when Finney hired the black pianist/baritone horn player/arranger Fred S. Stone, the orchestra's syncopation quotient increased. Stone's compositions were locally published, and he arranged them for use by the orchestra. These included two-steps ("Mackinac," "Ma Ragtime Baby"), a rag ("Bos'n Rag"), and a syncopated waltz ("Silks and Rags"). After Finney's death in 1899, Stone took charge of the orchestra and kept it playing ragtime for thirteen more years. Another black composer/arranger, Harry P. Guy, added his syncopated numbers—"Echoes from the Snowball Club," "Cleanin' Up in Georgia," and "Pearl of the Harem"—to the band's repertoire.

Arthur Pryor, who was born in St. Joseph, Missouri, in 1870, was Sousa's featured trombonist from 1892 to 1903, when he left Sousa to form his own band. The Pryor band toured incessantly into the 1920s. Unlike Sousa, Pryor did not shy away from ragtime in concert programming or recording sessions. The band was a mainstay of the Victor label from its first session in November 1903 until the mid-twenties. Pryor's trombone slashed its way through his own syncopated compositions ("Mr. Black Man," "A Coon Band Contest," "Artful Artie," "Frozen Bill"), as well as rags by Tom Turpin, Charles L. Johnson, Henry Lodge, and Percy Wenrich. He wrote a set of raggy numbers ("Southern Hospitality," "That Flying Rag," "Razzazza Mazzazza, A Trombone Sneeze") as showpieces for his slippery musical wit.

Omaha's star bandsman was Dan Desdunes, a black Louisianan who led local groups and conducted the band at Boys' Town from 1904 until his death in 1929. Des Moines boasted of T. Fred Henry, a native-born cornetist whose band was featured at state fairs throughout the Midwest for many years. Henry's syncopated compositions for band included "Eatin' Chocolates," "Cinders," and "The Ingersoll Tingle" (a two-step named for a Des Moines city park). The great circus band-masters were Midwesterners, too. Fred Jewell (born in Worthington, Indiana, in 1875), Karl L. King (born in Pointersville, Ohio, in 1891), and Merle Evans (born in Columbus, Kansas, in 1891) were given heroes' welcomes when their tours brought them back to their home states.

Even if there were no circus in town and no piano student in the house, the Midwesterner was not ragtime-deprived, because it was this region that led the nation in the manufacture and purchase of the rag-time machine, the player piano. Like salt-rising bread and the ice cream cone, the self-playing piano was also a Midwestern development. The spring-wound music box, a specialty of German manufacturers, had decorated vanity tables for years before John McTammany, a Scottish-born emigrant living in Canton, Ohio, built a hand-cranked mecha-nism for playing small, tabletop organs in 1868. American piano makers were fascinated by McTammany's invention, and they sought for three decades to make it marketable.

In 1898 their tinkering bore commercial fruit: the Aeolian Corporation's Pianola, which the company called a "piano player." This was a device that could be pushed up to the piano and aligned so that mechanical "fingers" could depress the keys, guided by tracks on a per-forated paper roll and powered by the pumping of pedals by an opera-tor. Priced around $250, the Pianola was an expensive item, but it was hailed by musicians and educators as a cultural treasure. With the advent of Pianolas, there was no reason for any home to be without music, they said, so the middle-class dug deep in their pockets and bought them. It was almost un-American not to, according to Aeolian's ads. An early campaign showed photos of the *Roosevelt*, Admiral Peary's ship, "which carried a Pianola twice to the Arctic," and of "the American Battle Fleet, which carried 26 Pianolas around the world."

Even as the Pianola was being touted as the last word in automatic music-making, piano engineers were still trying to improve on it and make it even more appealing. Soon they figured out how to miniaturize the mechanism and hide it inside the piano cabinet. By 1910 the "piano player" was obsolete, replaced by the "player piano." No more hauling and aligning, just insert a roll and pump. The player was even more expensive than the Pianola, costing from $700 to $1,000, but since it served as status symbol, dance accompanist, and baby-sitter, it seemed almost a necessity.

Piano makers advertised their players as fine furniture, and indeed they often were. Craftsmen managed to make the big, boxy objects look graceful by the gentle curving of lids and the fanciful carving of legs. Oaken cabinets were inlaid with more exotic woods: mahogany, ebony, and French walnut. The windows into which rolls were inserted were sometimes framed by pastel-colored stained glass. The visible hardware (on the sliding doors that hid the roll window, on the "expression levers," and on the lid) was usually brass. Pedals were padded, and their tops were often covered with velvet. The player looked like anything but a machine, yet it was a machine. It could play "Dill Pickles" by itself.

The Melville Clark Piano Company of Chicago had been in business only a year when, in 1901, it introduced yet another marvel, the first full eighty-eight-note player. Prior to Clark's "Apollo" model, player mechanisms could reach only fifty-eight or sixty-five notes, but eighty-eight notes soon became the industrywide standard. After the Apollo, any player with a shorter note span was not state of the art.

For the first fifteen or so years of mechanical music, roll-making had nothing to do with playing the piano. Perforations in rolls were machine-cut, precisely following the pencil lines drawn by an arranger on a paper master. "Arranging" consisted of planning the placement of holes to conform to the notes of published sheet music, then adding extra holes to embellish the sound. With the full-keyboard range of the eighty-eight-note roll, it became commonplace for arrangers to suggest the playing of a third or fourth hand.

In 1912 the Melville Clark company made another breakthrough by introducing the first hand-played rolls to the market. To make a hand-played roll, a pianist sat at a huge contraption that was half piano, half giant stylus, marking a master roll as he depressed each key. After the performance, editing began. Hand-played rolls could be embellished, of course, and mistakes could be erased simply by plugging any incorrectly punched holes. Lee Roberts was the first pianist to make a hand-played roll, when he "recorded" his "Valse Parisienne" for Clark.

Each advance required new hardware. To produce rolls in quantity, many manufacturers used the Acme Music Roll Perforator, a 1,600-pound monster that could perforate sixteen sheets at once at a speed of three to six feet per minute. Acme stressed that neither intelligence nor strength was required to run the machine. Manufacturers were reassured that unskilled laborers could do the job and that "some plants employ girl operators." The Leabarjan Manufacturing Company of Ontario, Canada, sold a small, "home" version of the perforator for amateurs who wanted to capture their own playing on rolls.

The mechanical player was a godsend for the small business owner—of a store, saloon, or brothel—who wanted music but couldn't afford musicians. In 1899 the Rudolf Wurlitzer Company, at 121 East Fourth Street in Cincinnati, marketed its Tonophone, the first popular coin-operated piano. In 1907 the J. P. Seeburg Piano Company, at 209 South State Street in Chicago, began its ceaseless competition with Wurlitzer in the mechanical music game. Shortly after the turn of the century, as the silent film became a weekly ritual for families, the mechanical music industry was ready to enhance the pleasure of movie-going. Wurlitzer offered professional film accompanists its "One Man Orchestra" for music and sound effects. Chicago's Photo Player Company introduced its Fotoplayer 50 model, which, besides music, could produce gongs, bird calls, wind, waves, horses' hooves, and auto horns at the touch of a finger.

Many of the older piano companies in the Midwest added players to their lines, and new companies that made only mechanical pianos sprang up to compete with them. Among the largest player piano manufacturers were Cincinnati's Baldwin and Wurlitzer companies, Milwaukee's Waltham Piano Company, and, in Grand Haven, Michigan, the Story & Clark Piano Company. (Melville Clark left Story & Clark to start his own company in Chicago.) Indiana had player companies in Connersville (the Krell-French Piano Company), Ft. Wayne (the Packard Piano Company), and Richmond (the Starr Piano Company). Rolls were made at Milwaukee's Staffnote Player Roll Company and at Cincinnati's Vocalstyle Music Company.

The hotbed of player- and roll-making was Chicago, home to five player piano manufacturers and five roll manufacturers in the first quarter of the century. (New York City had only four of each during this time.) Three of the Chicago piano makers (Cable, Melville Clark, and W. W. Kimball) also made rolls. The U.S. Music Roll Company, which had a deft and tireless arranger in Mae Brown, listed over 250 rag rolls in its 1916 catalog. Upon Melville Clark's death in 1918, the roll division of his company took the name of its most popular brand, QRS, and went on for decades to outlast every other maker of rolls. Clark's advertising said that its rolls were "so hot, we ship 'em in asbestos boxes."

Beginning in the mid-teens some companies began to issue rags as rolls only, rags that never appeared in sheet music form. Although these rag rolls sold well, there was no ensuing clamor for the music sheets, so many of the compositions went unpublished. The success of roll-only rags indicates a change in the ragtime landscape. Because they offered effortless perfection and instant fun, player pianos made a schism that was never there before: they separated the enjoyment of hearing ragtime from the enjoyment of playing it. As the player piano boom escalated to its peak years, 1919–1923, novelty rag composers, led by Charley Straight and Zez Confrey in Chicago, began to write in the third- and fourth-hand idiom of the music machines. They carried ragtime to such dizzy heights that amateurs couldn't play it, even with printed sheets to guide them. Many novelty rags were published, but few sold well in sheet music form. The amateur pianist simply didn't have enough hands to do them justice.

Another portent of the decline of ragtime was the failure of the QRS series of Educator Rolls. As modern-thinking musicians and teachers had praised the cultural advance of the Pianola, so did QRS trumpet its six Educator Rolls. The use of them would be like a piano education from a master teacher, they would foster the appreciation of all kinds of music, and they would instill correct playing by showing the correct playing of a ghost professor. The public nixed the Educator Rolls, preferring instant music to the bother of learning to play. When newer inventions, the phonograph and the radio, came along to offer even easier (and cheaper) music, the heyday of ragtime—and of family piano-playing—was over. By 1935 a player piano—even a fancy one with rosewood inlay, stained glass, shiny knobs, and brass levers—was hard to give away.

~⁀◞

Seven Profiles in Mid-American Ragtime

CHARLEY STRAIGHT

The first major composer/arranger of ragtime for piano rolls was Charles T. Straight, who was born in Chicago in 1891. Almost immediately after his graduation from Wendell Phillips High School, he began touring in vaudeville as accompanist for comic singer Gene Greene. His first compositions were specialty songs for Greene, "King of the Bungaloos" (in 1909) and "Mocking Bird Rag" (in 1912), both of which the team recorded for Pathé.

Straight was based in New York during his years with Greene, and his earliest songs and rags were published there. Witmark issued his first rag, "Humpty Dumpty," in January 1914, and nine months later the Victor Military Band recorded it. He placed three rags with Remick: "Let's Go" and "Red Raven Rag" (both issued late in 1915) and "Hot Hands" (issued in February 1916). "Hot Hands" made quite a stir, and Prince's Orchestra recorded "Red Raven." Straight was on his way up in the New York music scene when, in 1916, he got the job that took him back to Chicago.

Straight was hired to make piano rolls for the Rolla Artis label, a minor subsidiary of the mighty Wurlitzer company. Under the pseudonym "Billie King," he cut a few pop songs and one of his own compositions, "My Baby's Rag." His Rolla Artis work didn't get much

Charley Straight

distribution, but Straight found that he loved the process of making and doctoring rolls. Taking the roll as his medium and the rollicking rag as his compositional specialty, Straight was in a place to thrive. He would publish a few more songs and rags, but from 1917 on, his best musical ideas would be realized at the business end of a perforator. And there would never be another professional reason for him to leave his hometown.

In May 1917 Charley Straight made a roll of his rag "Out Steppin'" for the Imperial Player Roll Company, a subsidiary of the Cable Piano Company. He made a few more rolls for Imperial that year and, as word of his proficiency spread, several for QRS, Chicago's largest roll maker. Some time in late 1917 or early 1918 Straight was named production manager at Imperial. He stayed at Imperial for about three years, and during that time, such was his clout with his employer that he was allowed to continue making rolls for QRS, Imperial's only rival. Romping rags with cute titles poured out of him in the late teens: "Itsit," "Mitinice," "Playmor," "Sweet Pickin's," "A Dippy Ditty," "Fastep," "Mow 'Em Down," "Nifty Nonsense," and "Rag-a-Bit." The great majority of his rags were not published (nor did he even copyright them), but—because they were distributed by the two largest roll companies in the world, Straight's rags were heard more than anyone else's as America barreled into the 1920s.

Soon after Straight took charge at Imperial, a new Midwestern roll genius arrived at QRS to challenge him. Early in 1918, Zez Confrey, a twenty-three-year-old wunderkind from Peru, Illinois, was hired as pianist and arranger by Imperial's rival. Confrey had previously made two rolls for Imperial, but, as good as they were, they were not like "My Pet," which he made for QRS in the summer of 1918.

Zez Confrey

"Kitten on the Keys"—Confrey's perfect rag

"My Pet" was new in every way that a rag could be new: in its melodic and harmonic conceptions, in its structure, and in its use of roll-arranging techniques as compositional devices. It was simply the damndest thing ever to come out of a piano: a shifty, minor-keyed number in five sections with a dozen different rhythmic patterns woven into its melodies. From the sound of it, Confrey's pet must have been a tiger—it strode, prowled, and leapt. Its harmonies were liquid and dissonant, constantly shifting, sounding like Debussy on uppers. Nothing had prepared the world for "My Pet," but "My Pet" prepared the world for the novelty rag. Confrey quickly followed it with his masterpiece, "Kitten on the Keys," and he laced his pop song rolls with modernistic tricks. During his tenure at QRS, Confrey would play and arrange nearly 130 rolls in the novelty idiom.

Besides Confrey, QRS had another warhorse on its staff, the pianist/arranger Max Kortlander (born in Grand Rapids, Michigan, in

1890). Kortlander was not as harmonically adventurous as Confrey, but he cranked out dozens of infectious one-steps and fox-trots. Although Charley Straight did occasionally moonlight at QRS, he was enough of a company man to take up the Confrey-Kortlander challenge on Imperial's behalf. Imperial's philosophy was to go easy on the nonhuman embellishment, preserving the sound and style of the human performer. To compete with QRS's juggernaut, Imperial needed another terrific pianist, not a punchboard artist. In an audition in mid-1919, Straight found what he was looking for in Roy Bargy.

Roy Bargy was born in Newaygo, Michigan, in 1894, and he had grown up in Toledo, Ohio, where he listened carefully to black pianists in the sporting district. Bargy began his career as a silent movie accompanist, and he later formed a local dance orchestra. His army service had been curtailed when the war ended eight months after his enlistment, and he was back in Toledo at loose ends when a friend suggested that he go to Chicago to audition for Charley Straight. Straight was mightily impressed by his playing and asked him to make a test roll.

Bargy was given a pop song, and, although he had never made a piano roll, he devised a roll arrangement and played it. The test roll was so good that it went into Imperial's catalog, and Bargy was hired on the spot to edit the company's pop song rolls.

Inspired by his boss (and by the competition at QRS), Bargy began to write novelty rags, which were as energetic as Straight's and as rhythmically inventive as Confrey's. Bargy's trademark was his use of the "break"—the interruption of the melody by a rhythmic figure—as part of the melodic line itself. His supply of breaks was boundless. Imperial's pop songs began to sound as raggy as other companies' rag rolls. From 1919 to

Roy Bargy

1921, the four best roll artists in the world—Straight, Confrey, Kortlander, and Bargy—were all in Chicago, trying to outplay and outsell each other.

On April 17, 1920, the *Music Trade Indicator* carried an article by the Chicago *Tribune*'s music critic, W. L. Hubbard, who had been invited to the Imperial studio to see Straight and Bargy make a duet roll. What Hubbard heard and saw floored him:

> These two men sat at the pianos, and for an hour played one popular success after another. . . . Shades of Godowski and Hoffmann! . . . Both the youngsters are gifted with a technic [sic] which fears nothing and with a musical keenness that acknowledges no obstacle. During that hour of glorified rag and jazz I heard harmonies that Debussy, Ornstein, Scriabin, and all moderns have used for their most extreme and daring effects, and they were used here not in mere hit or miss fashion, but with real musical intent and for actual musical purpose. There were rhythms that would puzzle the most gifted theorist to analyze and classify, and yet they were made to skip along in most captivating and natural manner. . . . To watch them do it is like watching two deft jugglers whirl, toss, and keep in the air some fragile, shining objects. Only that in this instance these objects are tonal bubbles which, if they touch each other, would burst and crash into nothingness. The strange new harmonies flash and glitter and sting, but only for the instant. . . .

The twin demons at Imperial began to merge their musical personalities. They wrote pop songs together, and they edited each other's rolls. Early in 1920 Straight had the idea that Bargy should set himself the goal of writing and arranging one novelty rag per month for Imperial. The series began with Bargy's "Slipova" and "Justin-Tyme," released in the spring, followed by his "Sunshine Capers," "Jim Jams," and "Pianoflage" that summer.

Then the rag-a-month project started to run out of steam. Straight and Bargy were beginning to see the bottom of the bag when they looked into their bag of tricks. Their jobs required cleverness on demand—a relentless, assembly line cleverness that was always merry and bright and never repeated itself. Neither man was burned out as a composer, but neither wanted to be the Scheherezade of the piano roll industry. While still on the Imperial payroll, each began to look around for other musical projects. Late in 1920 Charley Straight formed his own dance band, and, on Straight's recommendation, Bargy was hired as director of the Benson Orchestra of Chicago.

Probably to keep the rag-a-month policy going during this time, Straight turned over to Bargy two of his own rags that he had previously made on Imperial rolls: "Knice and Knifty" (made in December 1917) and "Rufenreddy" (made early in 1918). They were out-and-out novelties, the most complex of Straight's compositions. They sounded more like Bargy than Straight, so Bargy was welcome to them. Early in 1921, Straight left Imperial, and Bargy left a few months later, never having made rolls of the Straight rags. Bargy had plans for them, however. He sent the two pieces, along with six of his own rags, to the Sam Fox Publishing Company in Cleveland, which issued all of them on music sheets. "Rufenreddy" appeared under the Fox imprint in November 1921, followed by "Knice and Knifty" in February 1922. (Because both Bargy and Straight skipped the manuscript-writing part of the compositional process and worked directly on the roll master, there were no manuscripts of these rags. Bargy sent eight piano rolls to Fox, and these were transcribed for publication. Two of these rolls must have been the ones that Straight made of "Rufenreddy" and "Knice and Knifty.")

The eight Fox publications of Bargy rags have a standard cover, with a large color photo of Bargy at the piano and a list of the rags in the series in the lower right corner. On the cover list, Straight's name is not appended to the two rags he composed, but on the title page each is credited to "Roy Bargy in collaboration with Charley Straight." Because of the delay between the composition and the publication of "Rufenreddy" and "Knice and Knifty," and because of their association with Bargy alone, Straight has been denied his place as a pioneer of novelty ragtime. Late in his life, Bargy told interviewers that he had written the rags and that Straight had contributed only "ideas and criticisms." Although Straight did not stay with novelty ragtime, it is undeniable that he got there first. The evidence is on the rolls that he made nearly two years before he met Roy Bargy and six months before he heard Zez Confrey.

Roy Bargy made a few more rag rolls in the early twenties (including "Rufenreddy" and "Knice and Knifty" for Melodee in 1922), but he was best known for his band work with the Benson Orchestra, Isham Jones, and his own orchestra. In 1928 he joined the Paul Whiteman Orchestra, and his piano breaks enlivened many of Whiteman's recordings for Victor. In 1943 he became music director for Jimmy Durante, a position he held for twenty years.

Zez Confrey kept his title as champion of novelty ragtime, outwriting and outplaying all comers, and composing and recording his rags into the mid-thirties. In 1922 he had three hit songs in the novelty idiom: "Stumbling," "Tricks," and "Dumbell." His "Kitten on the Keys" remained the most popular of all novelty rags. In 1923 Mills Music issued the definitive collection of Confrey's work, a folio called *Modern Novelty Piano Solos*, which stayed in print for forty years. In 1924 Confrey was one of two guest soloists with the Whiteman orchestra in its historic Aeolian Hall concert; the other was George Gershwin. Confrey was a vaudeville headliner throughout the 1920s, as well as a recording star. His shows and records featured a band, but at their center was Confrey, playing like a player piano, live and in person.

Max Kortlander stayed with QRS, composing and arranging rolls for each new dance fad that came along—the shimmy, the Charleston, the black bottom—with ragtime at the base of all his arrangements. He became president of QRS in 1931, and he headed the company until his death thirty years later.

Charley Straight's Chicago dance orchestra was the city's best throughout the 1920s. They were an elite outfit, playing the finest hotels and clubs and recording dozens of sides for Paramount and Brunswick. The piano roll industry dwindled in the late 1920s, but this did not affect Straight. He was not in the cleverness business any more.

CLARENCE M. JONES

The black pianist/composer Clarence M. Jones, a jack of all musical trades, was born in Wilmington, Ohio, in 1889. He was taught to play the piano by his mother, Carrie, who had some formal music education and who claimed to have played in bars as a young girl. When Clarence was about eleven, Carrie took him and his younger brother Harry to live in Cincinnati's West End neighborhood.

As a teenager, Clarence took piano lessons at the Cincinnati Conservatory of Music, and he began to play in the black theatres and clubs of the West End. His first publication was "Lightning Rag," issued by Groene Music Company in Cincinnati in 1908. His next rag, "The Candy," published by John Arnold in 1909, shows a highly advanced sense of harmony. Two more Jones rags, "Wild Grapes Rag" and "Oh You Sally Rag," were locally published before Clarence and his mother moved to Chicago in 1911.

Fanny Bloomfield-Zeisler, a Polish concert pianist who had retired from the stage to marry a Chicago lawyer, was impressed by Jones's talent and gave him lessons free of charge. His rag writing was at a standstill, but in the early teens he began to place songs with Chicago publishers. His "One Wonderful Night" was locally popular in 1914, and his "Thanks for the Lobster" got a recording by banjoist Fred Van Eps that same year. Around this time he was music director for Sherman Dudley, a dancing comedian (who used a mule in his act), at the Owl Theatre, at 4653 South State Street.

By 1916 Jones was able to open his own studio, at 3409 South State Street, where he did his writing and gave piano lessons. Among his pupils was a young man named Jimmy Blythe, lately arrived in Chicago from his native Kentucky. Blythe would be the best and most prolific of the race-label pianists of the 1920s. He disdained the lazy, splat-splat playing common to blues pianists at the time, and he attacked his accompaniments with the same vigor and imagination that he brought to his solo piano and band recordings. Blythe cited Jones as the primary influence on his style.

In January 1923 Jones made a solo piano recording of his masterful "Modulations," a shape-shifter that lives up to its title, ceaselessly winding harmonies around each other in surprising and satisfying ways. "Modulations" is a rare example of a novelty rag by a black composer. The stride playing of James P. Johnson and Willie the Lion Smith that was taking Harlem by storm had cut little ice in Chicago so far. With Charley Straight, Roy Bargy, and Zez Confrey in residence, novelty playing was that city's dominant style. It is not known whether Jones worked with Bargy during their roll-making days at Imperial, but "Modulations" certainly shows Bargy's influence. (In a 1972 interview Bargy recalled Jones as his favorite player among the pianists who passed through Imperial.)

After several years of making rolls for Columbia, Imperial, and Vocalstyle, Jones became a bandleader. He formed his own theatre orchestra in 1920, and in 1922 he and his three-piece Wonder Orchestra began a long stint at the Moulin Rouge Cafe. In 1923 Jones made his first recordings for Paramount, accompanying blues singers Ollie Powers and Monette Moore on that label's race series. He was still dabbling in ragtime as late as 1926, when he and an augmented eight-piece Wonder Orchestra made a hot recording of Fred Rose's "The Arm Breaker" for OKeh.

In 1932 Jones, his wife, and two sons moved to New York, where he worked as pianist/arranger/composer for a black male quartet called the Southernaires. He served as music director for the group's NBC radio show in the mid-thirties, and for a series of gospel recordings they made for Decca in 1939–1940. He worked as an arranger for Handy Brothers Music Company until his death in 1949.

HENRY FILLMORE

During the heyday of concert bands, audiences were awed by Sousa and they admired Pryor, but they loved Henry Fillmore. By his programming, compositions, and showmanship, the populace knew a populist was in charge when Fillmore was conducting. Even the light classics were too heavy for him. He viewed the band concert as an entertainment, and he thought that the making of band entertainment was the highest calling. On his list of more than 250 compositions, there is nothing that smacks of "art." He primarily wrote marches aimed at the foot and novelties aimed at the funnybone. Fillmore liked pep and polish in his ensembles, and he had the rehearsal techniques to put them there. As a child he loved the music he heard at minstrel shows and circuses, and, decades later, he carried the spirit of these institutions into concert halls and college band rooms. There is no title in Fillmore's catalog with the word *rag* in it, but the syncopated novelties he wrote for the trombone are nothing if not rags, with epaulets and plumes on them.

James Henry Fillmore, Jr., was born on December 3, 1881, in an upstairs room at his grandmother McKrell's boardinghouse, at 105 Broadway in Cincinnati. Henry's father and his uncle Frank owned the Fillmore Brothers Company, a successful publisher of hymnals and church music. (Two of J. H. Fillmore Sr.'s compositions, "Beautiful Garden of Prayer" and "I Know That My Redeemer Liveth," are still in Protestant hymnbooks.)

As a boy, Henry liked to sing, and he was interested in almost every instrument except the piano. He was especially fascinated by the trombone, and his mother bought him a used one for eight dollars. He took a few lessons on the instrument, but he mostly taught himself. The horn, the lessons, and the obsession had to be hidden from his father, who thought all band instruments to be

Henry Fillmore

snares of the devil. Henry began to compose almost as soon as he began to play, and it was his gift for composition that saved him from a thrashing when his father caught him practicing on the trombone. Henry explained that the piece he was playing was a hymn that he had written himself, and, although the elder Fillmore had never heard of hymns written for satanic instruments, he held his peace. The uneasy détente struck that day characterized their relationship until J. H. Fillmore's death.

As a boy, Henry rebelled in every way he could. In the summer of 1898, after a row with his father, he ran away to work as a laborer with a circus. After he came back, his father deposited him in the Miami (Ohio) Military Institute, with instructions to stay there until he graduated. Because he was allowed to organize an orchestra at MMI, Henry stayed. Upon his graduation in 1901, it was decided that Henry would go to work in the publishing company. (Fillmore Brothers was by this time occupying a five-story building at 528 Elm Street, and a retail store, Fillmore Music House, had been added to the enterprise.) In

1903 Henry Sr. sent his son to Europe to explore the possibilities of marketing church music there. Henry quickly abandoned his fact-finding mission and fell in with a small circus to play in its band for a week or so.

In 1904 Henry went to the World's Fair in St. Louis and came back with another reason for his father to disapprove of him. He was smitten with a cootch dancer named Mabel May Jones, and he was vowing to marry her. His scandalized family forbade it, so there was nothing to do but elope. In April 1905 Henry returned to St. Louis to claim his bride. Because there was no going home anytime soon, he and Mabel signed on with the Lemon Brothers Circus, a shady operation that roved the Midwest trailing a collection of pickpockets, ticket scalpers, and three-card monte dealers in its wake.

Henry was hired as a bandsman (at eight dollars a week), and Mabel tutored the children of the performers. Besides playing the trombone, Henry was expected to do whatever else needed doing. He loaded and unloaded the show, subbed for ailing clowns, and assisted the lion tamer. During parades his musical duties doubled. After playing the trombone in the bandwagon at the front of the parade, Henry would jump on a horse to take him to the rear of the parade, where he played the calliope that was hauled in the last wagon. The Fillmores' stint with the Lemon Brothers lasted five months, and Henry would remember it as the hardest work of his life. Rebellion was one thing, but exhaustion was another. He returned with Mabel to Cincinnati, knowing that his family would grudgingly accept the idea of their marriage and that his father would grudgingly take him back in the store.

A composer whose father was a publisher might expect to see his work in print, and Henry did, after a few years of persuasion. In September 1903 his first publication, "Higham March," was issued by Fillmore Brothers. Because his father thought it unseemly to put the Fillmore name on a piece of secular music, Henry used a pseudonym, "Will Huff." Not long after "Higham March" appeared on the counter at Fillmore Music House, Henry heard the Sousa band and was inspired to write more marches. Nine of them were published in 1904–1905. He wrote the occasional hymn or Sunday School song to appease his father, but his heart was in band music.

"Miss Trombone"

In 1908 Henry Fillmore wrote the first of his trombone rags, "Miss Trombone," which, because of its extensive glissando effects, was known as a "smear." (He was not the first to write a smear; Arthur Pryor and Fred Jewell wrote earlier ones.) The trombone is the only instrument capable of playing a melody entirely in glissandos, and nothing shows off "tromboneness" like a Fillmore smear. To see and hear one played is a distinctly American musical experience, Walt Whitman's "barbaric yawp" in brass. The smear constantly slides onto and off tones and replaces the do-re-mi scale with brrraaaats, wow wows, and grrrups. The tension between the bleary, skidding soloist and the strict accompaniment is released when they wind up together at the end of a phrase. A well-executed smear, like seeing the house *almost* fall on Buster Keaton, can make an audience gasp with delight.

Fillmore's second trombone rag was "Teddy Trombone," published in 1911 and dedicated to his friend Theodore Hahn, a Cincinnati orchestra conductor and ragtime composer. The third (from 1915) was everyone's favorite, "Lassus Trombone." Fillmore's series finally comprised fifteen of these showpieces, which were collected in a Fillmore Brothers folio of 1929 entitled *The Trombone Family: A Collection of Original and Humorous Trombone Novelties*. A 1917 ad offered five of the smears as arranged for full band (thirty cents each), full orchestra (forty-five cents each), and small orchestra (thirty cents each). Fillmore rarely made piano arrangements of his compositions, because he didn't want them played on the piano. The piano was all right, it just wasn't a trombone. Henry did not own one until 1922.

The various Fillmore bands would be the main exponents of the Fillmore novelties, of course, but other bands programmed them as well. By 1915 even Sousa had unbent enough to use "Miss Trombone" and "Lassus Trombone" as encores. Ford Dabney's Band recorded "Sally Trombone" in 1917, followed by "Miss Trombone" and "Lassus Trombone" two years later. Prince's Band (recording as the Columbia Orchestra) made "Lassus" and "Miss" in 1918. Henry's smears outsold everything else in the Fillmore catalog in the teens, so his father held his nose and kept publishing them. The only clash came in 1920, when Henry wrote a rag that paraphrased the "Hallelujah" chorus. To calm his enraged father, Henry changed its name from "Hallelujah Trombone" to "Shoutin' Liza Trombone."

Although Fillmore was considered the brightest composer for bands, he had not yet had a band of his own. Early in 1921, at age thirty-nine, he began to make his reputation as a conductor when he took over Cincinnati's moribund Syrian Shrine Temple Band. He weeded out "chair warmers" (by auditions and by embarrassing them during rehearsals) and turned it into a snappy unit, as sharp on the parade field as it was in the concert hall. In the spring of 1921, Fillmore's band was voted the best of those at the Shrine's Imperial Council gathering in Des Moines, Iowa. A year later, Fillmore showed off the band at home during the six days of the first Shrine Circus at Cincinnati's Music Hall. The band first drew national attention in 1923, when they attended the Imperial Council in Washington, D.C. As they paraded past President Warren G. Harding in the reviewing stand on Pennsylvania Avenue, they struck up "Men of Ohio," a march that Fillmore had written in 1921 and dedicated to Harding. A Harding aide found Fillmore after the parade and extended the president's invitation to an impromptu reception on the White House lawn. Harding asked to hear "Men of Ohio" again, and when this was done, a trumpeter serenaded Mrs. Harding with "A Perfect Day." Their next appearance was at Griffith Park, playing during a Senators–Yankees game. The following Sunday, at the request of New York manager Miller Huggins, they played at Yankee Stadium. On June 7, they were back at Griffith Park, front and center, as John Philip Sousa conducted the 6,200 men of the combined Shrine bands.

In January 1926 Fillmore introduced a new member of his band, his dog Mike, whom he had taught to bark on cue to add rural atmosphere to his composition "The Whistling Farmer Boy." Mike was a great hit, so Fillmore presented him regularly in concert that spring. (Fillmore would later write several pieces specifically to feature his gifted mutt, including "Mike Hunting Birds" and "Giving Mike the Ha Ha.") Mike's association with the Shriners was short-lived, however. In May 1926, after an ongoing dispute with the council about money for band trips, Fillmore resigned as the band's director. In a striking display of loyalty, all seventy-one of the bandsmen resigned from the band as well.

Fillmore's ex-bandsmen wanted to keep playing for him, however, and for a year or so they gave free concerts at orphanages and hospitals. Then Powell Crosley, Jr., of the Crosley Radio Corporation family, had an idea. He proposed that Fillmore assemble a band for broadcasts over Cincinnati station WLW, a Crosley-owned station. Fillmore assembled a twenty-two-piece band and began his weekly show (simultaneously broadcast over WLW and WSAI) on October 4, 1927. The show reached a wide audience throughout the Midwest, and the name Fillmore became synonymous with band music in millions of homes.

Radio listeners wanted to hear the band live, of course, and Fillmore was happy to oblige. In August 1928 he took his radio band to the Cincinnati Zoo and began a six-year tradition of summer concerts there. On October 1, 1928, the band (and Mike) recorded two sides for Columbia records (a march called "Golden Friendships" and "The Whistling Farmer Boy"), the only commercial recordings of a Fillmore band. A few weeks after the Columbia session, Henry and the band were the subject of a newsreel feature story filmed for Pathé's *Audio Review* in the WLW studio.

Keeping a band together was an expensive proposition during the Great Depression, and it was decided in the spring of 1930 that WLW could no longer afford Fillmore's group. (The show would be briefly reinstated two years later.) Henry enjoyed his celebrity from the radio show, but his pleasure was dimmed by Mike's passing in July 1932. He was the victim of rat poison put out in a neighbor's yard, but Cincinnati newspapers downplayed the details of his grisly death in their long, respectful obituaries.

The zoo shows continued, and in 1934, Cincinnati's city parks booked Fillmore for fourteen concerts. It was in the zoo-parks concerts that Henry began chatting with his audiences. He introduced numbers, kidded with soloists, and told jokes in a low-key and friendly way. The public loved it, and the parks department asked him for fifty-five concerts in 1935. When the Cincinnati Reds instituted baseball's first night games that year, Fillmore's band played at all seven of them.

Even a cherished institution gets tired, and Henry Fillmore's energy flagged in the mid-thirties. His father died in February 1936, and Henry inherited the task of running Fillmore Brothers. He juggled the business and the band for a while, but in the summer of that year, he disbanded the group after their final park concert. His last burst of composition came in 1937 (with a set of numbers for a Fillmore Brothers band book). In 1938 his doctor told him that he had a heart condition and that he had six months to a year to live. The doctor recommended sunshine and stress-free living for Henry's twilight days, so he and Mabel moved to Miami, Florida. The "dying" bandmaster was about to begin the busiest eighteen years of his life.

Although professional concert bands were declining in the late 1930s, school bands were booming. Fillmore was a hero to every college and high school band director, and those in Florida were quick to take advantage of his proximity. Not long after becoming a Floridian, he was invited to guest-conduct at Miami's Edison High School, DeLand High School, and Stetson University in DeLand. The stubby showman was a hit everywhere, of course, so more invitations poured in. Fillmore was invigorated by all the attention, so he accepted almost every invitation that he got. Because he had thoughtfully brought along his band books in his move, school bands all over Florida were soon giving out with "The Footlifter" and "Teddy Trombone."

Fillmore became the patron saint of the school band, personally arm-twisting thirty-two Florida school boards into creating band programs. He held workshops, conducted clinics, and judged contests. During the 1940s, he visited practically every school band—high school, college, and university—in the state. On New Year's Day 1943 he conducted the University of Miami band at the Orange Bowl Game, in the first of his seven appearances at the holiday ritual.

Fillmore had a half dozen minor heart attacks during these antic years, but he brushed them away like gnats. After a few days in a hospital, he would be on the podium again, at the university or in some back-country band room, showing a teenage trombonist how to smear. Honors came to him. On August 5, 1951, as the first guest conductor of Paul Lavalle's Cities Service Band of America on its NBC radio show, he programmed "Twelfth Street Rag" and "Pahson Trombone." On March 8, 1952, at Ohio State, he threw the American Bandmasters Association into a delirium of cheering when he led a college all-star band in "Men of Ohio" and "Shoutin' Liza Trombone."

Mabel died in 1954, but Henry kept going. In February 1956 he was given an honorary doctorate in music by the University of Miami. On December 7, 1956, Henry Fillmore died at Mercy Hospital in Miami. If he misses anything in the afterlife, it is probably the Orange Bowl.

BART HOWARD

Every American city large enough to have had a pleasure district had its local piano legends. The legends were male, most of them black, and all of them drifters. No one knew where they came from, and, in many cases, no one knew their last names. Some we know went on to shabby ends, but most of them just went on, vanishing as mysteriously as they had come. Each brought gaiety to the district in which he played, and each had a trick or two that caught the ear of younger pianists. But none of them published anything or made recordings, so their music lived exactly as long as those who had heard it being made. They are only names in books now, a roll call of ghosts, and there will be no new names added to the roll. Among them, in New Orleans: Albert Carroll, Alfred Wilson, Sammy Davis, John the Baptist; in Chicago: Plunk Henry, Johnny Seymour, Eddie James, Harry Crosby; in New York

City: One-Leg Willie Joseph, Jack the Bear, Jess Pickett; in Baltimore: William Turk, Sammy Ewell, and Big Head Wilbur.

One of the Detroit piano legends was Bart Howard, a small, cigar-chomping black man who, in the teens, was considered that city's rag-time king. We know a bit about Howard because, in the 1960s, the ragtime pianist/composer Tom Shea took the last opportunity there would ever be to find out about him. Shea sought out George Walls, Dewey Lee, and Don McCullough, three of Howard's admirers who long outlived him. They told of hearing him and of wanting to be that good.

They weren't sure about when Howard was born (probably around 1880) or where he came from (either Detroit or Toledo, Ohio), but each knew when and where he had been set afire by Howard's music. It was in 1915 at Detroit's Turf Cafe, at the corner of Mullett and Hastings streets, a tough joint in a tough neighborhood. Howard's playing was powerful and heavily ornamented with flips and fills. He was in his thirties at the time and still scrambling for a place among the pianists who had preceded him to Detroit's sporting world. There was a nameless, long-armed player (remembered only as "The Ape"); there was George Curtis (who, although he had all his fingers, chose to play with only three fingers on each hand); and there was "Snow" (a numbers runner who could play for ten hours or more without a break). At the Turf's piano contests, Howard's chief rival was Toledo's Johnny Waters (whose playing inspired another youngster, Earl Hines).

Johnny Waters had the edge on Howard because of his reach. Waters's hand span was so wide that he could hold a twelfth with his right hand and play three-note melodies with his inside fingers. To compete with Waters, Howard needed what nature had not given him. He went to a neighborhood "doctor," who snipped the skin between his forefingers and his thumbs to give him extra reach. While recovering from this career-enhancing operation, Howard wore gloves that held marbles between his middle fingers to increase their span also. When he was ready to play again, he could reach a tenth. It was not as good as what Johnny Waters had, but it was better than before.

The hallmark of Howard's playing was not treble-clef fireworks but an innovation that he brought to his bass. He broke up the usual octave-chord bass pattern of ragtime with sprightly left-hand running figures in octaves, fourths, and sixths. With his alternation between oompahs and runs, Howard had taken a step toward stride piano, and his trick was taken up by younger players. He composed a number called "Detroit Rags" to show off his bass idea.

Howard's wife, Corrine, was a singer, and when they worked up an act together, their fortunes improved. In the late teens they became the first black entertainers to work at the Griswold House, a hotel at the corner of West Grand Boulevard and Griswold. In the 1920s Howard led a dance band at the Royal Garden (a cabaret at St. Antoine and Madison) and at Thomas's Inn in Windsor, Ontario. He couldn't keep a band together during the Depression, so he became a bar pianist again.

Tom Shea's informants thought that Howard died in a rooming house somewhere, and thought that it must have been in the mid-thirties. Dewey Lee, the only one who remembered it, played "Detroit Rags" for Shea and showed him the tricky bass. Then the interview was over. Shea is gone now, and if Dewey Lee has left us, "Detroit Rags" is gone, too.

ALVIN MARX

One of the happy consequences of the ragtime revival (which has by now lasted longer than the ragtime era it celebrates) has been the recovery of lost or forgotten rags, including some works by major composers. A Sedalia friend of Scott Hayden's gave the manuscript of Hayden's "Pear Blossoms" to Bob Darch, who fleshed out its bass part and arranged for its publication in the 1966 edition of *They All Played Ragtime*. Also published in that book was James Scott's "Calliope Rag," from a manuscript given to Darch by Scott's sister. A piano roll collector found Joplin's "Silver Swan," an uncopyrighted and unpublished work from around 1914, in a box of rolls in his garage in 1970. Dick Zimmerman and Donna McCluer's transcription of it was published, and it now takes its place in the Joplin canon.

More typical of the recent finds are the works of ragtime's core constituency, the passionate amateurs. One of these locally published and long-forgotten rags was Alvin Marx's "Frigid Frolics." Its lost-and-found story bridges two ragtime eras that are decades apart.

Alvin L. Marx was born in Ashland, Wisconsin, in 1882. He was the second of the four sons of a railroad worker (who played the violin) and a housewife (who played the piano). The Marx boys all played the piano a bit, but it was Alvin who really took to it. His brother Richard recalled, "If Alvin got hold of a tune, he would start ragging it. That's how ragtime got into the family."

In 1902 the Marx family moved to Superior, Wisconsin, and Alvin got a job playing for silent movies at the Savoy Theatre. In 1905 he self-published his lively and folkish rag "Frigid Frolics." He probably ordered a hundred copies—the usual run for a vanity publication—to pass around to his family and friends. After the flash of pride at seeing Alvin's name in print, the friends and relatives put their copies away. Alvin could play it, and they couldn't. "Frigid Frolics" became a keepsake, a souvenir of Superior in 1905.

Alvin's father died in 1906, and whatever musical ambitions Alvin may have had died soon afterward. The rest of the Marxes returned to Ashland, but Alvin remained in Superior. He had extra responsibilities as family provider now, and he was recently married. It was time to get a steady job and stick to it. He found one with the Lake Superior Terminal & Transfer Railway, and, whether he intended it or not, Alvin Marx began a career.

Marx copyrighted a few songs over the years ("What Did Cleopatra Dance in Her Hey-Hey Day?" and "Don't Get Too Rosy with Rosie"), but he never made the effort to get them published nor did he publish them himself. His coworkers liked his piano playing, though. For years he was a fixture at socials given by the Switchman's Union of North America, Lodge No. 107, pumping out rags and songs. ("He sure could tickle the old ivory and make it shout," one of the lodge members said.) When retired switchman Alvin Marx died in 1956, his obituary did not mention that he was fun at parties.

One of those who remembered Alvin's music was his brother Richard. Early in 1985 Richard Marx (then ninety-one) attended a concert given by Yvonne Cloutier, a ragtime pianist and cofounder of the Lake Superior Ragtime Society. Richard enjoyed the music so much that he called Cloutier a few days later and asked if she might be interested in Alvin's rag. She came to his home, and he showed her his copy of "Frigid Frolics." Cloutier played it through on Richard's spinet and found it delightful. She promised that she would share it with the ragtime community. Cloutier and Tim Sandor worked up "Frigid Frolics" as a piano duet and introduced it at Sedalia's Scott Joplin Festival that summer. Alvin Marx's rag got a second chance at life. Young people still learn "Frigid Frolics," and audiences still enjoy it. No more is needed to keep a piece of music alive.

Richard Marx died in 1986. In his last year he was proud to see that his brother's rag had reached across eight decades. And it pleased him just to hear "Frigid Frolics" again. When he first heard Cloutier and Sandor's duet version, he said, "That was so nice. . . . I won't be able to sleep tonight. My ears are still ringing."

ADALINE SHEPHERD

Women were the target audience for published ragtime, and it is only natural that ragtime's main consumers would try writing rags. Because ragtime carried an aura of naughtiness and frivolity, female composers sometimes masked their identities by using only their initials when they signed their work (such as L. V. Gustin and N. W. Cocroft). When we see a list of unknown composers who use no first names, it is a safe bet that many of them were women. The old ruse still conceals their ragtime lives.

But the early century also saw the emergence of the New Woman, the one who, whether spurred by nerve or by economic necessity, left the house and went to work. Many of the New Women worked in the music business: as teachers, silent movie accompanists, and demonstrators and clerks in music stores. When they wrote rags, they thought no more of putting their names to them than they thought of endorsing their paychecks.

The first six women rag composers whose names we know were all from the Midwest: Zellah Edith Sanders (Chicago), Verdi Karns (Bluffton, Indiana), Frankie Gooch McCool (Indianapolis), Maie Fitzgerald (Sedalia, Missouri), Lina Mumford (Grand Rapids, Michigan), and Mattie Harl Burgess (Chicago). Between 1898 and 1902, they published one rag each. The women who followed them published a bit more, and in the teens and twenties, a dozen or so women worked as arrangers and roll and recording artists. Irene Giblin, of St. Louis, was the most-published woman of the ragtime era, with nine rags.

Adaline Shepherd (born in Algona, Iowa, in 1885) was the first woman to compose a nationally known rag. The brief arc of Shepherd's

Adaline Shepherd

career is typical of the female ragtimers of her day: early promise, a few publications, marriage, silence. Emancipation went only so far. Even the most successful of the female writers—like Shepherd, Irene Giblin, and May Aufderheide—were yanked back to amateur status shortly after leaving the altar. So, as amateurs have always done, they used their music to entertain their families. They became neighborhood "characters," middle-aged, then old, women who played roughhouse piano.

It isn't known what brought Adaline Shepherd from Iowa to Milwaukee, but by age twenty she was there, living on the West Side and starting to write rags. In 1906 she came up with one she liked enough to copyright, naming it "Pickles and Peppers." In the summer of 1907, she went to try it out on a local publisher, Joseph Flanner.

Flanner asked to see her manuscript first; she told him that she had none, the music was in her head. She played the number for him, and, although Flanner had never published a rag, he was intrigued. But he wanted a second opinion.

Flanner asked Shepherd to come back the next day, and when she arrived, he and a local bandmaster were waiting for her. Playing by ear, she again tore into "Pickles and Peppers." Flanner bought it, and the bandmaster offered to arrange it for publication.

"Pickles and Peppers" is a wide-awake rag, full of gusto and tricky syncopations, made trickier by the written-out variations in repeated sections. It became a regional hit, selling over 100,000 copies in a year. Its national reputation was made in July 1908, when, at the Democratic convention in Denver, "Pickles and Peppers" was played at every appearance of the presidential nominee, William Jennings Bryan. Considering its complexity, "Pickles and Peppers" was a bold choice for campaign music, but it was certainly catchier (and has lasted longer) than the Republicans' song, "Get on the Raft with Taft." In October Bryan was dining in a Milwaukee restaurant when the orchestra struck up "Hail to the Chief" in his honor. The master politician cemented his local popularity when he told the leader that he'd rather hear "Pickles and Peppers."

Bryan's defeat in November did not put an end to Shepherd's rag. "Pickles and Peppers" was recorded for Victor by Pryor's Band in March 1909, and it was also available in ten piano roll versions. Adaline Shepherd seemed to be on her way as a ragtime composer. In an effort to get better (and quicker) distribution for her rags, she shopped the next two in Chicago. Her "Wireless Rag" was issued by Standard Music in August 1909, and her "Live Wires Rag" was published by Harold Rossiter in 1910, the year of her marriage.

As the wife of insurance executive Fred Sherman Olson, Adaline Shepherd was assured a comfortable, upper-middle-class life in Milwaukee. The couple had three children, and Shepherd had one more publication ("Victory March" in 1917). "Pickles and Peppers" eventually sold another hundred thousand, and it remained Flanner's most valuable copyright until he went bankrupt in 1913. Arthritis plagued Shepherd in her last years, but she continued to play the piano. She died in Milwaukee in 1950.

ERIC SEVERIN

The bane of the self-publishing composer was distribution. Many vanity rags were excellent—and some of them are masterpieces—but Jerome Remick and Will Rossiter could always outpublish, outplug, and outreach their writers. By 1910 or so, a pianist in a middle-sized city was more likely to have heard the latest trifle from New York or Chicago than to have heard the work of a genius who lived across town. If by the writer's perseverance or good luck his local rag made a stir, it might be picked up by a major publisher, reissued, and rescued from oblivion.

Most of the composers on our checklist have one self-published rag to their credit. One disappointment was usually enough. Eric Severin tried more than once. He had a superior product, and he hustled like hell to sell it. As a preamble to the story of his persistence, let us recall two other gifted regional writers who had superior products, too.

Some of the one-shot rags are so good that, decades after they first appeared, they tantalize us and make us wish there were more from the minds that created them. One of these is Clarence Wiley's "Car-Barlick Acid." Wiley was a pharmacist in Oskaloosa, Iowa, when he copyrighted his souped-up folk rag in 1901. Like many of the early rags, "Car-Barlick Acid" is based on a simple syncopated figure like those in cakewalks, but Wiley's rag has more guts than any cakewalk. It is propelled by a bass line that marches all over the lower half of the piano, and it begs to be played fast. (The best recording of "Car-Barlick Acid" is Bob Darch's, on his *Ragtime Piano* LP, made for United Artists in 1960.)

Wiley published his rag in 1903, and the copyright was bought the following year by Giles Brothers, a publisher with offices in Hannibal, Missouri, and Quincy, Illinois. Piano rolls of "Car-Barlick Acid" began to appear (there would eventually be six). In 1907 Giles sold the copyright to Remick, and, six years after it was written, Wiley's "Acid" finally got national distribution. The wait was too long and the payoff too little. Wiley probably sold his work outright to Giles Brothers, and, if this is true, there was no payoff at all to him from the sale to Remick. If a masterpiece like "Car-Barlick Acid" could not earn out, it is small wonder that Clarence Wiley stayed in the drugstore and never published another rag.

The extra measures are extra music, not tags that repeat the last four bars but extensions of the melody itself. "Jungle Time" introduces Severin's compositional trademark, cascades of octave chromatics that race up and down the piano with the chromatic melody in alternating hands. The close juxtapositions of Ds in the left hand near Ebs in the right and the placing of Es near Fs put weird flashes of dissonance into the melody as it thunders by. "Jungle Time" has a piano-wide grandness to it, as well as textures that would not be heard again in rags until Artie Matthews's "Pastimes" ten years later.

"Jungle Time"

Despite its difficulty, "Jungle Time" was picked up by Arnett-Delonais, a Chicago publisher, in 1909. As Arnett began to place the rag with piano roll companies, Severin decided to write something in a more popular (and easier) vein. Indian intermezzos were still selling in 1910, so he wrote an "Indian" instrumental called "Mona," which was also issued as a song with lyrics by the composer. Even "Mona," a naked attempt at commercialism, bears the oddball Severin touch, with its unmodulated minor chords thrown into major key melodies.

In 1911 Severin's second rag, the magnificent "Sky Rockets," was published by the composer. Like "Jungle Time," it is a sunburst of chromatics, and it contains extra helpings of syncopation (one twenty-bar section and another of twenty-four). The hype of Severin the publisher was beginning to match the grandiosity of Severin the composer. On the title page of his new rag, he wrote:

Since publishing "JUNGLE TIME RAG" (a tremendous Hit) which was highly endorsed by the public, and one who's popularity it would seem, will never die, the composer has been swamped with requests from all over this country and abroad to give the public another Rag from the same Pen, hence, "SKY ROCKETS" which the writer has aimed to make a worthy successor to "Jungle Time," the result is a Rag which can be played over and over again, and instead of palling the listener develops new beauties and gives additional pleasure with each repetition, like Old Wine, SEVERIN'S RAGS improve with age, and by reason of this ones undoubted originality and the freshness of its melodies and style its popularity can be expected to extend for long years to come.

Like "Jungle Time," "Sky Rockets" got five piano roll versions, but, unlike the first rag, it was not picked up by a major publisher. While waiting for "Sky Rockets" to take off, Severin (probably inspired by Irving Berlin's "Alexander's Ragtime Band") issued a raggy song in 1912, "That Ever Lovin' Violin Man," with lyrics by J. Hayes Robinson and music by himself.

The 1914 Moline city directory says that Eric Severin "removed to Clear Lake, Iowa," and it is in that year that we begin to lose track of him. The directory does not mention Grace Severin going with him (were they separated?), but it says his mother resides at 428½ Eleventh Street. For the next four years there are no Severin publications or copyrights (and no indications of where he lived). Then he is back in Moline, at it again.

Severin published his "Rarin' to Go" in Moline in 1918. It is subtitled "Jazz Fox Trot," but it is actually a World War I song, with a drawing of General Pershing on the cover, riding a white horse and leading screaming doughboys into battle. On the back of the song is an ad for Severin's third and last piece of ragtime, "Grand Concert Rag," also issued that year. The ad carries his 1905 photo from "Jungle Time," and its copy, like John Stark's in the late teens, is shrill and defensive. He says that "Grand Concert" is the "MOST WONDERFUL RAG EVER WRITTEN" and calls it "*a Rag Classic of the highest order.*" The first blurb is questionable, but the second one is not.

Like Stark, Severin knew that he had something different, something, he said, "that would distinguish you from the average popular song thumper." And, like the old man in Missouri, he knew it was a hard sell. The back cover of "Grand Concert" indicates that he still has copies of his seven-year-old "Sky Rockets." Without giving an address from which to order them, he says he will send them "postpaid for 15 cents each."

The last Severin publication was a 1920 song called "I Am Always Having Pipe Dreams." The cover drawing shows a young man (looking like the 1905 Severin with a J. C. Leyendecker haircut) pondering a bag of money and a pretty girl's face that appear in wreaths of smoke from his pipe. We know Severin didn't get the bag of money, but we can hope that he got the girl.

<hr />

CHICAGO BEFORE RAGTIME
Out of the Mud, Out of the Ashes

Like most of its sister cities in the Midwest, Chicago grew from a cluster of traders' cabins to a metropolis in the first half of the nineteenth century. The first settler in the area was the trader/trapper Jean Baptiste Point de Sable, a Santo Domingan Negro who claimed the land between the north and south branches of the Chicago River as his own simply by building a cabin there in 1779. John Kinzie, another trader, bought de Sable's house and land in 1804 to establish himself as supplier of provender to the nearby Fort Dearborn, which had been erected the previous year. Because more traders came, the enterprising Mark Beaubien opened his Sauganash Tavern in 1826, and he inaugurated the city's musical life by playing his fiddle for dancing there. With the tavern as its nucleus, Beaubien's Sauganash Hotel, the first frame building in Chicago, arose in 1831.

In 1833 the Ft. Dearborn settlement, with a population of about 150, was incorporated as the village of Chicago. A village needed a piano, of course, and in 1834 Jean Beaubien, Mark's brother, imported one. A music teacher came to give lessons and to organize singing societies. Feverish speculation in land occurred in the mid-1830s, and the area boomed. Mark Beaubien soon had competition from Lincoln's Coffee House (a saloon built in 1835) and from Francis Sherman's Sherman House Hotel (built in 1837, with five stories and 300 rooms). In 1837 the village of Chicago (population 3,297) was incorporated as a city.

During Chicago's adolescence, the city was known for two things: its rapid growth and its mud. Most American cities of this time had dirt streets, but Chicago's were something else. Long winters and frequent rains kept the city writhing in mud, a distinctive Chicago ur-mud, viscous and smelly and often deep enough to mire a team of horses. Planking laid over it was sucked up when stepped on. Chicago's boosters saw their dreams for the city of the future literally bogging down, so in 1855 the local government began a huge engineering project. Over the next ten years the grade of the streets was raised twelve feet and virtually every building in the city, including the tallest, was jacked up and reset to align with a new topography. Chicago's victory over its mud was the first demonstration of the city's can-do spirit and its first triumph over natural disaster.

Chicago's real prosperity began with the opening of the Illinois-Michigan Canal, a water route between the city and the Mississippi River, in 1848. In February 1852 the Michigan-Southern Line completed the first rail connections to the East, and the city's future as a major trading and manufacturing center was assured. The Michigan Central, the Illinois Central, and the Rock Island Road soon joined the Michigan-Southern in moving goods and produce into and out of Chicago.

As commerce brought stability to the city, Chicago's cultural scene grew in quality and variety. In 1847, John B. Rice opened the first respectable (nonsaloon) theatre, and three years later, the Philharmonic Society, the first permanent orchestra, was founded. In 1847 the Lake Street firm of Brainard & Mould set up shop as the first music dealer in Chicago, and the first local instrument maker, G. A. Helmkamp, arrived that year. In 1848 the city's first music publisher, Griggs, Bross

& Company, began selling its songsters and school music at 121 Lake Street. James H. McVicker's Theatre hosted the acting companies of Edwin Forrest and the senior E. A. Sothern. John Wilkes Booth brought his acclaimed production of *Richard III* to McVicker's in 1862. There were four piano factories in Chicago by 1860.

In December 1858, the first important Chicago music publisher, Root & Cady, opened its doors at 95 Clark Street. The firm was founded by two music educators from the Northeast, Ebenezer Towner Root and Chauncey M. Cady; in 1860, the founders took in Ebenezer's brother, George Frederick Root, as a partner. With Ebenezer and Cady running the business and George directing the publishing arm, the company turned out parlor songs, marches, and quicksteps.

The outbreak of the Civil War threw Root & Cady into high gear. George Root was a music publisher with the "scoop" mentality of a newspaper publisher, and Chicagoans could practically follow the progress of the war through the lyrics of Root & Cady songs. The company issued the first Civil War song—George Root's "The First Gun Is Fired!"—on April 15, 1861, three days after the first gun was fired at Fort Sumter.

In 1862 the composer/lyricist Henry Clay Work began his long association with Root & Cady. With George Root and Henry Work as its most-published composers, the company turned out an impressive string of successes. Although the Roots, Cady, and Work were Northern sympathizers, their songs were popular everywhere because they had the common touch. Instead of publishing commemorative quicksteps named for generals and battles, Root & Cady issued songs that caught the emotions of young soldiers and the anxious families waiting for them at home. It took time for nineteenth-century songs to make their way around the country, so there were no instant "hits," but in the years 1862–1865, Root & Cady had fifteen nationally known songs, an achievement unmatched in so short a time by any other firm before the twentieth century. (Among them were "Kingdom Coming," "The Battle Cry of Freedom," "Just Before the Battle, Mother," "Come Home, Father" [a temperance song], "Tramp! Tramp! Tramp!," and "Marching Through Georgia.") Root & Cady showed the way to other local publishers: its success proved that there was money to be made in the pop music business, and that if one hustled, it could be made in Chicago.

Riding high on the sales of its Civil War songs, Root & Cady moved into new quarters in a new building in late 1865, taking offices and sales rooms in Crosby's Opera House, at 67 Washington Street. Uranus Crosby had laid out $700,000 to erect the grandest theatre that Chicago had ever seen, and to increase its commercial potential, he included in its design an art gallery and office spaces. There were few operas presented in the Opera House, but it bustled with other cultural activity: concerts, lectures, and entertainments of all sorts. In 1868 the Republican party's convention was held in the 3,000-seat theatre, and U.S. Grant was nominated there as the party's presidential candidate. The following year, Lydia Thompson brought in her British Blondes, giving Chicago its first look at burlesque. The famous dramatic/musical revue *The Black Crook* stopped there on its national tour.

As Crosby's stayed busy, so did Root & Cady. It bought the catalogs of five other publishers and issued their titles along with its own torrent of songsters and sheet music. Crosby and his tenants prospered until October 8, 1871, when an incident in a barn on DeKoven Street brought their downfall. It was there, at about 8:30 on a Sunday evening, that something (a cow kicking over a lantern?) or someone started a fire in the hay.

The fire was unstoppable. Despite the furious efforts of the fire department and citizen bucket brigades, it raged across the city for twenty-four hellish hours. A few days after it was finally brought under control, dazed and exhausted Chicagoans read the enumeration of its awful toll: nearly 300 dead; 17,450 homes lost; 90,000 homeless; 2,100 acres of the central city destroyed; and property loss of over $200 million, which represented about a third of the wealth of Chicago. Crosby's Opera House was among the hundreds of properties that burned to the ground. As George Root's office lay in smoldering splinters, his professional reflexes kicked in: he wrote a song about the calamity. "Passing Through the Fire" did not sell well; the city was still covered by a haze of smoke when the song went on the market.

Chicago's heroic response to the Great Fire earned the admiration of the world. Churches and government buildings sheltered the homeless. Soup kitchens fed the hungry. The rebuilding of many shops and stores began even before the fire was quelled. When insurance companies defaulted, many commercial and residential policy holders sold salvaged possessions and withdrew their savings to start over. In 1873 Chicago presented a symbolic progress report when it hosted the Interstate Industrial Exhibition. Local manufacturers proved by their elaborate displays of merchandise that Chicago was back in business, and regional manufacturers who exhibited there vouched their faith in Chicago as a good place to trade. That same year the bandmaster Patrick Gilmore staged a pageantlike "Peace Jubilee" to celebrate Chicago's recovery. The restoration would take another eight years to complete, but everyone knew that Chicago would not stop until the job was done.

As a grander Chicago grew out of the ashes, the city's cultural, as well as its commercial, institutions revived themselves. Chicago Musical College (founded in 1867 by Florenz Ziegfeld, the *Follies* producer's father) was up and going again by 1872, when it added the defunct publisher (but still-honored songwriter) George Frederick Root to its faculty. Uranus Crosby did not reopen his theatre, but James H. McVicker reopened his. In the 1870s and 1880s, at McVicker's and at Central Music Hall, Chicago saw the biggest stage stars of the day. Mme. Helena Modjeska depicted Camille, Buffalo Bill Cody reenacted his exploits among the Indians, and Oscar Wilde lectured on aesthetics to 2,500 Chicagoans who had never seen the likes of him. Sarah Bernhardt acted *Adrienne Lecouvreur* in French, and audiences paid the $5 top to follow the plot with English scripts in hand. (Bernhardt toured the stockyards during her visit, and she pronounced them "a horrible vision, a dreadful and magnificent sight.")

Although it was not boasted of by city fathers, one of the sights of the new, 1880s Chicago was the most notorious sporting district in the Midwest, a crucible of vice called the Levee. The district lay between Eighteenth and Twenty-second streets, bounded on the east by South Wabash Avenue and on the west by South Clark Street. (Chicago's Chinatown occupies much of the old Levee area today.) Within a few square blocks there were more than 200 brothels, ranging in size and style from filthy, one-woman cribs with a twenty-five-cent fee to elegant town houses that employed dozens of elegant girls. With whorehouses as the main attraction, the Levee was also home to the usual attendant diversions: dance halls, gambling parlors, dope dens, and peep shows. Despite the pretensions of upper-class madams, the Levee's hospitality was typified by Mickey Finn, the bartender/owner of the Lone Star Saloon. He served his "Mickey Finn special" (a combination of raw alcohol, water into which snuff had been dissolved, and a secret "voodoo" powder) to his unsuspecting customers, rifled their pockets after they fell unconscious, then threw them out into the street.

Traveling men, when they told their stories of the Levee, overlooked the sordid in favor of the grand. And many of the sporting houses actually were grand. Frankie Wright called her house "The Library" because it was filled with rare books; the action at Lizzie Allen's House of Mirrors was quadrupled by mirrored walls in every room; the House of All Nations offered girls of twelve nationalities in "native" costumes; men approaching Madam Carrie Watson's on South Clark Street were greeted by a parrot that she had taught to say "Carrie Watson's. Come in, gentlemen." The higher-class madams allied themselves in a professional organization, the Society of Friendly Friends. There were so many sinful options available to the Levee visitor that he needed a guidebook: in the mid-1880s, *The Sporting and Club House Directory*, the *Consumer Digest* of the Chicago underworld, was published to guide him.

The most lavish brothel was the Everleigh Club, a three-story double mansion of fifty rooms at 2131–2133 South Dearborn Street. The house had been the enterprise of Madam Effie Hankins until late in 1899, when it was taken over by Ada and Minna Everleigh, daughters of a Kentucky lawyer. The young sisters (both in their twenties) had saved a good deal of money during their time as co-owners of an Omaha bordello, and they laid out $55,000 of it to renovate their new workplace. They made twelve parlors and decorated and furnished each in a voluptuous manner (teakwood chairs and silken canopies in the Japanese room; a Copper room paneled in hammered brass; blue leather couches and pillows in the Blue room; and so on). There were several cut-glass chandeliers, gold spittoons, a fountain that spewed perfume, and a mahogany dining table that could accommodate fifty dinner guests. They opened their doors on February 1, 1900, and their astronomical prices did not deter callers. (Their lowest price for a session with a prostitute was $10, twice the highest price in any other Chicago house. There were also $25 girls and $50 girls. A bottle of wine was $12, and supper was $50 a plate.) On Sundays the Everleighs tried to make their house more like a home with Beau Nights, the evenings when the working girls could entertain their own boyfriends.

Itinerant pianists who were enticed to Chicago by stories of the Levee's elegance never got to see any of it. The Everleighs preferred small chamber ensembles (violin, cello, piano, and harp) to barrelhouse players. A few of the houses employed banjo players, but most of them, unlike the houses in New Orleans and St. Louis, used no music at all. The best pianists in the city held relatively low-paying jobs in black theatres and cafes.

Many musicians were drawn to Chicago in 1893 by the World's Columbian Exposition, and ragtime scholars have wondered ever since what they played and heard there. Scott Joplin and Otis Saunders came from Missouri; Ben Harney, from Kentucky; and Jess Pickett, from Baltimore. No surviving program or newspaper account of music at the World's Fair mentions the word *ragtime* or describes syncopated playing (except that heard in the various ethnic "villages" set up as living "exhibits"). We do know that the most heavily plugged song was Charles K. Harris's "After the Ball," which was played in shows and cafes everywhere along the Midway Plaisance. Most probably, the musicians, like everyone else, goggled at the electrical displays, took a peek at Little Egypt's hootchy-kootchy dance, marveled at the giant Ferris wheel and the Manufacturers Building (the largest building in the world), heard too much of "After the Ball," and then went home. The visiting pianists may have inspired each other (and may have reassured each other in the choice of a dicey occupation), but none of them left Chicago composing ragtime.

The city was ripe for ragtime, though, and in 1897 the breakthrough happened. In October of that year, the first rag ever published was issued in Chicago. It was "Louisiana Rag," a misshapen thing but the first to crawl out of the syncopated ooze of the mid-nineties and stand on its legs like a rag. Its composer was Theodore H. Northrup, a Chicago arranger about whom little is known except that he was among the first to have even a rudimentary grasp of composing in this new idiom. Northrup had previously published two cakewalks in 1897 ("Night on the Levee" and "Plantation Echoes").

In his "Louisiana Rag," as clunky as it is, Northrup finally crossed over into ragtime. The first two of its three strains are in the awkward

Theodore Northrup

key of D, and there is an eight-bar "dogfight" like those in marches of the period. Although it is fully syncopated, pianists have never liked "Louisiana Rag" enough to program it or record it. Its sales did not inspire its publisher, the Thompson Music Company, to ask for another rag from Northrup. (Thompson was primarily a publisher of church and school music. The biggest seller in its catalog was Will L. Thompson's hymn, "Softly and Tenderly.")

Theodore Northrup had another, more influential, publication in 1897. He provided the arrangements for the ten-page Sol Bloom folio, *Ben Harney's Rag Time Instructor*. Ben Harney, a white singer/pianist from Kentucky, was the first entertainer to specialize in syncopation. Although Harney never wrote a rag, his raggy songs were very popular on the vaudeville stage, so Sol Bloom commissioned the folio to take advantage of Harney's fame. The exercises and instruction illustrate what the arranger and the singer (and the public) thought ragtime was: Northrup writes out syncopated variations on "Annie Laurie" and "Come Thou Fount," among others, and advises the player to go and do likewise. A short preface (probably written by Northrup) assures the player that ragtime is "nothing but consecutive music, either in the treble or bass, followed by regular time in one hand." (In fairness to the *Instructor*, it must be said that there had so far been no published examples of real ragtime to draw on or to aim at as player or composer.) In 1897 and for a few years following, ragtime meant "songs" to most people, and the Northrup/Harney booklet simply confirmed what most pianists already knew: spicing up songs and hymns was great fun. There would be many good rags to come out of Chicago, but not because Harney or Northrup lit their way.

WILL ROSSITER

The most important publisher of popular music in Chicago was Will Rossiter, who was also the most prolific publisher of rags. He advertised himself as "The Chicago Publisher," but his methods were those of New York's Tin Pan Alley. Unlike Stark, Rossiter had no long-term relationships with composers, but his door was open wider than Stark's to newcomers. Rossiter was the first Chicago publisher to focus exclusively on pop music, and, as was the case with every other major publisher of ragtime except Stark, Rossiter's income from his songs subsidized his rags. As long as hit songs came, Rossiter rags kept coming, too.

Will Rossiter was born in Wells, Somerset, England, in 1867, and he emigrated to Chicago in 1881. He seemed set on a career as a draftsman, serving first as an apprentice, then running his own small drafting shop in the late 1880s. An evening at a vaudeville show in 1890 changed his life. He heard William Scanlan singing Irish songs in his act at the Bijou Theatre, and, for some reason, Rossiter took it into his head that he could write better Irish songs than the ones Scanlan sang. Rossiter went home and knocked out a song called "Sweet Nellie Bawn" and signed it "W. R. Williams," the writer pseudonym that he would use for the rest of his life. He showed it to publishers, and when "Sweet Nellie Bawn" was roundly rejected, Rossiter decided to publish it himself.

Will Rossiter

Rossiter wanted a hit, and he instinctively knew that publication was only the first step toward getting one. He went to music shops, department stores, and dime stores with copies under his arm and sang "Sweet Nellie Bawn" until it sold out or until he was thrown out. He persuaded (paid?) William Windom to make it his specialty number in Haverly's Mastodon Minstrels show, and through Windom, the song traveled beyond Chicago. "Sweet Nellie Bawn" did not make Rossiter rich, but it was successful enough to turn him from a draftsman into a music publisher.

By 1893, Rossiter had an office at 56 Fifth Avenue in Chicago and had also opened a New York branch. He had published fewer than ten numbers, but one of them was Harry S. Miller's "The Cat Came Back," his first nationally known song. When the World's Fair opened that year, Rossiter seized the opportunities it offered. He collected several of his less successful songs in a cheap folio and personally peddled it at the fair. (Rossiter was the first publisher to recycle songs in folios.) He issued Jim Thornton's "She Never Saw the Streets of Cairo," a comedy song about Little Egypt, the fair's most talked about performer. He was the first publisher to advertise his songs in show business trade papers, especially the *New York Clipper*, which was required reading for vaudeville performers. He provided financial backing to create acts and sent them out to plug his songs. He gave free music folders (with the Rossiter name emblazoned on them) to bands.

Rossiter's boldest stroke as a plugger came in 1898. He wrote to the New York variety impresario Tony Pastor, telling him that a popular Chicago singer, W. R. Williams, was coming to New York and that he wanted an engagement. Pastor replied that he would book Williams for one show to see if the public liked him. Rossiter went to New York, introduced himself as Williams, and took the stage at Pastor's music hall to sing his songs. Pastor was impressed with "Williams" and offered him an open-ended booking. Rossiter spent six weeks plugging his songs in Pastor's theatre and was paid $50 a week for the privilege. When Rossiter had had enough, "W. R. Williams" returned to Chicago, and Pastor was never the wiser.

In the late 1890s Will Rossiter began to dabble in syncopated product. He issued Warren Beebe's "Ragtime March" (which was more march than ragtime) in 1897. He published a folio of songs from Williams and Walker's *Sons of Ham* in 1899, the same year that he published a "Ragtime Fantasie" on "Turkey in the Straw," by Otto Bonnell, one of his staff arrangers. In 1900 the first Rossiter rag, Egbert Van Alstyne's "Rag Time Chimes," appeared. There were two rags that sold well in 1904, Charles B. Brown's "Policy King" and Charles E. Mullen's "Silence and Fun," but Rossiter's most prestigious publications of that year were Scott Joplin's "Sycamore" and Tom Turpin's "Buffalo Rag." Nonetheless, Fred Fisher's 1905 song "If the Man in the Moon Were a Coon" eclipsed them all; it was the company's first smash hit.

It was in 1909 that Rossiter entered the rank of major publishers. He had two rags that sold moderately well that year (Bernard Adler's "That Dreamy Rag" and Cora Salisbury's "Lemons and Limes"). And he outbid his New York competition to acquire the rights to songs from Bert Williams's new show, *Mr. Lode of Koal*, which yielded Williams and Henry Creamer's "That's a Plenty." Even "W. R. Williams" had a hit, "I'd Love to Live in Loveland with a Girl Like You." It was already shaping up to be a good year, but late in 1909 Rossiter purchased a song that would far outsell anything his company ever published.

"Meet Me Tonight in Dreamland" was by two local writers, Leo Friedman and Beth Slater Whitson, and a self-published edition had been on the market for three months before it came to Rossiter's attention. Friedman had paid for a 5,000-copy print run (an unusually large number for a self-published song), and when Will Rossiter expressed interest in it, the composer drove the price up to $5,000. This was hard bargaining from an unknown songwriter, but Rossiter had to have "Dreamland." He paid the $5,000 and he followed this with another show of faith by pouring $10,000 into plugging it. The payoff was huge and it came quickly. "Meet Me Tonight in Dreamland" sold a half million copies in its first year, and it did not stop selling for nearly a decade. Rossiter would eventually issue five million copies of "Meet Me Tonight in Dreamland," and since his practice was to buy songs outright, he owed none of his profits to Friedman and Whitson. The writers' price had been high, but it was not enough.

The success of "Meet Me Tonight in Dreamland" (and the resentment that it caused its composers) shifted the terrain of Chicago publishing. Will's brother Harold was on staff in the Rossiter firm during the song's takeoff, so he knew of the two disgruntled hit writers who would never sell another song to Will Rossiter. He saw the chance to start his own firm and to take Friedman and Whitson with him. In August 1910 the new Harold Rossiter Music Company published Friedman and Whitson's "Let Me Call You Sweetheart," which would surpass even the phenomenal "Dreamland" by selling six million copies. Hal Rossiter would have only one more hit ("When You're Smiling," in 1928), but his presence on the publishing scene continued to annoy Will until Hal closed his doors in 1929. Friedman and Whitson never had another big song, but since they were receiving royalties on "Let Me Call You Sweetheart," they didn't need one.

If his brother's coup had hurt him, Will Rossiter could at least take comfort in his hits. Shelton Brooks's "Some of These Days" (another previously published song, purchased by Rossiter in 1910) remained a hardy perennial throughout the teens, and Wilbur Sweatman's 1911 "Down Home Rag" was a staple for vaudeville acts. As the ragtime era wound down, Rossiter unknowingly ventured into jazz. In 1915 he published Jelly Roll Morton's "The Jelly Roll Blues," the first jazz number in print. He issued Shelton Brooks's "Darktown Strutters' Ball" early in 1917, but when Leo Feist made him an offer for the copyright a few weeks after its publication, he sold it. His willingness to sell a sure-as-sunrise hit seems to indicate that he was plugged out. In 1919 a fire destroyed Rossiter's stockroom and offices at 71 West Randolph Street, and he moved to 30 West Lake.

The best Rossiter rags came late in the ragtime era. In 1916 he issued the first of his four George Cobb rags, the harmonically rich "Midnight Trot." In 1918 Cobb's "Russian Rag" gave Rossiter his biggest rag hit. "Russian Rag," an adaptation of Rachmaninoff's

Prelude in C Sharp Minor, is an expression of the ragtimer's oldest impulse, the urge to kick a classic in the pants, and it sold over a million copies. It was so cleverly done that vaudevillians featured it for years. If Rossiter was too tired to plug "Russian Rag," instrumentalists plugged it for him in theatres all over America. After it had sold well for a few years, Rossiter asked Cobb to go back to the Prelude and find a follow-up. In 1923 Cobb's "New Russian Rag" translated Rachmaninoff into the novelty idiom.

"New Russian" was one of the last Rossiter rags. He also issued Roy Bargy's "Sweet and Tender" and Clarence M. Jones's "Modulations" in 1923, but they were too difficult to sell well. Rossiter changed the direction of his company in the mid-1920s and began issuing religious songs along with the reprints of his hits.

Will Rossiter stayed in business through the tough thirties and forties, hanging on during the time when the Hollywood-owned Tin Pan Alley firms drove most of the regional publishers out of business. Hits rarely came from anywhere besides New York or Los Angeles, and Rossiter had no more hits. Chicago still knew who he was, though, and in 1952, his adopted city honored him. At the Chicagoland Music Festival at Soldiers Field, he was wheeled out in a horse-drawn buggy before a cheering crowd to sing "I'd Love to Live in Loveland with a Girl Like You." It was Chicago's last look at "Uncle Will." He died, at age eighty-seven, on June 10, 1954.

ARNETT-DELONAIS COMPANY/F. J. A. FORSTER MUSIC PUBLISHER

Frederick J. A. Forster (1876–1956) was a Chicago publisher who, through his association with two companies, issued thirty-seven rags, two fewer than Will Rossiter. Forster learned the Chicago music business from the ground up, beginning as a mandolinist in his late teens, then working as a jobber. His jobbing firm was extremely successful, distributing music from many publishers to big markets in the West and Midwest, and he was able to open a branch office in New York by 1903.

With his jobbing firm well established, Forster enlisted as one of several founders of a publishing house, the Arnett-Delonais Company, in 1903. Arnett published its first rag right away: A. E. Groves's "Woozy." In 1906 Arnett issued two rags, "Noodles" and "Chestnuts," by Percy Wenrich, who would be the company's leading composer (with five of the firm's ten rags to his credit). The following year Arnett-Delonais published Wenrich's best rag, "The Smiler." (When Forster reissued "The Smiler" under his own imprint a few years later, he gave it a subtitle, "Joplin-Rag." Wenrich claimed that the subtitle was a reference to his home town, but like the 1950s stripper who called herself "Jane Mansfield," Forster must have hoped the public would draw its own conclusions.)

In 1910, after Arnett dissolved, F. J. A. Forster Music Publisher opened at 529 South Wabash. Forster needed some product in a hurry, so he reissued some of the Arnett music and bought the small catalog of Archie Scheu, a Cincinnati composer who had published all of his own rags. In 1911 he issued Louisville composer Al Marzian's only rag, the tasty "Angel Food." With the publication of "Sweetness" in 1912, Forster began a long association with Charles L. Johnson, who would be his firm's chief composer. Johnson produced two big numbers for Forster in 1913, "Crazy Bone Rag" and a waltz called "Dream Days."

In 1914 Forster acquired "The Missouri Waltz," the piece that would eventually be his biggest seller. The story of its crawl into public consciousness illustrates how music professionals used to make their own luck, good and bad. Forster had never heard of "The Missouri Waltz" until stores that used his jobbing firm began calling him to ask for it. It was an unusual request (such intercourse between a jobber and a store usually ran the other way). But if pianists wanted the number, Forster decided that he would try to track it down.

He discovered that a thousand copies of "The Missouri Waltz" had been issued in 1912 by Frederick Knight Logan, who was music director for the Chauncey Olcott shows. When Forster began negotiations to buy the number from Logan, he discovered

Archie Scheu

Lee Edgar "Jelly" Settle

that there was another name attached to it, that of John Valentine Eppel, an Iowa orchestra leader. So Eppel became a party to its sale. Forster bought "The Missouri Waltz" (with a royalty provision to Logan and Eppel) and published it as an instrumental in 1914. The cover bore one of the oddest composer credits in pop music: "From an Original Melody Procured by John Valentine Eppel," then, in larger letters, "Arranged for Piano by Frederick Knight Logan." Read: Something's fishy.

Eppel had "procured" the melody by writing it down on his shirt cuffs as it was being played by an intermission pianist at a dance in Moberly, Missouri. The pianist was Lee Edgar Settle, the pride of New Franklin, Missouri, known to his neighbors as "Jelly." When Eppel questioned him about the piece, Settle said that it was called "The Graveyard Waltz" and that he had no plans to publish it. Settle's "X. L. Rag," a fine folk number, had been published by A. W. Perry in Sedalia in 1903, and it had gone nowhere. Similar oblivion had also met his two self-published songs, so he was not in the mood to publish anything else. Satisfied that Settle would never do anything with "The Graveyard Waltz," Eppel renamed it, took it to Chicago, and sold it to Logan.

"The Missouri Waltz" was one of those tunes that, with no help from vaudeville performers or recording artists, stuck in the public mind. Logan couldn't get bandleaders to program the number, and neither could Forster. No professional musician (except Eppel) wanted to play it, yet everyone seemed to want to hear it. To hear it, you had to play it yourself, so the sheet music began to move a bit. Forster hired pluggers (Charles L. Johnson, Abe Olman, and Jack Robbins) to get "The Missouri Waltz" into band books, but to no avail. In 1915 the publisher tried again, reissuing it as a song, but no professional singers wanted to feature it. James R. Shannon, the lyricist, was offered royalties, but he didn't believe in it either, so he made his contribution as a work for hire for $100 cash.

In 1919 Forster went at the problem another way: he tried to create interest in "The Missouri Waltz" by issuing "Missouri Blues" (by Harry Brown and James Stanley Royce), whose chorus liberally paraphrased its model. There were no takers for "Missouri Blues." Only because Forster believed in it did "The Missouri Waltz" stay in print. Finally, its sales creeping along but never stopping, "The Missouri Waltz" acquired a sort of folklike status, that of a standard that was never a hit. (It is said that Eppel offered Settle a percentage of his royalties but that Settle turned it down in disgust. The song's progress was so glacial that Settle would have thought that he was not losing much anyway.)

In the 1940s "The Missouri Waltz" attached itself like a barnacle to Harry Truman. It was played wherever he appeared, at state occasions, parties, conventions, and parades. In 1949 (the year that Edgar Settle died broke), the Missouri legislature declared "The Missouri Waltz" the state's official song. Truman could never shake the association, even after he told a television interviewer, "If you ask me what I think, I don't give a damn about it. . . . It's as bad as 'The Star Spangled Banner' as far as music is concerned."

The Forster company's best and best-selling rags of the teens were those of its best-known writer, Charles L. Johnson. Perhaps the hard push for "The Missouri Waltz" had made the publisher skeptical about plugging instrumentals, but, in any case, it was Forster's songs that received most of his—and the public's—attention. He had "Oh, Johnny, Oh!" (in 1917), "Hindustan" (an "Oriental" one-step that was turned into a song, in 1918), and Charles Johnson's "Sweet and Low" (in 1919). Forster timidly issued two novelty rags (Victor Arden and Wheeler Wadsworth's "Marilynn" in 1919 and Roy Bargy's "Blue Streak" in 1921), but he published no more like them. His last big hit was a brainless ditty, "It Ain't Gonna Rain No Mo'," written by his promotions manager, Wendell Hall, in 1923.

VICTOR KREMER COMPANY

Victor Kremer is one of the few publishers, in Chicago or anywhere else, with hit rags but no hit songs. His company lasted only from 1899 to 1912 (and Kremer himself withdrew from it in 1910), but during its short life, it focused on ragtime more intensely than any other Chicago publisher. Located at 108–110 Randolph Street, Kremer began its ragtime publishing with the biggest name in syncopation, issuing as its first rag Scott Joplin's serene and graceful "Palm Leaf Rag" in 1903.

Victor Kremer

Theron Bennett

The Kremer company hired Theron C. Bennett, a young man from Pierce City, Missouri, as a traveling salesman to cover its Southern territory (which went all the way to New Orleans). While Bennett was on the road trying to place Kremer publications in department stores, he was also writing music. In January 1904 Kremer published a Bennett rag called "Satisfied," and seven months later, a better one, "St. Louis Tickle." Perhaps because the second strain of "St. Louis Tickle" quotes a "dirty song," the black folk strain known as "Funky Butt," Bennett signed the work with a double pseudonym, "Barney and Seymore."

"St. Louis Tickle" appeared at the height of the hoopla over the St. Louis World's Fair. Its cover shows black children dancing near a board fence, behind which loom the fair's domed buildings, a Ferris wheel, and a dirigible. The rag was played often at the fair, and its popularity continued long after the fair was over. Prince's Band recorded it in August 1905 for Columbia, and the Ossman-Dudley Trio (banjo, mandolin, and harp guitar) made it in January 1906 for Victor. The trio's recording was one of Vess Ossman's best-sellers, and it kept the rag in the repertoire of early country string bands. A song version (with lyrics by James O'Dea) was issued by Kremer in 1905. Piano rolls of "St. Louis Tickle" came for several years, keeping it among Kremer's steadiest-selling rags.

In 1905 another rag scored for Kremer: Joseph C. Northup's "Cannon Ball." Northup's rag was quite advanced for its time, with a recurring "three over four" pattern in its melody, trombonelike runs in the left hand, and dense chords in high octaves. "Cannon Ball" received more piano rolls than recordings, possibly because it was as much fun to watch it being played as to listen to it. In 1907 Theron Bennett (using the pseudonym "George E. Florence") gave Kremer another success with his "Sweet Pickles." The title is a knockoff of Charles L. Johnson's hit, "Dill Pickles," but the music is not. "Sweet Pickles" is a truly original folk rag, as brisk and funky as the B section of "St. Louis Tickle" itself. In 1909 Kremer published the last of his four Bennett rags, "Pork and Beans," which goes from a rattling opening to a mellow conclusion.

Thanks to Kremer's (or his professional manager's) keen eye for rags, the company prospered. In 1906 the firm opened a New York branch at Forty-first and Broadway, with W. C. Polla (who was hired away from Jerome Remick) in charge as business manager. Kremer acquired the catalog of Lee B. Grabbe in February 1909.

Kremer published more songs than rags, of course, but none of the Kremer songs caught on. Like all publishers of pop music, he tried a little bit of everything—flower songs, mother songs, jungle songs, baby songs, ethnic songs ("Abie the Sporty Kid," "Go On, Good-a-Bye," "Off Again, On Again, Gone Again, Finnegan")—but they were all stiffs. One Kremer song, "Little Puff of Smoke, Good Night," had a brief vogue in 1910 because its composers were local heroes. The lyrics were by the Chicago *Tribune*'s top sports writer, Ring Lardner, and the music was by G. Harris ("Doc") White, the lefty pitcher for the White Sox. Despite its pedigree, the "Southern croon" was probably outsold that year by Henri Klickmann's rag, "Knockout Drops."

In August 1910 Victor Kremer announced to the trade papers that he was leaving the company that bore his name. Starting over early in 1911, he was hired as business manager for the House of Laemmle, a small publishing firm recently created by Carl Laemmle. When the House of Laemmle disappeared after a year or so of struggle, Victor Kremer disappeared with it. The Victor Kremer Company ran without its founder until 1912, but in 1913 it was absent from the Chicago city directory.

THE CHRISTENSEN SCHOOL OF POPULAR MUSIC

Although he was neither a major composer nor a major publisher of rags—and although he has been belittled by pop scholars as grim as the classicists he decried—Axel Christensen is one of the three or four most important figures in the ragtime story. His pop music schools supplied America with ragtime pianists for more than thirty years, and as a proselytizer for the music, his passion equaled John Stark's but his reach exceeded Stark's. He was not the first to start such a school (Edward R. Winn began his School of Popular Music in Newark, New Jersey, in 1901), but Christensen's syncopated pedagogy was the most successful, musically and commercially. One of the few ever to get rich from ragtime, Christensen shared the wealth with his teachers, and he showed his students how they might turn a dollar, too.

Axel Christensen was born in Chicago in 1881. Although he stuck with his piano lessons as a child, no one would have foreseen him as a music teacher or even as a very good player. He hacked out his exercises and daydreamed of baseball. When he was fifteen, an incident at a party changed his attitude about music. He had dutifully played a few parlor pieces, then he was displaced at the piano by a nerdy boy with a large repertoire of coon songs. He was shocked at the degree to which the girls preferred "Ma Coal Black Lady" to "Silvery Waves." Axel became

Axel Christensen

determined to learn syncopated playing, and he discovered that he had a natural gift for it. Within a year or so, he could play all the raggy "extra choruses" appended to coon songs, and he could even add elaborations of his own. Soon he was tossing off "Maple Leaf" and was beginning to write down his improvisations. In 1902 he published a sample of what he was doing, his "Ragtime Wedding March (Apologies to Mendelssohn)."

Christensen and his peers were in the first teenage generation to be swept away by syncopation, the first to be rabid about ragtime. Axel realized that, among all of his friends who loved it, none had been taught how to play it, and that they all played it somewhat differently. In 1903, because no one else in Chicago was doing it, Christensen decided that he might try giving instruction in ragtime. He took an ad in the Chicago *Daily News*, with a headline that read RAGTIME TAUGHT IN TEN LESSONS.

His first "school" was a grungy studio, rented by the hour, and the twenty-two-year-old, semi-professional Christensen comprised the faculty. His new bride was the registrar, scheduling appointments and collecting the fifty-cent fee for each lesson. Students poured in. After a few weeks, Axel moved to larger quarters in the Fine Arts Building on Michigan Boulevard. His presence horrified the other piano teachers in the building, and they asked the landlord to throw him out. Christensen had demeaned their profession by his advertising, they said, and he was committing the unpardonable sin of teaching ragtime. When the landlord refused to remove Christensen, the teachers tried harassment, standing in the hallway during his lessons, chanting the junk man's cry, "Any rags? Bones? Old iron?" Christensen moved for a second time in 1903, not because the soreheaded teachers had driven him out, but because he needed additional studios—and a reception area and a waiting room. He already had more than a hundred students.

In 1904 Christensen began to issue his tips and exercises in folio form. Headquartered at 526 South Western, he self-published *Christensen's Instruction Book No. 1 for Rag-Time Piano Playing*. The "No. 1" in the title implied more books to come, and from 1906 through 1915, they came. The original folio was revised and enlarged five times during those years, and in 1912 Christensen issued the first of his five folios of instruction for the vaudeville pianist.

Christensen began to clone himself as teacher in 1909. The first branch school opened in San Francisco that year, quickly followed by one in Cincinnati, then one in St. Louis. By 1913 Chicago had four branches, and there were one or more in New York, Philadelphia, Boston, Buffalo, Des Moines, and Oakland. By 1918 Christensen had schools in twenty-five cities, including Los Angeles, Seattle, Kansas City, and Honolulu. His teachers were generally first-rate players, and several of them were good composers of ragtime (including Robert Marine in New York, Bernard Brin in Seattle, and Marcella Henry in Chicago). His students were those—of either sex, of any age or race—who wanted to play the piano. Some came to Christensen without any musical training whatsoever, and many came after years of boredom at piano lessons.

Christensen's system of franchising his schools was much like the "profit pyramid" structure used today by the Mary Kay cosmetics company. A local piano teacher who agreed to use the Christensen method bought a franchise, recruited students (using ideas and materials from the parent organization), and sent Christensen a percentage of the fees he collected. As enrollment grew, the franchise owner hired more teachers, paid them by the student-hour, took a percentage of their earnings, and sent a percentage to Christensen. Teachers and "principals" (franchise owners) received commissions on the Christensen books and materials sold to students. Christensen helped his managers enlarge their faculties and start new branches by advertising for teachers and students in his magazine, *The Ragtime Review*. (The rural ragtimer did not have to move to a city to pursue his passion: Christensen started a correspondence course in ragtime in 1913.)

His press had been running for four years before Christensen issued his first rag, "Irmena," in 1908. "Irmena" has a whiff of the piano lesson about it, and it is typical of his musically competent, but not very exciting, compositions. The Christensen rags are of middling difficulty, easy enough not to discourage beginners and hard enough so that advanced students could not play them on the first try. Christensen never touted himself as a composer, though. He venerated the John Stark catalog, and he cited these rags, rather than his own, as the best examples of ragtime literature. Like Stark, he used the phrase "real ragtime" to distinguish piano rags from syncopated songs and dance music. The school would eventually publish eight of its founder's rags, but, oddly, the best of its instructor/composers published elsewhere.

The Christensen schools spent little time on philosophical discussion, but the philosophy behind them was sound: the founder and his teachers knew the difference between "ragging" pop songs and playing "real ragtime"; they could do both themselves; and they would help students do either, according to the students' interests and abilities. Christensen's technical exercises would have passed muster by most of the music teachers who scorned him. He prescribed rigorous study of harmony, rhythm, fingering technique, and sight-reading as his classical rivals did, but because the reward was ragtime, Christensen's medicine went down easier. Very sensibly, Christensen wrote:

> A good ragtime number when played by a pianist who has mastered his tone and touch is beautiful, grand, and melodious. In addition to beauty and grandeur it possesses another quality that is not always found in classical music and that is rhythm—sparkling, lilting pulsations that add zest and relish to a melody that is already beautiful.
>
> Therefore, brother piano player, if you want to play real ragtime and play it well, do the following:
>
> Train and develop your touch until you can produce a firm, full, rounded tone.
>
> Learn to shade your tones from loud to soft as the requirements of the piece and your interpretation of it may require.
>
> Be sure to acquire a precise, even tempo, because a fluctuating tempo will kill the snappy, pulsating rhythm which is so desirable and so delightful in real ragtime.

Christensen's star teacher was Edward Mellinger, who opened the first St. Louis school, at 3121 South Grand, in 1909. Mellinger was a professional ragtimer himself, and he knew whereof he spoke. (He spent his "sabbaticals" playing on riverboats in the summers, when school business was slow.) By February 1910 Mellinger had enrolled over 200 students, so he opened a second branch, in the Odeon Building. He soon needed additional space, so he rented the entire fifth floor of the Holland Building, at Seventh and Pine streets, and installed a dozen pianos there. Most of his students wanted classes after their school day or work was over, so, from 5:00 until 9:00 P.M., pianists trooped in, twelve at a time, for half-hour lessons.

On April 24, 1910, a St. Louis *Times* article reported that all was not harmonious in the Holland Building:

> The success of the ragtime school is wormwood and gall to the ortho-dox teachers. They look upon the young professor as a serious menace to art. Four regular practitioners of music have studios in the same building and are forced to sit helpless and gnash their teeth while scores of pupils pass by their finely appointed studios and go on upstairs to worship at the shrine of ragtime.

Mellinger drove the spike further into his competitors' hearts when he began his popular series of student recitals (which were the first rag-time concerts). It was not uncommon for 500 or more to attend one of these events and to cheer as the students played in various combinations and as teachers played solos and in duets with their pupils. Mellinger was obviously a go-getter, so Christensen sent him to start new schools in Kansas City, Boston, New York, and Denver.

Christensen worked up a vaudeville act in 1913, and he cannily booked himself in cities where he had schools (or in cities where he wanted schools). Billing himself as the "Czar of Ragtime," he con-structed an eighteen-minute act that was very enjoyable. He ragged a couple of classics, played a classic rag, did a barn-burner like "The Entertainer's Rag," he joked, he sang Bert Williams songs. Promotion photos from his vaudeville days show him in his tux, wearing pince-nez and celluloid collars, with slicked-back blond hair and a slightly maniacal smile. He looks like the dotty scion of a noble family, Lord Haw-Haw at the piano.

In December 1914 Christensen began issuing his monthly maga-zine, *The Ragtime Review* ("Edited and Published by Axel Christensen, the 'Czar of Ragtime'"). Unlike John Stark's sarcastic screeds, the *Review* keeps a cheerful tone as it delivers its hodgepodge of ragtime chatter. There are playing tips and exercises, a "Notes on New Popular Music" column by the editor, snippets of music for silent film pianists ("Quarrel or Struggle Scenes," "Mysterious-Burglar Scenes," etc.), jokes (including some on ragtimers as well as on classical players), and cartoons.

Christensen's record label

The "news" mostly concerns the roaring successes of Christensen teachers: Miss Ruth Leonard (one of Mellinger's teachers in St. Louis) has just purchased a new Overland car and is "driving it herself"; Marcella Henry has recently enrolled "four new scholars"; students in Buffalo are getting jobs in silent movie houses; Edward Mellinger has a new Hudson, his fourth car since he opened his school. There are ads for Christensen's vaudeville dates, from music publishers, and from his competition. (Edward Winn's May 1915 ad for his ragtime method carried an endorsement from Scott Joplin, vouching that Winn's system was "wonderfully simple, easy and comprehensive.") Christensen's idea of a human interest story was typified by a January 1917 item about E. L. Leach of Knoxville, Tennessee. Leach had recently broken the world's record for continuous piano playing by staying at it for sixty-three hours in a contest held in San Antonio.

Best of all, each issue of the *Review* included music: Christensen's own rags (which he also issued as single sheets), waltzes, tangos, or pop songs. John Stark was a frequent advertiser and an occasional columnist

The Ragtime Review

for the *Review*, and he gave Christensen permission to reprint several Stark rags in the magazine. The *Review*'s reprints of these rags, especially the ones by Scott and Lamb, reached many more pianists than Stark's original editions did. The *Review* ceased publication in January 1918, but Christensen continued to share his commonsense views on ragtime through Walter Jacobs's *Melody* magazine well into the 1920s. He found other publishers willing to issue his rags, too: Forster brought out two in 1923, and Jack Mills issued two in 1924.

As new musical styles arose, Christensen kept up with them and devised methods to teach them. His "Jazz and Novelty" folio appeared in 1927, and his ideas on "Modern Swing Music," including a folio devoted to "Swing Breaks and Bass Figures," were codified in 1936. If changing musical tastes had been the only variables for Christensen to contend with, there would be Christensen schools today, teaching the fingering of Billy Joel and making medleys of Elton John songs.

The Christensen schools were big business, and, as was the case with other big businesses, the Depression hit them hard. Christensen's empire eroded at its base when those who wanted piano lessons could no longer afford them. As family incomes shrank, the fifty-cent lesson fee was hard to scrape up, and a dollar for an instruction book was out of the question. Throughout the 1930s the schools closed one by one, and by the early forties they had almost all gone. Christensen continued to run a handful of schools and to reprint his folios and sell them into the early 1950s.

There were a half million Christensen "graduates" by 1935, and they had got their money's worth. If the purpose of music is to lift the spirit, Christensen's alumni were well equipped to face the dark days of the Great Depression: most of them could play "Maple Leaf Rag."

MCKINLEY MUSIC COMPANY/FRANK K. ROOT & COMPANY

The McKinley and Root firms were the Siamese twins of Chicago publishing. Their sharing of officers, arranging staff, and production facilities have forever blurred their separate identities. They shared addresses, too, first at 158 Harrison Street and, after 1911, at 1507 East Fifty-fifth Street. The McKinley name is on almost all of the Root music, and vice versa. Root is often named as the copyright holder of McKinley songs, and McKinley's credit (as distributor) is often larger than Root's on Root publications. However little is known about McKinley and Root as individuals, the quantity and quality of their output show the two in perfect commercial sync: their aim was to publish tons of mediocre music and sell it cheaper than anyone else was selling music that was better. They specialized in clutter for the piano bench, and among the clutter they ground out were sixteen rags.

The McKinley company came first, entering the business primarily as a jobbing firm in 1897. William McKinley was the company's president, and Frank K. Root (the son of Root & Cady's co-founder, Ebenezer Towner Root) was, if not a founding partner, at least an early staffer. (Root was listed on the McKinley letterhead as that company's secretary/treasurer for years after he began publishing under his own imprint around 1900. To complicate Root's alliances even further, he was until 1928 also a partner in E. T. Root & Sons, a nonpublishing branch of the John Church Company of Cincinnati.)

Having built a distribution system that worked well for other publishers' music, the McKinley company began to issue its own songs and instrumental pieces. McKinley's first rag was Fred L. Ryder's "Jagtime Johnson's Ragtime March," published in 1901. The company's indifference to ragtime is shown by the seven-year interval before the appearance of its second rag in 1908.

The music publishing field was crowded by the time McKinley entered the game, and a new pop publisher needed a gimmick.

F. Henri Klickmann

McKinley's gimmick was to underprice everybody else, and he flooded the market with cheap songs. While other publishers' products cost from twenty-five to fifty cents apiece, music dealers were assured in ads that "McKinley 10c Music Is a Trade Bringer." The company's bargains were made possible by the low cost of producing them. Most of McKinley's music came either from first-time writers or from the company's staff, neither group in a position to haggle over purchase prices. Leo Friedman and Percy Wenrich were among the most published unknowns, and F. Henri Klickmann, McKinley's band and orchestra arranger, contributed many pieces to the catalog. Another cost-saver was low-quality paper. The McKinley/Root publications crumble at the touch today, while music sheets fifty years older do not.

If such a hotbed of mediocrity could be said to have a star composer, McKinley's was Percy Wenrich, who had come to Chicago in 1901 from Joplin, Missouri. He studied briefly at Chicago Musical

College, and he was working as a wine room pianist when he heard that McKinley was in the market for teaching pieces. (Although Wenrich said that he got nothing of value from his time at CMC, his training there probably gave him the facility to write on demand in various genres and to write quickly. The CMC piano teachers—Louis Falk, Jesse Dunn, and Frank Denhart—also provided a classical foundation for several other ragtimers, including Zez Confrey, Egbert Van Alstyne, and Charles L. Cooke.)

Wenrich started cranking out piano numbers for McKinley—at $5 each—and they were published by the dozens. Frank Root's first ragtime publication was a 1904 reprint of Wenrich's "Ashy Africa," which was published a year earlier, and the first original rag issued by Root was Wenrich's "Made in Germany" (written under the pseudonym "Karl Schmidt") in 1906. Four of the five rags issued by McKinley in 1908 were composed by Wenrich. His instrumentals were reprinted so often that Wenrich was finally given his own "imprint," a standard cover with his photo on it.

When Root began publishing black writers in the mid-teens, his catalog could, for the first time, claim some work of musical importance. Chicago, like the rest of America, was smitten with blues, and it was this vogue that opened Root's door to blacks. Root began his renaissance in 1915 with two "blue rags" by James (Slap) White, "Original Chicago Blues" and "Hot Off the Griddle." In 1916 the company had its first mainstream hit, Spencer Williams's "I Ain't Got Nobody," and this led to more Root songs by black writers, including James White, Spencer Williams, Maceo Pinkard, and Clarence Williams. In 1918 Root bought and reissued Hart Wand's 1912 classic, "Dallas Blues." The company's last rag was "Smiles and Chuckles," by its stalwart arranger, Henri Klickmann.

McKinley and Root, still joined at the hip, endured through the twenties and thirties by publishing easy and mid-level teaching pieces (selling for fifteen cents each) and by reverting to their original role as jobber and mail-order supplier of other publishers' music. In 1945 McKinley Music became a subsidiary of Targ and Dinner, of Chicago. Larry Spier, Inc., of New York, acquired many of the McKinley and Root copyrights during the 1950s.

MELROSE BROTHERS MUSIC COMPANY

Although Melrose Brothers of Chicago published only six rags, the company has a place in ragtime history because all six were written by Jelly Roll Morton. The company called itself "The House That Blues Built," but Melrose dealt little in blues. It dipped most of its wares from the seething cauldron of Chicago jazz. Under the Melrose aegis, improvisers like King Oliver and Louis Armstrong became published composers, jazz arrangers like Elmer Schoebel became songwriters, and matches were made between Melrose writers and record companies.

Walter and Lester Melrose had not the slightest interest in ragtime. They published the Morton rags because it was Morton who wrote them. He was the smartest and most exciting of the early Chicago jazzmen, and, whatever he wrote, they wanted. None of his six rags have the word *rag* in their titles, and it must have been hoped that the public wouldn't think of them as such. Coming late in the ragtime era, Morton's masterpieces, like Northrup's nonesuch of 1897, show a musical style evolving into another style. Because they were taken up by leaders and pianists, the Morton rags became staples of the hot band repertoire. Musicians who would have sneered at old-hat ragtime played them and recorded them, confident that they were something entirely new—and they were.

Walter Melrose was born in Sumner, Illinois, in 1889, and it was there that he opened his first music shop, in 1912. In 1915 he left Sumner to take a job with the Cable Piano Company in Chicago. The desire to have his own store never left him, and by 1918 he had saved enough money to do so. With his younger brother Lester and a silent partner, M. L. Blumenthal (who used the professional name Marty Bloom), he opened Melrose Brothers Music Company at Sixty-third Street and Cottage Grove Avenue. The store sprouted a second branch, then a third, and, in 1920, Walter Melrose decided to become a publisher.

Melrose Brothers began its publishing in a small way. Three pop songs comprised its entire output of 1920—and all three had words and music by Walter Melrose. Because there were no in-house composers and no out-of-house acquisitions, there was no need for a company arranger. Melrose farmed out its arranging chores to Harry L. Alford, a freelance arranger who had created his own firm in 1903. Alford had cornered the arranging market in Chicago, with a staff of thirty or so specialists who could write for any combination of instruments in any style. Despite their assembly line creation, the Alford company's arrangements were not hack work. The staff formed itself into various band and orchestral groups to play—and to correct—each of its products before sending it out. An Alford arrangement could make even an amateur composer like Walter Melrose sound as though he knew what he was doing. But even Alford's expertise could not put over the 1920 Melrose songs with the public. They lay on the shelves of the composer's stores, and for a year the company published nothing.

Then, someone (probably Marty Bloom) found the publishing niche that Melrose Brothers could fill. The country's newest musical passion was jazz, and Chicago's South Side was its epicenter. The cafes, clubs, and theatres of black Chicago were teeming with musicians who seemed to own jazz by divine right. Many of them were from New Orleans, but playing for Chicago dancers had put an urgency and a hotness into their music that was unknown in their native city. White listeners and dancers had taken notice of these players, and in clubs where integration would have been unthinkable even a year earlier, integration occurred every night because jazz-mad whites wanted to hear this music. Many of the black bands bypassed the pop repertoire and featured tunes of their own making, most of them unpublished. It was a source waiting to be tapped, and Melrose Brothers decided to tap it. In 1922 the company bought the copyrights to Clarence Johnson's "Sweetest Gal" and to Lil Hardin's "My Sweet Smellin' Man." (Walter Melrose rewrote the lyric to Hardin's song in 1923 and published it as "My Sweet Lovin' Man.")

Late in 1922 someone at Melrose heard a Jelly Roll Morton number called "The Wolverines" that was popular on the South Side and wondered about its copyright status. Melrose was told to send an inquiry to Spikes Brothers Music, a small Los Angeles firm at which Morton could be reached. Morton said later that the Spikes brothers intercepted the Melrose letter, wrote some lyrics on the lead sheet, renamed it "Wolverine Blues," and sent it to Melrose for publication. In May 1923 Melrose issued Harry Alford's arrangement of "Wolverine Blues," which would be the firm's first hit.

Morton was furious when he learned that Melrose had his tune, and he left Los Angeles for a showdown with the publisher. When he arrived in Chicago and heard "Wolverine" being played everywhere, his anger cooled. However Melrose had got his number, the company was at least promoting it, something no other publisher had done for Morton's work before. With the popularity of "Wolverine," Morton knew he held a trump, so he dropped in at the Melrose store and introduced himself to Lester. He commandeered a piano and played "Wolverine" for the startled customers, and he let it be known that he had dozens of other numbers that would be even bigger hits. If Melrose played its cards right, he said, the company could publish them.

Morton would never have a contractual agreement with Melrose as either composer or arranger, but his store performance on that spring day in 1923 bound him to the firm over six years. Melrose expressed interest in anything he had to sell, and the firm began paving the way for the Morton hits it was sure to have. Morton had earned some Chicago fame as a pianist and bandleader in the mid-teens, but he had spent the last five years in the West, so Melrose thought it best to revive his reputation as a performer before issuing any of his music.

Morton had no band (and no club connections any more), so Melrose made him a temporary member of the New Orleans Rhythm Kings, a popular white group with ties to the firm, and sent them all to the Gennett studios in Richmond, Indiana, to make some recordings. The NORK had made two sessions at Gennett in March, and these had produced hit records of "Wolverine Blues" and "Tin Roof Blues." The July 17–18 sessions with Jelly and the NORK would not make hits, but they would make social, as well as musical, history. They were the first interracial band recordings.

Morton played on five numbers with the Rhythm Kings, and his pianism sparked them to dizzy heights of improvisation. The band records are milestones, but the six piano solos that Morton made during the two days in Richmond are even more important. They are the first jazz piano records, and they offered listeners a first excursion into the mind of Jelly Roll Morton. Four of the six sides ("Kansas City Stomp," "The Pearls," "Grandpa's Spells," and "King Porter Stomp") are rags, but they don't sound like any ragtime that had come before them. They are not stately classics, showoff pop rags, or tricky novelties. They are in medium 4/4 time, always moving but never rushed. The variations on their themes are so intricately plotted that they must have been conceived beforehand. (If the variations were actually improvised at the piano, they are even more impressive.) Breaks, riffs, tangos, and walking bass lines blend in a kind of rhythmic gumbo. There is an undergrowth of dark harmonies, some of them as dense and eerie as a Plaquemines Parish swamp. Although they are fully syncopated, they only *feel* like ragtime rather than sound like it. This was ragtime on its way to somewhere else.

Jelly Roll Morton was not the hit-producing machine that Melrose hoped he would be. Walter Melrose, like many another publisher who had accidentally acquired works of genius, didn't know what to do with the Morton rags, so he did hardly anything. Three of them ("Kansas City Stomp," "Grandpa's Spells," and "The Pearls") were copyrighted—but not published—on August 20, 1923. "King Porter Stomp" was finally copyrighted in December 1924; "Shreveport Stomp" came in

Jelly Roll Morton folio

1925; and "Chicago Breakdown," in 1926. Two of Morton's songs ("Wolverine Blues" and "Milenberg Joys") sold well for the company, but his instrumentals, issued in such small numbers as to ensure failure, did not. (Elmer Schoebel, who had begun his career as pianist for the Friars Society Orchestra, became Melrose's staff arranger in 1924, and it was he who made the orchestrations of the Morton numbers of 1924–1925.) Finally, in 1927, more in the spirit of housecleaning than of a publishing event, Melrose collected twelve of Morton's pieces, including the six rags, and issued them in a folio. The collection got so little distribution that practically no one noticed it.

Morton made more effort for his Melrose numbers than Melrose did. In September 1926 he created a studio band called the Red Hot Peppers to fulfill a contract that Melrose had got him with Victor Records. In their five years with Victor, Jelly and the Peppers recorded many Melrose tunes (not all of them his own). There were a handful of hit records by the group ("Black Bottom Stomp," "Original Jelly Roll Blues," and "Grandpa's Spells"), but there was no sheet music in the stores with which to capitalize on them. The dozen or so jazz standards that Morton wrote achieved their status through the Red Hot Peppers recordings, not from Melrose's promotion of them.

Melrose's investment in jazz composers was only moderately successful. They provided their publisher with the occasional hit song (such as King Oliver's "Doctor Jazz" and Charlie Davis's "Copenhagen"), but Melrose, like Leo Feist before him with the Original Dixieland Jazz Band's tunes, found that published jazz had a built-in marketing problem. The interaction between instruments that made jazz so exciting could not be approximated on the piano. If a star soloist's breaks and licks were transcribed, as in Melrose's 1927 Louis Armstrong and Benny Goodman folios, the player of them was still a lone instrumentalist wishing he had a band around him. By 1926 Melrose Brothers was rethinking its commitment to jazz publishing.

The company set its sights on another seemingly lucrative but unexploited genre: college songs. Melrose began by issuing a few marches and fight songs associated with Midwestern schools, and, thanks to a recording by Fred Waring's Pennsylvanians, it found a hit in 1927 with a 1912 fraternity song, "The Sweetheart of Sigma Chi." "Notre Dame Victory March" and "On Wisconsin" were added to the catalog, and collegiate music began to supersede Melrose's jazz and blues. There were a few more nods at hot product in the 1930s. Melrose bought the copyrights to several Stark rags in 1935, and in 1936 issued "Pine Top's Boogie Woogie," the first of its genre in print. In 1940 the Melrose Brothers copyrights were sold to the Edwin H. Morris Company of New York.

CINCINNATI

From Losantiville to Bucktown

In December 1788 a trio of white land speculators moved into Miami Indian country to mark out four-acre lots for sale around Mill Creek in the Ohio River Valley. They had big plans for the town that would arise there, and they gave it a grand name, Losantiville (from the Latin *os* [mouth], the Greek *anti* [opposite], and the French *ville* [city]). It would not be a city for thirty years, but it was opposite the mouth of Kentucky's Licking River. In 1790 Arthur St. Clair, governor of the Northwest Territory, renamed the place Cincinnati, in honor of the Society of Cincinnatus, a fraternal organization of Revolutionary War officers to which he belonged. Cincinnati was incorporated as a town in 1801. Steamboat navigation began on the Ohio River in 1811, and the town grew toward its eventual incorporation as a city in 1819.

Waves of German and Irish immigrants poured into Cincinnati throughout the 1840s and 1850s. They came to build the docks, railroads, and factories of the booming port city, and many of them stayed to work at the places they had built. After the Civil War, thousands of ex-slaves, immigrants in their own land, made the symbolic crossing of the Ohio to work as laborers and stevedores in Cincinnati. The city's thriving commerce—in shipping, meatpacking, and wine making—needed all the labor it could get.

As Cincinnati prospered, a Louisville publisher, William Cumming Peters (1805–1866), looked up the river and saw a market for music there. W. C. Peters & Company opened its Cincinnati branch in 1846 on Fourth Street, between Main and Sycamore, and became the city's first music store to take publishing seriously. Peters issued Nelson Kneass's "Ben Bolt" in 1848, and had even greater success that year with a song that was currently winning acclaim in the Christy Minstrels show. Peters knew its composer, Stephen Foster, who was clerking in a Cincinnati office. He had previously published two of Foster's songs (and paid him in free copies), and now he wrote to Foster and asked for the manuscript of "Oh! Susanna." Foster was flattered by the request and complied. Peters sent Foster a "fee" of $100 and began turning out copies of the song that would eventually earn him $10,000. It was the first of many raw deals that Stephen Foster got from publishers.

Cincinnati's biggest and longest lived music publishing company was that of John Church, Jr. (1834–1890). In 1860 Church opened for business at 66 West Fourth Street, and in 1861 the company issued its first big song, "Aura Lea." (This beautiful melody was popular throughout the Civil War, and it was reincarnated in 1956 as Elvis Presley's first film hit, "Love Me Tender.") In 1876 the company had Thomas P. Westendorf's "I'll Take You Home Again, Kathleen," as well as "Punch! In the Presence of the Passenjare," a comic song about streetcar conductors with "Text by Mark Twain." Church issued several important Sousa marches of the 1890s, including "Stars and Stripes Forever," "El Capitan," and "King Cotton." "Mighty Lak a Rose," a refined coon song of 1901, was the last nationally known song to come from Cincinnati, and it made money for John Church & Company for years. In 1930 the large and valuable Church catalog was taken over by Theodore Presser Company of Philadelphia.

As John Church was printing his parlor songs, another kind of music was being heard in the less genteel parlors of Cincinnati. It was the countrified syncopation that accompanied the carousing of roustabouts, white and black, in the rough dens of the pleasure district. Cincinnati's "Levee" was a strip of riverfront between Broadway and Sycamore, which was sometimes called "Rat Row." Pickett's Saloon, at 91 Front Street, was the largest and wildest of the Levee's drinking establishments. The red-light district was a three-block stretch of George Street, between Central Avenue and Mound. The madams of George Street were mostly white (and all the houses catered to whites-only trade), but most of their cooks, cleaners, and musicians were black.

The black pleasure district was called "Bucktown," lying east of Broadway between Sixth and Seventh streets, ranging to Culvert Street. Cincinnati's two poorest ethnic groups, its blacks and its Irish, were uneasy neighbors there, and violent interracial brawls were a constant of Bucktown life. Because of the many murders that occurred there, the junction of Sixth and Broadway was accurately called "Deadman's Corner."

In a newspaper article written by Lafcadio Hearn, printed in the March 16, 1876, edition of the Cincinnati *Commercial*, there is a description of the music of underground Cincinnati. (Because Hearn openly carried on a liaison with a mulatto woman, Althea Foley, he was more welcome in Bucktown than other white reporters.) Hearn went to a dance in a basement room on the corner of Culvert and Sixth, paid his ten cents admission, and saw things that Cincinnati's more famous writer on black life, Harriet Beecher Stowe, had never seen.

Hearn wrote:

> With its unplastered and windowless limestone walls; sanded floor; ruined ceiling, half plank, half cracked plaster; a dingy black counter in one corner, and rude benches ranged along the walls, this dancing-room presented rather an outlandish aspect when we visited it. . . . A well-dressed, neatly-built mulatto picked the banjo, and a somewhat lighter colored musician led the music with a fiddle, which he played remarkably well and with great spirit. A short, stout negress, illy dressed . . . played the bass viol, and that with no inexperienced hand. This woman is known to the police as Anna Nun. . . . The musicians struck up that weird, wild, lively air, known perhaps to many of our readers as the "Devil's Dream." . . . The dancers danced a double quadrille, at first silently and rapidly, but warming with the wild spirit of the music, leaped and shouted, swinging each other off the floor, and keeping time with a precision which shook the building in time to the music. . . . Then the music changed to an old Virginia reel, and the dancing changed likewise, presenting the most grotesque spectacle imaginable. The dancing became wild; men patted juba and shouted; the negro women danced with the most fantastic grace, their

bodies describing almost incredible curves forward and backward; limbs intertwined rapidly in a wrestle with swaying bodies and tossing arms, and flying hair.

Old forms of music and movement fell away in this Bucktown basement as players and dancers inspired each other to leave traditional patterns of notes and steps. The "Devil's Dream" was a good choice to accompany their departure: its tune supplied endless possibilities for variation, and it could be made as hot as dancers wanted it. The rustic trio was not playing ragtime, but it had the mindset in which ragtime began. It was willing to break the rules to create something joyful. The first Cincinnati composer to publish a rag knew where this liberal musical impulse came from. Robert S. Roberts titled his rag "The Pride of Bucktown."

From "The Pride of Bucktown" (1897) to "Virginia Rag" (1916), piano rags were issued in Cincinnati. There were neither hits nor stylistic landmarks among the city's eighty-three published rags, but there was much solid work. The Cincinnati publisher with the widest distribution, John Church & Company, issued a handful of cakewalks in 1899 but no rags at all. A dozen or so rags have local references in their titles, and the city's ragtime seems typically aimed at a local market. Two major composers, Joe Jordan and Abe Olman, were born in Cincinnati, but neither published a rag there. (Clarence M. Jones published four rags in Cincinnati before he moved to Chicago at age twenty-two.) The Baldwin and Wurlitzer companies manufactured pianos and players, and Vocalstyle made piano rolls, but after 1916 there were no local piano rags to play on the locally made machines. (The trombone rags of Henry Fillmore, which were issued into the 1920s, were the best known pieces of Cincinnati syncopation.)

Cincinnati publishers' interest in ragtime precisely spanned the classic rag era. By the time ragtime pianist Artie Matthews arrived in town in 1918, ragtime had waned considerably. Matthews abdicated his role as St. Louis's preeminent composer and arranger of rags in 1915 and moved to Chicago to become music director for a Presbyterian church. Three years later, he took a church job in Cincinnati. When he opened his Cosmopolitan School of Music, a classical conservatory for black musicians, on West Ninth Street, in 1921, he was in the right place. Cincinnati's ragtime fever had cooled; it would not impede his work nor tempt his pupils.

JOSEPH KROLAGE MUSIC PUBLISHING COMPANY

The Joseph Krolage company, located on the southeast corner of Race and Arcade streets, was the first publisher in Cincinnati to pay even slight attention to the city's foremost ragtime composer, Homer Denney. Denney was the best known musician in town because he held the most visible—and loudest—job, as master of the calliope since 1901 on an Ohio River excursion steamer, *The Island Queen*. He self-published seven rags between 1905 and 1910, and he played them for the *Queen*'s passengers—and everyone walking along the riverfront—on endless trips back and forth to a riverside amusement park called Coney Island. (The boat, its setting, and its destination provided the titles for seven Cincinnati rags, including "Coney Island Dip," "Queen of Coney Island," "The River," "Water Queen," and Denney's own "Coney Island Girl.") Denney's music rang in the ears of Cincinnati publishers for years before the obvious struck Joseph Krolage. Here was a popular local musician with rags already in print: why not buy the copyrights and the plates and try selling them? In 1910 Krolage bought and reissued Denney's "Chimes" and "Cheese and Crackers," and thus entered the ragtime business.

Two new local-angle rags appeared under the Krolage imprint in 1911: Floyd Willis's "Queen Rag" (another reference to the pleasure boat) and Charles and Sylvester Hartlaub's "Caliope Rag," which was harmonized to imitate its namesake. A large photo of Homer Denney, in a yachting cap, standing at his keyboard on the *Queen*'s deck, is on the cover of the Hartlaub brothers' rag. Krolage issued another Denney rag ("Ham Bones," in 1912), bought a Harry Tierney rag by mail ("Louisiana Rag," in 1913), and ended his ragtime publishing with Clarence C. Jones's "Toodles Rag" in 1916.

After his publisher left ragtime, Homer Denney kept on playing his rags on *The Island Queen*. He also took another job, rebuilding and repairing instruments for the T. J. Nickols Company, a local manufacturer of calliopes. He often made out-of-town "house calls" to put a calliope-dependent circus or pleasure craft back in business. The *Queen*

"Caliope Rag"

sank in 1922, and it was Denney who hauled the calliope out of the Ohio River and refurbished it. When the boat was reconditioned and sent back into service, Denney resumed his noisy post. Fire destroyed *The Island Queen* while it was moored at Pittsburgh in 1947, and this time Denney could save nothing, not even his clothing. He returned to Cincinnati in a pair of borrowed overalls.

In 1952 Homer Denney began playing the organ at Cincinnati Reds games at Crosley Field, and when the Nickols calliope company shut its doors, the middle-aged Denney began a career in the city water depart-ment, which lasted twenty-five years. Although his decades at the instrument had left him nearly deaf, he continued to play the calliope in Shrine Circus parades, and at the closing of Coney Island in 1970, Denney's music was the last heard there. He died in 1975, at age ninety, in the Masonic Home in Springfield, Ohio.

MENTEL BROTHERS PUBLISHING COMPANY

Louis Mentel was born in Covington, Kentucky, across the river from Cincinnati, in 1880. Around the turn of the century, he opened a music store in Cincinnati and began to publish there. In 1903 Mentel Brothers issued its first rag, Louis Mentel's "Lagoon Breeze." With one exception ("Lagoon Rag," issued in Covington in 1907), all of Mentel Brothers' rags would come from Cincinnati. And from 1903 through 1912, all Mentel rags were written by Louis Mentel, with his 1906 "Gasoline Rag" a standout among them.

Louis Mentel wrote no more after 1912, but in that year his com-pany acquired the rag-heavy catalog of J. H. Aufderheide of

"Gasoline Rag"

Indianapolis. Several Aufderheide rags were reissued by Mentel Brothers during the teens, including Will Morrison and Cecil Duane Crabbe's "Trouble" and Paul Pratt's "Colonial Glide." The last Mentel Brothers rag was Bryant Gallagher's "Virginia Rag," issued late in 1916. The Cincinnati store, at 137 Fourth Avenue, remained open until Louis Mentel's death in 1955.

W. H. WILLIS COMPANY

The W. H. Willis Company, at the corner of Fourth and Elm streets, published piano rags for ten years. The firm was the first commercial publisher to issue the rags of Floyd Willis, a popular accompanist for silent films in Cincinnati. (Floyd Willis previously self-published two of his rags in Covington, Kentucky.) Willis also reissued two self-published folk rags, F. A. Walker's "Hot Air Rag" (originally published in

Mt. Healthy, Ohio) and Edward A. Blake's "Spots" (originally published by Blake and Kuhlman in Cincinnati).

In the summer of 1919 the W. H. Willis catalog was taken over by
G. Schirmer of New York.

CLEVELAND

Taking Care of Business

In 1796 the Connecticut Land Company, a private firm, undertook the
settlement of a town on the shores of Lake Erie, at the mouth of the
Cuyahoga River. It was named for Moses Cleaveland, the head of the
surveying team that laid it out. The place was incorporated as a village
in 1814, and in a rare instance of a town preceding its first drinking
establishment, the historic Dunham Tavern was built ten years later.

After the opening of the Erie Canal in 1832, the village began to
grow as a business and manufacturing center. Much of the armament
and equipment used by both sides in the Civil War was made in
Cleveland, and the city's prosperity after the war was assured when, in
1870, John D. Rockefeller established Standard Oil Company there.
For decades most of Pennsylvania's oil was refined in Cleveland. Steel
manufacturing came in the late nineteenth century, and this major
industry was precursor to another, the production of automobiles, in the
early twentieth century.

There are no colorful saloon-whorehouse stories of Old Cleveland;
aboriginal ragtimers who lived to tell their tales never mentioned playing there. If ragtime was played in Cleveland in the late 1890s, it was at
homes, on the pianos in the parlors.

The man who would be the city's most important publisher of
music in the nineteenth century moved to Cleveland in the year it was
granted a city charter. In 1836 a New Hampshire native named Silas
Brainard (1814–1871) opened the new city's first music store, at 38
Superior Street. S. Brainard & Company began to publish music in

1845 but did not have nationally known songs until 1862, when it issued Bernard Covert's Civil War ballad, "Can I Go, Dearest Mother?" and William Shakespeare Hays's "Evangeline."

Brainard's sons Charles and Henry entered the business a few years before the founder died, and, operating as S. Brainard's Sons, the firm took over most of the Root & Cady catalog in 1873. In 1879 Brainard moved its headquarters to Chicago, and in 1902, to New York City, where it remained in business until 1931. There was nothing remarkable about the Brainard product—no specialties, no obvious passions of its owners, no big hits—but there was enough know-how in the family to keep it coming for ninety-five years.

SAM FOX PUBLISHING COMPANY

The Cleveland publisher who got to ragtime first, and stayed with it ten years longer than anyone else, was Sam Fox (1882–1971). Fox, an amateur violinist, was clearheaded about his purpose. He entered the business as a publisher, not as a music store owner who intended to sell locally published pieces over the counter. And he staked out a publishing specialty: popular instrumental music. (Songs were added to the Fox catalog in the late teens, but there would be no hit songs until the 1930s.)

Sam Fox

It was an ambitious undertaking. To succeed, Fox would have to reach far beyond Cleveland, into the professional music world that didn't like outsiders. He would have to compete against the big boys without living in the big boys' neighborhood in New York. With Sam as president and his younger brother Harry as vice-president, the Sam Fox Publishing Company opened offices in the Arcade in April 1906. In

October Fox issued Charles Cohen's "Tatters," the first rag published in Cleveland.

Fox found local composers—and out-of-town composers found Fox. The company soon had a sizable catalog of waltzes, marches, and two-steps. Abe Olman, who was working as a music demonstrator at Cleveland's branch of the May Company, sold two piano intermezzos to Fox in 1907. The company had a success in 1908 with "Daisy Rag," the first published rag by Fred Heltman, Cleveland's foremost ragtime composer. (Heltman would become a publisher himself in 1909, and after 1913, there were no rags issued in Cleveland except those published by Fox or Heltman.)

"Harmony Rag" (1911) was sent by a Denver writer, Hal G. Nichols, and it was also a big seller. Fox was becoming a force in popular instrumental music, and the company's visibility attracted more submissions by out-of-towners, including Irene Giblin, Charles L. Johnson, and Theron C. Bennett. In 1911 Fox added a line to his logo stating that he now had European distribution, in London, Leipzig, Vienna, Zurich, and Paris. Fox's commitment to popular piano music brought him the honor of being the only publisher to have a rag named for him, George Howard's "Sam Fox Trot," in 1916.

John S. Zamecnik

In 1913 Fox issued J. S. Zamecnik's "Movie Rag," a composer-subject match that led to another Fox publishing specialty. Zamecnik was a Cleveland-born musician who had spent several years as first violinist with the Pittsburgh Orchestra. When he returned to Cleveland as music director of the Hippodrome Theatre, he began submitting compositions to Fox. Fox realized that he had something unique on his doorstep: a classically trained musician who was not a snob about ragtime and popular music. He decided to take advantage of Zamecnik's ability and attitude by commissioning him to create a series of piano folios for the silent film accompanist.

The Fox film series lasted from 1913 into the mid-twenties (and continued to be priced at fifty cents per folio). Zamecnik supplied compositions for any mood ("Love Scene," "Plaintive Music"), locale ("Oriental Dance," "Spanish or Mexican Scene"), or subject ("Horse or Automobile Races," "Indian's Grief," "Hurry Music for Combats, Struggles, etc.") that might appear on the screen over the head of an unsuspecting accompanist. It was audacious for a regional publisher to associate himself with film music, but Fox established his beachhead early and held it for three decades. He was one of the very few regional publishers to issue scores and songs from silent films and to have hit songs from sound films. When newsreels were added to the bill at movie emporia, Fox and Zamecnik were ready with pieces that evoked "European Army Maneuvers," "Paris Fashions," and "Aeroplane or Regatta Races."

For ten years, Fox had managed to make a prosperous music company without having a hit, but finally, in 1916, he had a big one. He bought a fox trot that had been published by its composer, Felix Arndt, in 1915. It was named for Arndt's wife, Nola. "Nola"'s melody is a flirtation between triplets and dotted eighth notes, and it is irresistibly catchy. It received dozens of recordings and piano rolls in the late teens and early twenties, and it had another round of popularity in a 1924 song version, with lyrics by James F. Burns. It was probably the success of "Nola" that prompted (and paid for) the opening of a Sam Fox office in New York in the summer of 1920.

Ragtime was at a crossroads between 1918 and 1921, and during that time Sam Fox published no rags at all. The music's popularity had taken a serious hit from the 1917 recordings by the Original Dixieland Jazz Band. The ODJB piled layer upon layer of syncopated lines, and, for the first time ever, ragtime seemed tame, compared to this onslaught from New Orleans. Three Chicago pianists, Charley Straight, Zez Confrey, and Roy Bargy, knew that ragtime had to get hotter and more complex or die, and they became the EMT that saved it. Their two-fisted novelties put the punch back into piano playing, and their roll-making showed how to get a combo's-worth of music from a single piano. Novelty rags daunted most amateur players, so their market would necessarily be limited, but when Roy Bargy approached Fox with a sheaf of them in 1921, Fox took up the challenge on ragtime's behalf. The publisher committed to novelties as he had committed to mainstream ragtime in 1906. Although they did not sell well, the only rags issued by Fox in the years 1921–1922 were those by Roy Bargy.

Zez Confrey was the preeminent novelty composer, and he was tied to Jack Mills of New York. If Fox could not have Confrey's work, he would have the next best thing. In 1925 Fox contracted to be the sole American publisher of the rags of Confrey's English counterpart, Billy Mayerl. Mayerl was then on the crest of his fame, a London star with Bert Ralton's hotel orchestra, the Savoy Havana Band. His flowery syncopations were a weekly feature on the band's BBC radio show, and a London publisher, Keith Prowse & Company, was issuing the Mayerl compositions. If no other American publisher wanted the Continent's most popular pianist, Sam Fox would be glad to have him. Fox began by issuing one of Mayerl's finest works, "Jazz Master," in August 1925, followed by another of his best, "Virginia Creeper," two months later. These rags didn't have the rhythmic kick of Confrey's (and they were even harder to play), but the twelve Mayerl rags issued by Fox gave American pianists something to chew on through 1928.

In 1929 a homegrown rag written by the reliable J. S. Zamecnik outsold everything that Fox had published by Bargy and Mayerl. "Polly" had been around since 1926, and had received recordings by Zez Confrey and the twin-piano team of Ohman and Arden, but for some reason it had never been issued in sheet music form. Pianists knew of "Polly" before it saw print, were waiting for it, in fact, and it quickly became one of the best-selling novelty rags of the decade.

Sam Fox continued to publish silent film themes and songs, and in 1925 he began his long association with William Fox, the nickelodeon entrepreneur turned film producer. (The producer, born Wilhelm Fried in Hungary, was no relation to the publisher.) After Fox films began to speak and sing in 1928, the publication rights to their songs became even more valuable. In the mid-thirties Sam Fox had his biggest hits, with songs from Fox movies starring Shirley Temple: "On the Good Ship Lollipop" (*Bright Eyes*, 1934), "Animal Crackers in My Soup"

(*Curly Top*, 1935), and "At the Codfish Ball" (*Captain January*, 1936). Another 1936 success was "You Turned the Tables on Me," from an Alice Faye film, *Sing, Baby, Sing*.

In 1942 Sam Fox moved to New York to establish his company's headquarters there, while Harry Fox stayed to oversee the Cleveland operation. The firm's New York coups included winning the publication rights to music from two Broadway landmarks, *Brigadoon* and *Man of La Mancha*.

INDIANAPOLIS

Hoosier Capital

There were plans for the city of Indianapolis even before there was a town called Indianapolis. In the spring of 1820, the Delaware tribe living in central Indiana was joined by George Pogue and his family, the first white settlers in the area. In the summer of that year, a state commission decided that the Pogues' homestead, at the junction of Fall Creek and White River, would be an ideal site for the state capital. Alexander Ralston, who had assisted Major Pierre L'Enfant in planning the city of Washington, D.C., was commissioned to design the city that would arise there. In 1825 (eleven years before Indianapolis was incorporated as a town and twenty-two years before it received its city charter), construction was completed on a capitol building, and the seat of Indiana's government was relocated from the temporary capital, Corydon.

German and Irish immigrants provided the brawn to build the Broad Ripple Canal in the 1830s and, in the next decade, the railroad network that reached from Indianapolis to every corner of the state. The city grew rapidly through the eras of war and Reconstruction. Stockyards were opened in 1877, and Indianapolis soon rivaled Chicago and Kansas City as a packing center. Automobile factories came in the late century, and by 1910 the city was fourth in the United States (after Detroit, Toledo, and Cleveland) in the production of cars. (In 1909 the Speedway was built for test-driving locally made autos, and in 1911 the first Indy 500 race was held there.)

Indianapolis's reputation as a show town dates from 1859, when the city's first theatre, the 900-seat Metropolitan, was erected at 148 West Washington Street. English's Opera House (with 2,000 seats), on Monument Circle, opened in 1880. The 3,800-seat Tomlinson Hall, built in 1886 at 200 East Market Street, was the largest venue for concerts and plays. The city's grand vaudeville theatres (the Empire, the Lyric, the Majestic, the Murat, and the Circle) made Indianapolis an important hub on Midwestern "wheels." In the early teens, there were more than twenty outdoor variety theatres (called "airdomes") in Indianapolis. The city's busy vaudeville reviewer at that time was a young journalist named Janet Flanner, writing for the Indianapolis *Star*.

There were no major publishers of music in nineteenth-century Indianapolis, but the city had a thriving music store, the Pearson Piano Company. Founded in 1873, Pearson eventually opened seven branches across the state. The original Pearson's boasted of its selection of 20,000 piano rolls in a 1918 ad, and by the early 1920s customers could sample the rolls in ten soundproof rooms the store had designed for aural browsing.

Several Indianapolis musical groups had commercial ties. John T. Brush, founder of the When Clothing Store, organized an employees' band in 1875. The When Band gave Saturday night concerts in city parks for years. From the 1890s into the 1920s, the Montani Brothers Band, five sons of a fruit stand owner, made music for society parties in Indianapolis. The Kioda Barber Band was a black group, with several barber shops represented in its membership.

In the early century the biggest black stars and their companies—Williams and Walker, Ernest Hogan, Billy Kersands, the Black Patti Troubadours, the Smart Set, the Cole and Johnson shows—made frequent visits to Indianapolis. At one point in the late 1890s, there were five black newspapers in the city, and through them readers could follow the careers of local black heroes who had gone on to wider fame, such as the vaudeville dancer Dora Dean and the comic actor Billy McClain.

The liveliest music of the ragtime era was made along the western stretch of Indiana Avenue, which bisected the city's largest black neighborhood. Cafes, theatres, and (later) movie houses featured pianists such as Bert King (sometimes billed as "Black Diamond"), Russell Smith (the only black composer to have a rag published in

Indianapolis), Jesse Crump (a regular at the Golden West Cafe), and Reginald DuValle (the musical mentor of Hoagy Carmichael). One of the last local military bandmasters was Frank Clay, who was known as the "Black Sousa." Among the youngsters drinking in the syncopation and show business that Indianapolis offered were J. Russel Robinson, Noble Sissle, and the kid who would write "Star Dust."

J. H. AUFDERHEIDE & COMPANY

For five years (1908–1912) in the middle of the classic rag era, a businessman, his daughter, and a few of her friends made Indianapolis a center of Midwestern ragtime. There were a handful of local rags before and after the Aufderheide period, but there was no other publisher as committed and no stable of writers as good as those Aufderheide had. Despite the nepotism of his firm, John Aufderheide must not be seen as merely a father with money enough to indulge his daughter's hobby. Aufderheide's interest in ragtime lasted only as long as his daughter was writing, but while it lasted, he was seriously committed to publishing. He took an office, hired a manager, and made his rags (fewer than a third of them written by his daughter) the best known of any written in Indianapolis.

John Henry Aufderheide (1865–1941), the son of a furniture manufacturer, was born in Indianapolis. As a young man, he played the violin semi-professionally in local orchestras. His sister May was an occasional piano soloist with the Indianapolis Symphony before she joined the faculty at the Metropolitan School of Music. If a musical career beckoned to John Henry, he ignored the call. He took a job as a bank teller, and this was followed by several years in a real estate office. When he was finally able to go into business for himself, he founded the Commonwealth Loan Company. He continued to play the violin for pleasure, and he shared the profits from his small-loan firm as a patron of the musical arts in Indianapolis.

His daughter, May Frances Aufderheide (b. 1888) was in her early teens when ragtime fever hit Indianapolis. She took piano lessons from her father's sister, but she much preferred popular music to the classics. It must have been while she was away at Pelham Manor, an Eastern finishing school, that May began to try to write rags. By late 1907 or early 1908, she had one that she liked enough to seek its publication. Making one of the oddest couples in ragtime history, the debutante found an ally in an itinerant Indianapolis sign painter named Cecil Duane Crabb.

It is not known (and can hardly be imagined) how they got together, but Cece Crabb obviously looked like a soul mate to the society girl with ragtime on her mind. Crabb, two years younger than May Aufderheide, grew up poor in Centerville, Indiana. A naturally gifted piano player, he had little formal education and no training in music. His teenage wandering had brought him to Indianapolis, where a local family, the Staleys, took him in. Crabb needed a trade, and when it was discovered that he could draw, F. D. Staley, Sr., set him up in business, painting outdoor signs and lettering bankers' and lawyers' names on their office doors. Crabb played on pianos wherever he could find them, and he began to try his hand at composition. In 1907 Crabb's two-step, "Fluffy Ruffles," was published locally by Will B. Morrison, a store clerk who was besotted with ragtime.

Crabb's musical credentials were slim, but he at least had the cachet of publication. May Aufderheide either met him by chance (perhaps at the Pearson Piano Company) or sought him out to show him her composition. Although Crabb was not a publisher, this did not matter to May when he offered to publish her rag. He drew a cover cartoon of a pop-eyed, big-lipped minstrel man, and he got his friend Paul Pratt (another teenager) to arrange the manuscript. In April 1908, "Dusty Rag" (the only rag issued by the Duane Crabb Publishing Company) arrived in Indianapolis music stores.

As "Dusty Rag" was making its debut, its composer was away in Europe, on the "Grand Tour" that well-to-do young ladies took to cap off a finishing school education. There was more to May Aufderheide's momentous year after her return from the Continent. Only weeks after she got back to Indianapolis, she married Thomas M. Kaufman, a young architect from Richmond, Indiana. By year's end—after May's graduating, publishing, touring, and marrying—the newlyweds were making a home in Richmond.

"Dusty Rag" was not even a local hit—Crabb's distribution extended only to the Indianapolis stores he could get to by streetcar to deliver copies—but its mere existence touched J. H. Aufderheide. Late in 1908 (as a wedding present; as a show of his belief in her?) he created J. H. Aufderheide & Company to publish his daughter's compositions. It was not a living room operation. Aufderheide took office space in the Lemcke Building and set up to sell music, including that of other publishers he handled in a small jobbing effort. (Perhaps it was Cecil Crabb who lettered his name on the door.) Aufderheide bought the copyright of "Dusty Rag" from Crabb and quickly reissued it (keeping the Crabb cover and the Pratt arrangement), and in December 1908 he published May's "Richmond Rag," named for her new husband's (and now her) hometown.

Like his daughter, J. H. Aufderheide was impressed with the teenage boys who had brought "Dusty Rag" to fruition. He hired Paul Pratt as manager of his music company, and the first 1909 rag issued by the company was Cece Crabb's "Orinoco," which was published in March. The following month the next Aufderheide rag, Paul Pratt's "Vanity Rag," was issued. Crabb became a partner in a sign-painting business in 1909, so music would be a sideline for him. But, under the aegis of J. H. Aufderheide, Paul Pratt and May Aufderheide Kaufman seemed set on musical careers.

In the summer of 1909 the Aufderheide enterprise attracted the attention of the *American Musician and Art Journal,* a trade magazine based in New York. Under a headline reading CLASSIC RAGS COMPOSED BY MAY AUFDERHEIDE, there is a photo of May, her hair piled high like a Gibson girl's, and an article that calls her a composer to "keep your eye (and ears) on." It says that "Dusty" and "Richmond Rag" are "now in considerable demand," and that there are "two new rags on the press that . . . will be sure winners." The two, published in September 1909, were "Buzzer Rag" and "The Thriller," and one of them would be her best known work.

"The Thriller" was immediately popular with players and listeners. It is a rich and graceful folk rag, and, with its feeling of serene forward motion, it could be the perfect accompaniment for figure skating. There were eight piano roll versions of "Thriller" and five of "Dusty." These two fine rags made May Aufderheide's reputation, and they were known far beyond Indianapolis. The New Orleans trumpeter Bunk Johnson committed them to memory as soon as they came out, and in a 1942 recording session, he proved that he still knew them.

There were two more May Aufderheide rags in 1910—"Blue Ribbon Rag" and "A Totally Different Rag" (with a cover designed by Cecil

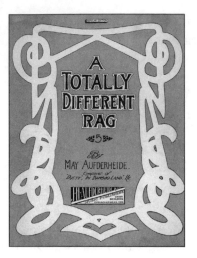

"A Totally Different Rag"

Crabb)—and two more by Paul Pratt. (It is not known if J. H. Aufderheide offered contracts to all of his composers, but Pratt recalled that he received a one-and-a-half-cent per copy royalty on his "Colonial Glide" of 1910.) Another new item in the Aufderheide catalog that year was "Candle-Stick Rag" by Abe Olman, who was currently manager of the sheet music department at the L. S. Ayres Department Store. The 1910 crop was so good that, in 1911, J. H. Aufderheide decided to open a second branch of his publishing company. He sent Paul Pratt to Chicago to open an office in the Randolph Building. Around this time the Kaufmans moved to Indianapolis from Richmond. The business was growing, May was back home, and the future seemed bright.

But the reason for the Kaufmans' move was that Thomas was not making it as an architect in Richmond. He took a job with an architectural firm in Indianapolis, but three years of failure in his hometown had sapped his confidence. There was stress at home, and it was taking a toll on May's writing. She wrote a few songs (several with lyrics by Paul Pratt), and in April 1911 J. H. Aufderheide issued "Novelty Rag," which would be her last piano composition. Crabb's "Klassicle Rag" appeared that same month (with a cover by the composer), as did Julia Lee Niebergall's "Horseshoe Rag" and Will B. Morrison's "Scarecrow Rag." These four numbers, all coming in the spring of 1911, were the final outpouring of ragtime from the Aufderheide company. Perhaps to encourage his daughter, Aufderheide commissioned J. Will Callahan to write lyrics to "Dusty Rag" and issued it as a song in 1912. "Dusty Rag Song" did not sell well, and its appearance did not inspire May to write any more ragtime.

Julia Lee Niebergall had taken over some of the arranging chores from Paul Pratt when he went to Chicago, and her "Red Rambler Rag," issued in the summer of 1912, was the last published by J. H. Aufderheide. The Aufderheide company vanished as quickly as it had come. Its founder sold his catalog to Mentel Brothers of Cincinnati, then closed the doors. Paul Pratt was left stranded in Chicago, and May Aufderheide Kaufman was left at home with her troubles.

The closing of the Aufderheide company was a blessing in disguise for Pratt. It threw him into the larger pond of commercial music, where, he was pleased to find, he could swim. He worked in Tin Pan Alley firms for a couple of years, then came back to Chicago to play and arrange piano rolls for the U.S. Music Company. He published several songs as well as three rags with John Stark in the mid-teens. As musical director for tab shows in vaudeville he made his way again to New York in the early twenties. Pratt led Broadway pit orchestras (for Vincent Youmans's *Wild Flower*, the 1926 *Ziegfeld Follies*, and Rodgers and Hart's *A Connecticut Yankee*, among others) before returning to Indianapolis to lead a dance orchestra in the early thirties. He turned a hobby into a profession in 1934, when he opened his own photography studio. He died in Indianapolis in 1948.

Julia Neibergall was one of the few ragtime women to have a lifelong career in music. Marriage did not derail her, because she was not married for very long. She divorced her husband, took back her maiden name, and went to work as pianist at the Colonial Theatre in Indianapolis. She made good money and spent it as she saw fit. She was one of the first women in the city to own an automobile. She left the Colonial to become an accompanist in a dance school, where she worked almost up to the time of her death, at age eighty-two.

In 1916 Thomas Kaufman gave up his dream of being an architect and went to work in his father-in-law's Commonwealth Loan Company. The firm grew steadily over the years, eventually operating eighty-one loan offices in eleven states. By 1930 or so, May wasn't playing the piano anymore. The marriage was financially secure but emotionally stormy. When J. H. Aufderheide died in 1941, his son-in-law became chairman of Commonwealth's board of directors. Six years later, Kaufman retired from Commonwealth and moved his family to Pasadena, California. Kaufman and their adopted daughter died in the late 1950s, and May was confined to a wheelchair by arthritis until her death in 1972. During May Aufderheide's decades of silence, her rags stayed in Midwestern piano benches—and in pianists' repertoires—where they had been placed by her loving father.

"Just Ask Me"

CHAPTER THREE

Ragtime in the South

Alabama, Arkansas, Florida, Georgia, Kentucky, Louisiana, Tennessee, Virginia, West Virginia

In Southern popular music, as in Southern literature, eccentricity abounds and is taken for granted. The South never quite lets go of any music that has been there, and aural ghosts linger everywhere. Disparate musical styles that would seem unlikely to have even nodding acquaintances have made long and happy marriages. It is in the South where spirituals ("When the Saints Go Marching In," "Bye and Bye," "Down by the Riverside") and marches ("High Society," "National Emblem," "Blaze Away") dug into the repertoires of the first jazz bands; where "Dill Pickles" and "Red Wing" became staples of traditional country string bands; where whorehouse pianists were expected to know a few operatic airs; where gospel singing—black and white—is often accompanied by barrelhouse piano playing; where the first country star, Jimmie Rodgers, borrowed tunes and paraphrased lyrics by Bessie Smith; where mourners followed hearses to cemeteries to the accompaniment of an old parlor song ("Flee as a Bird") and pranced back after the funeral to a pop song ("Oh, Didn't He Ramble?"). The South's musical motto might be "If it sounds good, play it."

The South began its acquaintance with ragtime when the rest of America did, in 1897, with the publication of New Orleans composer Paul Sarebresole's "Roustabout Rag," but it soon veered off the syncopated course that everyone else followed. The region used the same ingredients for ragtime—folk tunes, minstrel show syncopations, cakewalk rhythms—and had the same cooks—itinerant pianists—working in the same low kitchens—whorehouses and saloons. But it refused to accept St. Louis classicism as the recipe. While Southern pianists recognized "Maple Leaf Rag" as a fine number, and most of them cut their teeth on it, they did not take it as holy writ. They would not be bound by Joplin's idea of four sixteen-measure melodies in AA BB A CC DD order. Unlike the master's Chestnut Valley disciples, they never even agreed as to how long a melodic theme should be. Several Southern rags contain eight-bar melodies, a few have twelve-bar themes, and four- and eight-bar interludes between sections are common. The most complex structure in all of ragtime is in Harry Cook's "Shovel Fish" (published in Louisville in 1907), which has six melodic themes, three of which are eight measures long, strung together in INTRO AA BB A CC INTERLUDE C DD EE D FF order. Other regions venerated "Maple Leaf" and produced dozens of imitations of it, but the South produced only one (Al Morton's "Fuzzy Wuzzy Rag," published in Memphis in 1915).

The catchword for Southern ragtime in all its oddity is *folk style*. Like the folk rags of other regions, and like folk music in general, Southern rags have an anything-goes quality. There is craft in them but little compositional cunning. Most of them are a patchwork of (often borrowed) tunes presented as a medley, not as an original sequence of related melodies. Their single-note melody lines, along with the slurring up to and off notes in either hand, recall banjos and fiddles at country dances. Their harmonies are usually plain but are often salted with blue notes, dissonance, or crushed chords. They may have sudden, blunt key changes or no key changes at all. The use of "deeply flatted" keys, A♭ and D♭, gives many of them a rich, funky sound.

For a few years, Southern rags resembled those of other places that were drawing from the same folk well. But as ragtime matured

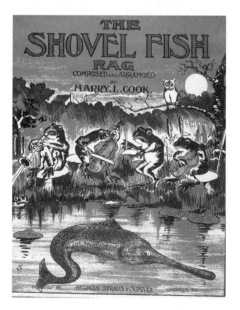

"Shovel Fish Rag"

in other sections of the country, its development as a form stopped at the folk level in the South. The vogue for locally published Southern rags was over by about 1910. There are few examples of "classic ragtime," even fewer "advanced" popular rags in the teens, and no published evidence that novelty or stride ragtime touched the South at all. The reason for this stunting of ragtime's growth is that while the rest of America was going through one pop revolution (ragtime), the South was undergoing three revolutions simultaneously (ragtime, blues, and jazz). Its rowdy siblings diverted attention from ragtime at a crucial stage in its life.

If there was ever anyone who should have been a lifelong rag player and composer, it was Jelly Roll Morton, who came of age at the height of the ragtime craze in the Mecca of Southern piano playing, New Orleans' Storyville. But as the adolescent Jelly wandered the district in the early century, picking up tricks and checking out his competition, he found little inspiration to take ragtime as his metier. He heard some good ragtime, of course, but he also heard players who were translating guitar blues to the language of the piano, imitating the guitar's scuffling rhythm and walking bass lines, playing twelve-bar tunes in a hundred variations every night. When a big spender called for something "down and dirty," this so-called honky tonk music was what he wanted. If a pianist could improvise a raunchy blues with the customer's name in the lyric, the tips poured like rain. The style would later be called "barrel-house," and still later, "boogie woogie," and although Morton saw it as the refuge of the musically illiterate, he knew he had to master it.

Morton's favorite players were generalists, just good "manipulators"—like Tony Jackson, Sammy Davis, and Albert Carroll—none of whom ever wrote down a rag and published it. The best musical minds in town left the writing of rags to amateurs. Morton, the boy who should have been ragtime's leading Southern practitioner, saw that, instead of specializing, one had better be able to do it all. Instead of becoming a local ragtime star, Jelly merely put ragtime on his list of various kinds of music to be improved on in the Morton manner. Storyville survivors did not reminisce about the tempestuous playing of rags; instead, they recalled the endless wrinkles that players brought to the blues and pop songs. There is a venerable New Orleans piano tradition behind Professor Longhair and Allen Toussaint, but it is not a ragtime tradition. And in backcountry jook joints, as in the cities, barrelhouse was the reigning style. Pine Top Smith and Cow Cow Davenport, both rural Alabamans, didn't grow up playing ragtime and probably never heard it played.

The predictability of blues and the freedom of jazz were attractive for several reasons, not all of them economic. Ragtime was constrictive, as jazz and blues were not. It was a *written* music, requiring memorization and practice. A player could not toss off "Original Rags" merely by having the impulse to do it and knowing where the chords were. Ragtime smacked of preparation and of study. In turn-of-the-century Storyville, it was the schoolmarm at the orgy.

Because piano ragtime was heard in New Orleans "houses," more than in New Orleans homes, its audience demographic was narrow: pianists, whores, and white men who were wealthy enough to patronize high-priced brothels. The piano rags that got the widest exposure were those arranged for dance bands. And they lost something in the translation.

In his autobiography, the bassist Pops Foster recalled that there were three basic musical styles among New Orleans bands: sweet (like John Robichaux's, one of the few bands in the city that used a piano); blues (like Frankie Dusen's Eagle Band); and ragtime (like the Magnolia Band and the Tuxedo Band). Classic rags were in the repertoire of the sweet bands and the ragtime bands, and Foster, describing the differences in their reading ability, sets the scene for the entrance of jazz:

> A band like the Magnolia Band would play ragtime and work the District. They'd play "Bag of Rags," "Frog Legs Rag," "Maple Leaf Rag," "Champagne Rag," and ones like that; they were all dance numbers. . . . John Robichaux got most of the dicty jobs. . . . His band played the country clubs, restaurants like Antoine's or Galatoire's, where the rich people gave dinners and had dancing, private clubs like Jackson Square Gardens or the Harmony Club, where they'd have parties. . . . [A]nd when you hired the John Robichaux Band, you had the cream of the crop. Robichaux's band played only what was written, but they did play some of the Scott Joplin tunes, and if you played what he wrote, you played enough. John had the best reading band in town. He wouldn't hire anyone who couldn't read. . . . When people ask me about who started jazz, I tell them I give the guys in New

Orleans the credit for playing it, but the ragtime composers most credit for writing the music. . . . The guys who wrote ragtime for us were Scott Joplin, Tom Turpin, and Walter Jacobs. [Jacobs was not a composer but a ragtime publisher in Boston. His name was on many orchestrations, and this is probably why Foster remembered him as a writer.]. . . In order to play Scott Joplin numbers right, you've got to be able to read. A whole lot of the guys back there couldn't read and didn't want to learn. They'd call the guys who could read "cute guys." . . . The fiddler usually could read and taught the rest of the band the numbers, and played a whole lot of everything.

So, as Robichaux and his troops were sailing through the arrangements in the *Red Back Book*, nonreading players in the Magnolia and Tuxedo bands were being coached in their parts by the "cute guy" who played fiddle. When harmony lines and counterpoints in complex numbers are passed out by rote, improvisation is just around the corner. The result was a statement of melody (by the violinist, the one who knew it), plus whatever the other players could remember/muster/improvise/harmonize to go with it. It was no doubt fun, and it was certainly danceable, but it was literally a rough idea of ragtime. Dancers may have heard "Champagne" and "Frog Legs" every week, but they never heard them the same way twice.

In the South, affection for ragtime did not run deep nor did it last long, because the South, unlike the Midwest, did not take ragtime home and get acquainted with it. During the years when parlor pianos in the Grain Belt rang with locally published rags, Southerners thought of ragtime as what the dance band played. It was new, it was fun, and, like all fads, it was sure to be supplanted by something else pretty soon.

The indifference of Southern publishers sealed ragtime's fate. There was no Southern publisher committed to getting ragtime into homes and keeping it there, and there were fewer than 125 rags published in the entire South (and only two or three of these were known outside the region). No Southern publisher had ten rags in his catalog, and no Southern composer had ten published rags to his credit. Not only were there no Southern counterparts to John Stark, there were no Victor Kremers or J. H. Aufderheides. One of the finest Southern rags, Irwin Leclere's "Triangle Jazz Blues," appeared in February 1917.

When questioned as to why he didn't compose more rags after his brilliant debut, Leclere replied, "Nobody asked me to."

Southern music publishers, including the oldest and largest of them (O. K. Houck, Philip Werlein, Henry A. French, Louis Grunewald, Frank G. Fite), were generally piano companies and/or music stores with a publishing arm. The piano companies' primary aim was to sell pianos, organs, band instruments, and, later, records and phonographs. They also sold sheet music, of course, but as a sideline to everything else. Music store-publishers issued the work of local and regional composers, but most of them did not seek distribution beyond their own branches. The most basic music-selling practices, such as plugging and jobbing into other stores, were unknown to them. In these publisher-stores, a new rag was the centerpiece of this week's counter display. A hundred or so copies would be printed, and after these were sold, there would be no second edition.

The South's most successful and influential pre-country publisher was James D. Vaughn, who did all of the businesslike things that the "sideline" publishers did not do. Vaughn began issuing his shape-note gospel songsters in Lawrenceburg, Tennessee, in 1903, and by 1912 he was selling nearly a hundred thousand copies a year. He set up singing schools to promote his products and, later, sponsored radio quartets to demonstrate them on the air. His recording company, Vaughn Records, which began in 1922, was the first to be based in the South. In the early twenties, Vaughn had sixteen quartets—made up of his singing school teachers—giving free concerts all over the South. These quartets not only defined the makeup and sound of the gospel quartet—four men and a piano—they also defined the quartet repertoire: Vaughn songs. Vaughn's publishing company lasted until 1964.

Although ragtime never got the promotion it deserved, it did lodge in the Southern consciousness. The first jazz records are saturated with ragtime, and if "Dill Pickles" has departed from the country repertoire, "Sugarfoot Rag" and "Steel Guitar Rag" have not. Ragtime propels the stomps of Jelly Roll Morton and guides the left hand of many a church pianist. Like so much in Southern culture, ragtime belongs to a past that is not past.

Five Profiles in Southern Ragtime

CHARLES HUNTER

Charles Hunter's eight rags are the most important body of work by a Southern ragtime composer. Hunter's mastery was evident in his first rag, which arrived without regional precedent or model. He was twenty-three when he wrote it, and he had lived nowhere except Columbia, his hometown, in middle Tennessee, and as a student at the Nashville School for the Blind. How did he know about ragtime? There had been only three rags published in the South before Hunter's earliest, and he could not have read them. Did friends lead him around to backwoods saloons? To Nashville's red-light district? Somehow, the gangly, good-natured redhead understood this new music well enough to set its standard in the South.

Charles Hunter learned piano tuning at the School for the Blind, and upon leaving the school, went to work for the Jesse French Piano Company in Nashville. He honed his self-taught piano playing there, and in 1899 he was ready to publish one of his compositions. Because his employer did not publish music, Hunter took his piece to a newer and smaller firm, Frank G. Fite, which issued "Tickled to Death" as its first ragtime publication.

"Tickled to Death," unlike most rags, actually exemplifies its title. Its relentless, burbling syncopations sound like a fit of the giggles. There are hints of older music in it (a call-and-response melody, basic cakewalk figures, a marchlike "Trio" that includes an eight-bar "dog-fight" strain in a minor key), but it is not a hybrid. It is an out-and-out rag, giddy with syncopation and superbly crafted. "Tickled to Death" was available on piano rolls for twenty years, and its recording by Prince's Band was popular in 1911.

Encouraged by the response to "Tickled to Death," Hunter took his next works to Nashville's leading ragtime publisher, Henry A. French (who had published two rags, compared to Frank Fite's one). "Possum and Taters" was issued by French in April 1900, and "A Tennessee Tantalizer" appeared the following November. Hunter's harmonic sense was maturing in these rags, and there is a bittersweet shadow behind their sunny facade. He published three more rags in Nashville (including "Just Ask Me") before he was transferred to the St. Louis branch of the Jesse French company in 1902.

Only a few blocks south of Hunter's employment, at 902 Olive Street in St. Louis, lay the tawdry temptations of Chestnut Valley, and within months of his arrival, the red-light district had Hunter in its clutches. He drifted away from his job, playing in houses and saloons, on the skids but enjoying the ride. The only identifiable photograph of a whorehouse pianist in his workplace is of Hunter, taken in St. Louis around 1904. He is facing the camera, slumped on a piano stool, hands in his lap, his sightless eyes staring at nothing. To his right are five plump girls in neck-high, floor-length dresses. Their eyes are as vacant as his.

Hunter sent one more rag back to Nashville for publication by Fite in 1903 ("Why We Smile"), and for a year after that, he wrote nothing. He must have had a health scare during that time, because he defiantly titled his last rag "Back to Life." Charles K. Harris of New York published it in 1905, and John Stark issued Hunter's "Seraphine Waltzes" that same year. Hunter died of tuberculosis in January 1906, four months before his thirtieth birthday.

Robert Hoffman

ROBERT HOFFMAN

Robert Hoffman, the son of a cotton broker, was born in a rural area of southern Alabama in 1878. His father died in 1889, and his mother and her four children moved to New Orleans the following year. Robert graduated from Spring Hill College in Mobile, Alabama, in 1898 with a degree in "commercial studies," and he returned to New Orleans, where he found a job as bookkeeper for the Southern Pacific Railway Company. Southern Pacific's new bookkeeper had musical ambitions, however, and he soon began to try to realize them.

In 1900 Robert Hoffman and T. A. Duggan published Hoffman's two-step, "A Dingy Slowdown." It is a patchwork of forgettable melodies, but, like his later, more syncopated numbers, it has an insinuating charm. "Slowdown" is the operative word for most of Hoffman's instrumentals. They pull the player into a loping, almost hypnotic tempo, and they rock like a chair. They are too slow for two-stepping, and they are nearly impossible to play fast. If Hunter's rags suggest a harvest time hoedown in Tennessee, Hoffman's evoke a sultry New Orleans bar on an August night.

The early century brought more bookkeeping jobs to Hoffman, and more publications. In 1901 Louis Grunewald issued his coon song called "Satisfied," which was dedicated to Ben Turpin, a local comedian. Cable Music Company published Hoffman's first rag, "Dixie Slow Drag," in 1903. His 1906 "Dixie Queen" (also published by Cable) achieved some regional popularity because it incorporated the melody of a folk song everybody knew, "Mama's Got a Baby Named Tee-Nah-Nah." (Grunewald published Harry Weston's rag "Tee Na Nah" in 1910. J. Russel Robinson would issue a song called "Tee-Nah-Nah" after a visit to New Orleans in 1912, and Jelly Roll Morton recalled the smutty original on a recording made in 1940.) "Dixie Queen" caught the attention of someone at the Victor Kremer Company, and the Chicago firm bought it in 1907, giving Hoffman his first out-of-town publication.

It must have been a relief to Hoffman when, in 1908, after ten years of eyeshades and ledgers, he could finally enter the music business as manager of the sheet music counter at D. H. Holmes Company. Roy Carew was a frequent customer at the department store, and he remembered Hoffman as a pleasant, sociable man who demonstrated popular music of all sorts in a "smooth and relaxed style." He preferred a chair to a piano bench or stool, and he played with the underside of his fingers rather than the tips. Browsers at Holmes probably heard Hoffman's 1908 rag, "A Black Hand," performed by its composer.

In 1909 Hoffman produced his best and best known rag, "I'm Alabama Bound." Its main theme is a folk strain or at least an old song. (The melody was included in Blind Boone's "Southern Rag Medley #2," which was published that same year. Jelly Roll Morton always claimed that he wrote it, and he recorded a vocal version called "Don't You Leave Me Here" in 1939.) Robert Ebberman was the original publisher of "I'm Alabama Bound," and he sold it to Puderer's Music Shop in 1910. The following year, the copyright was bought by Jerome

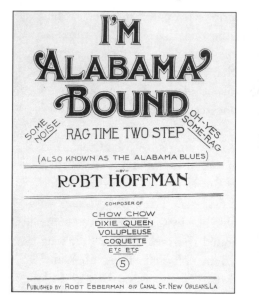

"I'm Alabama Bound"—original publication (left)
"I'm Alabama Bound"—Jerome H. Remick edition (right)

Remick of New York. Hoffman got $500 in the sale to Remick, the most he ever made on a composition. There would be only one more Hoffman rag, "Pussy Foot," issued by Walter Jacobs in 1914. "Pussy Foot" is not as sprightly as its title would suggest. Like the rest of Hoffman's rags, it sounds best in slow motion.

Hoffman left D. H. Holmes in 1910 to become an accompanist for the Fitchenburg Theatre Company, a regional vaudeville chain. He went to the rival Pierce Company theatres (earning a raise from $50 to $72 a week) in 1914. In the late teens he studied the pipe organ with Professor Beaudimular, a local instructor, so that he might work in the larger silent movie theatres. In the early 1920s, playing regularly at the Tudor and the Trianon, Hoffman was considered the best film accompanist in the city. By 1925 Hoffman was in charge of music at New Orleans' grandest movie palace, the Saenger. When the Saenger converted to sound in the late twenties, Hoffman held on to his job, performing elaborate preludes before the films and accompanying stage acts between showings of the features. In 1932 the theatre finally gave up on its live music policy, and Hoffman was let go.

In a desperate comedown from his glory days at the Saenger, Hoffman made a third and last career. He worked as a garage attendant for the city Sewerage and Water Board for twenty-four years before his retirement in 1956. He spent his last years with his wife in their house on Lake Ponchartrain. He played occasionally for church and community groups. After his death in 1964, his wife kept the little brown notebook in which he had listed the 150 numbers he knew by heart.

FERD GUTTENBERGER

For a hundred years, the words *Guttenberger* and *music* were synonymous in Macon, Georgia. The link between them was forged in 1849, when Phillip Guttenberger (1799–1874), a German immigrant, began teaching music at Wesleyan Female College there. Shortly before the Civil War, he was named head of the musical faculty, and, despite his blindness, he made a reputation as one of the South's most distinguished musicians and teachers. His nine children were all musically talented, and one of his sons, Ferdinand Alexander, decided to make music his profession after he returned from service in the Confederate army.

While studying with his father, Ferdinand supported himself by working at a local music store, J. W. Burke & Company, at 452 Second Street. He was a member of the Wesleyan music department from 1896 to 1901, and it was during this time that he bought the Burke store, renamed it F. A. Guttenberger & Company, and went into business for himself. Like his father, he sired nine children, and, like his father's, they were all musical.

Ferdinand Alexander Guttenberger, Jr., was thirteen years old when, in 1901, he wrote his first syncopated number. The family store was not yet publishing (and his father may have disapproved of low brow music anyway), so Ferd had to seek publication by mail. He found a taker in the M. D. Swisher company of Philadelphia, which issued his two-step, "Hobo Days in Georgia." If his father was proud of him for breaking into print, he did not show it by issuing any of his work.

After his father's death in 1905, seventeen-year-old Ferd took over the running of the business. He had helped out in the store since

Ferd Guttenberger

childhood, he knew how it worked, and now he could do things his own way. Syncopation still appealed to him, and he dabbled at writing rags. In 1908 he issued his "Log Cabin Rag," the first rag published in Georgia. To make sure it was up to date, he enlisted the Macon resident who seemed to know the most about popular music, J. Russel Robinson, to arrange it. (Robinson and his brother John, a drummer, had been trooping the South for several years as a vaudeville duo, and they had temporarily settled in Macon taking jobs accompanying silent films.) In 1909 Ferd self-published his best rag, the boisterous, break-laden "Kalamity Kid," in another Robinson arrangement.

"Log Cabin" and "Kalamity Kid" sold out their small first editions, and there were no more of them printed. Guttenberger would issue one more rag, his "Shaka Foot," in 1933, but it was probably composed many years earlier. In 1910 F. A. Guttenberger & Company became a full-service store, when it was authorized as selling agent for Victor Talking Machines and Victor records.

On the Tuesday evening before Thanksgiving in 1912, Ferd Guttenberger was shot by a neighbor who mistook him for a burglar as he was entering his home. The wound was so serious that he was given only a fifty-fifty chance for survival. Although, his recovery was slow, it was complete. He would have thirty-three more years as Macon's "Mr. Music." Using his store as a clearinghouse for community requests, he carried on the family tradition of supplying every kind of music for any kind of event. Until his death in 1945, he provided ensembles, of all sizes, from duos to orchestras, often drawing on the talents of his siblings and aunts, for lodge meetings, schools, churches, and dances. He sometimes appeared in nineteenth-century garb, dressed as his grandfather, for events and ceremonies at Wesleyan. Many of Macon's elders still remember him, not as the composer of Georgia's first rag, but as the nice man who played at their weddings.

Perhaps it was the Guttenberger rags that inspired the publications of another small-town music emporium, Cocroft Music Company, in Thomasville, Georgia. Christopher Columbus Cocroft opened the store in 1905, and in 1909 he issued "Pineywoods Rag," composed by his wife, Nellie (credited to N. Weldon Cocroft on the cover). In 1910 Cocroft published two more rags, "Cotton States Rag" (by Nellie's friend Annie Ford McKnight) and "Halifax Rag" (by H. D. Carter, the company's black janitor). The company built a catalog of a dozen or so numbers, including some two-steps and songs, but it stopped its publishing activity in 1917, when the composer of a fox-trot refused to pay his share for its printing. At this writing, the Cocroft store, the oldest family-owned music store in the United States, is still in operation at 105 South Broad Street, run by C. C. and Nellie's son Chris.

EDWARD B. CLAYPOOLE

There were two ragtime composers born in Baltimore in 1883. One of them, Eubie Blake, achieved international fame; the other, Edward Claypoole, stayed home, took a civil service job in 1905, and kept it until his retirement in 1948. It was Blake who garnered the honors, but it was Claypoole who had a hit rag.

Little Eddie Claypoole was one of those precocious children who see a piano for the first time and immediately know what it is for. He began playing at age five, sitting on pillows piled on the piano bench by his doting mother. She thrust him before audiences at every opportunity, and he impressed his neighbors at church socials, grange halls, and school exercises. He took piano lessons briefly but became impatient with them and quit, choosing to learn by doing. He began to compose songs in his early teens, and many of them were used in local minstrel shows and community theatre musicals. Because he could not transcribe his compositions, John Itzel, superintendent of music for Baltimore's public schools, wrote them down for him.

Claypoole began to send his compositions to New York publishers, and in 1900, when he was sixteen, he made his first sales. Joseph Stern took two cakewalks, "Prancing Jimmy" and "Cake Walk Lindy," and issued them that year. George Willig, a Baltimore publisher, bought his

1903 tune, "Fascination." In 1904 Claypoole went to play at the St. Louis World's Fair, and while he was there, he placed two instrumentals with Thiebes-Stierlin. One of these was a march called "Hike to the Pike," which was introduced by the Sousa band at the fair.

In 1905, after seventeen years of working toward a career in music, and some successes to show for it, Claypoole pulled back. He took a job in the Baltimore city court system. He would eventually become assistant chief deputy clerk, but his advancement would stop there. The job did not curtail his musical life by any means: he would eventually write nearly 500 pieces, and more than fifty of them would see publication.

Claypoole was moonlighting at music now, instead of working at it full time, but his activities remained about the same: He wrote songs for local theatre groups, especially the Paint and Powder Club; he played when he could; and he sent manuscripts to New York and took what he was offered for them. He sold two or three numbers a year, and his publishers occasionally plugged them well. Claypoole had two songs in *Nearly a Hero*, a 1908 Shubert production, and two in *The Echo*, a Richard Carle musical of 1910. His 1914 "Reuben Fox Trot," published by Stern, found its way into the score of the 1919 D. W. Griffith film *Way Down East*. In 1915 Will Von Tilzer's Broadway Music Company took Claypoole's first rag (in John Itzel's transcription) and went to work on it. It was called "Ragging the Scale," and, thanks to Von Tilzer's efforts, it became one of the biggest rag hits of all time.

Von Tilzer had a fine product in "Ragging the Scale." It rags the scale in five keys, and the syncopations are so varied that the simple idea never stales. In the trio the scale ascends and descends in whole notes as a syncopated figure dances between them. Bands took to it at once. It got recordings in the mid-teens by Prince's Band, the Pathé Dance Orchestra, Conway's Band, and the Emerson Military Band. The banjoist Fred Van Eps had a popular recording of it in 1916, and Charley Straight made it on a piano roll. "Ragging the Scale" would be one of the few rags to hold its popularity across decades, with recordings by Vincent Lopez (in 1923) and by Paul Whiteman, Jimmy Lunceford, and Joe Venuti in the 1930s. The publisher claimed that "Ragging the Scale" eventually sold two million copies of sheet music. Ed Claypoole could take pride, but no profit, in its success. He had sold it outright to Broadway Music for $25.

The one-sided payoff from "Ragging the Scale" did not sour Claypoole on the music business—because he was not really in it. He continued to send his compositions to New York and to take what strangers thought he should get for them. His second rag, "American Jubilee," was published by Broadway Music in 1916.

Claypoole wrote no more rags until he edged back into the genre in 1922 with a clever song called "Dusting the Keys." The lyric, by J. Edward Killalea, describes how "our maid Hannah plays piano in a funny kind of way, when she shakes a nifty dust rag on our baby grand Steinway." The accompaniment imitates Hannah's smeared tones, and there is an extra instrumental chorus that is to be played by wrapping a dust rag around the forefinger and flicking off black keys onto white ones. It is a novelty song that is almost a novelty rag. "Dusting the Keys" got several recordings, all of them instrumentals.

The success of "Dusting the Keys" led Claypoole to try the real thing, novelty instrumentals. He wrote four novelty rags, all of them published by Jack Mills, from 1922 to 1924. He also made test recordings of "Ragging the Scale" and "Skidding" for Victor in March 1927, but neither was released. The Irving Berlin company took a handful of Claypoole songs in 1928 and got several of them into films that year (*The Singing Fool, Synthetic Sin,* and *Show Folks*). None of them were hits, and Berlin bought no more from Claypoole.

Claypoole was in mid-career as a court clerk now but still a local celebrity as a frequent guest on Baltimore radio shows with his singing daughter, Audrey. After teaching himself to read and write music in the early thirties, he invented "Piano-Play," a piano teaching game for children in 1935. He continued to compose, and got the occasional publication, but his days of hit rags and film plugs were over. When he retired after forty-three years in the city court, he had the best musical career a deputy clerk could have.

EDWIN H. SEE

Eddie See, a one-shot rag composer who went on to a long career in music, was born in Lake Charles, Louisiana, in 1892. His father, Adolf, a German immigrant, was the contractor who built Lake Charles's Arcade Theatre in 1910. One of Adolf's sons became a boat builder and another entered military service at West Point. Eddie devoted himself

Edwin See

to the study of music. He would become known as a cornetist, trumpeter, and violinist, but his first love was the piano.

In 1913 See began to submit compositions to Henry Packman's Regent Music Company in Lake Charles. Regent took two numbers, "Regent Waltzes" and "Snappy Rag," as well as See's arrangement of "In the Summer Time," a song by R. D. Klock. The publisher had little distribution, and it sold most of its wares by mail order (twelve cents apiece, postpaid). But somehow its tiny catalog caught the attention of Axel Christensen. The November 1915 issue of Christensen's *Ragtime Review* mentioned See's syncopated waltz and "Snappy Rag" in a column, and it reprinted "In the Summer Time" in its entirety. (In 1914 Regent issued the second of its two rags, Henry P. Schaefer's "That Angell Rag.")

Eddie See forsook ragtime to hone his skills on the cornet, and the effort paid off. During most of the 1920s, See was a featured soloist with the Ringling Brothers and Barnum & Bailey band, and he played in the

"Snappy Rag"

off season with Merle Evans's resident band in Sarasota, Florida. When the shortened and musically refurbished *Birth of a Nation* was rereleased in 1931, it was See's trumpet that carried the film's majestic themes. In 1936 See became band director for the Harley Sadler Circus.

Returning to Lake Charles in the late 1930s, See established himself as a teacher, taking private students as well as directing bands for several parochial schools in south central Louisiana. During this time he also served as first violinist and concertmaster of the Lake Charles Civic Symphony Orchestra. In 1948 he was named band director and instructor of brasses at McNeese State College. He adapted the Cajun classic "Jolie Blon" to become the school's fight song. His wife, Donita, was piano accompanist for his students at concerts and contests. The beloved brass teacher retired from McNeese in 1954, and he died in Lake Charles in 1963.

NEW ORLEANS

Souvenirs of Carnival

New Orleans was more than a hundred years old before the first piece of music was published there in 1837. The city had worn three nationalities by then (French, Spanish, and American), developed a sugar industry that was the strongest in the world, weathered a failed revolution (French settlers against their Spanish government, in 1769), survived a great fire (in 1788), and been a focal point in a great war (in 1812). Louis Moreau Gottschalk, the New Orleanian who would become America's first internationally known concert artist, had already left the city (at age thirteen, in 1832) to study music in Paris.

And New Orleans had long been known as a cosmopolitan, pleasure-loving place. Dancing, at public balls and in private homes, was the center of social life. After the Louisiana Purchase in 1803, the citizens were apprehensive about their new government's position on the activity. William C. C. Claiborne, the new American commissioner of the Louisiana Territory, took pains to reassure them that the United States had no plans to interfere with their public dancing.

Dancing schools were a growth industry in New Orleans in the early nineteenth century. Madame Angelina taught the waltz, the polka, and the mazurka at her academy at 139 Royal Street. Rivalries flared in ball-rooms between those who preferred the old-fashioned French quadrille and those who called for the English version of the quadrille, the newfangled lancers. Fad dances, like "the Grasshopper," came and went. The city was saturated with music, but no one thought much about where it came from or why there was none published in New Orleans.

In 1822 an Austrian immigrant named Emile Johns set himself up as a piano teacher in a studio at 56 Canal Street. He began to deal in pianos and musical supplies, and in 1837 he became the first music publisher in New Orleans. Like many of the early publishers, Johns mostly churned out bootleg editions of classical music that had been previously published elsewhere, but he also issued a set of eight descriptive piano pieces called "Album Louisianais," which set the tone for local publications for years to come. The first original music from New Orleans was about New Orleans.

All cities had music on local subjects for local enjoyment, of course, but New Orleans was musically preoccupied with itself to an inordinate degree. Publishing there was a ritual of commemoration of New Orleans events, New Orleans people, New Orleans places. As publishers in other regions began to discover that music on wider subjects—home, mother, romance—reached wider markets, New Orleans stuck to celebrating itself. There was not yet a "hit" mentality among publishers in the 1850s, but the idea had dawned that some songs sold better than others and acquisitions were made accordingly. That decade saw the publication of "Camptown Races" (in Baltimore), "Darling Nelly Gray" (in Boston), "Listen to the Mocking Bird" (in Philadelphia), "When You and I Were Young, Maggie" (in Chicago), and "The Old Folks at Home" (in New York). In New Orleans the 1850s brought "The New Orleans and Great Northern Railroad Polka," "The Fireman's Funeral," "The Beauty of Esplanade Street," and "Eulogy on the Death of Henry Stephen Green" (a local church choir leader). Obsolescence was built into such numbers. Who would want to hear "The Fireman's Funeral" a year after the funeral had occurred? Would "The Beauty of Esplanade Street" appeal to anyone who lived even a few blocks away from its subject?

During the Civil War, those New Orleans publishers who reached from city topicality into regional topicality suffered grave consequences. Armand E. Blackmar, a Vermonter who had begun publishing in New Orleans in 1860, was jailed in 1862 by federal occupation troops for issuing the Confederate anthem, "The Bonnie Blue Flag," the previous year. Philip P. Werlein, who had issued "The Grand March of the Southern Confederacy," had his stock confiscated and sold at public auction. (Most Southern publishers simply shut down during the war. A regionwide shortage of paper left them unable to operate.)

After the Reconstruction government withdrew from New Orleans in 1876, it was back to home rule, and business as usual, for the city's publishers. The tradition of the Mardi Gras parade (which began in 1857) grew into a monthlong party, attracting tourists from all over the world by the end of the century. The annual carnival, and the various groups involved in its preparation, inspired much local music: "Mardi Gras March," "Merry Fifty" (a carnival organization), "Kickapoo Waltz" (dedicated to another carnival club, the Phorty Phunny Phellows), "Les Folies du Carnaval," "Momus," "Rex," and "Krewe of

Proteus." Public improvements ("Gas Light Galop," "Tramway Galop," "Trolley Polka"), institutions ("L.S.U. Waltz," "Y.M.H.A."), newspapers ("The Algiers *Herald* March," The *Daily States* Dudes"), clubs ("Check-Mate Waltz," "Shakespeare Gavotte"), local color ("Convent Chimes," "The Creole Pieman's Song")—all inspired musical souvenirs. By the time the intricate saloon music from St. Louis got to New Orleans, the city was too busy for it. When you live from holiday to holiday, with diversion all around you, there is no time to practice.

LOUIS GRUNEWALD COMPANY

The first New Orleans publisher to issue a rag was Louis Grunewald (1827–1915). A native of Hanhofen, Bavaria, Grunewald came to the city as a youth. He was well known as a church organist (at St. Alphonsus, St. Mary's, and, later, St. Patrick's) before he opened a music shop on Magazine Street in 1856. He had published only a handful of pieces before the Civil War, none of them considered seditious, so the federal army allowed him to keep his store open during its occupation of New Orleans from 1862 to 1865. Unbeknownst to Union general Benjamin Butler, the officer in charge of the occupation, Grunewald made fifes and drums for the Confederate army during the conflict.

Having curtailed his publishing activities for three years, Grunewald came back strong after the war. Within five years or so, he was the most prolific and successful publisher in the city. In the early 1870s he built Grunewald Hall, a grand complex of performance spaces, in which he also kept his music shop. (Grunewald Hall was destroyed by fire in 1890, and the Grunewald Hotel was erected on its site in 1893. When the hotel passed from the family's hands, it was renamed the Roosevelt, and in the 1970s, it became the Fairmont.)

Grunewald's music was the typical, topical New Orleans product: quicksteps, waltzes, and polkas named for current events and for prominent civic groups. In 1879 the company published "The Silver Wedding Waltz," by Robert Meyer, dedicated to Mr. and Mrs. Louis Grunewald on their twenty-fifth wedding anniversary. In 1880 the founder decided to withdraw from the business, so he called his son William (1857–1915) back from his study of music in Europe to take over as manager of the store and publishing arm. (In choosing William, he passed over his son-in-law, Joseph Flanner, who later became a music publisher in Milwaukee.) In 1884 William issued a march called "127" to announce the company's new address, 127 Canal Street.

"*Roustabout Rag*"

In 1897, with no syncopated precedents in its catalog, the company published Paul Sarebresole's "Roustabout Rag." It is a romping rag, with a progressive three-over-four melodic pattern, and no hint of the cakewalk about it. The city seems to have taken little notice of this milestone, as there was not another rag published there for six years. Grunewald issued a few cakewalks (one with the triply misleading title "Raggedy Ragtime Rags") before its next rag in 1904. The main store was then located at 785 Canal Street, and one had only to ask sheet music manager Henry B. Kranage for a demonstration of anything in stock.

Grunewald's last rag, Glennie C. Batson's "Electric Rag," came in 1914, then, like that of most regional publishers, the company's output dwindled in the late teens. Among its last publications was a World War I song, "Asleep in the Fields of Flanders."

P. P. WERLEIN

Philip P. Werlein, another European immigrant, came to the United States in 1831, when he was nineteen years old. In 1842 he founded the House of Werlein, a small but grandly named music shop, in Vicksburg, Mississippi. As partner in Ashbrand & Werlein, he relocated to New Orleans in 1853 to open a store at 93 Camp Street. By 1854 he was ready to strike out on his own, and he bought the stock of an established New Orleans music dealer, W. T. Mayo. In a stroke, Werlein became a major player in the city's music trade. (The new company used only its founder's name, and it still does. P. P. Werlein remains in business in New Orleans.)

Werlein was shut down by federal fiat in 1862, but he gradually regained his status after Reconstruction. In the mid-1880s *Werlein's*

Journal of Music appeared, offering monthly cultural news, piano pieces, and short stories to the company's customers. In 1887, following Grunewald's lead, Werlein issued "135 Canal Street Waltz," as a reminder of his address.

In 1901 Werlein published its first syncopated number, a cakewalk called "Knotty Rags." The first Werlein rag, "Something Doing Soon," came four years later, shortly after the company had taken new and larger quarters at 605 Canal Street. (Howard Winburn was manager of its sheet music department at this time.) Three rags issued in 1909 were among the last Werlein publications.

CABLE MUSIC COMPANY

Cable Music Company was a piano manufacturer, at 914 Canal Street, that issued a handful of syncopated publications and little else in the early century. Its first ragtime publication was Robert Hoffman's "Dixie Slow Drag," in 1903, and its most successful was Hoffman's "Dixie Queen," in 1906. Cable's store manager, Fred C. Schmidt, contributed "Happy Sammy" to his employer's small catalog in 1906, and "Jolly Molly" in 1910. The company's most significant contribution to pop history was as distributor of the first published blues, A. Maggio's "I Got the Blues," in 1908.

HAKENJOS PIANO MANUFACTURING COMPANY, INC.

Hakenjos was another piano company that dabbled in ragtime. During the ragtime era, the Hakenjos music shop was located at 930 Canal Street, and Annie Brown was its manager. Only a few coon songs had appeared under the company's imprint before its first rag, Sebastian Lutz's "Dat's It," was issued in November 1903.

In 1904 Hakenjos published the best of all New Orleans rags, Al Verges's "Whoa! You Heifer." Despite its hokey title and cartoony cover, Verges's only rag is an extremely sophisticated work. There are several kinds of syncopation in each of its melodies, and part of the fun of listening is to find the patterns in their seamless blend. When a pattern is interrupted by two bars of stop time, the effect is startling. "Whoa! You Heifer" was bought from Hakenjos and reissued by F. J. A. Forster of Chicago. A recording by the Columbia Orchestra, along with a Connorized piano roll version, made it one of the few

Southern rags known outside the South. At the time he wrote "Whoa! You Heifer," Al Verges was serving an apprenticeship in his father's butcher shop. In 1907 he was hired to sell Hakenjos pianos, and a few years later he became the company's manager.

~~~

NASHVILLE
Music City Before Country

In the early eighteenth century, French trappers began to compete for game with the Cherokees, Chickasaws, and Shawnees around the Cumberland River in the area that is now north central Tennessee. In 1779 pioneers from North Carolina, led by James Robertson and John Donelson, established a settlement on the Cumberland and named it Ft. Nashborough, in honor of a Revolutionary War hero, General Francis Nash. The Cherokees were especially contentious neighbors, frequently attacking the settlement, but the Carolinians held their ground. In 1784 the growing town was given the upscale name Nashville, and in 1796, Tennessee entered the Union as the sixteenth state. A city charter followed ten years later, and in 1843 Nashville was selected as the permanent state capital.

Steamboat traffic on the Cumberland brought trade and prosperity to Nashville, and its population grew steadily. In the 1850s two shopkeepers opened stores to supply the city with music. The first was James A. McClure, who entered business at 33 Union Street in 1855; his rival, Charles D. Benson, came three years later, with a store uncomfortably nearby at 34 Union Street. Benson was a sometime composer, and he began issuing his own compositions almost immediately. Both music dealers were fervent secessionists, and as war loomed, they became firebrands for the Southern cause. Benson issued his "Secesh Battle Flag March" in 1861, and McClure's "Song of the Southern Boys" appeared that same year.

When Nashville fell to the Union, federal troops moved in to occupy the city, and it was no place for rabble-rousing music publishers. Both McClure and Benson fled to Memphis. McClure held his silence there,

but Benson kept cranking out Confederate morale boosters in his
adopted city, eventually issuing more than thirty such titles under his
imprint. Both would return after the war to find Nashville in shambles.
They reopened their stores, and each published a bit, but both would
spend the Reconstruction struggling to reconstruct their trade. Benson
lasted until 1881, and McClure closed his doors a year later.

One of the brave enterprises that began in Nashville's gloomy business climate during Reconstruction was the Jesse French Piano
Company, which was founded in 1872. As America wanted movies
during the Depression, it wanted pianos after the Civil War, so the
company grew quickly. Within ten years of its beginning, the French
factory was booming, and there were branches in St. Louis, Little Rock,
Memphis, and Birmingham. In the early 1880s French had seventy-five
Nashville employees and thirty-five piano salesmen on the road.

In 1887 the company incorporated, with Jesse French as president,
and moved into the five-story Jesse French Building at 240–242 North
Summer Street. The building was among the city's first to boast an elevator, and the array of more than 200 pianos, of all shapes, brands, and
sizes, was mind-boggling. The Jesse French Piano Company did not
publish, but its splendid physical presence was a daily reminder to
young Nashville hustlers that a fortune could be made in music. In the
late 1890s, two men decided to provide some syncopated software for
all of those Jesse French pianos, and each began to publish rags.

H. A. FRENCH

Henry A. French began in the music business as bookkeeper for his
older brother Jesse's piano company. When Jesse incorporated and
expanded his enterprise in 1887, Henry set himself up as music dealer
and publisher nearby at 237 North Summer. The H. A. French company soon opened two more Nashville shops, and by the early 1890s its
owner was receiving more unsolicited manuscripts than he cared to look
at. In his catalog he warned hopeful composers that unless they "happen
to be well-known and have written a number of salable pieces," they
would be expected to share the cost of publishing their work. A hundred copies of an ordinary four-page number (including the title page)
cost $13.55. To dissuade the starry-eyed from overreaching, he set a
price of $15.55 for each hundred copies after the first edition.

H. A. French published several syncopated pieces in the late nineties (such as Carrie McKee's two-step, "Vanity Fair," in 1897), and in 1898 he issued Nashville's first rag, "Mandy's Broadway Stroll," by Thomas E. Broady. Broady's number is a sort of hip cakewalk, hung with such a variety of syncopated fillips, fills, and suspensions that it qualifies as a rag. There were two more Broady rags (both published by French), but after his "Whittling Remus," in 1900, the mysterious composer, possibly tired of subsidizing himself, disappeared from the scene.

Broady's place in the French catalog was taken by Nashville's best rag composer, Charles Hunter. French published two Hunter rags in 1900 and a third in 1901. His adventurous ragtime publishing did not pay off, however, and H. A. French closed shop some time around 1904. His stock was bought by Claude Street, Jr., the owner of a small Nashville piano company. Street couldn't move the French numbers either, and, years later, he recalled throwing most of them away.

FRANK G. FITE

Frank G. Fite (1865–1917) was another Nashville music store owner who did a bit of publishing. Fite began as a dry goods merchant shortly after graduating from Vanderbilt University, and he converted to the music business around 1899. His store was located at 531–533 Church Street, and his trade was not enough to keep even his core staff busy. His secretary, Olney Davis, found time to serve as secretary/treasurer of Davies Piano Company and as vice president/manager of O.K. Houck's Nashville branch concurrently while working for Fite.

Fite earned his place in ragtime history, however, as the first to publish Charles Hunter. He issued Hunter's first rag, "Tickled to Death," in 1899 and the superb "Just Ask Me" in 1902. Like French, Fite found the marketing of ragtime beyond his capability. He closed shop around the same time French did and embarked on another career, as a salesman for the Fidelity & Casualty Insurance Corporation.

LEW ROBERTS MUSIC COMPANY

Henry Lew Roberts was a native New Yorker who sold an odd assortment of things at the store he opened at 40 Arcade in 1907. He had a line of cutlery, some cheap novelty jewelry, and some rags he had written himself. When his own inspiration ran dry after two rags, he issued a handful of syncopated numbers by others.

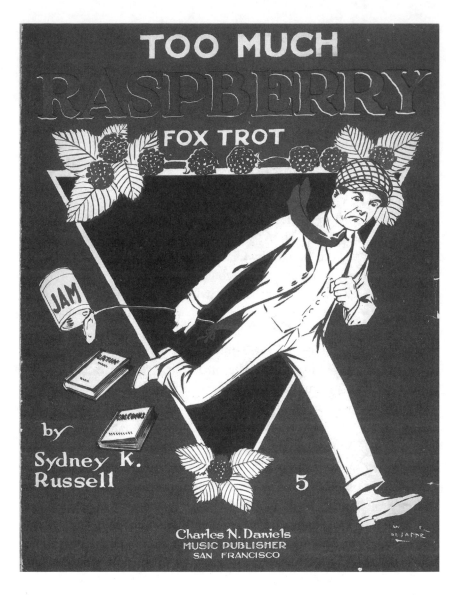

"Too Much Raspberry"

CHAPTER FOUR

Ragtime in the West

Alaska, California, Colorado, Idaho, Montana,
Nevada, North Dakota, Oklahoma, Oregon, South
Dakota, Texas, Utah, Washington, Wyoming

Ragtime came late and—with the city of San Francisco as the sole exception—left early in the West. During the ragtime era, the region was still undergoing growth pangs that the East and Midwest had passed through a hundred years before, and there was no regionwide support for commercial music of any kind. Well into the twentieth century, there were territorial disputes to be fought or adjudicated (including some disputes with Indians and Mexicans), deserts to be irrigated, railroads to be built, rowdy towns to be tamed. Parts of the West had yet to be carved into states and gathered into the national fold. The area was in the United States but not completely *of* it.

In the 1840s the area that now comprises Idaho, Montana, Wyoming, Utah, Colorado, and New Mexico was labeled "Unorganized Territory" on U.S. maps. Oklahoma's panhandle was "No Man's Land" because it seemed to belong neither to Texas nor to the United States. America's northwest section was called Oregon Territory until Oregon entered the Union in 1859; the corner that was left became Washington Territory, to await the statehood that came thirty years later. Carving off chunks of territories stepped up after Reconstruction. Ten states were added to the union between 1876 and 1912, all of them in the West.

Achieving statehood was something to be proud of, but it was no guarantee of prosperity. In the late nineteenth century, the region held hundreds of communities begun by homesteaders and miners, all hoping that a railway company president thousands of miles away would smile on them and order the crossties that would connect them with the rest of the country. "Civilization" (read: trade) came on the train, and if the train did not stop at their settlement or very nearby, growth would be slow or not at all. A hundred ghost towns were created with the plotting of every railroad route.

The earliest white settlers in the West were drawn there by its size. Possibilities were vast because the West itself was vast. One could grow large things, like trees, horses, and cattle, and could grow them in great numbers. With so many vacant places in which to look, one might, with luck, find silver, gold, or oil. Pioneers did not go there for the society but for the isolation that improved life's odds. If no one else were around, one could be the first to homestead in a virgin forest, to build a sawmill, to fence a grassland, to find nuggets in a Colorado stream, to corner the market in something that latecomers would want. The spaces were
really wide open, and the prairies were really lone. That was the point of going.

Isolation was good for pioneers but not for ragtime. Although clapboard-and-canvas saloons dotted the old West, including the wilderness areas, most had no music in them. Many drinking establishments were actually wagons, rolling up to campfires and crossroads to sell homemade beer and whiskey to those as transient as the wagonmaster himself. They did not carry pianos, but there is no record of anyone taking his trade elsewhere due to a lack of music.

City barrooms had more amenities, often including piano playing, but the great distances between cities precluded "saloon circuits," like the ones in many areas of mid-America. City bars were often ethnic social clubs, where lonesome immigrants could go to hear the old country's music, talk the old language, and be among those like themselves. In the pre-ragtime years, when Midwestern pianists were reinventing popular music by their musical and intellectual intercourse, no such communication was going on in the West. Pianists were too far apart to hear each other. (The saloons of eastern Oklahoma—in Tulsa, Enid, and El Reno—were, because of their proximity to Missouri, stops on the Midwestern players' "wheel." They were the only places in the West to see the light of ragtime as it was dawning.)

Western cities had their sin strips, of course—Houston's "Smoky Row," Dallas's "Deep Ellum," Denver's Blake Street, San Francisco's Dupont Street, Cripple Creek's Myers Avenue—where many saloons (and some whorehouses) offered opportunities for pianists. A player who won a reputation in one of these demimondes tended to stay there. He would have to go a long way to find a comparable string of workplaces. There were doubtless many fine saloon pianists in the West, but because they didn't circulate enough to wind up in anyone's memoirs, and because they seldom published their music, their names are lost.

One of the few Western musicians to describe his whorehouse days in any detail was George Morrison, a black violinist who spent the teens working for a Denver madam named Mattie Silks. Silks ran an upscale place, with beautiful girls, champagne at the ready, and elaborate suppers by appointment. Her regular pianist was Hugh Thomas, and Morrison played in a small combo (which she called an "orchestra") she hired for dancing. The minimum tip for an orchestra request was $5. Morrison remembered that the madam liked classical pieces (especially "Humoresque"), but that the customers preferred hotter stuff, like "Cubanola Glide," "Darktown Strutters' Ball," "Blue Bell," and "Red Wing." "Blue Danube" was the standard waltz number, and, when Silks loaned her orchestra out to play at a whore's funeral, she wanted "Good Bye, Little Girl, Good Bye." In the Denver headquarters of Bacchus and Venus, Morrison did not recall playing a rag.

Three Profiles in Western Ragtime

JAY ROBERTS

The Western player and composer who best lived up (or down) to ragtime's scandalous image was a rakehell from Oakland, Jay Roberts. He wrote three good rags (one of them enormously popular), and almost everything known about him comes from newspaper accounts of his serious brush with the law and his violent death.

Roberts's father was a clerk for Oakland's Railway Mail Service, and in 1909, when Jay was about nineteen, he got his son a job as a substitute postman. The swift completion of his appointed rounds was not for Jay, however, and in 1910 the Oakland city directory lists him as a musician, living away from home for the first time, in his own apartment on Page Street. Roberts teamed with a comic singer named Lee D. Lloyd that year, and together they created an act for Bay Area roadhouses.

Keeping the usual pecking order of vaudeville acts, Lee Lloyd, the singer, was more prominently featured, but Roberts's playing was so impressive that reviewers never failed to mention it. The duo performed the latest raggy songs, such as "Casey Jones" and "Oceana Roll," but Roberts wrote much of their material himself, including some piano specialties. He would later tell a reporter that he began taking opium around this time to reduce the "brain fag" of writing songs.

Although the giant Orpheum chain was headquartered in San Francisco, Lloyd and Roberts could not get a hearing there. In the spring of 1911 they booked seven weeks on the rival Keith circuit in the Northeast, playing New York City, Brooklyn, Hartford, Buffalo, and Philadelphia. Having made a name for themselves out of town, the local boys were welcomed home with a booking at the San Francisco Orpheum in early September. Their reception made them welcome at Orpheum theatres for two years to come. In December 1911 two of Roberts's piano specialties, "Joy Rag" and "Jay Roberts' Rag," were issued by Forster Music of Chicago and touted as compositions by "The California Ragtime King."

Another Roberts rag, the one that made his name as player and composer, would be published by Forster the following year. "The Entertainer's Rag" was the first, and gaudiest, of the showoff pieces that Roberts wrote for the act. It was originally published in September 1910 by Pacific Coast Music Company of Oakland (which was probably Lloyd and Roberts themselves). It is extremely progressive for its time, and the most difficult to play of all the rags that have ever

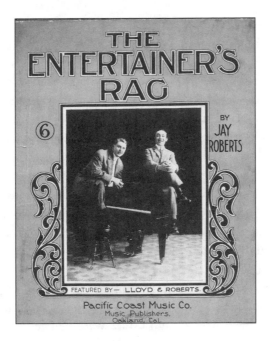

"The Entertainer's Rag"

achieved wide popularity, but players still find its effect on audiences worth the effort required to master it.

"The Entertainer's Rag" was obviously designed to bring down the house, which it is still capable of doing. There are six melodic themes in it, all lushly chorded, all scampering the width of the keyboard. Roberts builds excitement by the use of four-bar, fanfarelike intros within the number and with breaks played in octaves. An eight-bar theme, in which "Yankee Doodle" is played underneath a relentlessly syncopating right hand, is not only tricky in itself, it foretells more trickiness to come. One strain and one key change later, it comes, with "Yankee Doodle" striding along in the left hand as "Dixie" simultaneously rings out from the right. The rag ends with a maestoso section (marked "Largo") that suggests a duet by left-hand tympani and right-hand flutes. Only the vaudeville vernacular does it justice: "The Entertainer's Rag" is a socko number.

Forster Music bought the Pacific Coast copyright and reissued "The Entertainer's Rag" in 1912. It got a few recordings, but its widest renown came from piano roll versions (roll-makers didn't actually have to play it). Roberts said that he received $3,500 from its sale and that he eventually made "about $65,000" from its publishing and mechanical rights. Both of these sums seem wildly inflated, although Roberts was undeniably living beyond the means of a vaudeville accompanist in the early teens. He invested in San Francisco restaurants; he hung out with sports, including some professional ones, like the black heavyweight champion Jack Johnson. Another expensive passion—aviation—seized him around 1915. He bought a plane, and by 1916 he was listing himself in the San Francisco city directory as an aviator. He gave exhibitions of stunt flying, and, at one of these in Seattle, he met Grace Rodgers, the girl he would soon marry.

The San Francisco police began to have dark suspicions about where Roberts's money was coming from, and at 2:00 A.M. on July 16, 1916—twelve days after he and Grace were married—they raided the newlyweds' home. They found a small box of opium, a bottle containing an opium-brandy solution, and a vial of heroin. The police thoughtfully brought along a photographer from the San Francisco *Examiner* to get a picture of the "perp walk" after the arrest. Jay Roberts, pasty-faced and bleary-eyed—but snappily dressed in jacket, tie, and cap—is on the left, and in the center, being led out by detectives, is C. M. Davis, Roberts's airplane mechanic. Davis's trunk was found in the Roberts house, and it held items that could be construed as burglar tools (by the police) or as a detective kit (by Davis). Grace Roberts was not marched out with the suspects, but the *Examiner* ran a photo of her sitting in Roberts's plane when it broke the story the next day.

Although the amount of drugs confiscated did not indicate anything beyond a pathetic habit of their owner, the arresting agents were quick to speculate for the press. Roberts had made unscheduled flights to Mexico, they said, probably to get opium for resale in California. He was also probably smuggling arms and ammunition to Pancho Villa. Roberts was contrite, saying, "I swear that I've tried to quit the hop." He was charged with possession of opium and released on $100 bail. If the case ever came to trial, it was not recorded by the *Examiner*.

The arrest diminished Roberts's life. There would be no more high living for him, no more real estate, no more unscheduled trips to Mexico. The sporting world, because of embarrassment or wariness, turned its back on him. The 1917 city directory found him and Grace living with his mother, but Grace vanished from the directory, and from Roberts, in 1919. Forsaking all conventionality, he would spend the rest of his life wandering.

Roberts became a piano player again, not on the vaudeville stage this time, but in bars. He played around Oakland, drifted to Alaska, and, some said, to Europe. In 1921 he passed through Panama, and in 1923 he took up residence there. He worked at one club in Balboa for four years, took supplemental jobs in the Canal Zone, and was occasionally heard on Panamanian radio.

On July 28, 1932, Jay Roberts killed himself with a .38 revolver in his room above a store in Panama City. Beside his body were found a sealed letter to his mother and a suicide note. The *Panama American* printed the note in full. He said goodbye to two of his Panamanian friends, and he expressed a wish to be cremated. As for his reasons to take his own life, he wrote, "Just tired of life and pain. Insomnia, knotting muscles, and nervousness. Really, it is a long story, but that is enough for you to know. . . ."

RAY SOLADAY

The first flickers of ragtime in the West occurred in, of all places, South Dakota. O. H. Andersen, from Redfield, had his "Dakota Rag" published by S. Brainard's Sons in Chicago in 1899. The first rag published in the West was "South Dakota Rag," issued in Canova by its composer, Joseph Liljenberg, in February 1902.

A 1915 rag by Ray Soladay, of Fulton, is like the output of his South Dakota predecessors and like that of most rag writers: it is a talented amateur's sole syncopated work; it carries a local reference in its title; and it was made to sell in his hometown. There were more sparrows than peacocks in ragtime's aviary, and Soladay typifies the ordinary bird who once, and only once, had a ragtime itch.

Ray Stewart Soladay was born in Lena, a small town in the northwest corner of Illinois, in 1892. His father, Arthur William Soladay, moved the family to Fulton, South Dakota, in 1905, and Ray completed

Ray Soladay, third from right, in 1914 orchestra

elementary school there. There would be no more formal schooling for the boy, but he took correspondence courses in music and bookkeeping in his teens. Ray worked for three years as a printer's apprentice at the local newspaper for $25 per month. In February 1913 Arthur Soladay, seeking a drier climate to relieve his tuberculosis, took his brood to Carlsbad, New Mexico. The following month Ray purchased the Carlsbad Bottling Works (probably with help from his father) and set himself up in business.

The young newcomer mingled easily in Carlsbad's social and church life. He played in the local band and orchestra, he taught Sunday School at the Methodist church, and he was elected president of the Epworth League. It was a sad surprise to the town when he left, two days after marrying Ethel Stephenson in November 1914, to return to Fulton to become a farmer.

Soladay farmed for three years, but he kept his hand in music during that time, giving lessons in violin, cornet, and piano. In September 1915, the Fulton *Advocate*'s printshop, where he had apprenticed as a boy, published Ray Soladay's "Corn Palace Rag." It is a lively number and easy to play, its only quirks being a few flashes of minor harmonies. Its trio is marchlike, with melody in the left hand and offbeats in the right.

The original edition of "Corn Palace Rag" is prized now more for its cover than for its music. The sheet carries a striking photograph of one of America's oddest buildings. The Corn Palace was built in Mitchell, South Dakota, in 1892 to house an agricultural exhibition, and it was the state's main tourist attraction before the carving of Mount Rushmore. It is comprised of eight Moorish-looking towers of varying heights, seven onion domes and one pyramid, all topped with banners on flagpoles. If the structure itself is exotic, its decoration is outright bizarre. The Palace is covered with murals showing scenes of South Dakota life, and the medium in which they are done is grain. In the autumn the exterior is stripped, and thousands of bushels of multi-colored corn kernels, cobs, oats, and milo are stuck on to make new pictures. Inside, tapestries made from shucks, stalks, and grasses cover the walls. The Corn Palace looks like it was designed by a committee of medieval Turkish architects and painted by Roy Lichtenstein.

A job offer from the Wells-Fargo Express Company lured Ray and Ethel Soladay back to Carlsbad late in 1917. The following year he became director of the town's municipal and junior bands, a position he would hold until 1938. In September 1922 he retitled his "Corn Palace Rag" and offered it to the newspaper, the Carlsbad *Current*, for publication. "The Pecos Valley Rag-Two Step" ran in three installments, beginning September 29, and readers were assured that they would "appreciate the number as much for its authorship as for the beauty of the piece itself."

Until his death in 1960 Ray Soladay served Carlsbad as businessman and booster. He was a member of the city council from 1924 to 1932, and a mainstay of the Rotary Club and the First Methodist Church for decades. After he left his job as agent for Wells-Fargo, he became postmaster. He was what they used to call an upstanding citizen, and he lived the kind of life that would have horrified Jay Roberts.

NACIO HERB BROWN

Nacio Herb Brown was one of the most important composers for films during the first decade in which movies sang. He wrote only two rags, but both of them were hits. Although musical films had little use for ragtime, it was these rags that got his toe in MGM's door. A local composer with national hits had to be given a try. Brown walked through the door that ragtime opened and made himself at home. His string of successful movie songs was unmatched by anyone in the all-talking, all-singing era.

Brown was born in Deming, New Mexico, in 1896, and he moved to Los Angeles with his family at age eight. During his years at Musical Arts High School, his father became a deputy sheriff of L.A. County. After his musical schooling, Brown did what any gifted pianist with a penchant for pop would do: he became a vaudeville singer's accompanist. He toured California's Orpheum theatres for a year, backing the vocal stylings of Alice Doll, and he hated it. He saw the vaudeville route as a rambling and ill-marked road, and he knew there was not necessarily a pot of gold at the end of it. As soon as he had saved enough money, he returned to Los Angeles and opened a tailor shop.

The tailoring business was small, but it quickly attracted an elite clientele. In the late teens Brown and his seamstresses clothed Hollywood royalty, including Charlie Chaplin, Rudolph Valentino, and Wallace Reid. Brown was still dabbling in music during this time, occasionally submitting songs to Sherman, Clay in San Francisco, the largest nearby publisher. In 1920 Sherman, Clay gave him his first publication, a song called "Coral Sea" (with lyrics by King Zany). As prominent bandleaders passed through Los Angeles, Brown offered them custom-made outfits in return for plugging his songs. When Paul Whiteman recorded "Coral Sea" in October 1920, he may have been wearing a Brown suit.

The tailor shop made Brown a small fortune, and in the early 1920s, he decided to risk it in hope of making a larger one. Noticing the boom in Hollywood property, he opened a real estate office. The stars who had given Brown their tailoring trade began to list their houses with him. Looking like a movie star himself, the suave, mustachioed realtor strolled his properties with the famous, showing them Mission-style mansions and supplying the exact dimensions of swimming pools.

In his heyday as a real estate mogul, Brown kept up his secret musical life, still sending submissions to Sherman, Clay. In 1927 the company published the piece that would blow his cover by making him nationally known as a composer.

The number was "Doll Dance," a Novelty Lite rag that listeners couldn't get enough of in the late twenties. "Doll Dance" has only two melodies, and none of the rhythmic kick of Confrey's and Straight's work, but it is one of the few rags that is easily danced to, and it is so good-natured that it can still bring a smile. Sherman, Clay plugged it heavily, and it began to get band recordings (by Carl Fenton, Sam Lanin, and Nat Shilkret) in March 1927. Pianists soon took it up, and it was off on its career. The piano duo of Constance Mering and Muriel Pollock recorded it in April, Rube Bloom in June, and, best of all, Frank Banta (using the pseudonym "Jimmy Andrews") in August. Its takeoff was so strong that its publisher saw the chance to issue a song version. Brown himself supplied the words, and "Doll Dance" became the song hit of a 1927 stage show, the *Hollywood Music Box Revue*.

Sherman, Clay wanted another just like "Doll Dance," and in 1928 Brown produced "Rag Doll." Brown's second "doll rag" sold about a half million copies, a smash by any standard in 1928, but it did not approach the sales of his first. Brown was still a realtor, but he was a realtor with a very lucrative sideline.

In 1929, as MGM was about to take the plunge and make its first all-sound musical, Nacio Herb Brown, the best known composer in Los Angeles, was asked by Irving Thalberg, the studio's production chief, to write its score. He was teamed with Arthur Freed, a lyricist from Charleston, South Carolina, and they delivered three hits in *The Broadway Melody*: "You Were Meant for Me," "Broadway Melody," and "The Wedding of the Painted Doll." *Broadway Melody* was a great success, starting a vogue for backstage musicals and winning the Academy Award for best picture of 1929. For MGM's *Hollywood Revue* that same year, Brown and Freed came up with their biggest song, "Singin' in the Rain," which was introduced by Cliff Edwards and the studio's top stars in slickers, with Brown himself at the piano, just out of range of the shower provided by the special effects department. Finally, after two hit rags and four hit songs, Nacio Brown rethought his career: maybe he wasn't a realtor who wrote music, maybe he was a composer who sold real estate.

Brown and Freed were both signed to MGM, and their hits continued in a steady stream: "Pagan Love Song" (in *The Pagan*, 1929), "Should I?" (in *Lord Byron of Broadway*, 1929), "Paradise" (in *A Woman Commands, 1931*), "Temptation" (in *Going Hollywood*, 1933), "All I Do Is Dream of You" (in *Sadie McKee*, 1934), and "You Are My Lucky Star" (in *Broadway Melody of 1936*, 1935).

Real estate beckoned again in the early 1940s, and Brown began to deal in property once more. He lived in Mexico for a few years and returned to Los Angeles in 1948. In 1952 his early film songs were used to make what is generally considered the best movie musical of all time, *Singin' in the Rain*. A full sixty of the film's 103 minutes are given to music, most of it by Brown and Freed. Their last song together, "Make 'Em Laugh," was written for *Singin' in the Rain*. Although Brown had not stayed with ragtime, it took him where he needed to go.

SAN FRANCISCO
The Best Dollar Dinner on Earth

By 1880, when the city was less than forty years old, San Francisco was already considered the most cosmopolitan of American cities. Its physical and architectural charms were undeniable, even to the snootiest of visitors from the Old World. Its reputation was that of a food-loving, fashion-conscious, high-living place, without airs or affectations. San Franciscans liked fine things, and if quality cost more, many of them were willing—and extremely able—to pay for it. There was no new money/old money schism in its society, for all of its money was new, or at least recent. And the money was made in *American* ways: through pluck, luck, and the hard work of pioneering. Many of those with vast fortunes could remember empty pockets not so long ago, and the memory gave an anchor to their urbanity. San Francisco was elegant and down-to-earth at the same time.

San Francisco began in 1776, as an unnamed settlement nestled between the Presidio, a military outpost, and a Catholic mission. During the 1820s, when California was claimed by Mexico, the settlement grew to number its residents in the dozens. In 1835 the place was finally given a name, Yerba Buena, for the locally grown "good herb" with which its residents made tea. The area was occupied by the U.S. army and navy during the Mexican War in 1846, and the war's outcome left all of California under American jurisdiction. The following year Yerba Buena, with a population of around a hundred, changed its name to San Francisco. In January 1848 gold was discovered on the Sacramento Valley property of Captain John A. Sutter, and the face and future of northern California was transformed overnight.

By May 1848 over 2,000 uninvited guests had overrun the Sutter property, straining pans of mud from every stream and turning over every rock and clod of dirt, looking for gold. Just enough grains of gold were found to keep the rumors of riches flying and to keep the wild-eyed invaders coming. As gold fever spread across the region, San Francisco ballooned from hamlet to metropolis. In 1849 more than 40,000 prospectors (fewer than 300 of them women) came to San Francisco, which had, by default, become their supply center.

Most of the gold diggers had left home in a hurry, and their packing had been minimal. They needed everything, and local merchants found that they would pay almost anything to get it. Apples sold for $1 each, flour was $40 a barrel, and a dozen eggs was a bargain at $10. A shovel cost $25, and a butcher knife, $30. A saucepan was $5, a blanket, $40. Those who wanted to homestead found pioneering expensive: a twenty-foot plank cost $20, and bricks were $1 each. A pound of gold (valued at $16 an ounce in 1848) bought a pound of iron tacks. Those who sought alcoholic or pharmaceutical relief from the crazy prices found that this too came high: a quart of whiskey cost $30, and laudanum was $1 a drop. More fortunes were made by gouging the deluded than by finding gold.

By 1850 San Francisco, with a permanent population of about 25,000, was undeniably a city, and it incorporated as such. Most cities took decades to grow, but the gold rush had robbed San Francisco of its childhood and adolescence. Many of the city's homes, shops, hotels, and saloons were tents and shacks, but they were owned by wealthy people who were too busy making money to build anything permanent. When gold fever cooled, the city was ready to see what its money could buy. In the quarter century that followed its incorporation, San Francisco methodically went first-class in its development and in its taste. America's youngest large city became its most elegant.

Railroad and real estate barons—Huntington, Stanford, Hopkins, Crocker—built great mansions on Nob Hill. The aptly named, 1,000-room Palace Hotel arose in 1875. The first exhibition of electric lights took place on the roof of St. Ignatius College on July 4, 1876, and the city's pretty streets were lit with them soon after. Night shopping became a vogue. Kearny Street, the "Broadway of San Francisco," kept its stores open until 10:00 P.M. Cable cars, the city's unique combination of mass transit and thrill ride, began to swoop over its hills in 1873. By 1879 San Franciscans were talking with each other over the telephone.

Many San Franciscans could afford to travel, and those who took the Grand Tour came home with a taste for French cooking. Restaurants, such as Marchaud's, the Maison Dorée, and the Maison Riche, opened to accommodate them. A complex dinner of many courses could be had for what a miner had paid for a plate of beans thirty years earlier. The city's favorite French restaurant, the Poodle Dog, advertised "The Best Dollar Dinner on Earth." Each of the first-class saloons invented a powerful specialty cocktail and kept its recipe a secret. The Bonanza, the Black Velvet, the Stone Wall, and, especially, the renowned Pisco Punch set many a diner to nodding over his elaborate French meal.

During its hasty maturation San Francisco became known as the best show town in America. The city loved entertainments, high and low, and show troupes working their way west would play any number of decrepit town halls along the way to get there. The first large theatre, the California, was erected in 1869 on Bush Street near Kearny, and within a few years its competition included Morosco's Grand Opera House (which boasted the largest chandelier in the United States) and the first vaudeville palaces in the West, the Orpheum (built in 1887 on O'Farrell Street) and the Tivoli (on Eddy).

International stars, such as Dame Nellie Melba, Emma Calvé, Enrico Caruso, Adelina Patti, Henry Irving, and Ellen Terry, made frequent stops in San Francisco in the 1880s and 1890s, as did American stage royalty: Maurice Barrymore, Edwin Booth, and James O'Neill. San Franciscans were loyal to the variety performers Lotta Crabtree and Emma Nevada, who had entertained many of them at torch-lit shows in mining camps a generation earlier. In the early 1890s Bert Williams and George Walker were in residence with a San Francisco minstrel troupe. Not yet ready to turn pro in the early nineties, the teenaged Isadora Duncan was teaching dancing in her family's house on Van Ness Avenue, and chubby Elsa Maxwell was playing piano and singing naughty songs at neighborhood parties.

San Francisco's love for music, like its other cultural enthusiasms, was indulged during the city's remarkable spurt of growth. The first piano in town was ordered from the East by General M. G. Vallejo in 1843. By 1850 there were enough piano players to need a music shop, and so a music dealer and publisher, Joseph F. Atwill, opened a San Francisco branch of his New York store at 158 Washington Street. Atwill published a few local-interest numbers (such as "The California Pioneers" and "The San Francisco Quadrilles"), and he was followed by several other dealers who dabbled in publishing.

Unlike that of most cities, San Francisco's popular music scene was not energized by its red-light district in the ragtime era. The notorious "Coast" (bounded by Dupont, Broadway, and Clay streets) was wiped out by the fires that followed the earthquake of 1906, before San Francisco had taken up ragtime to any degree. (Ferde Grofé, the most famous piano-playing alumnus of the Coast, wrote two novelty rags in the 1920s.) The best known of the early San Francisco rags was Wally Herzer's "Everybody Two-Step," published by its composer in 1910. The best of them was "Meadow Lark Rag," written by the black pianist Tom Pitts and published in San Francisco by Charles N. Daniels in 1916. Another fine number, Sydney K. Russell's "Too Much Raspberry," was published in nearby Berkeley the same year.

Although San Francisco was by no means ragtime crazy, it was a good market for sheet music, and in the teens and twenties many Eastern publishers established branches there. In the late 1920s the building at 935 Market Street, with its dozen or so publisher occupants, was known as the "Tin Pan Alley of the West." Another San Francisco publishing company was too big for a cubbyhole on Market Street, however. It was the city's greatest musical success story, a local operation that flourished on the corner of Kearny and Sutter streets for over a hundred years.

SHERMAN, CLAY AND COMPANY

Leander S. Sherman (1847–1926), the son of a Boston cabinetmaker, arrived in San Francisco at age fourteen and immediately apprenticed himself to a jeweler. He learned to repair watches and clocks, and when he took a second job, at A. A. Rosenberg's music store, his skill was adapted to the repairing of music boxes. As he always would, Leander worked hard and saved his money, and in 1870 he was able to buy the Rosenberg stock and set up his own tiny music shop at the corner of Kearny and Sutter. Needing capital, he took in F. A. Hyde as partner in 1871, and the store operated as Sherman & Hyde for five years.

Sherman's banker, Clement C. Clay, an ex-Tennessean who kept his Civil War rank—"Major"—in front of his name, noticing the large and frequent deposits made by Sherman & Hyde, decided to join Sherman in the music business. In 1876 Major Clay bought out Hyde, and Sherman, Clay & Company was born. With Clay acting as financier, Sherman as merchant, and an Italian harp as its logo, the company quickly became a force in San Francisco's musical life. By the early 1880s there was no larger or more active music store in town. Sherman, Clay began its own line of pianos, and when a pipe organ manufacturer defaulted on his debt, the company took over his factory and manufactured those instruments for several years.

The first of many branch stores opened in 1883, at Grant Avenue and Market Street. In 1892 Sherman, Clay bought out Mathias Gray Company (which had previously bought out Joseph F. Atwill, San Francisco's first music dealer). With the purchase of Gray, the company acquired the San Francisco franchise as agent for Steinway pianos. In mid-year 1892 Sherman, Clay incorporated for $1 million, with its founder as president and Major Clay as vice-president. Another important distributorship came in the late 1890s, when Sherman, Clay became the exclusive Pacific Coast agent for Victor Talking Machines.

Sherman, Clay acquired copyrights (some of them going back to the Atwill era) when it took over Mathias Gray, but it reissued few of these locally published numbers. It was not until the late 1890s that

Sherman, Clay decided to activate its publishing arm. The tentative nature of this decision was shown by the hiring of an eighteen-year-old, Edward P. Little, to effect it. Although he would not have nationally known hits for twenty years, Little would stay at his post until his death in 1932, and his obituary in *Variety* would call him "the dean of western music publishing." It was Little who found San Francisco's first rag, Sydney S. Barker's "Johnny Jump-Ups," published by Sherman, Clay in 1905.

Edward P. Little

In the early twentieth century Sherman, Clay began to expand its empire beyond San Francisco. In 1902 Fresno got a Sherman, Clay store, and Tacoma, Washington, got one in 1905. With all of its activities humming, from piano sales to mandolin repair, the company expanded and reorganized again, adding the bosses' sons, Frederick R. Sherman and Philip T. Clay, to its board of directors. Major Clay died in 1905, and after a respectful pause in his memory, the company went back to its growing business. Sherman and Clay had created a musical monolith that seemed unshakable, but at 5:12 A.M. (PST) on April 18, 1906, it, along with the rest of San Francisco, was shaken badly.

Leander Sherman was in New York on business when the earthquake hit. A few minutes before 1:00 P.M. on April 18, he received a wire from his son:

> Terrible earthquake, fires, no water. Broken glass our only damage. Business will be paralyzed. Advise cancel all orders for present. Will give further details later.

At first it seemed that the damage to Sherman, Clay was minor. Its treasurer, Leonard George, on being awakened by the first rumble, had

run to the office and removed the books and business records. It took
three loads in a rented one-horse wagon (with each trip more expensive
than the last), but by 10:00 A.M. all the company's files were safe in
George's home. If the fires could be contained, Sherman, Clay would be
all right. But they could not be contained. The nearby Palace Hotel
burned steadily through the day, and surrounding buildings lay in heaps
of ashes by noon. The blaze made its way to Sherman, Clay, and during
the evening, the building and all its stock were lost. Leander Sherman
wired his son from New York on April 20:

> I return San Francisco tonight. We can work Coast trade from
> Oakland and Portland. Keep up your courage and brace up the boys.

Sherman, Clay moved its operations to the Oakland store and filled
what orders it could from the Oakland stock. A temporary office was
opened in Philip Clay's home, and, using the records saved by Leonard
George, the company began to sort out its business. (Philip Clay's own
piano and talking machine were sold to fill an order.) In the fall a
Sherman, Clay store opened at 1635 Van Ness, in the new business district that was rising to supplant the old, charred one. In December the
Steinway company sent twelve complimentary grand pianos to
Sherman, Clay as a Christmas present, "a token of our appreciation of
your splendid business in Steinway pianos."

Late in 1907 a magnificent new Sherman, Clay building arose at
the old location, on the corner of Kearny and Sutter. It was the first
major construction to be completed in the rebuilt downtown area, and
all of the company's enterprises were gathered into its eight floors (plus
mezzanine and basement). It was less like an office building than like a
small city unto itself, a city that trafficked in music and nothing else.
Salesrooms, stockrooms, soundproof demonstration rooms, an entire
floor of player pianos, sheet music, a department for talking machines,
records, and rolls, a recital hall—Sherman, Clay offered it all, along
with rest rooms and public telephones. A rent-free ticket concession
counter was provided to those promoting local concerts and musical
events. A browser in the sheet music department might run into Ignace
Paderewski, Leopold Godowski, or Edward MacDowell, among the
many artists who were frequent browsers themselves. Satellite stores—

in San Jose, Spokane, Sacramento, Los Angeles, Stockton, and Vallejo—sprang up to make Sherman, Clay the most successful and far-reaching musical enterprise west of the Mississippi. Professional offices opened in New York, Chicago, Detroit, and Denver.

So far, publishing had been the sluggard among the Sherman, Clay interests, but even that branch felt the company's momentum in the mid-teens. There were enough outlets to guarantee at least break-even sales for almost anything, and it was time to take advantage of them. Ed Little began to go after pop music that would sell anywhere, not just in San Francisco. Sherman, Clay's 1916 publication of Chris Smith's "San Francisco Blues" exemplified the company's hopes for some really popular pop music. The song seemed to be a triple threat: it was a fox-trot (currently the vogue in social dancing), with the city's name as well as *blues* in its title. "San Francisco Blues" did not set the world afire, but it indicated a new direction to Ed Little's acquisitions. Sherman, Clay would have its near misses for a while, but an impressive string of hits came, beginning in 1920, the year that Leander Sherman retired from his presidency of the company to become its chairman of the board.

Ben Black, the head of Sherman, Clay's professional department, moonlighted as banjoist in Art Hickman's orchestra at the St. Francis Hotel, and it was probably through Black that Hickman began to publish with the company. In 1918 Sherman, Clay bought the copyright of "Rose Room," a Hickman instrumental originally self-published in 1917, and got Harry Williams to write a lyric for it. "Rose Room" would become a standard during the big-band era, but it stumbled in the short run, as did another future Sherman standard, a 1920 song called "Do You Ever Think of Me?"

Art Hickman was invited to New York to record for Columbia in September 1919, and he brought with him a song that he had written with Ben Black called "Hold Me." Hickman's record began to take off in the winter, and Sherman, Clay published "Hold Me" early in 1920. Finally, the record/song sheet symbiosis had occurred in San Francisco, giving a hit to a local bandleader and a local publisher. Jerome Remick bought "Hold Me" from Sherman, Clay late in 1920, and, thanks to Remick's muscle, the song became a late addition to that year's *Ziegfeld Follies* score.

The company had another big song in 1920, from Paul Whiteman's August recording of "Whispering," by the Schonberger brothers, John and Malvin. Sherman, Clay's capital stock increased to $4 million in 1921, and rose to $7 million two years later. The publishing division was, for the first time, a major contributor to its parent's good fortune.

In 1923 the company got a hit from an unlikely source, an old-time composer named Adam Geibel. Geibel had had one previous hit ("Kentucky Babe," in 1896), and most of his catalog consisted of kindergarten and glee club songs. He had been blind since babyhood, and now, at nearly seventy, he was in his thirty-eighth year as organist at the John B. Stetson Mission Sunday School. Geibel submitted the manuscript of a waltz song called "Sleep" to Sherman, Clay, and it was signed with a pseudonym, "Earl Lebieg." In one of his smartest moves, Ed Little bought it. Fred Waring and His Pennsylvanians recorded "Sleep" in October 1923 (with another Sherman, Clay song, "The West, a Nest and You," on the other side), and the record's success led to the band's adopting it as its closing theme. Waring's band, one of the rowdiest of the 1920s, used "Sleep" to end its revels for the rest of the decade. During his later years on radio, a more sedate Waring used "Sleep" to send his elderly audience to bed.

Ed Little had done well by following the fads, so he kept following them. He tried some pop blues in the early twenties ("Teddy Bear Blues," "Ozark Blues," "Rock-a-Bye My Baby Blues"), some "state" songs ("Louisiana," "California Lullaby," "I Love You, California"), and even a Charleston ("Hayfoot-Strawfoot Charleston"). Movie themes by Erno Rapee and Lew Pollack brought Sherman, Clay two near-million sellers: "Charmaine" (featured in *What Price Glory?* in 1926) and "Diane" (in *Seventh Heaven*, 1927). The popularity of novelty rags led Sherman, Clay to try one, Bernard Barnes's "Dainty Miss," in 1924. Barnes's "Dainty Doll" was published ten years later; both of his "dainty"rags still remain in print. Nacio Herb Brown's "Doll Dance" (1927) and "Rag Doll" (1928) were the company's only hit rags. The company's publishing began to wane in the late 1920s, and an undistinguished output of the early 1930s finished it off ("The Wedding of the Birds," "If I Can't Have Anna in Cuba, Then I'll See Esther in Spain").

Leander Sherman died in 1926, but his rock-solid organization did not falter. In 1932 the Sherman heirs bought out the interest of the

Bernard Barnes

"Dainty Doll"

Clay heirs in the corporation, and five years later, ownership passed completely to the Sherman family. Sherman, Clay rode out the Depression by closing several of its smaller stores and by discontinuing its higher-priced items (radios, phonographs, and amateur moviemaking equipment). During World War II the company did its bit by becoming a giant clearinghouse for musical instruments given by the public for military personnel. Sherman, Clay donated the services of its repair shop to refurbishing the instruments and sent them, without charge, to bases in Europe and the Pacific. After the war the company saw great expansion, and in 1949 Clay Sherman, Leander's grandson, was named president. At this writing, Sherman, Clay & Company is still serving the musical needs of San Francisco.

DALLAS

The Cowtown with Manners

Although French traders from Louisiana had visited the Caddos's tribal lands in east Texas since the early eighteenth century, it was not until 1841 that a white settler decided to put down roots there. John Neeley Bryan, an Arkansan, claimed his piece of the Republic of Texas by erecting a hut on the banks of the Trinity River that year, and he induced three families to join him in his adventure a year later. Texas joined the Union in 1846, and, early in the statewide demarcation process, the cluster of pioneers around the Trinity were informed that they were now residents of the seat of Dallas County. The progression from outpost to county seat was fast but orderly. There was a stability to Dallas from its beginnings, and its growth through the rest of the nineteenth century, while eventful, would not be tumultuous. Dallas was woolly but not wild.

In 1849 two bellwethers of civilization arrived in Dallas on the same oxcart: the town's first printing press and its first piano. The cultural tone of the area got another lift in 1854, when about 350 French,

Belgian, and Swiss socialist-intellectuals arrived (by way of New Orleans), looking for a place to set up a Utopian colony. They chose a location about four miles west of Dallas to begin the experiment in communal living that they called La Reunion. The Europeans were good at painting pictures, writing political tracts, and making music—good at everything, in fact, except homesteading. They gave up trying to live off the land after three years and moved into town, bringing their books, art, and musical instruments with them.

Dallas incorporated as a town in 1856, and as a city in 1871. Its commercial traffic was four-legged (horses pulling stagecoaches and cattle on their way to market) until 1872, the year that the Houston and Texas Central railroad came. The iron horse did not displace the flesh-and-blood horse by any means, but it brought the city's first boom in trade. By 1873, the year that the Texas and Pacific line arrived, the population had doubled (to 6,000, from 3,000 in 1872). By 1886 six rail lines had converged in Dallas, and the city (now at 30,000) was the Southwest's clearinghouse for wheat, wool, sheep, and cattle. Dallas's first cotton mill, built in 1886, added another commodity to the list of those that needed hauling in and out of town.

In the late nineteenth century the fortunes made by cattle barons, like C. C. Slaughter and J. B. Wilson, began to manifest themselves in grand homes and gracious living. (The *Dallas Red Book*, a local social register, was first issued in 1895.) The city's hospitality was legendary and lavish. Invitations might have been extended as "y'all come," but what they often implied was "y'all come to the mansion." Professional decorators were often called in to make the grand grander, and everybody knew what society columnist Mrs. Hugh Nugent Fitzgerald meant when she wrote that "Mrs. [Jules] Schneider has one of the most beautiful interiors in Dallas."

Much show business traffic came through Dallas, along with the cotton and cows. Field's Theatre, the city's first large performance hall, was built in 1872, and it quickly became a mandatory stop for acting troupes. The San Francisco–based Orpheum chain franchised a Dallas Orpheum, which was the city's main vaudeville house until the opening of the Majestic, at Commerce and St. Paul streets, in 1905. The Ella B. Moore Theatre, at 428 Central Avenue, was a major link on the Theatre Owners' Booking Association's black vaudeville chain. The great catchall was the Dallas Opera House, which hosted stage plays—the Dandy Dixie Minstrels, Black Patti's Troubadours, Cole and Johnson's *The Shoo-Fly Regiment*—and even the occasional opera.

From the 1880s into the ragtime era, a vice industry wove its way through Dallas. The red-light enclave was originally in the area of Houston and Young streets (near the site of the later Union Terminal Railroad Station), then it moved eastward to Record Street, where Clara Barclay, Kitty Wilson, and Fanny Harris were among the most prosperous madams. The sporting neighborhood next gravitated to lower McKinney Avenue, with a satellite of sin on a short stretch of Emma Street (now Federal Street), just off St. Paul. On Griffin Street, in the McKinney area known as "Frog Town," there was a sort of weekly trade show, a parade of whores on horseback. To Dallas males, the only shocking thing about this sight was that they rode astride the horses, not sidesaddle as ladies should.

"Deep Ellum," the black amusement and shopping district on Elm Street, between Preston and Good, was where the city's hottest pianists were to be heard. Like their counterparts in New Orleans's Storyville, they all played a little ragtime, but no one was a purist about it. They doctored it with blues, with walking bass lines, with much improvisation. It wasn't the genuine article, but who cared? It was Texas piano, a pretty good thing in itself.

BUSH & GERTS

There were no full-time music publishers in Texas during the ragtime era. A composer could issue his work through a music store, or he could publish it himself. The most important Texas-born composer, Scott Joplin, left his native state as a teenager and published none of his rags there. Euday Bowman, second only to Joplin in importance among the native-born, published most of his work himself in Ft. Worth, occasionally selling copyrights and new pieces to J. W. Jenkins in Kansas City. So the three dozen or so published Texas rags (more than half of them by women, higher than the female-male ragtime ratio of any other state) came from ragtime's grass roots, amateurs who were in love with the music. "Amateur" does not necessarily mean "untalented," and this is especially true of Texas rags. Lone Star ragtime is extremely pianistic and full of gusto. It is great fun to hear and play, and there is no artiness in it.

The first and most important of the Texas music store-publishers was Thomas Goggan & Bros., which began its operation in Galveston in 1866. Goggan opened its first branch in Houston, and by the end of the nineteenth century, there were Goggan stores in Dallas, San Antonio, and Waco. Several rags appeared under its imprint, along with some blues and parlor pieces in the teens. San Antonio Music Company purchased the Goggan sheet music department in 1931, but the company remained in business as a jobber well into the 1940s.

The Bush & Gerts Piano Company of Texas, although its publishing was short-lived, was more committed to ragtime than Goggan. In two years as publisher, Bush & Gerts issued about a third of the Texas rags. Founded by W. L. Bush and Richard Gerts (who had designed pianos for the Mason & Hamlin company), the company was headquartered in the center of Dallas's musical activity, in Bush Temple, at 1311–1313 Elm Street. There were fourteen music teachers in the building in 1912 (nine of them piano teachers), most of them on the faculty of the Bush Temple Conservatory. The studio pianos that they used were no doubt from the Bush & Gerts line.

Bush & Gerts got into publishing late in 1912, issuing two songs by William Renick Smith and a reprint of a Clarence Woods rag, "Slippery Elm," which had been previously published by its composer. In 1913 two more rags appeared under the company's imprint. These two copyrights were retained by the composers, M. Kendree Miller and Margaret Agnew White, which may indicate that the writers paid Bush & Gerts to publish their work. The company also issued a landmark of Texas blues, Leroy (Lasses) White's "Nigger Blues," that same year.

In 1914 Bush & Gerts issued eight rags, the most from any Western publisher in a single year. The company owned five of the eight copyrights, which means that most of them were bought and paid for. Bush & Gerts's distribution was mostly to its five stores, so none of the firm's fine rags came to national attention through performers' plugs or recordings. As abruptly as Bush & Gerts began ragtime publishing, the company abandoned it. There are no more Bush & Gerts rags after

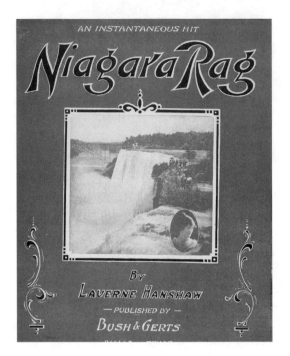

"Niagara Rag"

Billie Talbot's "Imperial Rag" of November 1914. The company's treasurer, Joseph Goodpasture, probably convinced its president, W. L. Bush, to pull the plug. The Bush & Gerts rags are treasured today, but by January 1915 they must have looked like an experiment that didn't work.

THE RAGTIME REVIVAL IN THE WEST

The number of published rags in the West was relatively slight—about 120, with California and Texas accounting for about two-thirds of them—but they do not tell the glorious second half of the story, which is that, beginning in the early 1940s, Westerners spawned and shaped fifty years of renewed interest in ragtime. Through festivals, recordings, and publications, Western players, producers, writers, researchers, and fans nurtured an international revival that has by now lasted longer than the era from which its music came. The spark flared toward the end of the big-band years, and it has outlasted a dozen pop trends that succeeded it. It was not doused by rhythm and blues, Elvis, or folkies. It continued to burn during the British invasion, and it survived the neglect of Top 40 radio programmers. It was not daunted by disco. When the ragtime revival is described as a grassroots phenomenon, think crabgrass, the toughest thing in the yard to kill.

This renaissance was not sponsored by academe. People did not listen to ragtime in the early 1940s because they were supposed to. There was no historical aura around the music. It had been out of vogue for only about fifteen years, and, like all old pop forms, it seemed dead as a hammer. The few recorded rags of the late 1930s were on such small, obscure labels as to be practically unobtainable. Only a handful of rags remained in print. "Nostalgia" was not a category in record shops, and "Americana" was not a buzzword, even in art galleries. Ragtime was not yet "classic," but it was no longer "popular." It won its new audiences in the simple way it had won its old ones: musicians liked to play it, and listeners liked to hear it. Lu Watters found when he organized a small band in San Francisco in 1941 that many listeners were, in fact, starved for it.

Lu Watters was a trumpet player from Santa Cruz who had played in various hotel bands and combos throughout the West since he was fifteen. In 1938, at age twenty-seven, he took over the leadership of an eleven-piece dance band at Sweet's Ballroom in Oakland. He was a constantly working musician, firmly established in the Bay Area music scene, and terminally bored with the kind of music he was making. When several of his friends, equally successful and equally dissatisfied, complained about the mush in their band books, Watters decided to do something about it. In a move so audacious that it bordered on professional suicide, he created a band that specialized in old-fashioned styles, and he booked the band into the Dawn Club in San Francisco. The Yerba Buena Jass Band lit into their twenties jazz tunes, cakewalks, and rags, and crowds went wild for it.

The Yerba Buena's fame quickly grew from citywide to regional, so a Los Angeles record company, Jazz Man, came to record them in December 1941. The first two sides they released were "Maple Leaf Rag" and "Black and White Rag," both propelled by the bounding piano of Wally Rose. In March 1942 the group shrank to a quartet to record Rose on "Hot House Rag," "Temptation Rag," and a remake of "Black

Wally Rose at piano with Yerba Buena Jass Band rhythm section

and White." Jazz Man was a small label, but the YB sides eventually made their way around the United States, serving notice that a handful of wild cats in San Francisco were making music the way they used to. Rough-edged pop was an acquired taste in the smoothness era, but, thanks to the records made by Watters and his boys, many acquired it.

Wally Rose created a local demand for period piano, and San Francisco discovered that it had another fine player in the moody, eccentric Paul Lingle. For those San Franciscans who liked their ragtime with the symphonic touch, Professor Albert White created his

Ragtime's biggest selling recording

Gaslight Orchestra in the mid-1940s. Using musicians from the city's symphony, White recorded two LPs of surprisingly gutsy ragtime-era orchestrations on the San Francisco label in the early 1950s.

Military call-ups broke the Yerba Buena's stride, but by 1946 they were back in step. In 1947 they took up residence at Hambone Kelly's, a new club that opened to present them. Lu Watters suffered a stroke in 1950 and left the band business, but his place—and his niche—was quickly filled by his trombonist, Turk Murphy. Murphy's band, featuring the pianist Pete Clute, carried the Watters repertoire, rags and all, through the 1950s, and in 1960 Murphy and Clute opened their own club, Earthquake McGoon's.

Watters's records sold steadily in the late 1940s, but in small numbers. Finally, in 1948, a major label stumbled onto the success that Watters and Jazz Man had been looking for. Capitol Records accidentally discovered that, although there had not been a hit rag recording in twenty years, ragtime could sell records again.

The Pee Wee Hunt band, like several others signed to Capitol, was required to make recordings of half-hour radio shows for the company. These programs, containing music by Capitol artists interspersed with commercials for the latest Capitol releases, were sent free to local stations in the hope that any of their unoccupied time slots might be given over to plugging Capitol records. Early in 1948 Hunt paused in mid-tour to make one of these radio programs in a Nashville recording studio. When the session ended, the engineer told Hunt that he had a few minutes left over if he would like to record something just for fun. The band chose their doo-wacka-doo arrangement of "Twelfth Street Rag," laid it down, had a laugh over it, and left, knowing that Capitol's engineers in Los Angeles would remove it before the program was sent out.

Through an oversight, the tune was not discarded, and the half-corny, half-thrilling "Twelfth Street Rag" popped up, unannounced, at the end of the Hunt show all over the country. Listeners everywhere called in with the same two questions: What was that thing that Pee Wee Hunt had just played? and When could they hear it again? Capitol seized the moment and released Hunt's "Twelfth Street" as a single in May 1948. By late June it had edged onto the *Billboard* charts. It stayed there for thirty-two weeks, in the Number 1 position for eight of them. When Capitol began reissuing its 78 hits on 45s in the early 1950s, "Twelfth Street Rag" scored again in the new format. The recording eventually sold over three million copies and received countless hours of air play. Hunt's hit (and his own and others' imitations of it) melded ragtime and Dixieland so firmly that it would take a generation to pry them apart. However, after its success, ragtime would never be totally absent from record stores again. It took the taint of esoterica off ragtime, as only a smash could have done.

It was Lou Busch who restored the piano to its place at the center of ragtime. Busch, a Kentuckian, was a trained pianist and self-taught arranger who was hired by Capitol Transcription Service in 1946. He supervised the making of radio shows, and he endeared himself to company executives by playing ragtime at their parties. As the fluky "Twelfth Street Rag" lingered on the charts, Capitol's bosses wondered if there was more gold where that came from, and Lou Busch was the obvious choice as prospector. He was promoted to A&R man in May 1949, and he began to pepper the records of Capitol's singers and bands with his ragtime piano choruses and breaks. (Jo Stafford's "Ragtime Cowboy Joe" was a hit, but Ray Anthony's "Spaghetti Rag" was not.) In April 1950 Busch gave himself a jokey pseudonym, Joe "Fingers" Carr, to use on his Capitol recordings. Carr's raggy version of "Sam's Song" spent the summer on the *Billboard* charts.

Late in 1950 Lou Busch created the first all-ragtime LP. It was called *Honky-Tonk Piano*, and it featured eight unnamed numbers, performed by three uncredited solo pianists. (They were Marvin Ash, Ray Turner, and Busch himself.) The company's marketing strategy was bold and brilliant: instead of selling a sound, it sold an *image* of a sound.

Joe "Fingers" Carr

The cover drawing said it all: a shirtsleeved, derby-hatted, suspendered pianist sitting at an ornate upright, pounding it out for a bare-legged, whory-looking showgirl leaning against the piano. The not-so-subliminal message was "This is raunchy and it's fun. That's all you need to know." Coming at the time when the pop charts were at their nadir of blandness, it was a powerful and appealing message. The album was released in four formats (first as a 10-inch LP, then as a 45-rpm double EP, as a four-record 78 rpm set, and as a boxed set of four 45s). *Honky-Tonk Piano* sold well in the United States, and it was a whopping success in Europe. In 1953 four tunes were added to make a 12-inch LP, and orders from England, Germany, and Spain kept it in print for fourteen years.

With "Twelfth Street Rag," Capitol had inadvertently revived ragtime, and now, under Busch's calculated effort, rags became a specialty of the label. Busch (as Carr) made thirty-six ragtime singles and fourteen albums before he went to Warner Brothers Records in 1958. He wrote seventeen rags during his time at Capitol, and six of them were published. Busch did not deal in pastoral classics nor twenties novelties. His repertoire centered on the commercial rags of the teens, the easily accessible, straight-ahead ragtime that anyone could enjoy. His album cover photos show him as the living embodiment of the guy on *Honky-Tonk Piano*.

The steady sales of the Carr records inspired other labels, large and small, to try some ragtime. In 1955 Dot Records had the first million-selling piano single with Johnny Maddox's "Crazy Otto Medley." (The record was a note-for-note copy of an earlier recording made by a German pianist, Otto der Schrage; the first melody heard in the "Medley" was Lou Busch's "Ivory Rag.") None of the major labels knocked Elvis off the charts with their ragtime, but all had some to offer in the late 1950s. Ragtime was thought of as an adjunct to pizza-eating (in the Shakey's and Red Garter chains) and to sing-alongs (in banjo bars and on the Mickey Finn television show), but, thanks to Hunt, Busch, and Maddox, it was at least thought of.

In October 1950, around the time that *Honky-Tonk Piano* was released, *They All Played Ragtime* appeared in bookstores. It was the first history of the music, and its timing couldn't have been better. Just when Lou Busch was presenting ragtime as a living, vital sound, Harriet Janis and Rudi Blesh supplied the evidence that ragtime was musically important and that it had a fascinating past.

Harriet Janis, a New York dealer in modern art, had the idea to write the book, and she thought that her friend Rudi Blesh, an interior designer and knowledgeable jazz buff, was the one to write it with her.

They All Played Ragtime *book jacket*

He wasn't so sure. Blesh had heard some ragtime as he was growing up in Guthrie, Oklahoma (he was born there in 1899, when the area was still Indian Territory), but hot jazz became his passion while he was an architecture student at the University of California at Berkeley in the early 1920s. In 1943 he gave a series of lectures on jazz at the San Francisco Museum of Art, illustrating his points with material from his huge record collection. His erudite presentations won him a place as jazz critic for the San Francisco *Chronicle*. In 1944 the publisher Alfred A. Knopf asked Blesh to write a history of jazz, and two years later, his book *Shining Trumpets* appeared. Like most experts of his day, Blesh considered ragtime merely a stop along the way to the real thing, small-band jazz. He didn't know that ragtime needed a history (or had one), but, after Janis twisted his arm and Knopf offered a contract, he agreed to help find out what it was.

Blesh and Janis spent the calendar year of 1949 researching the book. They dashed about the country looking up one old-timer after another, unearthing yellowed and wrinkled rags from libraries and piano benches, reading reviews and articles in obscure and long-dead periodicals. (Shep Edmonds, retired from both his careers, as songwriter and as the first black private detective, received them at his home in Columbus, Ohio. Edmonds told them how to find the oldest black musicians in any city: go to the local undertaker and ask for their addresses. The tip invariably worked.) If *They All Played Ragtime* was researched in a hurry, it was written in a whirlwind. Blesh and Janis turned in their manuscript to Knopf in February 1950. Although their perspective was occasionally askew, the two nonmusicians created a masterpiece of pop music literature.

The importance of *They All Played Ragtime* lay in its identification of the earliest ragtime giants. It placed Scott Joplin highest in the pantheon, where he belongs, and it made the reputations of Joplin's prolific followers, James Scott and Joseph Lamb. Although the book slights some important figures (Confrey, Christensen, and Berlin) and belittles the commercial ragtimers of the teens, it throws the spotlight accurately on the main characters in ragtime's first act and illuminates its setting in St. Louis. We take Joplin's genius for granted today, and almost anyone could, at least roughly, describe the milieu in which it flowered. But his genius and its milieu were news in 1950, and *They All Played Ragtime* was not just important, it was necessary. The book has been in print for most of the five decades since it was issued, serving as reference, inspiration, and springboard for more research. It was timely in another way as well: within a year of its release about half of the hundred or so subjects interviewed by Blesh and Janis had died.

They All Played Ragtime established ragtime's integrity, and a few pianists were inspired to reclaim it. The most important and adventurous of these was Robert Russell Darch, who, in 1955, walked away at the midpoint of a military career to play ragtime. The ragtime idea had been planted in him during his childhood in Detroit. His piano teacher was Gene Turpin, a nephew of Tom Turpin, and the lessons consisted of Turpin playing and the boy trying to imitate him. Darch chose a military career rather than music, but fourteen years in the U.S. Army Corps of Engineers could not quench the call. He left the army, determined not only to play authentic ragtime but to live an authentic ragtime life, that is, to be a nomad and to make a living in bars. He was not looking for faux-retro places like Shakey's, where children drank Cokes and ate pizza and sang "On Top of Old Smokey" to the accompaniment of a teenage pianist in sleeve garters. He wanted the real deal, places where whores, sports, losers, and loudmouths gathered of an evening for some fun and music. He went west, where there were some saloons.

"Ragtime Bob" Darch found a base in Virginia City, Nevada, and he traveled from there to Colorado, Toronto, Alaska (still Yukon Territory in the mid-1950s)—wherever there was a smoky joint with a piano. In the late 1950s he began to take any job he could get in Missouri, because it was there that he wanted to do some missionary

Bob Darch with Arthur Marshall at piano

work. He went to Sedalia first in 1957, and he returned many times, ostensibly to play in clubs but really to grab the town by the lapels and tell it who Scott Joplin was. He brought Arthur Marshall back for a concert in 1959. He played Chamber of Commerce breakfasts at 7:00 A.M., after ten-hour shifts in bars. He offered free concerts to any schools that would have him. He went to Carthage on behalf of James Scott, and he preached about Blind Boone in Columbia. He dug up local history that even the oldest locals had forgotten was theirs. He found sheet music, gravesites, composers, and composers' widows; he poked around in rotting buildings that had once rung with ragtime. He took photos, he gave interviews, he was a walking feature story. The

Dick Zimmerman

conversion that Darch sought for the Midwest would not come until the mid-1970s, but, after twenty years of his evangelizing, it came.

Max Morath, a native of Colorado Springs, took ragtime to another audience. His mother had been a silent movie accompanist, and she played ragtime at home after her professional life was over. There was no discussion about ragtime, nor were there lessons in it: it was just there. Max stayed with his piano studies through high school, but when he enrolled at Colorado College, he chose English as a major. His early professional life seemed shapeless, a conglomeration of jobs as radio announcer, television director, and accompanist to the burlesque melo-dramas given in the summers at Cripple Creek. Finally, in 1959, it all came together for him when he was asked to create a series of programs on ragtime for National Educational Television. The twelve-show series was called *The Ragtime Era*, and Morath turned out to be the music's perfect television spokesman. He was an excellent pianist and singer and a charming, low-keyed raconteur. *The Ragtime Era* won awards and, even better, attracted a surprisingly wide audience.

Even the networks noticed NET's ratings and decided that a little ragtime couldn't hurt. ABC's *Lawrence Welk Show* kept a ragtime pianist in residence (first Tiny Little, Jr., then Jo Ann Castle). CBS's *What's My Line?* ended its weekly games with Lou Busch's "Roller Coaster" as its closing theme. Bil Baird often took his ragtime-playing puppet, Slugger Ryan, to visit Jack Paar. Jelly Roll Morton's "Naked Dance" opened every visit with *Lucky Pup*. The theme of Joe Franklin's TV show (for forty years) was "Twelfth Street Rag." NBC presented a one-hour Morath imitation, *Those Ragtime Years*, as a "Project Twenty" special in 1960. There was an obvious demand for more on NET, so in 1961 and 1962, Morath hosted a fifteen-show series called *Turn of the Century*.

Morath's television shows made him America's best known rag-timer, and they opened the doors for him to theatres and concert halls, venues that had never presented such entertainment before. He was a tireless trouper, popping up at college auditoriums, in community con-cert series, joking with Arthur Godfrey on the radio, and recording for half a dozen labels. He had a four-month off-Broadway run with his one-man show, *Max Morath at the Turn of the Century*, and he was a favorite guest of the Boston Pops Orchestra. Morath did more than anyone to "legitimize" ragtime in the public mind, and he presented it as a natural American delight, not as a history lesson. He took the high

Trebor Tichenor

road and Darch took the low, but they wound up at the same place: on a plateau of new respect for ragtime, wherever it was heard.

By the mid-1960s there were so many ragtime fans that they needed an organization through which to share news of festivals, concerts, and publications. On May 28, 1967, Dick Zimmerman, a Los Angeles–based professional magician as well as a professional pianist, along with pianist-bandleader Dave Bourne, called California enthusiasts to the first meeting of the Maple Leaf Club. More than a hundred showed up at Spencer Quinn's Hock Shop, a Hollywood club, and they were pleased to find that this organization was about music, not parliamentary procedure. Zimmerman led off with a rousing "Maple Leaf

Rag," and Doug Parker, a banjoist, played "Pickles and Peppers" and "Grandpa's Spells." Jim Hession, a university student, offered "Cataract Rag" and "Carolina Shout." The only motion passed at the first meeting was to do it again, every month.

Word of the L.A. ragtime club got around, and its mailing list grew accordingly. In July 1967 the first issue of *Rag Times*, the Maple Leaf's newsletter and journal of record, was issued. Edited and published by Zimmerman, the *Rag Times* continues to be the best source of articles, festival news, and book and recording reviews for the ragtime aficionado, and its readership is international.

The enthusiasm of Westerners for ragtime has echoed throughout the United States. St. Louis held its first ragtime festival, on the Goldenrod Showboat, in 1965. The Goldenrod's gatherings ran for twenty-eight years under the inspired leadership of Trebor Tichenor and Don Franz. Sedalia followed suit with occasional Joplin festivals in the early 1970s and has had an annual festival since 1983. Fresno, Boulder, Sacramento, Detroit, and Savannah have hosted yearly gatherings for ragtime fans. Ragtime enters the new century as it entered the last one, as a regional music with a devoted national following.

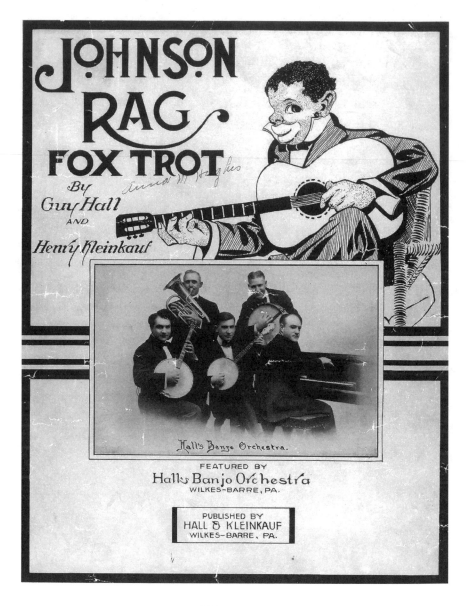

"Johnson Rag"

CHAPTER FIVE

Ragtime in the Northeast

Connecticut, District of Columbia, Maine,
Massachusetts, New Hampshire, New Jersey, New
York State, Pennsylvania, Rhode Island, Canada

Most of the music published in America before 1860 came from the Northeast, so almost all of our musical "firsts" occurred in that region. Because of the original colonists' disapproval of nonchurch music, these "firsts" were a long time in coming. There was no secular music published at all for nearly 150 years after the Pilgrims' arrival in 1620. The Europeans brought folk tunes with them, of course, but these were learned by hearing them sung. There was no point in printing music that everyone already knew. The only public place for music was church, and church music was a bone-simple (and noncommercial) affair. Most churches forbade instrumental accompaniment to singing. Hymns, like folk tunes, were learned by rote, by a leader's "lining out" and the congregation's repetition of or "answer" to the leader's line. The churches that used hymnals at all used the ones that their worshipers had brought from Europe.

Finally, in 1640, a growing dissatisfaction with standard hymnals led to the first book-length publication in the United States, a lyric collection called *The Whole Booke of Psalmes* (commonly known as *The Bay Psalm Book*), which was issued in Cambridge, Massachusetts. At twenty-three pence apiece, 7,000 copies were sold. The ninth edition of this hymnal, called *Psalms, Hymns and Spiritual Songs*, which appeared in

225

1698, was the first American publication to contain both words and music.

The Bay Psalm Book did not revolutionize publishing or music in America. Neither did the first published secular piece (and the first single-sheet music publication), "The Liberty Song," issued by Mein and Fleeming in Boston in 1768. Until the end of the eighteenth century, a published "song" was usually a lyric printed on a one-page broadside. The customer was given the name of the borrowed melody it should be sung to, and he was expected to know the tune. These "songs" were sold in the bookstores and print shops that ground them out. The first American merchant to specialize in the sale of music seems to have been John Aitken, a Philadelphia silversmith who opened shop at 60 South Second Street in 1785. Aitken eventually published several tunes before he went out of business in 1811.

The Revolutionary War inspired many American songwriters, but most of their work was taken to the streets, not to publishers. War songs served their fiery purpose at rallies, and they spread like folk music, through the performances of listeners who carried them on. Even the most famous of them, such as "Yankee Doodle" and "Hail Columbia," were not published in U.S. editions until after the war.

It was during the Revolutionary War era, however, that the church's suppression of music finally gave way. The idea that the enjoyment of music would not call down hellfire gained gradual acceptance in the early eighteenth century. Imported European instruments (mostly violins and flutes) began to enliven evenings around colonial firesides, and in 1769 the first American "spinnet" piano was made by John Harris, in Boston. As cities grew, musical entertainments became a part of city life. The first auditorium used (occasionally) for public entertainment was built in Williamsburg, Virginia, in 1716, and fifty years later, the first building used exclusively for theatrical performances arose in Philadelphia. In 1787 Thomas Dobson, a Philadelphia publisher, issued an important just-for-fun folio, *A Selection of the Most Favorite Scots Tunes.* The following year, Dobson published the first secular folio of a U.S.-born composer, Francis Hopkinson's *Seven Songs for the Harpsichord or Forte Piano.* In 1793 Moller and Capron, of Philadelphia, became the first American firm to specialize in the publication of music. "Negro songs" began to find their way into parlor music cabinets in the 1790s.

Philadelphia led the way in early American music publishing. The firms of John Aitken, Benjamin Carr (at 136 High Street), Thomas Dobson (who was prosperous enough to open a branch store in New York in 1784), and George Willig (the longest-lived of the early firms, and the first American publisher of "Yankee Doodle," in 1798) were colleagues and rivals in a brand-new trade in the 1790s. Boston's publishing activity began to surpass Philadelphia's, and to equal New York's, in the 1830s. Regional publishing houses sprang up as America pushed its border west during the mid-nineteenth century, and a few of them, such as Root & Cady of Chicago, gave strong competition to their Northeastern counterparts. It was not until the rise of the Tin Pan Alley firms in the 1880s and 1890s that New York clinched its domination of the music business.

The oldest, best established, and best connected firms in the United States were in New England, and it would be expected that these companies would lead the way when the publishing of popular music became big business. Yet they did not. Even those who had had hits in the mid-nineteenth century ceded the pop turf to the young upstarts of Tin Pan Alley. Most of them chose not to publish pop music at all, and those who did kept it as a negligible sideline. These old-line publishers had created the pop music trade. They literally knew the territory; they had markets, products, and reputations; several of them had even solved the hardest riddle, that of distribution. They were strategically poised to dominate a sprawling music market, but they left the field without a fight in the 1890s.

Four Boston firms, all established before 1880, lasted well beyond the ragtime era, yet none of them published rags. Two of the Philadelphia firms established in the early 1880s somehow survived a century in a pop music world without publishing much pop music. One of them, Theodore Presser, published no rags; the other, M. D. Swisher, published two. These companies refused to play the crass game invented by the teenage Witmark brothers, along with refugees from the garment district (Stern and Marks) and an ex-dairyman from Detroit (Remick). An innate Puritan propriety held them back.

The old firms had shown some hustle in their day, but their hustle was the kind that expressed itself in filling orders promptly. But the business was not about filling orders any more, it was about the shameless hawking of songs. It involved handing out song sheets to drunks in saloons, flattering singers and orchestra leaders, and harassing vaudeville performers until they gave in and featured your company's music. If backslapping, arm-twisting, and harassment failed, it was time to take out the wallet and try bribery. Music publishing was not a business for gentlemen anymore, even gentlemen with distribution and solid reputations. When the pirates took over the ocean, the old-timers held close to shore and made few ripples. Some of them beefed up their lines of school and church music, some of them went classical. As they had always done, they published catalogs and waited for orders to come in. Like Bartleby the scrivener, they preferred not to get involved.

A handful of Northeastern publishers entered the business about the same time the Witmarks, Sterns, and Remicks did. They had no reputations to protect and no stodginess to overcome. They were keen students of the song business, and they learned the Alley's lessons well. It was these younger Northeastern publishers, as cheeky as their New York counterparts, who planted modern popular music, including ragtime, in Pilgrim soil.

Four Profiles in Northeastern Ragtime

GEORGE L. COBB

The best and most prolific composer of ragtime in the Northeast was George Linus Cobb, who was born in Mexico, New York, in 1886. (Mexico is about thirty miles north of Syracuse and just south of Texas, New York.) Cobb was a fine pianist as a youngster, and in 1905 he enrolled in the School of Harmony and Composition at Syracuse University. After graduation, he lived in Buffalo for a year or so. His rag "Buffalo Means Business" won a local music competition in 1909, with publication as the prize. It was probably the hoopla over this rag that prompted Jack Yellen, a local teenager who had emigrated from Poland in 1897, to seek out Cobb. Yellen was working as a reporter for the Buffalo *Courier*, but he had ambitions to be a songwriter. The two became friends and wrote a few songs together, but the partnership was severed almost as soon as it began when Yellen left Buffalo to attend the University of Michigan.

It was fine to win a prize for a piece of syncopated boosterism, but a more important career step was taken in 1909, when Cobb sent his "Rubber Plant Rag" to the publisher Walter Jacobs, of

George L. Cobb

Boston, and it was accepted. "Rubber Plant" is a testament to Jacobs's good eye for rags, and it is also proof of Cobb's attentiveness at the Syracuse School of Harmony. Its harmonic surprises come thick and fast, as in silent movie music, yet it is not a showoff piece. It is a satisfying rag of middling difficulty, and, like most of Cobb's rags, it sounds harder to play than it is. The professional relationship between the composer and publisher of "Rubber Plant Rag" would become one of the most important in the history of ragtime.

In 1913, newly graduated from the University of Michigan, Jack Yellen stored his diploma in a cool, dry place and headed to where he wanted to be all along, Tin Pan Alley. He renewed his friendship with Cobb there, and they plunged into songwriting together. Success came with their first try, "All Aboard for Dixieland." They pitched it to a singer named Elizabeth Murray, and—when she was cast in the new

Rudolf Friml operetta, *High Jinks*—she insisted on interpolating the song as her specialty number. They also scored on their second try, "Bring Me Back My Lovin' Honey Boy," which was published by Will Rossiter, in Chicago. Songwriting was proving to be a lucrative side-track to Cobb's ragtime career, and for two years he wrote no rags at all. He wrote both words and music to "Just for Tonight," a hit for Will Rossiter in 1914.

The big year for the Yellen-Cobb team was 1915. Early that year, Elizabeth Murray introduced their "Alabama Jubilee," Remick published it, and Arthur Collins and Byron Harlan made the first of its many recordings. In the spring their classic strut, "Are You from Dixie?," was published by Witmark and recorded by Billy Murray and Irving Kaufman. Staying with their lucky subject, they wrote "Listen to That Dixie Band" and had a third big seller. Their "Dancing Around the U.S.A." found a spot in a 1915 Broadway revue, *Maid in America*. Cobb had not yet had a hit instrumental, but he kept writing dance numbers and sending them to Walter Jacobs. Jacobs published two of Cobb's one-steps ("Rabbit's Foot" and "Levee Land"), but when Cobb began writing rags again in 1916, he sent them elsewhere.

Cobb stayed abreast of musical fads and tailored his instrumentals accordingly. His 1913 "Bunny Hug Rag" was an attempt to cash in on a dance craze, and his first rag after his two-year dry spell was the musically topical "Good Bye Blues," issued in 1916. Both were published by Charles E. Roat, of Battle Creek, Michigan. In April 1916, Cobb's best rag, "The Midnight Trot" (a maxixe written for the vaudeville dancer Maizie King), went to Will Rossiter. Jacobs, who had given Cobb his start in 1909, must have been alarmed to see Cobb's hit songs and clever rags sailing under the banners of Tin Pan Alley, Battle Creek, and Chicago. In September 1916, to cement the "gentlemen's agreement" he thought he had, Jacobs offered Cobb a staff job. To the publisher's eventual regret, he did not secure Cobb's exclusive services as a composer, but instead hired him as an arranger and as a columnist for his new trade magazine, *The Tuneful Yankee*.

Jacobs did get a few rags from Cobb in 1917–1918, including "Nautical Nonsense," "Cracked Ice," and "Irish Confetti" (Boston slang for "potato peelings"), but the company's star composer spent most of his time arranging the work of others and writing his column.

Because Cobb's rags were occasionally reprinted in *The Tuneful Yankee* (renamed *Melody* in 1918), he signed two of his new ones with the pseudonym "Leo Gordon," so he wouldn't seem to be hogging space in the magazine.

The column was called "Just Between You and Me," and in it Cobb critiqued the songs and instrumentals sent to him by his amateur-composer readers. The tone of the writing is cheerful, but the old pro took no guff, musical or verbal, from the nascent Gershwins and Berlins who offered him the first look at their work. He told "A.M." of South Pekin, Illinois, that "I Can Hear the Chime of the Church Bell Toll" was "a long, dreary, melancholy, and morbid affair." "A.L.E." of the Bronx was informed that his song was "squirrel food." "G.L.B." of Belt, Montana, must have been disappointed to learn that the story he told in his song was "as old as the flood, and there is absolutely nothing new in the rhymes." "W.C.R." of Brighton, Massachusetts, got the news that his "Dear Old Hawaii" was "the same old dope about 'strumming ukuleles' and 'singing natives.'" Cobb pounced on plagiarists ("Did you think I was so young or so old that I wouldn't remember 'The Red Rose Rag' by P. Wenrich?"), and bullying letters did not wring apologies from him ("Yes, we still have your manuscript and also your threat to sic a lawyer on us if we do not return your pet poetry. Send us three cents' worth of fresh U.S.A. stamps and we will mail your maudlin material back to you."). His kindest advice: " . . . go to college, fit yourself for a professional career and if you must write songs, do so as a side-line."

In 1918 George Cobb finally got his hit rag, a syncopated version of Rachmaninoff's Prelude in C Sharp Minor called "Russian Rag." There were no congratulatory parties thrown for Cobb at the Jacobs offices, however, as he had sent "Russian Rag" to Will Rossiter, who reaped great profit from it. Jacobs did get another Cobb shakeup of a classic that year, the one-step called "Peter Gink," adapted from Edvard Grieg's *Peer Gynt* Suite. Walter Jacobs received scant reward from the sales of "Peter Gink," but somehow its composer remained on his payroll.

After the out-of-town success of "Russian Rag," Cobb was mostly a company man. (He did succumb to Rossiter's request for a novelty follow-up, called "New Russian Rag," in 1923.) Keeping up with musical trends, he had by 1923 moved completely into the novelty rag idiom.

His "Piano Salad" and "Chromatic Capers" are especially fine examples of Cobb novelties. The last of Cobb's twenty-eight rags (and Jacobs's last rag publication) was "Snuggle Pup," a reworking of Nacio Herb Brown's "Doll Dance," in 1929. Cobb died on Christmas Day 1942 in Brookline, Massachusetts.

GUY HALL AND HENRY KLEINKAUF

Nothing was more prized by Tin Pan Alley publishers than a truly infectious tune, and in 1939 Robbins Music had such a jewel placed in its lap by a bandleader who had carried it in his head for more than twenty years. It was "Johnson Rag," the sole composition of two journeymen musicians who spent their lives playing hotel jobs and college dances in eastern Pennsylvania. "Johnson Rag," by all rights, should never have been heard south of Harrisburg, and the story of its finding its way into jukeboxes all over America is both fluky and inspiring. It is the kind of story that keeps amateurs and small-timers pursuing their dreams.

Guy Hall and Henry Kleinkauf grew up in Wilkes-Barre, Pennsylvania, and, as aspiring musicians in a small city, it was natural that they would find each other. Guy Hall organized a dance band in the early teens, and he asked "Heine" Kleinkauf to be his pianist. The other instruments in Guy Hall's Banjo Band were two banjos, a baritone horn, and a bandolin (Hall's instrument, which was an ungodly amalgam of snare drum, banjo, and mandolin). Kleinkauf was a good player, but no one could hear him in the banjo-heavy group.

At a Phi Kappa party at Penn State in the mid-teens, a boy approached Hall as the band was setting up. He casually asked what was new, and Hall said that "Heine" had recently written something. Hall went to the piano and played a one-finger version of a jagged, and still unnamed, tune. The boy, John McLaughlin, remembered years afterward that he had heard the unadorned melody of "Johnson Rag" and that when the band played it later in the evening, the dancers wouldn't let them stop.

"Johnson Rag" was published (with Hall named as co-composer) by Hall and Kleinkauf in Wilkes-Barre in September 1917. The band was currently in residence at the Oneonta Hotel (a resort on Harvey's Lake, about fifteen miles west of Wilkes-Barre), and Hall said that the rag was named for a popular black waiter there. The original "Johnson Rag"

Guy Hall (left) and Henry Kleinkauf (right)

is subtitled "Fox Trot," but its tempo marking is the slower "Tempo di Drag." The piece stays in the mellow key of A♭, and there are three strains, each of them nothing more than the age-old flirtation between tonic and dominant chords. The teasing between the two is powerful, though, and if the "Drag" tempo is kept, the rag has a lazy, sensuous feel. The world beyond Wilkes-Barre did not see or hear "Johnson Rag," but hometown sales were good enough to inspire Hall and Kleinkauf to issue a song version, "That Lovin' Johnson Rag," also published in 1917.

Guy Hall led regional bands in northeastern Pennsylvania throughout the 1920s and 1930s (often using Kleinkauf as his pianist), and all of his groups kept "Johnson Rag" in their repertoires. Among the musicians who drifted through the Hall bands on their way to bigger things were Bill Challis, who would become a Whiteman arranger, and future orchestra leader Hugo Winterhalter. Another Hall alumnus was the trombonist Russ Morgan, who came to fame as a leader of a pleasant and extremely danceable big band in the late 1930s. Morgan was visiting his folks in Scranton in 1939 when he remembered Hall and wondered if he were still playing that catchy tune. He sought out Hall in Wilkes-Barre and asked if he could arrange for its publication. Hall agreed, and the copyright of "Johnson Rag" was sold to Robbins Music Company of New York.

Robbins had high hopes for "Johnson Rag," seeing its potential as a song as well as an instrumental. Jack Lawrence was hired to write a lyric, and his conversion of "Johnson Rag" was masterful. His lyric was good, but what he did to the tune was even better. Lawrence used only the A strain of the rag, and he added the one extra note that made all the difference, the one-note pickup that slides up to the first note of the original melody. He put the *ya* into the famous *ya-daaa* opening, setting up the call-and-response that we know as "Johnson Rag" (*ya-daaa—ya-da, ya-da, ya-da*). He wrote a lightly syncopated melody for the bridge, and he made a lyric entirely out of hepcat slang.

Despite Robbins's and Morgan's faith in "Johnson Rag," its first recordings did not do well. Morgan's disc lay in the record stores alongside those by Will Bradley and Larry Clinton early in 1940. "Johnson Rag" was undeniably cute, but record buyers could live without it. Hall and Kleinkauf had had their shot, and, since they had never written anything else, there was no second shot to take. They stayed in Wilkes-Barre, working in bands of all sizes, and they kept their regional following. Hall discovered the vibraphone in the early 1940s, and organized a small group in which he featured himself on the instrument. Kleinkauf died in 1942.

But, Scott Fitzgerald to the contrary, there are second acts in American lives, and the second act began for Hall in 1949. Capitol Records had made ragtime a household word again, and publishers started to look through their file drawers to see if they owned any rags. Someone at Robbins found "Johnson Rag" and offered it to bandleaders. Russ Morgan was first to accept, of course, and late in 1949 he made a Decca recording with his vocal group, the Morganaires. The Morgan recording edged onto the *Billboard* charts in December, to begin a ten-week stay in the Top 40. It was joined there early in 1950 by the Jimmy Dorsey version (eleven weeks), the Claude Thornhill version (four weeks), and the champ of them all, the Jack Teter Trio version (twenty-three weeks). At one point, all four recordings were simultaneously occupying various positions in *Billboard*'s weekly listing of hits. Royalties poured in to Robbins Music, and to Hall.

In 1958 Hall and his wife, Clara, moved to Harrisburg, where Hall began a second career as a drum teacher for Thorpe's Music House. He taught in Harrisburg for sixteen years, justly lionized as a local boy who had written a big, big hit.

WILLIE ECKSTEIN

Canadians have had an affinity for ragtime since its earliest days. The first rag published in Canada was S. Em. Duguay's "Club Cabin," issued by La Passe-Temps in Montreal in 1903. The major Canadian pop composers—such as Charles Wellinger, A. Lorne Lee, and J. B. Lafreniere—all dabbled in ragtime, and Toronto and Montreal have

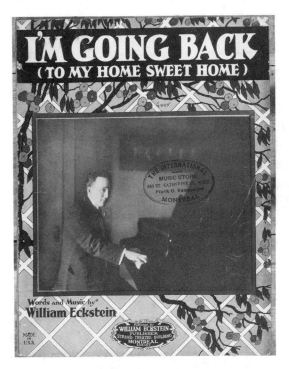

Willie Eckstein

been focal cities in the music's revival. And for more than forty years, Montreal could boast that one of its native sons, Willie Eckstein, was considered by many to be the best ragtime pianist in the world.

William Eckstein was born in Pte. St. Charles in December 1888, and as a child he seemed to possess almost supernatural musical gifts. By the time he was ten or so, he could read any music that was placed before him, and he could play all of it that his tiny hands could reach. At age twelve he gave the classical recital that won him a music scholarship to McGill University, and in his early teens he was earning about $15,000 a year as a "child wonder" pianist in American and Canadian vaudeville. In 1902 he played at the Wisteria Grove Roof Garden in New York City, on a bill with Elsie Janis (and billed above her). In 1905 he was back in Montreal for an acclaimed recital at Karn Hall before swinging around the vaudeville circle again. In 1906 he gave a private performance for Teddy Roosevelt and his family at the White House.

Then, around 1910, something happened that derailed Eckstein's career: he grew up. He was still a wonder at the keyboard, but he wasn't a child wonder anymore. Although he was barely five feet tall at his adult height, he was twenty-two and he looked it. He made the alarming discovery that his appeal lay not so much in his music as in the fact that a youngster was making the music. Without his youthful persona, he was merely a fine classical pianist, and there was no call for such in vaudeville. His vaudeville past had, of course, tainted him as far as classical concert promoters were concerned. His genius was obvious, but no one would book it for an entire season. By 1911 he was back in Montreal for good, playing bar jobs at $18 a week, plus food and drinks.

Because the classical world had renounced him, Eckstein renounced the classics by turning his prodigious talent to popular music. He wrote the surprisingly tame "Some Rag," issued in Montreal in 1911, and he began to turn out songs with any lyricist who would work with him. In the teens and twenties he had dozens of locally published songs on generic Tin Pan Alley subjects: pretty girls ("Captivating Kitty Green"), weather ("In Sunny Summertime"), and places ("Where the Niagara Flows"). Several of his songs were dedicated to various members of the royal family. *The Ed Wynn Carnival*, a Broadway revue of 1920, was the only show to feature an Eckstein song ("Goodbye Sunshine, Hello Moon," with lyrics by Gene Buck).

In 1912 Willie Eckstein found the perfect venue in which to use his otherworldly skills as player and improviser. He became the "cinema interpreter" at Montreal's premiere silent movie house, the Strand Theatre. With only a trap drummer at his side, he became a sort of D. W. Griffith of movie accompaniment, creating musical impressions of wars, floods, trains, forest fires, comedy chases, and saloon brawls as striking as those that flickered above his head. He seemed to know every march, rag, song, and classical theme ever written, and he wove them in any configuration—quoting only a few bars or playing the entire work—to suit the action on the giant screen. He could play octave runs so fast that they sounded like *glissandi*, and he could augment the *glissandi* made by his thumbs, filling in fourths and fifths with his free fingers. His chords were as thick as the ice floes and strong as the sea waves they were meant to evoke. For tense dramatic situations, he had a special double tremolo, in which he broke a chord in half, trilling two sets of two notes with each hand instead of merely rattling one set of four. The power of his small hands was exceeded only by the power of his imagination, and those who heard him "interpret" a film never forgot the experience.

Visiting pianists of every stripe were taken to the Strand by their Montreal hosts to hear Eckstein. Axel Christensen marveled at his ability and asked why such talent was frittered away in a silent movie theatre. When it was explained that Eckstein was making $250 a week plus 25 percent of every ticket sold, he had his answer. Eckstein's music was so popular with the Strand's audiences that the theatre delayed its entrance into the sound era by four years, booking silent films into 1932, so that they could hear him play.

If there was a drawback to Eckstein's job at the Strand, it was that it hampered his recording career. He could pop into New York occasionally to make a few sides for Pathé or OKeh, but most of his records were made for Canadian Victor and did not receive the distribution they deserved in the American marketplace. He was a novelty composer's dream, as his early twenties recordings will attest. He made Confrey's "Coaxing the Piano" and "Nickel in the Slot," Bargy's "Knice and Knifty," Larry Brier's "Fine Feathers," and Ted Shapiro's "Putting on the Dog," in each of which complexity is layered onto complexity and tossed off with an almost casual aplomb. In 1923 Eckstein made the first piano recording of "Maple Leaf Rag."

In 1932 the Strand reluctantly admitted that audiences wanted to hear actors talk more than they wanted to hear Willie Eckstein play, and it changed its programming policy to sound films. Eckstein looked for another steady job and immediately found one, in a nightclub called the Chateau Ste. Rose, where he was in residence for twenty years. He rounded off his career with several years at the Lido (just across the street from the Chateau Ste. Rose), playing there almost up to the time of his death in 1963.

BOSTON

The Athens of America

Boston's cultural tone was set for two centuries by its first white settlers, John Winthrop and the 800 Puritan souls who came with him from Charlestown to occupy the peninsula between the Charles River and Boston Harbor in 1630. They immediately changed the name of the place from Shawnett (what it had been called by its original inhabitants, the Massachusetts Indians) to Boston (in honor of the English town from which many of them had emigrated). By 1632, the year that Boston became the capital of the Massachusetts Bay Colony, the town was already the colonies' principal port. For most of the seventeenth century, it was a village of farmers, craftsmen, and ministers, and its rectitude was protected by the fact that only Puritans were allowed to hold city offices. The "Beantown" nickname came from travelers who couldn't find anything but beans to eat on Sunday. Cooking was forbidden on that day, so housewives and innkeepers made pots of beans on Saturday and served nothing else for two days.

As the leading industrial, fishing, and shipbuilding center of colonial America, Boston held both strategic and symbolic importance during the Revolutionary era. Britain's control of Boston was the keystone to its commercial and governmental dominance of the colonies. As

America's nationalistic feelings grew, the mother country began to remind restless Bostonians of their status as residents of an occupied city. Six were killed by British troops in the Boston Massacre of 1770. In 1773, immediately after the Boston Tea Party, England closed the port to prevent any other such dramatic expression of protest against taxation. Finally, after years of skirmishes in Boston's streets, General George Washington and his soldiers drove the British out on March 17, 1776, in the first major colonial victory of the Revolutionary War. The victory inspired the first well-known song published in Boston, William Billings's war anthem "Chester," issued by Draper and Folsom in 1778.

In the becalmed Boston of the 1790s, a handful of local book publishers began to carry their own music imprints in their shops. In 1792 Thomas and Andrews added music to its literary line at 45 Newbury Street. In 1796 three bookstores, William Norman's (at 75 Newbury Street), Gottlieb Graupner's (at 10 Jarvis Buildings), and Francis Mallet's (on Union Street) entered into competition with Thomas and Andrews for Boston's music trade. In 1798 the city's first all-music store, P. A. Von Hagen, Jr. and Company, opened at 62 Newbury Street. None of these early publishers had distribution beyond their own neighborhoods, and Graupner was the only one to last more than ten years or so. (It stayed in business until 1835.)

Boston was incorporated as a city in 1822, and in the next quarter century, it would grow into a commercial and industrial giant. It was a magnet for immigrants from all over Europe, especially those leaving Ireland in the late 1840s. It would attain a worldwide reputation for its culture and learning and would become home to the Abolitionist movement in the 1830s. It was this influx of diversity that changed the city's cultural face. Though it had not forgotten its Puritan roots, Boston could not remain a Puritan city. Many kinds of people poured in, people with broader notions of how to entertain themselves and how to spend their money. They provided a market for purveyors of worldly pastimes: show producers, concert promoters, and those who published music that had no purpose beyond enjoyment.

Boston's most important nineteenth-century music publisher was Oliver Ditson, who opened his doors at 107 Washington Street in

1835. Ditson not only sold music, he bought it. Almost as soon as he established himself on Washington Street, he began acquiring the stock and the stores of small local firms, creating instant branches of his company all over town. Ditson would expand this practice and make acquisitions throughout the East and Midwest, owning or controlling the interest in dozens of music companies. (Ditson's firm was itself acquired by the Theodore Presser company, of Philadelphia, in 1931.)

Before the days of vaudeville and recordings, there was no such thing as a hit factory, but Ditson's company came as close as any in the East in the mid-nineteenth century. It had the popular "Blue Juniata," an Indian song by M. D. Sullivan, in 1844. In 1856 there were three big numbers under the Ditson imprint: "Darling Nellie Gray," Gottschalk's piano showpiece "The Last Hope," and "Root, Hog, or Die." James Pierpont's "Jingle Bells" was the firm's major acquisition of 1857, and five years later "The Battle Hymn of the Republic" took its place of honor in the Ditson catalog. In 1864 the firm got another Gottschalk piano number, "The Dying Poet," as well as a Civil War favorite, "Tenting on the Old Camp Ground." Ditson's pop output took an arty turn in the 1860s and 1870s, with song settings of Longfellow poems and such numbers as "Beautiful Bird, Sing On" and "Eilleen Allanna."

Boston pop—Ditson's and everyone else's—declined in the 1880s, but a local show business venture would help to revive it. In January 1883 a grifter named Benjamin Franklin Keith, with his partner William Austin, established a showplace on Washington Street. Keith was a New Hampshire native whose prior entrepreneurial experience consisted of selling a phony blood-testing device on the side lots of small circuses. It was an unlikely training ground for a future theatrical magnate, but Keith learned a lot about audiences by watching circusgoers. He knew that freaks held a powerful attraction for most people, and that ticket buyers like a lot of show for their money. With these principles in mind, he and Colonel Austin opened a dime museum. It was crammed with grotesque exhibits, some real and some fake. For a dime, one could stay as long as he liked in the thirty-five-foot-long building, leisurely goggling at midgets and baby midgets, fire eaters, bearded ladies, and deformed animals. The place did good business, but Colonel Austin had had enough by May. He bailed out and Keith found a new partner, nay, a soul mate, in a former scalper of circus tickets: Edward Franklin Albee.

Keith and Albee had dreams beyond freaks and small, stuffy buildings to show them in. They decided to open a real, respectable theatre together. They had no money, of course, but that was no hindrance to grifters. They threw up a bootleg production of *The Mikado*, and with the profits (including those that should have gone to Gilbert and Sullivan), they opened the Bijou Theatre in 1885. There were no freaks in the new Keith-Albee enterprise, but there was novelty: they were the first showmen in Boston to offer variety acts in continuous performance, from 10:00 A.M. until 10:00 P.M. Admission was a dime, but for five cents more one could sit in a chair.

Like the *Mikado* that had launched the pair, the continuous-performance idea was a theft of intellectual property: Tony Pastor, a New York impresario, had been presenting continuous variety for several years. Keith and Albee gave their show a fancy name—vaudeville—and the customers flocked in. Pastor thought the term was sissified, that "variety" was the honest way to say what it was. But Pastor's influence over the genre he had created was even by then beginning to dwindle. He was in charge of only one theatre; within a few years Keith and Albee would own dozens of them.

The Bijou was the first link in what would become the Keith-Albee chain. In 1893 they opened the magnificent Colonial Theatre in Boston, as well as the Union Square Theatre in New York. By the turn of the century they owned or controlled major vaudeville houses in Cleveland, Providence, Philadelphia, Portland, and Pittsburgh. Several cities had as many as three or four Keith theatres. The routing of acts among their theatres created the Keith Circuit, the biggest in big-time vaudeville. By 1910 Keith and Albee controlled all of the major vaudeville houses east of Chicago. As they ran out of large theatres to buy, they began to buy into small suburban ones. Keith and Albee not only ran the big-time, they had much to say about what went on in the small-time. The Colonial, their Boston flagship, remained their pride. To keep it immaculate, the Colonial's house staff, in 1907, numbered 139.

With Keith and Albee running their empire from Boston, the city became a hotbed of auditioning, booking, and refurbishing of vaudeville acts. Singers, bands, and instrumentalists converged on Boston, hoping to get a hearing by the czars. Jugglers, dog acts, magicians, acrobats, wire walkers trooped the city's small stages, hoping for the break that would put them on its large stages. Variety—with a capital *V*—came in giddy profusion, and the only thing the acts had in common was a need for music. The music they chose to present got free and overt advertising all over the East. Vaudeville and the pop music business were locked into a perfect symbiosis. They fed and promoted each other, and they used each other in creating a demand for the latest things in song and dance. In the 1890s, just before the ragtime era, several Boston music publishers, younger and more aggressive than the mainline firms, came forward to help vaudeville "artistes" with their selections.

WALTER JACOBS

In 1894 Walter Jacobs (1868–1945), a native of Oberlin, Ohio, opened a music publishing company at 165 Tremont Street in Boston. He had little money for acquisitions, so his earliest publications were of folk songs and ancient pop from the public domain. A folio of Jacobs's roy-

Walter Jacobs

alty-free standards, *The Columbia Collection of Patriotic and Favorite Home Songs* ("125 Songs 25¢"), sold well for years. There was prosperity enough to buy original material in the late 1890s, and Jacobs began to hire staff arrangers around this time. One of these early employees, R. E. Hildreth (who was born in England and reared in Holyoke, Massachusetts), would soon become Jacobs's chief arranger, the position he held for twenty years. The company expanded, and a professional department was added, with Don Ramsey placed in charge. The firm's first big instrumental seller was "The National Emblem," which Sousa himself called "one of the most effective street marches," written by E. E. Bagby and published in 1906.

In December 1904 George J. Philpot's delightful "Lazy Luke" became the first of the thirty-two rags issued under the Jacobs imprint. Jacobs did not plunge into ragtime publishing for another ten years, but he issued a rag every year or so along the way. Joseph M. Daly, a Jacobs competitor, made news when he issued Scott Joplin's "Rose Leaf Rag" as his first ragtime number. (Jacobs would far outstrip his rival as a ragtime publisher. Daly would publish only nine rags, none of the succeeding eight by Joplin, and none of them remotely as good as "Rose Leaf.") The best Jacobs rags from this early period were Mae Davis's low-down "Virginia Creeper" (in 1907) and Percy Wenrich's great folk rag, "Persian Lamb" (in 1908). "Rubber Plant Rag," the first of nineteen George Cobb rags issued by Jacobs, came in 1909.

Before George L. Cobb began his long tenure on the Jacobs staff in 1916, the firm's star composer was Thomas S. Allen, a Boston violinist and leader of one of the first "singing orchestras," which played regularly at Norumbega Park. Two of Allen's coon songs, "By the Watermelon Vine" (in 1904) and "My Dusky Rose" (in 1905), were the Jacobs company's first nationally known hits. Allen also contributed syncopated numbers to the Jacobs catalog, including three rags. His "Dance of the Lunatics," a schottische, was popular enough to warrant published arrangements for seventeen different instruments or combinations.

More than any other publisher in the Northeast, Jacobs made a concerted effort to sell music to professional musicians through self-published trade journals and memberships in the company's band and orchestra clubs. Thomas S. Allen was a frequent contributor of string arrangements for *Jacobs' Orchestra Monthly*, which was first issued in June 1910. Other Jacobs magazines for the working musician were *The Cadenza* and *The Dominant*, two other monthlies. These publications offered sample arrangements of Jacobs numbers, as well as performance tips and business advice. Each issue was, of course, laced with ads for Jacobs music. Those who paid dues in a Jacobs band or orchestra club received all the magazines, along with special discounts on folios and arrangements ordered in quantity. Jacobs was among the first publishers to create a line of folios for the silent movie accompanist.

In the mid-teens the Walter Jacobs company (now located at 8 Bosworth Street) beefed up its commitment to ragtime. Joseph Daly had stopped publishing rags in 1913, so the local field was open. Jacobs hired his sometime compatriot George L. Cobb as a sort of ragtimer in residence. It was expected that Cobb would publish with Jacobs, of course, but his main duties were as arranger and as contributor to another company magazine. The new Jacobs monthly was called *The Tuneful Yankee*, and it was designed for the musical public, not the professional musician. As editor-in-chief, Jacobs chose an old Tin Pan Alley pro, Monroe H. Rosenfeld, a hit writer of the 1890s. The first *Yankee* reached newsstands in January 1917, at fifteen cents a copy.

The browser of the *Yankee*'s first issue got an eyeful. There were articles by Monroe Rosenfeld (on the origins of ragtime), Al Bryan (on lyric writing), J. Bodewalt Lampe (on arranging music), and Edward R. Winn (on ragtime piano playing). There were record and sheet music reviews, along with gossip, "Funny Incidents in the Rambles of Music Men," and the announcement of a songwriting contest with a $50 prize. There were six complete musical numbers, three songs and three piano solos (a waltz, a novelette, and a one-step). Cobb wrote a salty column for amateur composers. (Later, after amateurs began sending him their work, the column got saltier.) The magazine was renamed *Melody* in January 1918, and its price was lowered to a dime. *Melody* continued to publish into the 1930s.

Walter Jacobs had no more big sellers after "Our Director," a march issued in 1917, but the company continued to flourish through the 1920s. At the main office (now at 120 Boylston Street), Cobb continued to turn out his brilliant rags and to look askance at would-be songwriters. Movie folios continued to sell well, as did the band and orchestral music. In 1943 the company was taken over by a Hollywood firm, but the Walter Jacobs imprint remained on its music. Walter Jacobs died in Boston in May 1945.

WILLIAMSPORT
Proud Past, Promising Future

Throughout the history of Williamsport, Pennsylvania, nature has been the city's best friend and worst foe. Topography was its first problem. Its location in the Appalachian Mountains (in the West Branch Valley of the Susquehanna River) kept it sparsely settled until the 1830s. Because all wagon roads avoided the rough terrain, the area was bypassed during the westward migration of the mid-nineteenth century. Indigenous pine and hemlock forests put the town on the map as a lumber center, but frequent floods on the Susquehanna played havoc every few years with the lumbermen's mills, bridges, and shipping facilities. Humanity, as well as nature, was often hostile to Williamsport. Disputes with various Indian tribes, especially the Iroquois, led to a series of armed skirmishes, called the Yankee-Pennamite Wars, that lasted fifteen years, from 1769 to 1784.

The town's first resident, a land speculator named Michael Ross, convinced the Pennsylvania legislature to carve a new county out of western Northumberland County and to name 111 undeveloped acres of his holdings as the county seat. Despite the fact that the place had only one building (the Russell Inn), no name, and no permanent population, the Pennsylvania legislature created Lycoming County in 1795 and proclaimed Ross's pasture the seat of Lycoming's government. A county seat needs a name, of course, so in 1796 Ross named it after his son William.

In 1800, only 131 people called Williamsport home. Most of the trades had only one practitioner there (one tailor, one tanner, one blacksmith, one distiller, etc.), but there were two attorneys, two carpenters, and several taverns. The Susquehanna was impassable for large boats, so there was not much business activity until the opening of the West Branch Canal in 1834. The canal was Williamsport's first link to the outside world, making it possible to export the town's most valuable resource, timber. In the decade before the Civil War, a great lumber industry arose, along with an offshoot craft, furniture-making. An influx of workers in the timber trades led to Williamsport's incorporation as a city in 1866. In 1870 the population was 16,030 (nearly triple the 1860 census figure), and most of this growth was due to the boom in lumber. Williamsport first made national news in 1872 when its mill workers struck, demanding that their hours be reduced from twelve to ten a day, to earn the same daily wage, $1.50. Pennsylvania's governor sent 400 militiamen to put down the "Sawdust War," and the twelve-hour day held firm.

Culture followed prosperity, as usual, and in 1867 Williamsport's first major concert hall, the 1,000-seat Ullman Opera House, was erected on Market Square. In 1869 a small conservatory, the Williamsport Academy of Music, opened its doors. The Ullman and the Academy of Music were sources of local pride, but the town had another musical organization that was known beyond its borders. This was the Repasz

Band, a community group, formed in 1831, that covered itself in glory during the Civil War. The Repasz bandsmen joined thousands of Pennsylvanians in volunteering for the Union army, and they served as musicians for two hard-fighting state regiments. It was the Repasz Band that provided the background music at Appomattox, playing "The Star Spangled Banner" as Lee surrendered to Grant.

Williamsport boasted a journalistic institution as well as a musical one: the *Grit*, a weekly paper that began publishing there in 1882. Saturday was "*Grit* day" for nearly a hundred years in rural and small-town homes across the United States. The paper was light on news but long on cheer. It celebrated farm living, offering cooking and canning tips, photos of prize-winning animals, and feature stories with happy endings. Many a barefoot boy began his business life as salesman and local fulfillment manager for the *Grit*.

In the mid-1880s the local lumber barons awoke to the fact that the unthinkable was happening: they were running out of trees. Like many cities blessed with a vast natural resource, Williamsport had never given a thought to conserving the blessing. Fifty years of harvesting every tree in sight had cut the mountains clean, and no seedlings had been planted to replace the white pines and hemlocks. Mills closed, workers drifted away, property values plummeted, and the town was paralyzed. The paralysis lasted into the early 1890s, when the city government took action. It created the Williamsport Board of Trade, a kind of high-powered and very aggressive Chamber of Commerce, to rove the Northeast and Midwest touting the city as the perfect place to open a business or a branch. The board enticed diversified businesses—retail stores, insurance companies, a pipe fitting firm, a hinge company, several banks—to move there, and the local economy righted itself at the dawn of the ragtime era. The most recent book-length history of Williamsport fails to mention that during this new prosperity, the city was home to an important regional publisher of pop music. After Walter Jacobs in Boston, and outside of New York City, no one in the Northeast published more ragtime than Vandersloot Music Company.

VANDERSLOOT MUSIC COMPANY

Frederick William Vandersloot (1866–1931) founded his music publishing company in Williamsport in January 1898. There was no shortage of music to issue, because the founder's brother Carl wrote marches

Frederick W. Vandersloot

and waltzes by the dozens. Vandersloot overreached almost as soon as he began, by opening a New York City branch, at 42 West Twenty-eighth Street, in 1899. On the cover of one of his first New York pieces is a list of his distributors, and, for a newcomer to the game, the list is quite impressive. Less than two years old, Vandersloot had music for sale in Milwaukee, Detroit, Philadelphia, St. Paul, Chicago, New York, and Toronto.

As soon as the company established itself in New York, a hack composer named Lee Orean Smith attached himself to it. The first Smith item in the company's catalog was an 1899 cakewalk, "Campin' on De Ole Suwanee." Even more prolific than the publisher's brother, Smith ground out bad marches, bad reveries, bad intermezzos, and bad songs—and Vandersloot seems to have bought them all. Smith's near-monopoly of the catalog was not broken until Vandersloot closed his New York branch around 1903.

Back in Williamsport, Fred Vandersloot met Harry J. Lincoln, a composer/arranger from Shamokin, Pennsylvania, whose work would be the ballast of the company. In 1904 Vandersloot published a Lincoln march, "Heaven's Artillery," and, more importantly, he bought a copyright from Lincoln that would give the company its only hit: "Repasz Band," a march credited to Charles C. Sweeley and published by Sweeley Music Company in 1901. When he learned that Vandersloot was interested in "Repasz Band," Lincoln dropped his mask and admitted that he was Sweeley and that he would be happy to sell the number. ("Charles C. Sweeley" was the first of several pseudonyms used to cloak the identity of Harry Lincoln. He also wrote under two other names besides his own—H. A. Fischler and Abe Losch.)

Harry J. Lincoln

Vandersloot issued the perky, triplet-laden march in 1904, with a photo of its subject on the cover and Lincoln credited as its arranger. Over the next several years, local sales grew into regional sales. By 1915 or so, "Repasz Band" was in the repertoire of every school and community band in the United States, with Lincoln credited as composer. Vandersloot sold it in arrangements for every possible combination of instruments, and in 1920 it was reissued as a song, with lyrics by Ray Sherwood.

In April 1909 Vandersloot Music issued its first ragtime composition, Charles L. Johnson's "Apple Jack." Johnson was riding high as the composer of the hit "Dill Pickles" and was still operating his own publishing business in Kansas City at the time. Why he would send a major rag like "Apple Jack" to Vandersloot, who had published no previous rags, is anybody's guess; maybe it was offered as a test, to see what the Williamsport publisher could do with it. In any case, "Apple Jack" was a strong entry into ragtime publishing for Vandersloot. The company's ragtime list had nowhere to go but down, and it did. (There was no

Williamsport competition to spur it to excellence. The only rag from
that city not published by Vandersloot was J. C. Halls's "Fuss and
Feathers," issued by United States Music in 1909. It has recently been
learned that "J. C. Halls" was another pseudonym of Harry Lincoln.
When Vandersloot hired Lincoln as staff composer and arranger, he co-
opted his only possible local rival.) Frank Hoyt Losey, the
composer/arranger who had founded Losey's Military Band School in
Erie, Pennsylvania, joined the company's staff around this time. Losey
contributed his first rag to the Vandersloot catalog in 1909.

Vandersloot Music published four more rags after its first in 1909,
and they, not "Apple Jack," characterize the company's syncopated
product. Harry Lincoln was on the Vandersloot staff by then, and he
contributed three of them. His "Rastus Rag," issued in September, typifies Vandersloot's output: it has single-note melody lines and thin harmonies, making it very easy to play, and there is a busyness about its
syncopation that borders on the nervous. The "Rastus" cover is typical,
too: the huge face of a cartoony black man in a stovepipe hat. Unlike
most ragtime imprints, Vandersloot covers often have a racist tone, and
many of them bear the signature of their illustrator, W. Dittmar.

The big year for Vandersloot rags, with eight original publications
and one reprint, was 1910. Charles L. Johnson gave Vandersloot a second and last try with his "Golden Spider," and the Lincoln-Losey
machine was in high gear, contributing six of the eight originals. The
reprint was of Charles Cohen's "Riverside Rag." Cohen had self-published "Riverside" in Binghamton, New York, earlier that year, with a
drawing of Binghamton's Riverside Park on the cover. When the rag
was issued by Vandersloot, it was given a drawing of alligators ogling
black children at a swimming hole.

Harry Lincoln's last rag as a Vandersloot staffer was "Black
Diamond," published in 1914. A few years later, Lincoln went to
Philadelphia to start his own publishing company. Losey remained a
Vandersloot employee, and the ever-dependable Carl Vandersloot came
back into action in the late teens, thrown into a frenzy of composition by
World War I. Carl's marches and war songs made up much of the
Vandersloot list until the hostilities were over. In 1920 Carl entered the
Jazz Age with his "Spooky Ooky Blues." There were no Vandersloot rags
between 1914 and 1928, when Harry Lincoln tried his hand at a novelty,
"Hickory Nuts Rag" (using the pseudonym "Abe Losch"). The firm's last

rag was Giff Fahrmeyer's "Ivory Kapers" in 1929. The Vandersloot company went out of business with the death of its founder in 1931.

WASHINGTON, D.C.

Southern Efficiency, Northern Charm

In 1783 the U.S. Congress heard the first proposal to establish a permanent capital city in the new republic. After much partisan debate, there was no clear mandate as to where the capital should be, so the matter was tabled for seven years. In 1790 compromise won the day, and it was decided to choose a site in the middle of the country (that is, in the middle of the ex-colonies along the eastern seaboard). President George Washington himself selected the place, a sparsely populated area on the Potomac River, bordered by Maryland and Virginia. The following year Andrew Elliott, a white surveyor, and Benjamin Banneker, a black mathematician, worked together to delineate its boundaries. Pierre L'Enfant, a French engineer, laid out the city, and in 1800 the federal government made its official move from Philadelphia to the city of Washington, which did not yet quite exist. In 1802 Congress established a local government for the upstart capital and adjourned, believing that growth and prosperity would surely follow their anointing of it.

But growth and prosperity did not come. Tradesmen and entrepreneurs saw no reason to leave homes and businesses in older, better-established cities to set themselves up in Washington. Even politicians resisted moving there. Bostonians, Philadelphians, and New Yorkers knew urbanity when they saw it, and they didn't see it in Washington. When British troops sacked and burned the town during the War of 1812, the skittish were confirmed in their fears. Washington was not only small, dirty, and jejune, it was a target for foreign aggressors.

The restoration of Washington was as slow as its startup had been. By 1840 there were only about 50,000 residents, and, although most of the rebuilding was over, there was much still left undone in L'Enfant's original building plan. It was not until 1846 that Washington was incorporated as a city. The city's real growth and expansion of commerce did not come until the Civil War years, when bureaucracy bloomed as a result of the complex military effort. In 1874 the Baltimore & Potomac Railway Station was built, and the city was finally linked to the nationwide railway system.

Among the businessmen who were not drawn to Washington were music publishers. The only nineteenth-century publisher who specialized in music—and who lasted more than a year or so—was John F. Ellis, who opened shop at 306 Pennsylvania Avenue in 1852. In 1871 the Ellis company, now under the imprint of Mrs. John F. Ellis, moved to 937 Pennsylvania Avenue, N.E., where it remained until it went out of business in 1912. Although it operated well into the ragtime era, Ellis published no rags. D.C. had a ragtime publisher, though, and he almost figured out how to make the riskiest of all musical enterprises into a sure thing.

THE H. KIRKUS DUGDALE COMPANY

Horace Kirkus Dugdale (1890–1980) was king of the vanity publishers in the ragtime era. He sold his publications, not to music stores, but to those who had written them. If a writer was confused or daunted by the difficulty of getting published, Dugdale was there to serve. Whatever anyone sent him, he would publish. If a number was musically or lyrically awkward, his arrangers would make it look presentable, neaten it up, give it a cover, and print it. He took away the bother and the risk of rejection for amateur composers and lyricists. If the composer's object was merely to get his song into print (and to see his name on a published tune), Dugdale was his man.

Dugdale's advertising implied that he had connections in the mainstream music business, but he never promised to place a song with a vaudeville star or with a larger publisher. He didn't pledge to make a song a hit, or even to plug it. That was the concern of the writers themselves. Because Dugdale ran a mail-order business, his rags are rarely seen today. They went back to the small towns from which they came, where they gladdened the hearts of their writers for a few weeks, then disappeared into oblivion. Most of the Dugdale composers' estates probably contain multiple copies.

H. K. Dugdale grew up in Baltimore and moved to Washington with his family when he was a young man. Horace took a job in a large music store, Sanders and Stayman Company, and acquired his knowledge of the inner workings of the music business there. He had some ambition to be a composer, and in 1907 he self-published his "Ginger Snap Rag." When "Ginger Snap" failed to attract any notice, and Sanders and Stayman began to look like a dead end, Horace decided to go at commercial music in another way. In 1908, when he was eighteen, his father set him up in business with a "manuscript-writing studio." Amateurs would send him "song-poems," which he would set to music for a fee. He had a flair for setting the unsettable, and as word of his ability got around, his assignments multiplied. Of course, a lyricist who had bought a melody for a song was still faced with the awesome task of getting it published, and Dugdale saw a way to take his services a step further.

He began to advertise in trade journals, proclaiming his H. Kirkus Dugdale Company a publishing enterprise. Amateur writers had only to submit their songs, and Dugdale would do the rest. If a song needed a melody, he would supply it. If a tune had no lyric, he would write one. He could fix up anything. For $50 Dugdale would print 300 copies. The composer received 298, and the other two were placed on deposit with the copyright office in the Library of Congress in the composer's name.

The first rag from the Dugdale company was "Rattle Snake Rag," written by Clyde W. Headley of Galva, Illinois, in 1910. Three more Dugdale rags followed in 1911, bringing cheer and encouragement to Kenneth W. Bradshaw (in Thornton, Indiana), Harry Bussler (in Beresford, South Dakota), and Len Larimer (in Westboro, Missouri). Although neither Washington nor Tin Pan Alley ever heard of his products, Horace Dugdale was, by age twenty-one, D.C.'s premier publisher of ragtime and of pop music in general. In 1912 the company incorporated, with a capital stock valued at $250,000.

Dugdale moved his firm into the Dugdale Building, at 1435 U Street, N.W., in the summer of 1913, and the founder issued a promotional brochure in celebration. He boasted of the two-story structure's modernity, its plentiful lighting, its ventilation, and its location (across the street from a post office substation and a fifteen-minute ride from the copyright office). In the basement was a recital hall, called the Olympic Theatre, which he said was used for showcasing songs. (He did not say to whom the songs were showcased.) There was an office where his monthly magazine, *Musical Progress*, was prepared for publication. A large general area contained work spaces for the thirty employees—composers, stenographers, and clerks—who processed everything. In Dugdale's own office was a piano, on which "new compositions are tried over and approved." His proudest possession was a four-drawer file cabinet marked "Testimonials," which contained hundreds of letters from satisfied songwriters. Dugdale said the place was "the only building in Washington devoted entirely to the publication and sale of sheet music," and this was true.

The elation over the new facility was dampened somewhat when, a few months after moving in, Dugdale and two of his executive staff were arrested for using the mails to defraud. Evidently three amateur songwriters (one each from Newark, New Jersey, Allentown, Pennsylvania, and St. Michaels, Maryland) expected more than they had got from Dugdale, and they were now claiming that they had been enticed by his advertising. Dugdale, his vice-president (who was his younger brother George), and his secretary/treasurer were released on $2,000 bond, and a hearing was set for October 13. Music trade magazines make no more mention of the matter, so the charges must have been dropped. In any case, the arrest hardly broke the stride of the thriving company. In late 1913 and early 1914, parcels of freshly published rags went out to M. Mae Serviss (in Ontario), to Ray Collins (in Newport, Kentucky), to Cliff Irvin (in Chillicothe, Missouri), and to Ermon Smith (in El Paso, Texas), among many others.

Perhaps the expense of the building and the large number of staffers took its toll. Perhaps Dugdale's father had been bankrolling the business all along and simply ran out of money or patience. Whatever the reason, the Dugdale company went bankrupt and closed its doors in July 1915. Even if it ended badly, the company could only be called a success. Dugdale had his cabinet full of testimonials, and he had the satisfaction of having come very close to staying afloat in the pop music business without ever having a hit or even going for one. And, at twenty-five, he was still a young man. He went into advertising and stayed with it all of his life.

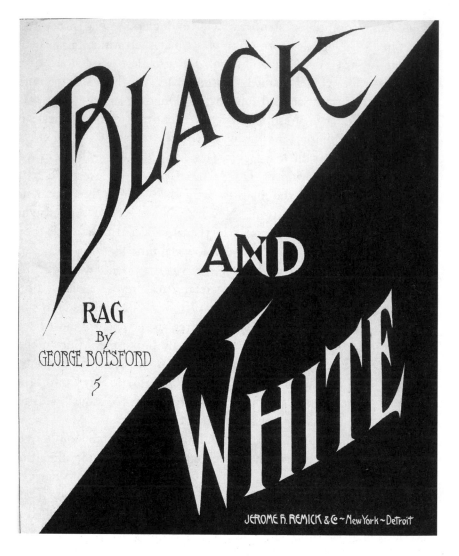

"Black and White Rag"

CHAPTER SIX

Ragtime in New York City

The Italian navigator Giovanni da Verrazano was the first European explorer to see the area that became New York City, in 1524, but it was an Englishman, Henry Hudson, sailing for the Dutch East India Company in 1609, who first had the idea of colonizing it. The Dutch built a few trading houses there in 1613, and the following year a permanent settlement was established. The place was (optimistically) called New Amsterdam by 1625. Its prospects were so promising that Governor Peter Minuit, acting for the Dutch government, purchased the entire island of Manhattan from its original Indian settlers in 1626. New Amsterdam's nationality, and its name, changed in 1664, when a military regiment sent by the Duke of York wrested the area from the Dutch in a violent takeover. In 1686 New York was chartered as a city, and it remained under British control throughout the rest of the colonial era. In 1783 New York became an American city, with the expulsion of the British by the Continental Army. The new United States Congress convened in New York City from 1785 to 1790, and George Washington's inauguration as president took place there. European immigrants swarmed into New York in the late 1700s, and the city's perennial shortage of elbow room began with their arrival.

It was during the years immediately after the Revolutionary War that publishing became a profession in New York. Music was still a commercial sideline to books and periodicals, but a handful of New York houses began to issue songs with some regularity. G. Gilfert & Company (at 191 Broad Street), William Howe (at 326 Pearl Street), and John Paff (at 112 Broadway) were among those printer-publishers who ventured into music in the 1790s. The city's first all-music publisher was probably the Manhattan branch of Philadelphia's Thomas Dobson company that opened at 230 Queen Street in 1787. The first music dealer was the jack of all peddlers, John Jacob Astor, who added tunes to the stock in his horse-drawn emporia in 1786.

Until late in the twentieth century, the names of music publishing firms often ended with the phrases "and Brother[s]" and "and Son." Family connections, as partnerships or as nepotism, have permeated the music business and have been of great importance in its history. The first American music publishing dynasty arose in New York in 1794, when James Hewitt established a firm on the south end of Greenwich Street, near the Battery. Hewitt's output, like that of most American publishers before 1865 or so, was largely of foreign origin. No international copyright law protected composers or publishers, so pirated, royalty-free editions of foreign works could be made for the cost of printing them. Any pieces of music, especially the classics, that found their way to America from Europe were taken by as many publishers as wanted them. Some American editions presented these stolen goods in their original form; other pieces were edited—"arranged," simplified, or merely bowdlerized—for local markets.

As Hewitt's rivals from the 1790s fell by the wayside, Hewitt sailed into the new century. He opened a branch store in Boston in 1812, and in 1825 his son, James L. Hewitt, entered the business, opening both a New York store (at 129 Broadway) and a Boston store (at 34 Market Street) in his first year. Another son, Horatio N. Hewitt, started in a small way in 1830, with a music shop in a private home on Boston's Norfolk Avenue. A third Hewitt son, George W., opened a music store at 70 South Third Street in Philadelphia in 1839. In 1827 the senior Hewitt issued the first internationally known American song, "The Minstrel's Return from the War," written by his brother, John Hill Hewitt. The composer's grandson, Horatio D. Hewitt, would extend the dynasty beyond the Northeast by establishing stores in New Orleans and Baltimore. (Another important musical family was that of W. C. Peters of Louisville. Three of Peters's sons—in various combinations—were partners in stores in Cincinnati, St. Louis, New York, Louisville, and Baltimore for nearly forty years, beginning in the 1850s.)

The idea of "hits"—songs that outsold other songs and sustained a demand beyond a first printing—dawned slowly, beginning in New

York in the early nineteenth century. Joseph F. Atwill, the owner of Atwill's Music Saloon, at 137 Broadway, saw possibilities in the songs of "blackface delineators," the Negro impersonators of the variety stage. In the late 1820s Atwill had big sales with "My Long-Tail Blue" and "Jump Jim Crow." "Zip Coon," the best known of the early minstrel songs, was issued by Atwill in 1834.

The first New York publisher to have a working concept of hits and how they were made was John Firth, who entered the music business as an instrument salesman in 1815. Five years later, in partnership with William Hall, Firth began publishing music at 362 Pearl Street. In 1840 Firth, Hall had its first nationally known song, a minstrel ditty called "Jim Along, Josey." A third partner, Sylvanus B. Pond, joined the firm in 1843. When Hall withdrew in 1848, the company became known as Firth, Pond & Company. As the popularity of blackface shows grew in the 1840s, Firth and Pond saw the effect that the minstrels' programming had on sheet music sales. If a song were heard in a show and if there were copies of the song for sale in the theatre lobby after the show, people were likely to buy it. Their 1851 publication of "The Arkansas Traveller" (the "Zip Coon" melody with a new lyric) was a minstrel-related success, as was their edition of "Dixie," in 1860.

When Stephen Foster's "Oh! Susanna" became the hit of the 1848 minstrel season, Firth and Pond marked Foster as a writer to watch, indeed, a writer to go after. Dealing through the impresario Edwin P. Christy, the company acquired the publishing rights to two Foster songs in 1849. Firth, Pond was never the exclusive publisher of Foster's work, but the company had all of his big songs after 1850, including "Jeanie with the Light Brown Hair," "Massa's in de Cold Ground," "My Old Kentucky Home," "Old Black Joe," "Old Folks at Home," and "Ring de Banjo," among many others. After the composer's death in January 1864, it was William A. Pond (Sylvanus's son) who issued Foster's posthumous smash, "Beautiful Dreamer."

Song hits trickled, rather than poured, out of New York in the 1870s and 1880s, but the pace of the trickle increased during that time. Some of these successes were the result of calculation, of finding talented writers or thriving theatrical companies as sources of material and of making sure that show-related songs were available while the shows were running. (William Pond's songs from Harrigan and Hart shows proved the profitability of show-song synchronization.) Some were happy accidents ("There Is a Tavern in the Town," "Rock-a-Bye Baby," "Where Did You Get That Hat?"), songs that unexpectedly caught on with college students, tapped a primal emotion in a simple way, or caught new slang expressions just before they peaked.

At the dawning of the pop song era, several truisms emerged:

1. an untried song usually requires something to hook listeners into paying attention to it (a show, a star, a fad, a well-known event as its subject)

2. money must be spent to command attention to a song

3. old subjects (mother, love, home) usually need a new twist

4. blatant imitations of last year's big songs are pretty safe bets

There were other lessons yet to be learned, but these would do for twenty years or so. If the underlying premise of the business was "you never can tell about a song," the modern addendum was that *trying* to tell was worth doing. Fortunes were being made in music by 1880, and many new publishers were inspired to go after them. As always, the young thought they could do it better, and in this case they could. New York's neophyte publishers of the 1880s and 1890s created something new under the sun—a unique industry built on nerve, liquid assets, and a pinch of art: the pop music game.

By 1890 New York City was the U.S. entertainment capital. It was the center of activity for each of the three main components of show business: musical theatre, vaudeville, and the publishing of popular music. In the 1890–91 season, sixteen new musical shows were produced in New York and nearly as many revivals held the stage. There were more than two dozen major playhouses (all but three of them below Thirty-fourth Street), presenting everything from big-time vaudeville to operetta to Shakespeare. Real estate tycoons Marcus Klaw and Abraham Lincoln Erlanger were on their way to owning enough theatres to exercise the near-dictatorial control that they would soon hold over the legitimate stage. The Keith–Albee chain, headquartered in Boston, had a toehold in New York by 1893, and would rule vaudeville by 1900, as the Klaw–Erlanger syndicate ruled legit. William A. Pond, Frank Harding, and Willis Woodward were the most successful pop music publishers of the day. These titans of legit, vaudeville, and pop recognized that they were all in the same business: that shows sold songs and that songs sold shows. Another piece of common knowledge was that they all needed a steady supply of whatever was new.

Ragtime hit New York even before it was new. It was taken out of the oven, half-baked, in 1896 and served by Ben Harney (1871–1938) to vaudeville audiences, who ate it up. Harney, a white Kentuckian, was a pianist-singer who specialized in performing coon songs of his own authorship. He was no great shakes as a piano player, but he didn't have to be to put his songs across. When he hit the stage at Tony Pastor's variety theatre (in the Tammany Hall building, on Fourteenth Street between Irving Place and Third Avenue) in the spring of 1896, he was a bundle of novelty, playing and singing and doing things unlike anybody else. Although he didn't perform in blackface, he opened with a "black" song, "Mr. Johnson, Turn Me Loose." He syncopated the hell out of it, musically and vocally, finally rendering the lyric in a kind of raggy pig-Latin. When his song was answered by a singer in the gallery, Harney invited the stranger to the stage. As Harney's partner, Strap Hill, climbed over the footlights, the audience

Ben Harney

gasped when it realized that Hill was black. Harney and Hill fooled around for a while, doing animal imitations and eccentric dancing. To further confound the racial element of the act, Harney's wife, Jessie, wearing blackface, sprang out from the wings, and the three sang "I Love My Little Honey," two-stepping off, with Jessie adding a cartwheel for good measure. Harney called his music "rag-time," and New York took him at his word.

Harney and his songs made a sensation. Here was something new, all right, and whatever it was called, publishers and vaudeville bookers wanted it. Witmark was his primary publisher, issuing three of his hits ("Mr. Johnson," "You've Been a Good Old Wagon," and "The Cakewalk in the Sky") and ten or so of his lesser numbers. May Irwin, the preeminent coon-shouter (as interpreters of this type of pop song were known) of the day, used Harney songs in her vaudeville act. When she opened at the Bijou Theatre in a musical called *Courted into Court*, in December 1896, she took "Mr. Johnson" with her. Long after he had been displaced by better singers, pianists, and songwriters, Harney played the inventor of ragtime on the vaudeville stage.

If Ben Harney's performance at Pastor's wowed his audiences, it electrified Pastor's music director, Mike Bernard. Bernard was nineteen when he first saw Harney, and the experience changed his life. Before the Kentucky juggernaut hit Fourteenth Street, Bernard had had no thoughts of musical exhibitionism. He had been a child prodigy, beginning two years of study at the Berlin Conservatory at age nine, and playing a command performance for the Kaiser to cap his stay in Germany. As his prodigy's appeal waned, Bernard had drifted into popular music, arranging and conducting for variety acts. As a vaudeville musician, he must have thought that he had seen it all, but he had seen nothing like this. Harney took pop songs and literally tore them to tatters, and the effect was liberating. Seeing audiences go wild over "ragtime" night after night, Bernard was transformed. He resolved that he would perform the "rag-time," too. His act would be radically different from Harney's, though. Mike Bernard didn't need to horse around with stick dancing or coon-shouting; he could play the piano.

When Harney finally left Pastor's after a long-extended engagement, Bernard took his place as ragtimer-in-residence. Whatever the weekly changes of the acts on Pastor's bill, one featured performer was always Mike Bernard. Like Harney, Bernard dealt in coon songs, not ragtime compositions, but, unlike Harney, he could impress audiences by his piano playing alone. By 1900 "ragtime" had become a catchword in New York's entertainment circles, and although the city had not yet heard much real ragtime, New York liked what it thought it knew about it. With his rowdy playing of simple songs, Mike Bernard spread the idea of ragtime as good-natured desecration.

On the evening of January 23, 1900, Richard K. Fox, the publisher of the *Police Gazette*, sponsored a ragtime piano-playing contest at Pastor's and offered a diamond-studded medal as the prize. At 1:40 A.M., before a huge, restless, and half-drunk crowd, the playing finally got underway. None of the players were top-drawer—a woman who was so nervous that she was practically paralyzed, a German who called his brother out to help him finish his piece—but three finalists, including Mike Bernard, were chosen. One of them, a black pianist named Duke Travers, played something soft and lyrical; a man called Warnick played "The Stars and Stripes Forever"; Bernard played the latest coon hit, "I'd Leave Ma Happy Home for You," and took home the medal. It wasn't exactly Rosebud-Café quality, but New York had had a piano contest and the local favorite had won. Bernard would trade on his notoriety and make a long vaudeville career, as Harney had done before him. For years his name led all the rest in New York ragtime, and in December 1912 he was invited by Columbia Records to make the first piano ragtime recording on disc, Wallie Herzer's "Everybody Two-Step."

New York's introduction to ragtime, at the hands of Harney and Bernard, colored the city's idea of the music for decades. Manhattan associated rags with vaudeville, because that was the site of its first acquaintance, and ragtime would continue to be seen from a show-business perspective, as a spectator sport. Ragtime would serve as the medium for outrageous acts, singers (often in blackface) who spouted rhythmic nonsense, and pianists whose trademarks were noise and flying hands. When ragtime was no longer a novelty, it became merely background music, accompaniment for acrobats, jugglers, and clowns. Trickiness was thought to be the core of its appeal. In the Midwest, the region that loved ragtime most, the music came in through the living room and made itself at home in the parlor. In New York, ragtime was something that you went out to see, rather than something you stayed home to hear. The timing was right, though: when New York ragtime was young, it attracted some vigorous and well-heeled suitors in the pop music business.

Two Profiles in New York City Ragtime

HENRY LODGE

It was nearly ten years after the first ragtime publication (in Chicago, in 1897), that ragtime began to be accepted by New York publishers as a genre that was here to stay. Up until that time, the city's few ragtime hits had been imports, written and first published in the Midwest. The only famous composer of ragtime was Scott Joplin, although working musicians would also have known the rags of Tom Turpin, James Scott, or Charles L. Johnson. (The first New York rag to attain renown was George M. Cohan's "Popularity," published by F. A. Mills in 1906.) Around 1906–07 Jerome H. Remick & Company, under the guidance of Charles N. Daniels, a Kansan who cut his ragtime teeth in Missouri, stepped up its purchase of rags from Midwestern composers: Irene M. Giblin, Percy Wenrich, Charles L. Johnson, Julia Lee Niebergall. Daniels's idea was to offer good ragtime in original editions, not reprints, and Remick's infusion of brand-new, high-quality rags energized the market. And in 1907 the biggest name in ragtime, Scott Joplin, moved to New York and began to offer his work to Tin Pan Alley publishers (Joseph Stern the first among them). As rags consistently outsold coon songs and cakewalks, New York publishers finally got the message: coon songs and cakewalks were the fads, not ragtime. Although there had been only a handful of rag hits, several of them had been huge ("Maple Leaf," "Dill Pickles," and "Frog Legs"), and none of the big ones had come from New York. Having been scooped for a decade by out-of-town publishers, Tin Pan Alley finally put its mind (as well as its money and energy) to selling rags.

Henry Lodge

One of the first composers to flourish in this new, hyper-commercial ragtime scene was Henry Lodge. Over a ten-year period he wrote fifteen rags, most of them of extremely high quality, and he had two solid hits. Although he was never under contract as staff composer or arranger, all but one of his rags were issued by major New York firms. In an environment where professionalism was as highly prized as musicianship, Lodge was a hard-working and reliable professional.

Thomas Henry Lodge was born on February 9, 1884, in Providence, Rhode Island. His father was a textile worker who had emigrated from Manchester, England, and his mother had her hands full tending the little Lodges, who eventually numbered five. When

Henry was twelve, a family friend stored a piano in the Lodge home, and he got his first up-close look at the instrument. He took to it at once, and his experimentation inspired him to ask for piano lessons. His father's death curtailed his formal study after three or four months. Instead of spending money, Henry was expected to earn it, so he took a job at Meiklejohn's Music Store. He kept practicing on his own, and he was soon promoted to the position of piano demonstrator and salesman.

It was in 1904, when Henry Lodge was twenty, that his first compositions appeared in print. He started his own ball rolling by self-publishing his schottische "At the Ball," and later that year a Providence publisher, M. Steinart & Sons, issued his waltz song "Down to Rhodes," a salute to a local city park. He also sent a song called "Say That You Love Me, Carrie" to Eckerson Music Publishing Company, a small Boston firm, which published it.

Lodge married Sarah Agnes Mackie in 1906, and they lived for a year or so in Pawtucket, where their only child, Mary, was born in 1907. By 1908 Henry was back in Providence, listed in the city directory as a music teacher. With a new family to provide for, he could not accept the risks inherent in a musical career, but he resolved to keep writing and publishing. In 1909 he placed "Skylark—An Intermezzo for Piano" with N. Weinstein, a New York publisher, and "Old South—A Plantation Dance" with Vinton Music of Boston. Another Lodge composition of 1909 was his first rag. He sent "Temptation Rag" to M. Witmark & Sons in New York, and it was this rag that would eventually uproot him from Providence.

Witmark had published only one rag before "Temptation" (Stephen Howard's "Sakes Alive" in 1903), but the company knew what to do with a good number when it had one. With nearly a quarter-century of successful song-plugging under its belt, in September 1909 Witmark went to work on "Temptation Rag." The firm first pushed it into the hands of vaudeville orchestra leaders, and they quickly took it up. "Temptation"'s lyrical, sweet-and-sour tonalities began to be used as accompaniment to dance teams and acrobatic acts. Prince's Band made a Columbia recording within six weeks of its publication and Arthur Pryor's Band recorded it twice for Victor in June 1910.

By the time of the Pryor recordings, "Temptation" had proved such a winner in its instrumental version that Witmark decided to issue a song version. Louis Weslyn was hired to write the lyric (to two of its four melodic themes), which Arthur Collins was first to sing, on a Columbia record made in the spring of 1910. Lodge's compositional trademarks—long, flowing melody lines and bittersweet harmonies—permeate "Temptation Rag," and these devices kept it a favorite among dance orchestras long after the ragtime era had passed. "Temptation" would be one of the most-recorded rags through the 1920s, and it would have a new burst of popularity during the early revival era.

Resisting "Temptation," Lodge was not yet ready to give up the security of teaching music in Providence. He was keen to write more rags, however, and in 1910 he saw three of them published. He placed his "Sure Fire Rag" with Victor Kremer in Chicago and his "Sneaky Shuffles" with Remick in New York. But it was Witmark's December publication and plugging of his fine "Red Pepper" that gave him his follow-up hit. Prince's Band recorded it in 1911, as did the Empire Military Band and the banjoist Fred Van Eps. Encouraged by "Red Pepper"'s instrumental sales, Witmark hired theatre lyricist Harold Atteridge to turn it into a song.

Finally, in 1912, Henry Lodge answered the siren call and moved to New York City. Having given Witmark two hits, he might have been taken into the firm as a staff arranger or composer, but he chose to play in vaudeville and cabaret orchestras instead. (Lodge obviously longed for stability, so it is odd that he never worked for a publishing house. Perhaps he did not know that such jobs existed when he moved to New York.) Although Lodge was not a Witmark employee, the company was the exclusive publisher of his rags during his first two years in New York, and the firm had a near-hit with his "Black Diamond" in 1912. In early 1914 Lodge served as pianist for the tea dances and private instruction sessions at Vernon and Irene Castle's elegant Castle House, on East Forty-sixth Street.

In late 1915 or early 1916, perhaps still chasing security, Lodge moved to Atlantic City, where he played in the dance orchestra that held forth on the Million Dollar Pier. His rag output waned in the mid-teens, but in 1917, possibly inspired by the progressive work of Charley

Straight, he came back strong. Remick issued two Lodge rags (each with the catchword "blues" in its title), and Witmark issued his final three rags the following year. Lodge's late rags, unlike his earlier ones that band leaders so loved, are very pianistic. They are extremely complex, full of odd harmonies and textures, and perhaps too unusual to have been popular.

Sarah Lodge died in 1918, and there were no more Lodge compositions for three years. Henry moved back to New York in 1920, taking a job playing in a gamblers' hangout, Murray's Café. In the early 1920s he began spending his winters in West Palm Beach, where he organized society orchestras for New York nabobs who had fled the snow. He remarried and began a second family during this time, and he began to compose again. His song "Fooling Me" was published by Robert Norton Company in New York in 1921, and he had a mild success with "That Red Head Gal," written with the singing duo Van and Schenck, in 1923. One of his last publications was a song, "Indian Butterfly," written with Edgar Leslie and Billy Stone and published by Leslie in 1927.

After seesawing between New York and West Palm Beach through the 1920s, Lodge decided in 1930 to give Los Angeles a try. A year or so of writing background music for films was enough for him, and he returned to New York. Henry Lodge died in West Palm Beach, at the height of the season, in February 1933.

GEORGE BOTSFORD

George Botsford's career in ragtime almost precisely parallels that of Henry Lodge in duration and accomplishment. Two of Botsford's seventeen rags were hits, and he had hit songs as well. But the two professional lives were very different in that Botsford found the security that eluded Lodge. Not long after his arrival in New York, Botsford joined the staff of Jerome H. Remick & Company, and for more than twenty years, he knew where he was going when he got up in the morning.

George Botsford was born in Sioux Falls, South Dakota, on February 24, 1874. Little is known of his early life other than that he grew up in Iowa, and nothing is known of his musical background or training. His first published composition was a cakewalk, "The Katy Flyer," which he issued himself in Centerville, Iowa, in 1899. Botsford

George Botsford

obviously had large ambitions, however, and he knew where to go to realize them. Somehow he made it to New York and began peddling songs in Tin Pan Alley.

In 1906 the Remick company had published two of the biggest hits of the current cowboy-and-Indian song vogue ("Cheyenne" and "Iola"), so when a Westerner arrived with a Western song in hand in 1907, he got a hearing. The "cowboy" composer was George Botsford, and the song was "Pride of the Prairie," with lyrics by Harry Breen. Although the song was not the biggest hit of its kind, it was successful enough to keep the vogue, and Remick's stake in it, alive. Botsford had some rags for sale, too, and in January 1908 he placed one ("Klondike Rag") with a small publisher, William R. Haskins Company.

"Pride of the Prairie" got Botsford's toe into Remick's door, and in 1908 he called again, this time with a number called "Black and White Rag." Remick bought the rag and published it that year but did not plug it heavily at first. (Remick's initial lack of enthusiasm for "Black and White Rag" is reflected by the fact that the company never bothered to copyright it. After fifteen years of popularity in vaudeville and on recordings, "Black and White Rag" was finally secured by a Remick copyright in 1924.) Even if the publisher was not wild about it, the public loved the way "Black and White" rattled along, with a three-over-four pattern in each of its three boisterous melodies heightening its gaiety.

Albert Benzler's version of "Black and White Rag," released by U.S. Everlasting in 1908, was the first cylinder recording of solo piano ragtime. However, Botsford's rag sold tens of thousands of sheet music copies before it was available on discs. The Victor Orchestra made the first disc recording of "Black and White," in June 1909, and a Columbia disc, made by Prince's Band, was issued two months later. In spite of Remick's stumble in getting "Black and White Rag" into the market-place, it went on to sell over a million copies. Like Lodge's "Temptation," "Black and White" remained popular into the 1920s, and it firmly held its place in the rag repertoire during the 1940s and '50s revival.

Although Botsford had given Remick a big song and a hit rag (as well as three other rags in 1909), the company made no move to secure exclusivity of Botsford's services, so he was still a freelancer. He took his first rag of 1910 to Ted Snyder, and its reception must have caused a general gnashing of teeth at Remick's. Snyder published "Grizzly Bear Rag," another three-over-four concoction, named for the first of the "animal dance" fads, in April 1910. Snyder's faith in the "Grizzly Bear" melody was so strong that, even before it was in general release as an instrumental, he asked his lyricist partner, Irving Berlin, to put words to it.

The song version, called "The Dance of the Grizzly Bear," hit the music stores simultaneously with the piano version, and both were hugely successful. Sophie Tucker immediately snapped up the song for her vaudeville act, and it also became a featured number in the *Follies of 1910*, which opened in June. Ziegfeld's 1910 edition was the raggiest of all the *Follies*, using syncopated songs by Lewis F. Muir, Harry Von Tilzer, and Joe Jordan, and "The Dance of the Grizzly Bear" was the raggiest of all its numbers. Arthur Pryor's Band made the first instru-mental recording of "Grizzly Bear," for Victor in September 1910, and Arthur Collins's song version, on the Sonora label, was released the same month. Around the time that the Snyder-owned "Grizzly Bear" began its climb to million-seller status, George Botsford was offered a staff arranger's job at Jerome H. Remick & Company.

Botsford worked in Remick's vocal department, arranging choral and quartet numbers for publication. And with his employment he became, of course, an exclusive Remick writer, to be published by no one else for the rest of his life. He would eventually become chief of the "harmony and quartet division," and he would remain there until his retirement, remembered by his colleagues only as a "silent man" with no discernible personality or eccentricities. He found a way to turn his vocation into civic service in his later life, giving of his time for two decades as director of the New York Police Department Glee Club.

Beginning with "Chatterbox Rag" in October 1910, there were seven more Botsford rags issued under the Remick imprint. There were no hits among them, but his two fine "flower" rags of 1911, "Hyacinth" and "Honeysuckle," represent his most graceful and mature work. Two Botsford rags, "Universal Rag" (1912) and "The Buck-Eye Rag" (1913), were written for piano roll companies and were never published.

Botsford, composing under pseudonyms, tried his hand at theatre writing in 1912. As "Will H. Becker," he provided music (and several lyrics) for *Mama's Baby Boy*, a nine-performance flop at the Broadway Theatre in May of that year. Three months later, as "William Becker," he and lyricist Jean Havez contributed the score to *The Girl from Brighton*, a forty-nine-performance flop at the Academy of Music. Botsford and Havez got their song "Join Our Jubilee" into *All for the Ladies* in 1913, and this interpolation marked the end of the composer's theatre career.

Although Broadway was not clamoring for Botsford-Havez songs, Remick was. Botsford's employer issued several numbers by the team in the early teens, reaping a huge hit with their "Sailing Down the Chesapeake Bay" in 1913. "Chesapeake Bay"'s raggy melody and boundless energy made it the perfect closer for musical acts, and its built-in lyric break is irresistible ("All aboard for Baltimore and if we're late they'll all be sore"). The tune received many recordings, the duet version by Henry Burr and Albert Campbell being the biggest seller. With his profits from "Chesapeake Bay," George Botsford began his own small publishing company. In doing so, he was not jeopardizing his job at Remick because his firm issued music so odd that neither Remick nor any other pop publisher would want it. Botsford had been experimenting with the idea of short operas, using three or four singers, and he had to try his experiments in the marketplace. After two years of trying, Botsford closed his mini-opera factory in 1915.

There were no more Botsford hits after 1913, and only one Botsford rag ("Boomerang Rag" in 1916). Botsford's bouncing rags and punchy songs were perfectly attuned to his time, but his talent did not transcend its era. As an evolving music business whirled around him in the late teens and twenties, he stayed in place, arranging other people's songs at his desk at Remick's. George Botsford died in New York City on February 11, 1949.

～⌐

M. WITMARK & SONS

Although ragtime accounted for only a small part of the Witmarks' enormous output, it is proper to begin the story of ragtime publishing in New York with them, because this remarkable family practically invented the modern pop music business. They were the first systematically to diversify their musical products, to departmentalize their business organization, to recognize the size of the amateur show market and to cater to it, and the first in America to establish ties to European publishers. The Witmark boys were fierce pluggers during the 1890s, but they had a goal that went beyond day-to-day plugging. The idea, like most great ideas, was a simple one: to acquire the most likeable theatre and pop ballads in the world and to keep them in print, to sell them over and over. Of course, the brothers dabbled in musical fads, such as coon songs and topical numbers, but it was the "heart songs" in the "Witmark Music Library" and the "Black and White Series" that fattened good years and ameliorated bad ones. They had their share of hits, but, even better, they had literally dozens of standards.

Marcus Witmark arrived in New York City from his native Prussia on July 4, 1853. An older brother had preceded him to America and had set himself up as a dealer in housewares in Ft. Gaines, in southeast Georgia, so Marcus immediately went south to join him. After a few years of peddling his brother's goods from a horse-drawn wagon, he opened his own store in Ft. Gaines, built a house there, and bought a few slaves to work the cotton acreage he had acquired. At the outbreak of the Civil War, he organized his own volunteer company, equipped and trained it, and received a commission as lieutenant in the Confederate army. Lieutenant Witmark was briefly the overseer of military activities at Macon, Georgia, and he later commanded a battery at Richmond. He was granted a battlefield promotion to the rank of captain shortly before he was wounded and taken prisoner at the Battle of Gettysburg in July 1863. Captain Witmark was held in a prison camp at Johnson's Island, near Sandusky, Ohio, until the war's end. He returned to Ft. Gaines to find his home and business in ruins, so he sold the cotton he had left and headed for New York. At a neighborhood party there, he reunited with his childhood sweetheart, Henrietta Peyser, who had recently emigrated from Prussia, and they were married in October 1866.

Marcus and Henrietta Witmark would eventually have eight children, none of them strangers to work, and it was of course their two eldest who went to work first. Isidore (1869–1941) started as a delivery boy for his father's liquor business, and he later sold magazine subscriptions door to door. For six months he apprenticed himself to the United States Pianoforte Company, where he learned to tune and repair (and taught himself to play) the rental pianos that the firm placed in homes for twenty-five cents a week. Julius (1870–1929), who had won amateur contests with his startlingly pure tenor voice, sang with a local minstrel troupe for $10 a week. Jay (1872–1950), the third oldest, was the math whiz of P.S. 28. In 1883 he turned in a perfect arithmetic paper and won a school prize, a toy printing press. Among the first items produced on Jay's press were business cards that read "Witmark Brothers, Printers" and gave as their company's address 402 West Fortieth Street, their home on the edge of Hell's Kitchen. They also cranked out homemade greeting cards and were so successful at peddling them that their father bought them a gas-powered press, to make a more professional-looking product.

The collective skills of the Witmark boys made them prime candidates for the music business, but it was the duplicity of a publisher that pushed them into it. Isidore began writing songs, and in 1885 he placed two of them with Willis Woodward & Company. Woodward offered no money up front for the songs, but he promised generous royalties. Around the time that Isidore made a bargain with Woodward, his brother Julius made one, too. Because Julius was, at fifteen, the star of the Thatcher, Primrose & West company, Woodward sought him out and offered him a percentage of the profits on a new Woodward song, "Always Take Mother's Advice," if Julius would feature it in the show. Isidore's song, "A Mother's a Mother After All," racked up respectable sales, and Julius' singing of "Mother's Advice" created a demand for the music, as it was supposed to. When Isidore went to Woodward for their money, the publisher reneged. Furious at being stiffed, Isidore resolved to become a publisher himself. If he could profit from his own writing and Julius's plugging, he would do it. If he could drive Willis Woodward out of business, so much the better. In 1886 the Witmark boys entered publishing literally with a vengeance.

The only impediment to the enterprise was the youth of the founding partners. Isidore was seventeen, Julius was sixteen, and Jay, the born treasurer, was fourteen. None of them was old enough to sign a legal document. Their father solved the problem by offering to establish the business in his own name. Marcus Witmark knew nothing about music publishing and never intended to learn. He signed what Jay told him to sign and came up with cash when there was a shortfall. For more than fifty years, M. Witmark's name stayed on the company's products and on its masthead, as a gesture of appreciation for the faith he had shown in his teenaged sons.

The first Witmark publications were all-Witmark products. Isidore composed them, Julius plugged them in shows, and Jay arranged for their distribution. Sneering rivals called their firm "The Hatchery," because it was run by fledglings, but they quickly outgrew their Hell's Kitchen nest. Early in 1888 they rented space in the Union Square area, at 32 East Fourteenth Street, where they kept the office open during the great blizzard of March 12, in case some doughty vaudevillian should brave the ten-foot snowdrifts and come looking for songs. (No one did.) They moved around the corner to 841 Broadway in 1889, and in 1891 the Witmarks became the first publishers to settle on West Twenty-eighth Street, the strip that would later be known as Tin Pan Alley.

Although most of the early products bore Isidore's name as composer, there was no mistaking the Witmark firm for a vanity press. The brothers were ferocious pluggers, and their chutzpah eventually attracted manuscripts from outside the family. Vaudevillians who dabbled in songwriting (J. P. Skelly, James Thornton, and William Collier among them) began to place their tunes with the Witmarks, and the firm finally had its first hit in 1891, with a tearjerker bought from Charles Graham for $15, "The Picture That Is Turned Toward the Wall." The black balladeer Gussie Davis first published with the brothers in 1892. In 1893 Julius Witmark began a three-year stint as a singer in the longest-running show of the decade, *A Trip to Chinatown*. As a star of New York's most popular musical, he was a magnet for songwriters, and he steered the most promising of them to Jay, who offered them his standard buyout contract and his standard $15 fee for anything that Witmark purchased.

Isidore displeased George M. Cohan by overhauling the lyric of "Why Did Nellie Leave Her Home?" before he issued it, but he gave Cohan his first published number in 1893. He did similar surgery on "All Coons Look Alike to Me" in 1896, and the company's arranger, Max Hoffman, provided a "Choice Chorus, with Negro 'Rag' Accompaniment" to the Ernest Hogan tune, which was the firm's biggest hit up to that time. Two other coon songs swelled the Witmark coffers that year: Ben Harney's "Mr. Johnson, Turn Me Loose" and Barney Fagan's "My Gal Is a High Born Lady." In 1898 the company issued songs from *Clorindy*, Will Marion Cook and Paul Laurence Dunbar's musical that was the first black show in a Broadway house, and had hits with "Darktown Is Out Tonight" and "Who Dat Say Chicken in Dis Crowd?"

The Witmarks seized on headline events for song subjects in their early days, but they read the rest of the paper, too, and shaped their business accordingly. In 1891 a change in the international copyright law initiated protection for foreign compositions published in the United States. Other publishers merely despaired at the loss of royalty-free imports from Europe, but Isidore Witmark saw the change as a chance to make his firm a global enterprise. He went to London in 1892 to negotiate with several British publishers for exclusive American rights to their songs. The titans of Denmark Street were taken aback by the brash twenty-three-year-old, but Isidore won them over. By the time he left London, the musical traffic was flowing both ways: into and out of the House of Witmark. Isidore had gained the right to take his pick of the product of his British colleagues, and he had established a Witmark office in London, the first American pop enclave on European soil.

In 1893, while taking advantage of a gigantic plugging opportunity, Julius established a family beachhead in Chicago. His reputation as one of New York's most popular singers had brought him a chance to perform at the World's Fair, and the first order of business was to sing all

Witmark songs all the time. Julius moved a lot of his company's product from his stand at the midway's music hall, and he saw a need for a permanent presence in the Midwest. He established a Witmark office in Chicago and placed a young hustler named Sol Bloom in charge of it. Over the next fifteen years, other addresses would be added to the Witmark letterhead, as offices arose in San Francisco, Paris, and Melbourne. The flinging of the Witmark organization around the world was not arrogance, it was just good business. The brothers kept an eye on where songs were selling, and this rudimentary market research showed them that any song had a better chance outside New York than it had in their native city. In his autobiography, published in 1939, Isidore Witmark wrote:

> . . . taking as a whole the fifty years of the Witmarks in the business of music publishing, it is a statistical fact that New York City was the worst center for sales in all America. Perhaps this was because the people of the city, except during such holidays as New Year's, had less home life than the smaller communities and did not make such constant use of their pianos.

The watershed year for the Witmarks was 1898, when the thirteen-year-old firm solidified its success by taking over a five-story building at 8 West Twenty-ninth Street, by establishing *The Witmark Monthly* (the first Tin Pan Alley house organ), and by snaring the services of Victor Herbert, the most popular composer in America. Witmark was not the exclusive publisher of Herbert's work, but beginning with the score of *The Fortune Teller* in 1898, the company issued the cream of his compositions for twenty years. "Gypsy Love Song" was the smash from *The Fortune Teller*, and as Herbert's hit shows poured forth—*Babes in Toyland, Mlle. Modiste, Dolly Dollars, The Red Mill, Naughty Marietta, Eileen*—Witmark issued their hit songs.

Herbert's work gave literal and figurative weight to the Witmark catalog, and although it did not turn the brothers from generalists to operetta specialists, it certainly shifted the emphasis of their acquisitions. They began to sign other operetta writers, such as Julian Edwards, Gustav Luders, Karl Hoschna, John Stromberg, and A. Baldwin Sloane. Although none of these composers had an ounce of

Herbert's talent, their scores yielded ephemeral hits and the occasional standard (such as Stromberg's "Ma Blushing Rosie" and "Come Down, Ma Evening Star," or Hoschna's "Cuddle Up a Little Closer" and "Every Little Movement"). In 1919 the Witmarks began a long professional relationship with Sigmund Romberg, who kept their operetta quotient up throughout the 1920s.

Another composer who greatly influenced the content and texture of the Witmark catalog was Ernest R. Ball. Ball's specialties, the grandly declarative love song and the Irish ballad, made him the company's most dependable hit-producer after Herbert himself. Ball gave the company two huge songs—"Will You Love Me in December as You Do in May?" in 1905 and "Love Me and the World Is Mine" in 1906— and they earned him an unheard-of twenty-year contract as a staff composer. He made himself useful to the Witmarks in many ways: as in-house demonstrator, vaudeville accompanist plugging Witmark songs, and musical handyman, touching up the work of others and writing with any staff lyricist who came his way. The company's first Irish hit had been Chauncey Olcott's "My Wild Irish Rose" in 1899, and when Ball was loaned out to compose for Olcott shows in 1910, shamrocks again sprouted on the Witmark list. With various lyricists, Ball composed "Mother Machree," "I Love the Name of Mary," "When Irish Eyes Are Smiling," "A Little Bit of Heaven," and "She's the Daughter of Mother Machree," among many others. His big, wide ballads included "Let the Rest of the World Go By," "As Long as the World Rolls On," "Dear Little Boy of Mine," and "Till the Sands of the Desert Grow Cold."

During the ragtime era, the Witmarks' bread was undeniably buttered on the ballad side, so their staff writers were a decidedly unsyncopated lot. Along with the tenderhearted Ball, others who punched the company's time clock included Arthur Penn (who wrote "Carissima" and "Smilin' Through"), Caro Roma ("In the Garden of My Heart" and "Can't You Hear Me Calling, Caroline?"), and Rida Johnson Young (a frequent lyricist partner of Victor Herbert). Their work, along with that of freelancers ("Because," "When You Were Sweet Sixteen," "Sweet Adeline," "Too-ra-loo-ra-loo-ra"), constituted the core of the Witmark Music Library, "the largest collection of Vocal Concert Numbers and Excerpts in America," an extensive reprint service and amateur production guide that the company launched in September 1898. The following year, the Witmark Minstrelsy Department, a lowbrow counterpart to the Music Library, was established. Through the full-service minstrel division, the amateur producer could purchase jokes, blackface makeup, and props for his show, along with Witmark's coon songs and cakewalk orchestrations.

On August 4, 1903 (Henrietta Witmark's birthday), the Witmarks moved again, this time into a new building that they had erected at 144–46 West Thirty-seventh Street. Victor Herbert wrote a commemorative march for the opening ceremonies, and he chose for its title the company's motto, "Success Is Work." The Witmark Building was a six-story beehive of getting and spending, with two additional basement floors devoted to the packing and shipping of music. "Toyland" and "Sweet Adeline" were topping the firm's song sales that year, and the Music Library and Minstrelsy department were booming. The Black and White Series, a plain-cover reprint line, was the newest thing in recycling old successes. Although the fact probably went unnoticed by everyone except a bookkeeper or two, 1903 saw the publication of the first rag to bear the Witmark imprint, Stephen Howard's "Sakes Alive."

The 1903 rag made so little stir that the Witmarks did not publish another one for six years. The second Witmark rag was Henry Lodge's "Temptation Rag," issued in September 1909. A recent change in the copyright law (for which Isidore had lobbied in Washington) made the million-selling rag even more profitable than it would have been otherwise. The big change was the recognition that copyright holders deserved payment for mechanical use of their music. For the first time, record and piano roll makers were required to pay for the music they chose to record. The rate was set at two cents for each cylinder, disc, and paper roll manufactured, and to a publisher with many recorded numbers, such as Witmark, it meant tens of thousands of dollars of additional income over the course of a year. Lodge's "Temptation," one of the most recorded rags of its time, would bring profits to Witmark for more than twenty years, long after its sheet music sales had stopped.

Witmark had a success with Lodge's "Red Pepper" in 1910 and with Julius Lenzberg's "Haunting Rag" in 1911. Although the company's ragtime list was more than respectable, it was an afterthought to the other Witmark products. No one at the firm nurtured it by wooing new composers or by taking its plugging as a specialty. Lodge and Lenzberg were the only rag composers to be published more than once by Witmark (Lenzberg was published twice), and even their rags, the company's most successful, were dwarfed in the long shadows cast by Herbert and Ball. The brothers remained loyal to Lodge, at least, publishing his last efforts (also their last rags, except for one novelty in 1927) in 1918. When Eubie Blake became a Witmark writer in 1919, it never occurred to anyone to ask him for ragtime compositions.

In 1923 the Witmarks sold their building and made one more move, to two rented floors at 1650 Broadway, where they prospered through the rest of the 1920s, acquiring new hits and recycling their old ones. They merged their Music Library with that of their rival Arthur W. Tams in 1925, and four years later the Witmark brothers' company was bought by the Warner Brothers studio.

JOSEPH W. STERN & COMPANY/EDWARD B. MARKS MUSIC CORPORATION

The Joseph Stern company may be said to have compiled the strongest ragtime catalog in New York because it, alone among the Tin Pan Alley firms, went after the work of the black pianists who were the best rag writers and players in town. The driving force in the firm was Stern's cofounder, Ed Marks. Although Marks's name was not on the logo and he was technically the "silent partner," it was he who was the more visible and aggressive of the two. He was universally respected in the music world, not only for his business acumen but also because he was a gentleman. Ed Marks was approachable, so he was approached by many writers,

Edward B. Marks

including black ones. His openness to talent, whatever its color, gave the Joseph Stern Company an enviable list of rhythmically progressive songs, dance numbers, and rags.

Edward B. Marks (1865–1945), a native New Yorker, was a notions salesman who liked to tinker at writing lyrics. In the sample cases of hooks, eyes, and whalebone that he lugged around the Northeast were notebooks in which he jotted rhymes and song ideas during train rides. In 1890 he won a $100 prize given by the Samuel French company for a poem promoting a French-owned stage comedy called *Doctor Bill*. He decided to investigate the possibility of writing songs, and he went to see Frank Harding, Jr., who had taken over his uncle E. H. Harding's publishing business in 1889. Harding put Marks in touch with a hack composer named William Loraine, and together they turned out a song, "December and May," which Harding published in 1893.

After Marks placed several more lyrics with Harding, the publisher asked him to carry some Harding songs with him on his notions route, to take orders from music stores and to plug them if he could. Marks knew his songs were selling, because he was selling them, but when he saw his first dismal royalty statement from Harding, his heart sank. Harding was making much more from Marks's effort than Marks was. It was the realization that it was more profitable to own songs than to write them that made Ed Marks determined to become a publisher. Needing capital as well as some tunes, he turned to a friend whom he had met on the road, a necktie salesman named Joseph W. Stern (1870–1934). Stern, a mediocre pianist and composer, knew that his songs would never see print unless he published them himself, so he joined Marks in his venture. Just as the partnership was born, Marks got cold feet. Fearing that their company would fail, he kept his name off of it, and the enterprise that Ed Marks would steer for twenty-six years was named Joseph W. Stern & Company.

In 1894 Stern and Marks opened a small office in the basement of 304 East Fourteenth Street and issued the first song that they wrote together, a tearjerker called "The Little Lost Child." The song tells a sappy story about a policeman who sees a little girl crying and offers to help her find her way home. When she says that her name is Jennie, he recognizes her as his own daughter, who has been raised by his estranged wife. "The Little Lost Child" was taken up by vaudeville singers Lottie Gilson and Della Fox, but its success really came from a new plugging method devised by its writers. Stern and Marks decided to drive a desire for this musical melodrama into the brain by visual as well as aural means. They hired an off-duty policeman and a friend's daughter to pose for a series of lantern-slide photos, illustrating the situations in the lyric, to be projected when the song was performed in nickelodeons and vaudeville houses. Stern and Marks's "Lost Child" was the first song to be promoted in this way, and there would be many others to follow.

Stern and Marks's second success also came from their own pens. This was "Mother Was a Lady," a sob song of 1896, inspired by Marks overhearing a waitress's retort to a rude customer. This was even bigger than "The Little Lost Child," and the partners' remarkable batting average, two hits out of fewer than ten publications, made the industry take notice. The secret was, of course, the hard work of plugging. Ed Marks wrote in his 1935 autobiography: "The best songs came from the gutter in those days. Indeed, when I began publishing in 1894, there was no better way of starting a song off to popularity than to get it sung as loudly as possible in the city's lowest dives."

So off they went to the lowest dives—Bowery beer halls, small-time vaudeville houses, dance halls, saloons—Marks hitting about sixty joints a week and Stern about forty. They shoved manuscripts at band leaders and pianists. They carried lyric sheets to pass out, in case they could coerce a room full of drunks to have a sing-along. They offered professional copies to singers and dog acts.

As Stern and Marks made their rounds, songwriters made rounds, too, and the Stern office became a regular stop for them. James Thornton gave them "On the Benches in the Park"; Gussie Davis gave them "Down in Poverty Row"; Maude Nugent gave them "Sweet Rosie O'Grady." In addition to their song successes, a lawsuit that they brought against Witmark resulted in another infusion of cash. In 1898 the Witmarks issued James Thornton's "When You Were Sweet Sixteen," and Ed Marks thought it sounded familiar. He looked into his files and found that he not only owned the song, he had purchased it (for $15) before Thornton had sold it to Witmark (also for $15). Stern sued Witmark to stop the song's sale, and Witmark, knowing that it had a highly valuable commodity, settled out of court by paying Stern $5,000.

It was in the late 1890s that Ed Marks began to reach out to black writers. Irving Jones offered the company "Take Your Clothes and Go" in 1897, and Bert Williams and George Walker began their association with Stern that same year. Stern would be the primary publisher of songs from the Williams and Walker vaudeville musicals. Ernest Hogan, as well as the Bob Cole–Johnson Brothers team, would soon be added to the list of Stern's black theatre writers. Stern was scooped on several 1890s musical fads (Witmark had bigger coon songs, and F. A. Mills cornered the market on cakewalks), but most of the black writers published by Stern had talent enough to transcend fads. Ed Marks's interest in them was neither social work nor a democratic impulse: it was an investment, and it paid off handsomely in hits over three decades.

Someone at the Stern company (possibly its black arranger, Will Tyers) had heard of Tom Turpin's "Harlem Rag," which had been published in St. Louis in 1897. Somehow it was decided that Stern should buy the copyright of "Harlem Rag" and reissue it. Although it was "arranged" beyond recognition by Will Tyers, the Stern version of "Harlem Rag," which appeared in 1899, was the first rag published in New York City.

Like most other New York publishers, Stern gave ragtime a good letting alone for nearly ten years. Max S. Witt, the company's professional manager, had written a few coon songs, but he was not keen on ragtime. There were a few Stern rags issued from 1903–07, but the hits and the historic firsts came in other genres. Cole and Johnson's songs were the company's biggest-selling theatre music during that time. Eddie Leonard's "Ida" did well in 1903. The hottest items in the pop line were two previously published numbers reissued by Stern: Paul Dresser's "My Gal Sal" (1906) and the company's all-time best-seller, Paul Lincke's "Glow-Worm" (first issued in Germany in 1902 and republished by Stern in 1907). Two major writers, Jerome Kern and Irving Berlin, were given their first publications, but their numbers were flops (Kern's piano piece "At the Casino," issued by Lyceum, a Stern subsidiary, in 1902 and Berlin's song "Marie from Sunny Italy," bought for seventy-five cents and published in 1907). On the day before Christmas in 1906, the Stern offices were moved to spacious quarters in a nine-story building at 102–104 West Thirty-eighth Street.

In the summer of 1907 Stern's reputation as a ragtime publisher took a giant leap when Scott Joplin appeared, unannounced, with rags for sale. Joplin had recently moved to New York, and he had no doubt heard of Stern's accessibility to black composers. He began his exploration of Tin Pan Alley with a visit to Ed Marks. Marks couldn't believe his good fortune. He didn't know much about ragtime, but he knew that Joplin's name would add luster to his catalog. He bought two Joplin rags, "Gladiolus" and "Search Light," and thus became the first New York publisher of ragtime's premier composer. (Stern would also issue Joplin's "Stoptime" in 1910 and "Scott Joplin's New Rag" in 1912.) Joe Jordan, another major St. Louis figure, added his "That Teasin' Rag" to the Stern list in 1909. Jordan's rag was successful in its first incarnation, and it was again highly profitable in 1917, when its trio was paraphrased by the Original Dixieland Jazz Band in their "Original Dixieland One Step." Marks pounced on the ODJB and claimed copyright ownership of the band's hit record. After hours of negotiation with the ODJB's leader, Nick LaRocca, Stern wound up with two-thirds ownership of the tune and the right to publish it under the title "Original Dixieland One-Step: Introducing 'That Teasin' Rag.'"

It was the craze for social dancing in the early teens that brought New York's best rag composers into the Stern fold. At the height of the vogue, in 1913–14, no other publisher had such high-quality rags, most of them by black writers breaking into print for the first time. Although the company marketed them as numbers for dancing, rather than for listening, they are indubitably ragtime, and they have been happily listened to over the eighty-five years since the dance fad that spawned them passed. Stern's professional manager during this dance-mad time was the songwriter L. Wolfe Gilbert, himself no stranger to the syncopated urge, and the firm's chief arranger was the black conductor Will Vodery. Between Marks's and Gilberts's acquisitions and Vodery's arrangements of them, the company amassed an unbeatable collection of "dance rags."

The first of the Harlem piano giants to be published by Stern was Luckey Roberts, who had hits in 1913 with "The Junk Man Rag" and

"Pork and Beans." "Junk Man" is a sunshine-bright tune, its melody ringing out in treble octaves, and "Pork and Beans" is a sparring match between feisty minor and major harmonics. Even in the printed scores that were simplified from Roberts's performances of them, both are harmonically rich and rhythmically nifty. Another black master who got his first publications from Stern was Eubie Blake. In 1914 his "Chevy Chase" and "Fizz Water" entered the dance band books, to resurface decades later as concert numbers. The black trombonist and bandmaster Frederick Bryan contributed his "Sunset Rag" and "Bell Hop Rag" to the Stern catalog in 1914, and Wilbur Sweatman's "Old Folks Rag" was also a steady seller that year. The company had major hits with the song version of "Junk Man Rag" (lyrics by Chris Smith and Ferd Mierisch) and with the king of "dance instruction songs," "Ballin' the Jack," by Chris Smith and Jim Burris.

Stern's biggest coup of 1914 was the signing of James Reese Europe, the black composer/conductor for Vernon and Irene Castle, the couple who had sparked the dance craze from its beginning. Over a two-month period, Stern issued ten Castle-related numbers composed by Europe (eight of them co-composed with Ford Dabney, one of them being "The Castle House Rag"). This set of Europe-Castle pieces represents the strongest publisher-composer relationship of the dance era. Again Ed Marks had bet on talent, and again he won. As the Castles' newest innovation, the fox trot, began sweeping the country, it was Stern's house man, Will Vodery, who got the first one into print, his "Carolina Fox Trot," issued in July 1914. When the dance craze cooled in the mid-teens, Stern's "dance rags" stopped coming, but there was one late masterpiece, Ford Dabney's exquisitely sexy "Georgia Grind," in 1915. Oddly, the Stern company did not plunge into the next musical vogues, blues and jazz, as it had into ragtime.

Joseph Stern retired in late December 1920, and Ed Marks kept on running the company he had always run, which was renamed the Edward B. Marks Music Corporation. Marks had his triumphs in the 1920s (one of them as publisher of Rodgers and Hart's first hit, "Manhattan," in 1925) and he had great success in the early 1930s with American versions of Latin hits ("Malaguena," "La Cucaracha," "What a Difference a Day Made"). At Marks's death in 1945, the company was taken over by his son Herbert.

There was one last burst of ragtime from the Marks organization, in the 1970s. As Ed Marks had recognized the cachet of ragtime's first star, Scott Joplin, someone at Marks recognized Eubie Blake as the star of ragtime's revival. In 1971 Marks issued *Sincerely, Eubie Blake*, a folio containing nine numbers (including seven rags) transcribed by Terry Waldo and all published for the first time. Another Marks collection of that year, *Giants of Ragtime*, put several classics back in print for the first time in decades. The company also issued the rags of William Bolcom, and its 1976 collection, *The Ragtime Current*, was a generous sampling of new work, including rags by Max Morath, Terry Waldo, and Donald Ashwander, among others. If, as Ed Marks said, the best music came from the gutter, he made sure that it didn't stay there.

JEROME H. REMICK & COMPANY

The most prolific and successful music publisher in the years between the Teddy Roosevelt era and the dawn of the jazz age was Jerome Remick, and his company's history is an object lesson in macromanagement.

Jerome H. Remick

Remick was a thoroughly unmusical man who never wrote a melody or a lyric, who purportedly could not even carry a tune. Unlike the Witmark brothers, Joe Stern, and Ed Marks, he never entered a Bowery dive with a stack of manuscripts under his arm, never bought a steak for a saloon pianist, and never slipped payola under a dressing room door in a vaudeville house. Not a day of his life was spent in a grimy office on Union Square. This *grand seigneur* of Tin Pan Alley did not even live in New York. Remick's music went everywhere, but after his company got rolling, Remick himself divided his time between two places: his palatial Detroit offices and his palatial home in Grosse Point.

Remick bought an already successful music company and, by relying on the people he hired, grew it into an empire. He did not publish to his own taste, and he never questioned a decision if he trusted the employee who made it. His function was to pay the bills and to reap the profits. Although the enterprise bore his name, the founder's hands-off approach very nearly removes him from the Remick story. Moral: Hire Smart and Stay Out of the Way.

Jerome H. Remick (1869–1931) was a rich man long before he entered the music business. He had amassed two fortunes, in lumber and real estate, and was building a third, as owner and president of the Detroit Creamery Company, when he decided to diversify further by buying out a local music publisher. Whitney-Warner, the company he bought in 1902, was not yet ten years old, but its roots recalled the heyday of nineteenth-century Detroit publishing. It reached back to the Reconstruction era as the C. J. Whitney company, the city's premier publisher before the merger in the early 1890s that created Whitney-Warner. From its headquarters at 10 Witherell Street came the new company's first hit, Anita Owen's "Sweet Bunch of Daisies," in 1894.

The question must be asked: Why did the nonmusical Jerome Remick buy a music company? The answer can only be that it looked like good business to do so. Whitney-Warner had thrived since its inception, producing steadily selling numbers and taking leases on music departments in department stores. Through these self-made franchises (constituting near-monopolies in several cities), it re-created music departments in its own image and spurred the sales of Whitney-Warner tunes. Under the direction of business manager Fred Belcher (1869–1919), the company was obviously well run, and it had a good-looking product. (Many of the Whitney-Warner covers were drawn by Gene Buck, a local illustrator who would in later years become a respected Tin Pan Alley lyricist and president of ASCAP.) The company's star composer was Fred Stone, a black bandleader who contributed waltzes, songs, and syncopation to its catalog. A black arranger, Harry P. Guy, prepared many of the firm's numbers for publication.

Whitney-Warner had done well with Stone's "Bos'n Rag" in 1899, and when Remick began looking it over, it was enjoying a smash hit with J. Bodewalt Lampe's cakewalk "Creole Belles," published in 1901. Perhaps Remick liked the Gene Buck covers, or perhaps Fred Belcher divulged the markup on a fifty-cent song sheet that cost a penny or two to make. In any case, Whitney-Warner seemed an attractive proposition, and Jerome Remick bought it outright. The first perspicacity shown by the new owner was that he didn't try to fix what was not broken. In one of the wisest decisions of his professional life, he kept Fred Belcher as business manager of the Remick-owned Whitney-Warner company.

During Remick's first three years in the music business, he went on a buying spree, and it must have been Fred Belcher who advised him to embark on it. Late in 1902 Remick acquired Daniels, Russell & Boone, a small St. Louis firm, from its founding partner, Charles N. Daniels. When Daniels realized how much Remick wanted DR&B's Indian intermezzo, "Hiawatha" (which had been endorsed by John Philip Sousa), he drove the asking price for his company up to $10,000. Amazingly, Remick agreed to the deal, and, even more amazingly, the deal paid off for the buyer. "Hiawatha" was a hit for Whitney–Warner, and another

Fred Belcher

Daniels song, "You Tell Me Your Dream and I'll Tell You Mine," would be an even bigger hit a few years later. Remick was so impressed by Daniels, as a composer and as a negotiator, that he hired him as general manager and editor-in-chief for Whitney-Warner. It was Daniels, a ragtime man from ragtime land, who would turn Remick into the most prolific publisher of rags as well as the publisher with the most rag hits. Daniels's first acquisitions for Remick were two syncopated prizes from Kansas City: Scott Joplin's "Original Rags" and Harry Kelly's "Peaceful Henry," both originally published by Carl Hoffman and both strong sellers for Whitney–Warner.

Still in a buying mood in 1903, Remick acquired Louis Bernstein's half-interest in a flourishing Tin Pan Alley firm, Shapiro, Bernstein & Company, and established a New York presence for himself (and for Whitney-Warner) in the heart of Tin Pan Alley, at 45 West Twenty-eighth Street. Shapiro, Remick & Company soon needed new letterhead, however, as Remick bought out Shapiro late in 1904. On January 1, 1905, Jerome H. Remick & Company, with Fred Belcher in charge, opened its doors at Shapiro, Bernstein's old address.

In each of his two earlier buyouts, Remick got more than a list of copyrights and a stack of stock, he also found a valuable employee who would serve the Remick interests for years to come (Belcher from Whitney-Warner and Charles N. Daniels from DR&B). And Remick acquired another topnotch employee when he bought out Shapiro. During the yearlong life of Shapiro, Remick, Fred Belcher had noticed the growth of the company's Chicago branch, and he recommended to Remick that the branch manager, Moses Edwin Gumble (1876–1947), be invited to move to New York to head the professional department of Jerome H. Remick & Company. It was another wise hire. With Charles Daniels running the editorial operations in Detroit and Belcher and Gumble tending to business in New York, Remick had assembled a championship team almost before the game had got underway.

Remick didn't know much about the making of his product, but he wanted it to be technically precise. Daniels and Gumble must have told him stories about arranger errors and sloppy typesetting, for he resolved that Remick music would be correctly copied and printed. Toward this end, he hired the meticulous W. C. Polla as his chief band and orchestra arranger, with J. Bodewalt Lampe as his assistant. (Lampe was hired in 1906. He would take over as chief arranger in 1910 and would remain in that position until 1923.) In 1910 George Botsford took over vocal arranging in Remick's "harmony and quartet" department. The boss's demand was met: Remick's numbers came closer than anyone else's to being bug-free.

Jerome H. Remick & Company began its life with plenty to sell (the combined catalogs of Whitney–Warner, DR&B, and Shapiro, Bernstein) and with much talent to sell it. There was also a substantial budget for acquisitions. Strong new titles were added to the old ones in the catalog, and hits began to roll in immediately. In 1905 Remick had one of the big ones, "In the Shade of the Old Apple Tree," as well as Eva Tanguay's saucy theme, "I Don't Care." Over the next four years several Remick songs became instant standards: "Chinatown," "Shine On, Harvest Moon," and "By the Light of the Silvery Moon." Percy Wenrich became a staff writer in 1908, and during his five years with Remick he earned his keep with "Rainbow," "Put On Your Old Gray Bonnet," and "Silver Bell," among many others. The company's volume grew so great that in 1907 Remick bought his own printing plant.

After two years of setting Remick's various houses in order, Charles N. Daniels could finally turn his attention to ragtime. There were only two rags in the Remick catalog before 1905 (Whitney–Warner's "Bos'n Rag" and Shapiro, Remick's "Southern Roses"), but in that year Daniels began to step up his purchases of ragtime. And he knew where the good rags came from. Six of the eight Remick rags published in 1905–06 were by Missouri composers. The biggest seller among them was Irene Giblin's "Chicken Chowder." In 1907 a reprint of another Missouri rag, Charles L. Johnson's "Dill Pickles," began its climb toward a two-million-copy sale. Daniels's judgment in rag-picking was confirmed the following year by the sales of George Botsford's "Black and White Rag," Remick's second rag to sell over a million. In 1910 the company had two more successes in the ragtime department: Albert Gumble's "Chanticleer Rag" and Jean Schwartz's "Black Beauty."

Daniels left Remick in 1912 to move west for his daughter's health. His successor, Mose Gumble, was equally passionate about ragtime, so the Remick rags kept coming. Two rags from 1913, Wallie Herzer's "Tickle the Ivories" and Julius Lenzberg's "Hungarian Rag" (based on Liszt themes), each sold a million. Oddly, the chief composers/

Remick Building in New York City

arrangers on the staff—Daniels and Lampe—contributed only a few rags each to the catalog. The wallflower George Botsford was the most published rag writer among the Remick team. There was no distinctive "Remick rag sound." Daniels and Gumble simply bought the best of what came to them, from Missouri classicism to oddities like Ford Dabney's "Haytian Rag" to dance rags in the mid-teens. As Remick published the most of everything else in its heyday, it also published the most rags, nearly 130 originals and dozens of reprints, the longest rag list of any publisher.

In 1912 Jerome Remick & Company took a twenty-year lease at 219–221 West Forty-sixth Street. The building housed the firm's shipping department and stock room, as well as a twelve-man arranging department, a 200-seat auditorium, and fifteen piano cubicles for demonstrating songs. From his third-floor office, Vice-President and Secretary Fred Belcher, with his assistant, Jerome (Joe) Keit, oversaw the activities of fifty Remick branches and a retail store.

There were no rag hits for Remick after 1913, but the company had huge songs in the teens, including "It's Tulip Time in Holland," "Memories," "Pretty Baby," "Sailin' Away on the Henry Clay," "Smiles," "Til We Meet Again," and "I'm Forever Blowing Bubbles." For three years in the mid-teens Remick's star demonstrator was George Gershwin, who pounded out the firm's tunes in a piano cubicle for $15 a week. Gershwin was not able to place his own songs with his employer during his tenure, but in June 1917, three months after he left, Remick published his only rag, "Rialto Ripples" (co-composed with Will Donaldson). Vincent Youmans served a year or so in a Remick piano cell, beginning in 1919, and the company gave him his first publication, a song called "The Country Cousin," in 1920. Richard A. Whiting, a Remick plugger based in Detroit, was much more successful than Gershwin or Youmans at getting his work published by the company.

In September 1919 Fred Belcher died of appendicitis at age fifty-two, and his private secretary, Jerome Keit, succeeded him as head of the New York office. Keit steered the firm successfully through the 1920s, and in late 1928 he bought the company from Jerome Remick. In September 1929 Keit sold Remick to Warner Brothers, but he continued to run the Remick organization for his Hollywood bosses. The music factory that Jerome Remick had assembled in the early century continued to hum into the 1940s. Tin Pan Alley's best boss died on July 15, 1931, in Detroit.

SEMINARY MUSIC COMPANY/ROSE & SNYDER/TED SNYDER COMPANY/ WATERSON, BERLIN & SNYDER

Ted Snyder and his partner, Henry Waterson, in their various (and overlapping) capacities as owners, managers, and officers in four publishing companies and a music distribution company, were major figures in the dissemination of Tin Pan Alley ragtime. Snyder was a journeyman songwriter with a flair for syncopation, and Waterson was the managerial wheeler-dealer who juggled their musical enterprises. Before stability settled on them in 1912, Snyder and Waterson operated under several company names, all of them at the same address. There seemed to be no organizational problem that the creation of a new company couldn't solve. Waterson is the common link in the multicompany story, as backer or as partner, but, because he was professionally involved with three other Snyders besides Ted, it is impossible to know precisely the working dynamics—or even the structure—of the Snyder–Waterson enterprises. It is certain, however, that their shared office was the place where the old ragtime gave way to the new. In 1910, the year that Waterson's Seminary Music was touting itself as the New York publisher of Scott Joplin's rags, the Ted Snyder Company was celebrating the sales of "Grizzly Bear Rag" and the rag songs of Irving Berlin. At 112 West Thirty-eighth Street, ragtime's sunset and dawn occurred simultaneously.

In 1904 twenty-three-year-old Ted Snyder arrived in New York from Chicago, where he had worked for several years as a song plugger and demonstrator. The composer-publisher F. A. (Kerry) Mills gave him his first New York job, as staff pianist in Mills's company. Snyder, often teamed with lyricist Ed Rose, published a few songs with Mills, and he was quick to demonstrate these to any vaudevillian who dropped into his boss's cakewalk factory. Mills became annoyed at Snyder's constantly plugging his own work and fired him. Snyder took the dismissal as the occasion to form his own company, and he talked Ed Rose into joining him. With startup money borrowed from a Boston jobber named George Krey, Ted Snyder and Ed Rose became Rose & Snyder in 1906.

Although Rose and Snyder's catalog was only about a page long, they needed a distributor for their handful of publications, and it must have been the search for a jobber that led Ted Snyder to Henry Waterson early in 1908. (Perhaps it was nepotism that brought them together. Waterson's partner was named Herman Snyder, but it is not known whether the two Snyders were related.) Waterson ran a distribution house called Crown Music at 12 East Seventeenth Street. Being middle-aged and practically deaf, he seemed out of place in youth-oriented Tin Pan Alley, but there was a touch of the pirate in him. He was a sometime diamond merchant and full-time gambler, and he didn't let his scant knowledge of music stand in the way of his selling it. Crown was a small operation, but it had recently taken on a very prestigious customer, when Scott Joplin chose the firm to act as selling agent for his self-published set of six exercises that he called the "School of Ragtime."

If it was impressive to distribute Joplin, it was even more impressive to publish him, and Henry Waterson and Herman Snyder were about to do just that. They had begun a publishing company called Seminary Music late in 1906, and they made its headquarters at a desk in the Crown Music offices. (Seminary's owners of record were Mary Waterson and Mary Snyder, and its officers were Henry Waterson and Herman Snyder.) Joplin must have been pleased with Crown's handling of his "School of Ragtime," because in April 1908 he granted Seminary the publishing rights to his new rag, "Sugar Cane." A few weeks after acquiring "Sugar Cane," Seminary and Crown took larger offices, at 112 West Thirty-eighth Street.

Joplin's imprimatur must have marked Waterson as a comer to Ted Snyder, and Snyder's hustle must have impressed Waterson. In any case, they were partners by midsummer 1908. Waterson was the one with cash, so it was he who bankrolled the Ted Snyder Company. Snyder was president, and Waterson was named treasurer/manager. In July the new firm squeezed in with the two older ones at 112 West Thirty-eighth. In September Snyder bought the handful of Rose & Snyder copyrights from George Krey and Ed Rose. The administration of Rose &

Snyder's business—along with that of Crown, Seminary, and the Ted Snyder Company—meant that four music firms were sharing space (and officers) in one headquarters. But because each firm was mostly a daydream, requiring little space for such corporeal items as stock, there was room for all of them.

The daydreams soon started to come true for Snyder and Waterson. In September 1908 Snyder's first rag publication, his own rambunctious "Wild Cherries," began to take off. Vaudeville pianists seized on it as a favorite showpiece, and the house orchestras at Victor and Zonophone made popular recordings of it soon after its sheet music release. In October Seminary scored a coup by adding a second Joplin number, "Pine Apple Rag," to its otherwise tepid catalog. Besides giving the company a fine piece of music, the signing of "Pine Apple" signified that tiny Seminary Music had wooed and won Joplin from Joseph Stern & Company, who had been the first to publish Joplin in New York. (Stern's looming presence in its nine-story building, five doors away, at 102-104 West Thirty-eighth, must have daunted the small squad of Seminary employees on their way to work.)

Seminary's tie to Joplin held for a year. The company was his exclusive publisher in 1909, issuing four rags ("Wall Street," "Country Club," "Euphonic Sounds," and "Paragon"), as well as a waltz ("Pleasant Moments") and the haunting "Solace." In March 1910 Joplin received the closest thing he ever had to a recording plug when the Zonophone Orchestra recorded his "Wall Street Rag," only a year after the sheet music appeared. Seminary's last Joplin publication was a song version of "Pine Apple," with lyrics by Joe Snyder, another shadowy Snyder in Waterson's orbit, and possibly a relative of Ted/Herman/Mary. The Ted Snyder Company's luck held, too. In April 1910, while "Wild Cherries" was still selling like crazy, it published another hit rag, George Botsford's "Grizzly Bear." Much of Snyder's luck was embodied in the skinny frame of one of his new employees. About a year earlier, he had put a genius on the payroll, at $25 a week.

Early in 1909 Amy Butler, a vaudeville singer who was a friend and customer of Snyder's, had taken him to Jimmy Kelly's saloon on Union Square to hear the smutty song parodies delivered by a brash young waiter named Irving Berlin. Snyder appreciated the cleverness of Berlin's rhyming, but he knew that such risqué material could never be published. There was obviously no place for Berlin in his firm. Refusing to let Snyder thwart her professional matchmaking, Amy Butler attacked the problem from the other end. She suggested that Berlin take his smartest (and cleanest) lyric and go around to see Mr. Waterson. Berlin took "Dorando," a topical comic verse about an Italian barber who loses his shop by betting on the wrong marathon runner in the recent Olympic Games in London. He shouted his lyric to the deaf Waterson, and the older man got the jokes. He offered Berlin his standard $25 fee for the words and music to the song. Of course, Berlin had no melody for his words, but he knew that this was a chance he must not pass up. He improvised a tune on the spot, as one of Waterson's arrangers took it down. The Ted Snyder Company published "Dorando" in March 1909 and had a local hit with it. The opportunistic Berlin was taken in by the opportunistic Snyder as a staff lyricist.

Berlin was hired to supply words for Snyder's melodies, and during his first two years with the firm, this was mostly what he did. His name is on fifty-four songs published by Snyder in 1909–10, forty-four of them naming Snyder as composer and seven others with melodies that Snyder had purchased from various tunesmiths. Snyder's syncopated tunes and Berlin's jokey lyrics were a good match, and the team quickly began producing successful songs. Soon after "Dorando" they had "My Wife's Gone to the Country (Hurrah! Hurrah!)," and in the summer of 1909 there came "Do Your Duty, Doctor," as well as a Berlin lyric for Snyder's rag "Wild Cherries." By the end of 1909 the public took Berlin's name on a song sheet to mean that cleverness lay therein, and, while his name did not guarantee millions in sales, it guaranteed tens of thousands. In April 1910 George Botsford's "Grizzly Bear" was published by Snyder, and Berlin's song version of the rag, called "The Dance of the Grizzly Bear," appeared in stores the same month. Berlin was as quick as Snyder to smell a trend. If the public wanted raggy songs, he would supply them, melodies and all.

Berlin's first serious attempts at writing melodies came late in 1909, and they produced mostly Snyderesque syncopated songs. In November he wrote "Stop That Rag" and "Yiddle, on Your Fiddle, Play Some Ragtime"; in December he had great success with "That Mesmerizing Mendelssohn Tune" (a ragtime treatment of "Spring Song"). In April 1910 he came up with "Draggy Rag." In March 1911 Snyder published the Berlin song that practically blew away the memory of all other rag-songs that had come before it, "Alexander's Ragtime Band." It was the megahit of the year, and its popularity has never waned. In a stroke, Berlin (who never wrote an instrumental rag) displaced Scott Joplin in the public mind as the "King of Ragtime." And in the same stroke, Berlin displaced Ted Snyder as the star composer of the Ted Snyder Company.

Even before Berlin's first royalty statement for "Alexander's Ragtime Band" was due (in December 1911), Snyder and Waterson realized that it would be cheaper to take Berlin in as a partner than to pay him hundreds of thousands of dollars twice a year. On December 13, 1911, the deal was done. Waterson, Berlin & Snyder opened that day, or rather, remained open, where the trio had always come to work, at 112 West Thirty-eighth Street. For the next seven years, the company's story is mostly the story of Irving Berlin.

Ted Snyder remained committed to instrumental ragtime, and kept publishing it, but his rags were inevitably outsold by Berlin's rag-songs. In 1911 Snyder thought he had discovered a star on the ragtime horizon, and he published eight rags by Harry Tierney. (This is the largest number of rags to come from a composer-publisher team in a single year.) The combined sales of Tierney's 1911 rags did not approach those of a single Berlin song, "Everybody's Doing It Now." In 1912 Harry DeCosta's "Bunny Hug Rag" was left in the dust by Berlin's "Midnight Choo-Choo" leaving for Alabam'. In 1913 Les Copeland's advanced "38th Street Rag" was rendered obsolete by Berlin's "Snooky Ookums" and "That International Rag." Berlin showed his sentimental side in 1912 with his first ballad hit, "When I Lost You," and, with its publication, he became the compleat composer, still clever as hell but capable of tenderness, too.

The Berlin hits were dutifully demonstrated and plugged by the company's hotshot staff pianists. Milton Ager, lately arrived from Chicago, took over a WB&S cubicle in 1914, alongside another piano-pounder, Pete Wendling. Fred Ahlert became a Snyder arranger in 1915, and Harry Ruby served as a demonstrator in the late teens. George Gershwin applied for a demonstrator's job in 1914, but Berlin talked him out of it on the grounds that he had too much talent for such an occupation. Gershwin thanked Berlin for the compliment and immediately took a job at Remick, where he would work as a demonstrator for three years.

Waterson's Crown Music held on to its tenuous connection to Scott Joplin in the early teens. Joplin formed his own publishing company late in 1913, and he kept Crown as the distributor of his works. If Joplin had been seriously writing rags, Waterson, Berlin & Snyder would probably have been their publisher, but he was deep into his obsession with his opera *Treemonisha*, which everyone in town had turned down. He self-published two numbers from the opera's score, "Prelude to Act III" and "Frolic of the Bears," and Crown sent them out into an indifferent world. Crown couldn't do much with "Magnetic Rag," the last rag from Joplin's pen, either.

Not long after Waterson, Berlin & Snyder took new offices in the Strand Theatre building at 224 West Forty-seventh Street in May 1914, Irving Berlin began implementing a plan to escape from his partners. He had dark suspicions that Henry Waterson was dipping into the communal till to pay gambling debts, and he resented Snyder's share of profits made largely from Berlin hits. He created Irving Berlin, Inc., ostensibly to publish his theatre songs, but actually designed as a holding company for the Berlin copyrights that he would buy back from his partners over the next few years. When he owned all of his own work, he would leave Waterson, Berlin & Snyder. In January 1919, now the sole owner of his songs, he severed his connection with WB&S and entered the publishing business with the most valuable catalog of a single composer in the history of Tin Pan Alley. He did not part friends with Ted Snyder because they had never been friends, merely collaborators. They did not keep in touch, and they seldom saw each other again.

Oddly, Berlin's leaving the firm seemed to energize Waterson, Berlin & Snyder. Snyder and Waterson, recognizing that their hits would not come from across the room any more, began to buy and plug aggressively. In 1919 they had "How Ya Gonna Keep 'Em Down on the Farm?"; in 1920, "Margie"; in 1921, their biggest non-Berlin hit, Snyder's own tune, "The Sheik of Araby." Ted Snyder proved that he still had his composer's chops in 1923, when he wrote "Who's Sorry Now?" with Bert Kalmar and Harry Ruby.

In the summer of 1927 Snyder answered the call of Hollywood before it had actually come. He sold his share of the business to Henry

Waterson and moved to Los Angeles, on the understanding that he would be taken into the music department of the Fox studios. The understanding was a misunderstanding, and there was no job for Snyder at Fox. He retired from music and opened a Hollywood café, called Snyder's, in 1930. He poured money into the place, but he could not make it a success. He closed Snyder's in 1932.

Irving Berlin's premonition about Henry Waterson's gambling habit proved true in 1929. In the two years since Snyder had left, Waterson had run their successful company into bankruptcy. In 1931 Jack Mills bought the Waterson, Berlin & Snyder catalog of copyrights for $5,000—a bargain at, roughly, a dollar a song.

JACK MILLS, INC./MILLS MUSIC INC.

Jack Mills

Most music historians give 1917 as the year of ragtime's death, but like the rumor of Mark Twain's demise in 1897, this report is greatly exaggerated. Some writers pinpoint the precise date on which ragtime keeled over: April 1, 1917, the day that Scott Joplin died and the day on which the first recording by the Original Dixieland Jazz Band went into release. It is true that the classic rags, along with the small-timers who were the primary publishers of them, had had their day by 1917, but America had enjoyed a decade of "commercial" ragtime (beginning in 1907 with Remick's reprint of "Dill Pickles") by then. A second generation of rag players, the pianists and composers who dealt in hotness, had already arrived. They weren't about to give up ragtime simply because five guys from New Orleans had made a record. And the five guys from New Orleans were not asking them to. The ODJB itself, along with its many imitators and offshoots throughout the 1920s, used ragtime, not the blues, as their musical basis. What was original about the Original jazz band was improvisation, and most of their improvisations, as well as most of their compositions, were based on the syncopations of ragtime. Instead of playing rags as written, they played them as they were not written, making up arrangements as each player took a part and cut loose. The rhythmic liberation of ragtime made possible the melodic and harmonic liberation of jazz.

Ragtime broke into racial halves around 1920, its black players pursuing stride piano and its white players inventing novelties. Each of these forms is musically important, but the larger story is that both of them, through jazz, were absorbed into mainstream popular music. The dance rhythms of the 1920s—especially the Charleston, the black bottom, and the shimmy—were closely akin to the hot rhythms of teens ragtime. Before Earl Hines, the major jazz band pianists (James P. Johnson, Fats Waller, Frank Signorelli, Rube Bloom, Roy Bargy, Arthur Schutt) were really rag pianists, playing (and composing and improvising) in a somewhat freer version of the rag style.

The first Tin Pan Alley publisher to look behind the gaudy mask of jazz and see ragtime's face was Jack Mills. In 1921, after everyone else had given up on ragtime, he made it the specialty of his publishing business. He would issue more than seventy-five novelty rags before 1930 (only one of them with the word "rag" in its title), and his company would be the publishing home of the most brilliant piano minds of the 1920s. As his ragtime catalog (and, later, his song catalog) attests, Jack Mills was a rarity among publishers in that he was not afraid of complexity. He knew that the best instrumentals and songs were not necessarily those that could be hummed after one hearing. He published to his own taste, and because his taste was both sophisticated and democratic, he immeasurably enriched American music.

Little is known of the early life of Jack Mills (1891–1979) other than that he was born in Russia and that he somehow made his way to New York. He began his career as a song plugger for various firms, and he worked his way up to the position of professional manager for the (Joe) McCarthy & (Fred) Fisher Company. He did such a good job at McCarthy & Fisher that he was given a cash bonus in the spring of 1919. Mills surprised his employers by using their largesse to set himself up in competition with them. In July 1919 he opened a publishing company, Jack Mills, Inc., at 152 West Forty-fifth Street, with himself as president and his younger brother Irving (1894–1985) as vice president.

Because Jack Mills, Inc. had nothing to sell, its founder decided to compose a song. With lyricists Ed Rose and Willie Raskin, he turned out "I'll Buy the Ring and Change Your Name to Mine." The tune is awkward, and its lyric is downright silly. ("And if I call you Buttercup, Dandelions may eat you up.") Although the song had no commercial chance in 1919, and deserved none, it gave Jack Mills something to carry under his arm when he visited music stores. (The only performer to remember it was George Burns, and his breakneck, out-of-time rendition was the only way to smooth out its rhythmic lumps.)

Jack Mills published nothing except a few undistinguished fox trots in 1920, but his fortunes took an upswing in 1921, when Enrico Caruso died. Mills rushed into the marketplace with "They Needed a Song Bird in Heaven (So God Took Caruso Away)," and it became the first big-selling song issued by Jack Mills, Inc. (Despite Mills's own progressive taste, there would always be room in his catalog for the "dead celebrity" song. In 1926 he marked the passing of Rudolph Valentino with "There's a New Star in Heaven Tonight," and in 1935 he issued "There's a Vacant Chair for Will Rogers in Every Home Tonight.")

Henry Creamer and Turner Layton, a black songwriting team, placed two songs with Jack Mills in 1921. "Strut Miss Lizzie" was a mild success, and "Dear Old Southland" was a hit. Besides the profits they brought in, the Creamer–Layton songs were important to the company because they announced to the small world of Tin Pan Alley that the doors of this new white firm were open to black writers. The most talented of them would be published by Mills over the next three decades.

In April 1921 Jimmy McHugh, a young man who had recently relocated from Boston, appeared in the Mills office looking for a job. His experience in the music business consisted of riding his bicycle to saloons and music stores around Boston, plugging songs published by the Ted Snyder Company. He was a good pianist and he seemed to know enough to be useful, so the Mills brothers hired him as their professional manager. One of McHugh's first suggestions to improve the company's product was that Mills issue some of his songs. Jack Mills's 1921 publication of McHugh's "Ladies Day in Dixie" (lyrics by Phil Ponce) was the beginning of one of the most important composer-publisher relationships of the 1920s.

Another stroke of good fortune befell Jack Mills, Inc. in 1921 in the person of a dispirited young man from Illinois. Zez Confrey, as the top arranger-performer for the QRS piano roll company in Chicago, seemed to have everything going for him, but he was frustrated as a composer. He had arranged and played more than a hundred rolls for QRS, including many of his own compositions, but except for a handful of songs, he couldn't get publishers interested in his work. Following the trail blazed by Charley Straight, he was now writing and thinking in that most complex of piano genres, novelty ragtime. Whirlwind tempos and impressionistic chords were second nature to him, and his two hands could do the work of four. He had made rolls of his first three novelties in 1918, and they had sold well enough to let him know that listeners liked them. But he had been told over and over that his compositions were too hard for the average player and that there was no market for them as sheet music. Expecting to be turned down again, he halfheartedly showed his wares to Jack Mills.

Mills knew that not every intermediate-level player could knock off Confrey's rags, but he also saw their musicality. And he made the judgment that the fun of playing them would outweigh the difficulty of learning them. In March 1921 he bought "My Pet" and "Kitten on the Keys." Zez Confrey knew that Mills had his work cut out for him in selling them, and he resolved to do what he could to help. In April Confrey recorded both of his newly published rags for the Brunswick label, and he made two other recordings of "Kitten on the Keys" before the year was out. One of these was made in September for Emerson, and the other in October for Arto/Bell. (His Emerson recording was also released on the Banner label that year, crediting the playing to "Vi Palmer.") Thanks to the brilliant Confrey recordings, players heard what was possible to achieve if they worked at "Kitten on the Keys," and the records and sheet music began to sell each other. The impossible-to-play rag sold more than a million copies in its first year. It established Zez Confrey as the king of novelty rag writers and Jack Mills as the nerviest publisher in New York.

Jack Mills issued five Confrey rags in 1921, reaping four hits and a smash. On August 16 he announced to the trade press that his company had given Confrey an exclusive contract. (The contract was not really exclusive. Confrey's three big songs of 1922—"Stumbling," "Tricks," and "Dumbell"—all went to Leo Feist, as did Confrey's "Nickel in the Slot," in 1923.)

If Mills were surprised at the number of customers for novelty ragtime, he must have been amazed at the number of composers who wrote in the idiom. After the success of "Kitten on the Keys," his company attracted them like flies. During the years 1922–29, Jack Mills, Inc. published the "too-difficult" rags of Henry Lange, Arthur Schutt, Rube Bloom, Max Kortlander, Vee Lawnhurst, Frank Signorelli, Pauline Alpert, and Frank Banta, among many others. Confrey remained the company's star composer of novelties, and "Kitten on the Keys" remained its best-seller. Confrey folios were steady sellers, too. *Modern Novelty Piano Solos*, a collection of Confrey rags published in 1923, remained in print for forty years, and Confrey's *Ten Lessons for the Piano* was the bible among novelty instruction manuals.

Paying obeisance to the ragtime that had come before his own, Jack Mills began to buy older rags and reissue them. Two of these were J. Russel Robinson compositions. "That Erratic Rag" became "Erratic," and "That Eccentric Rag" (originally issued by an Indianapolis publisher in 1912) was renamed "Eccentric." Both "Erratic" and "Eccentric" were republished by Mills in 1923. And Mills did what Henry Waterson could not do in 1914, which was to get national distribution for Scott Joplin's "Magnetic Rag." The master's last rag was given a subtitle, "Syncopations Classiques," and issued in a Mills folio of "Novelty Piano Solos" in 1923.

As Confrey and his disciples led the sales of Mills instrumentals in the mid-1920s, the company's own professional manager, Jimmy McHugh, provided its best-selling songs. In 1922 McHugh contributed "When You and I Were Young Maggie Blues" to the catalog, and this was followed by "Hinky Dinky Parlay Voo?" (1924), "My Kid" (1924), "When My Sugar Walks Down the Street" (1924), "Everything Is Hotsy Totsy Now" (1925), and "I Can't Believe That You're in Love with Me" (1926). Mills didn't publish much theatre music, but the Jimmy McHugh–Dorothy Fields score for *Blackbirds of 1928* yielded two huge hits: "Digga Digga Doo" and "I Can't Give You Anything But Love." In 1924 McHugh and Al Dubin wrote one of the few songs about a songwriter. They commemorated Irving Berlin's marriage to socialite Ellin Mackay with "When a Kid from the East Side Found a Sweet Society Rose."

Jack Mills continued to champion black writers, and he became a presence in the blues business in 1923, with the publication of Alberta Hunter's "Down Hearted Blues" and "Chirpin' the Blues." He also created a subsidiary that year, Down South Music Publishing Company (at 1658 Broadway), for the purpose of publishing blues by black composers. The pioneer jazz and blues arranger Fletcher Henderson was placed in charge of Down South Music. Mills issued the songs from Sissle and Blake's *Chocolate Dandies* score in 1924, and he began buying occasional songs from Fats Waller and James P. Johnson in the mid-twenties. In 1929 Mills bought the songs from Waller and Andy Razaf's *Hot Chocolates* (reportedly for the bargain price of $500) and had the hit of the year with "Ain't Misbehavin'."

Mills's catalog (and his personal taste) expanded in the mid-twenties to include compositions that crossed the line between the unusual and the unwieldy. But his faith in his hard-to-hum acquisitions often paid off. In 1925 he published Hoagy Carmichael's good-natured but slightly bizarre piano number "Riverboat Shuffle," and the following year he issued Carmichael's unblueslike "Washboard Blues." These two tunes paid their way in mechanical rights, and, more important, they brought Carmichael to Mills in 1929 with his oddest composition yet, the harmonically crazy "Star Dust." Mills published "Star Dust" as an instrumental in January 1929 and four months later issued it as a song. The sprawling, impossible-to-remember ballad became one of the biggest selling pop songs of all time.

The person who turned the trick for "Star Dust" was Mills's staff lyricist, Mitchell Parish. Parish's specialty was supplying the poetic conventionality that was needed to make difficult melodies accessible to listeners. Unlike Porter, Hart, and Ira Gershwin, Parish did not deal in clever wordplay and delightfully smartass references. The tunes that Mills assigned to him were tricky enough without adding verbal trickery to them. What they needed was lyrics for the listener to hang on to while their complex melodies were curling into the ear. Parish was a master of the common touch, and his way with simple (mostly one-syllable) words and everyday imagery made hundreds of Mills's oddball melodies memorable and made dozens of them into hits. Besides "Star Dust," Parish brought his gift for the ordinary to "Sophisticated Lady," "Sweet Lorraine," "Emmaline," "Cabin in the Cotton," and Carmichael's "One Morning in May" and "Riverboat Shuffle," among many others.

In 1928 Jack Mills, Inc. changed its name to Mills Music, and the following year Jack Mills celebrated his company's tenth anniversary by buying up the catalogs of Gus Edwards Music, Stark & Cowan, Harold Dixon, McCarthy & Fisher, and Fred Fisher. In 1931 Mills Music became the beneficiary of Waterson, Berlin & Snyder's woes, when it bought the bankrupt company's enormous catalog for $5,000.

Along with Mills's consolidation came diversification. In 1925 Irving Mills became the manager of an up-and-coming bandleader named Duke Ellington. Irving Mills supervised many Ellington recording sessions with various ensembles, and, as Ellington began to write tunes, it was natural that Irving would steer them to Jack's company. After Mills had published a few pieces by Ellington, it was decided to create a second "black" subsidiary, Gotham Music Service, primarily for the purpose of issuing Ellington songs and instrumentals. Beginning with "Black and Tan Fantasy" in 1927, most of the classic Ellington work of the next six years was published by Gotham: "Creole Love Call" (1928), "Black Beauty" (1928), "Rockin' in Rhythm" (1931), "Mood Indigo" (with an uncredited lyric by Mitchell Parish, 1931), and "Sophisticated Lady" (in both song and instrumental versions, 1933). Irving Mills often cut himself in as lyricist or co-composer of Ellington's work, but this practice did not drive Ellington away from Mills Music. In the mid-1930s, Mills created two other subsidiary imprints, American Academy of Music and Exclusive Publications, Inc., and both of them issued Ellington numbers. Exclusive also published two Confrey rags, "Mouse's Hoofs" and "Giddy Ditty," in 1935.

In October 1932, when many other Tin Pan Alley publishers were on the ropes, Mills Music moved into fine quarters in the new Brill Building, at 1619 Broadway. The company sailed through the Depression on hits from Duke Ellington, Cab Calloway, Fats Waller,

and Hoagy Carmichael. The bloom was off novelty ragtime, but Jack Mills showed that his taste for the hard-to-play was still intact when he began issuing the rags of Willie the Lion Smith in 1935. Mills published Smith's "Sneak Away" (1937) and his relentless "Keep Fingering" (1938). The "new classicism" pieces by Morton Gould, such as "Pavanne" and "Deserted Ballroom," which Mills issued in the late 1930s, were almost as rhythmically and harmonically complex as Willie the Lion's rags. In the early rag revival era, Mills was the primary publisher of the rags of Bill Krenz. A 1964 folio called *Ragtime Treasures* put thirteen recently discovered rags by Joe Lamb into print for the first time.

Jack Mills sold his company to a generically named conglomerate, the Utilities and Industries Company, for $5 million and retired in 1965. The hippest publisher in Tin Pan Alley died in Hollywood, Florida, on March 23, 1979.

RICHMOND-ROBBINS/ROBBINS-ENGEL/ROBBINS MUSIC CORPORATION/THE BIG THREE

Jack Robbins's love of ragtime was second to none among New York publishers. The three companies that he headed in his lifetime published nearly forty rags, almost all of them novelties, without ever having a hit. He spent the 1920s poaching Jack Mills writers (and he even wooed Confrey away from Mills in the mid-thirties), but their best sellers always went to Mills, not to Robbins. And his catalog of loss-leading rags was not subsidized by hit songs. Hits did not happen for Robbins until 1929, after he had been in business for seven years; up until that time he stuck with his unprofitable passion, the highly advanced novelty rag.

John J. (Jack) Robbins (1894–1959) entered the music business at its lowest level, through the stockroom. In the late teens he worked as a clerk at Emerson Music Supply, a small shipping and jobbing house, and, unlike most clerks, he took the time to look at and hum through the song sheets that he packed for mailing. One of the prettiest songs on Emerson's shelves, Robbins thought, was "Smiles," and it seemed odd to him that there were never any orders for it. "Smiles" had been self-published by its composer, Lee S. Roberts, in Chicago in 1917, and

Jack Robbins

it was meeting the indifference that befell most self-published works by unknown writers. Jack Robbins thought "Smiles" deserved a better fate, so he took it to Mose Gumble at Remick's and talked Gumble into buying its copyright from Roberts. Remick's 1918 edition of "Smiles" sold more than two million copies, and Robbins received a handsome finder's fee for bringing it to the company.

In 1919, as "Smiles" was still beaming in music stores, Robbins's uncle, Maurice Richmond, gave him a job as general manager of Richmond Music Publishing Company, at 1552 Broadway. Richmond had bought the F. A. Mills catalog in 1915 (for $3,000), but these numbers were mostly duds on the market. Mills had built his company on the two most unrevivable fads of the late 1890s, cakewalks and coon songs, and there was no call for them in the Vernon and Irene Castle era. Richmond was by default more a jobber than a publisher, but it was under his tutelage that Robbins learned the music business.

Late in 1921 Richmond and his nephew decided to cast their lots together and get serious about publishing, and on January 1, 1922, the new firm of Richmond-Robbins opened at 1658 Broadway. Because

Jack Mills's novelty rags were currently the rage, the new partners decided to get themselves some novelty rags, too. They found Phil Ohman, one of the few novelty rag writers whom Mills had not nailed down, and issued three of his rags in their first year. Like Confrey, Ohman was a prodigious player and arranger for the QRS roll company, but he did not have Confrey's prankishness or his melodic gift. The title of his first published rag, "Try and Play It," tells his story as a composer. Advanced players might want to imitate a kitten on the keys, but they did not want to take Ohman up on his dare. The Ohman rags flung out a technical challenge, and learning them seemed to be more work than fun. Richmond and Robbins had bet on the wrong horse. Needing an infusion of cash to keep going, they sold a third interest in their firm to Harry Engel in June 1923.

By the summer of 1924, Maurice Richmond had had enough. He left the business to his partners, who renamed their firm Robbins-Engel. Still chasing novelty gold, they bought rags from every piano whiz who came along. They published Louis Alter's sparkling "Piano Phun" in 1925, and they issued three oddly funky novelties by Willard Robison in 1926. They lured Harry Jentes away from Mills for one publication ("Twinkles"), and another Mills writer, Arthur Schutt, gave them what is probably the most difficult rag ever published, "Bluin' the Black Keys." In January 1925 Robbins-Engel tried to shore up the sales of their new numbers by buying some old ones. The partners acquired the catalog of E. T. Paull, the composer-publisher of dozens of marches and piano showpieces, for $25,000. Although the company had no hits, it had prospered enough to need larger offices, and it found them at 799 Seventh Avenue. By the time the move was made, on February 1, 1927, Robbins-Engel was missing a partner.

In January 1927 Harry Engel chose security over entrepreneurship by taking a job as sales manager for Irving Berlin, Inc. With Engel's leaving, the firm became Robbins Music Corporation, and for the first time Jack Robbins was solely in charge of a publishing company that bore his name. Finally, in 1927, Jack Robbins found his first hit song since "Smiles," Eugene Ford's wistful ballad "Rain." And, of course, Robbins continued to publish his adventurous rags. In 1927 he issued Bix Beiderbecke's moody and highly syncopated "In a Mist," and in 1929, Ralph Rainger's sparkling and urbane "Pianogram." Robbins

Dave Jasen

Music's best-selling rags were two by Rube Bloom that it published in 1931, the sprightly "Aunt Jemima's Birthday" and "Southern Charms."

In 1929, during Hollywood's buying up of Tin Pan Alley firms, Jack Robbins entered into an unusual agreement with MGM. Instead of selling his firm to the studio, he contracted to be the primary publisher and distributor of MGM's movie songs. The deal brought him the best of both worlds, autonomy as a publisher and a steady supply of movie-related—and highly promotable—songs. MGM's star songwriting team at the time was Nacio Herb Brown and Arthur Freed, and the Brown–Freed hits ("Broadway Melody," "Pagan Love Song," "Should I?," "Singin' in the Rain," and "Temptation") were channeled directly to Robbins for publication.

Jack Robbins kept his arm's-length arrangement with MGM for six years, before he sold his company to the studio in 1935. MGM had previously purchased the catalogs of Leo Feist and Miller Music, and the

Robbins copyrights were combined with those to form the Big Three Music Corporation. A Big Three folio called *Ragtime: 100 Authentic Rags*, issued in 1979, was the last major collection of rags from a Tin Pan Alley publisher. The book includes rags from the catalogs of each of the Big Three, along with those of other publishers. The rags span eighty years, beginning with the 1899 "Maple Leaf Rag" and ending with ten new rags by David Jasen.

At the time the folio appeared, all of the ragtime eras were over, but ragtime was not over. Since the revival took root in the early 1970s, we have seen a perpetual ragtime era. We are as likely to hear a Joplin rag as a Brahms quartet on any "good music" radio station. Record companies have plundered their vaults to make their once-forgotten rags available on CDs. Ragtime is still in the American air, and we are not surprised to find it anywhere: in hotel bars, in elevators, on concert stages at non-ragtime events. And there are still kids at living room pianos, hacking away at "Maple Leaf Rag," digging into its mysteries and slowing it down to get the fingering. "Maple Leaf" will hold them, will keep them working to get it right. And when they have it under control and up to speed, they will own something powerful and joyous and fine.

Ragtime Composers by Birthplace

ALABAMA

Donald Ashwander   b. Birmingham   July 17, 1929   d. New York City   October 26, 1994

James Reese Europe   b. Mobile   February 22, 1881   d. Boston, MA   May 9, 1919

Robert Hampton   b. Tuscumbia   August 10, 1890   d. Los Angeles, CA   September 25, 1945

Robert George Hoffman   b. South   September 19, 1878   d. New Orleans, LA   December 8, 1964

ARKANSAS

Will Nash   b. Hot Springs

Will Skidmore   b. Little Rock   April 9, 1880   d. El Paso, TX   November 13, 1959

Blanche M. Tice   b. Eureka

CALIFORNIA

Allan Clark   b. Los Angeles   October 20, 1907

James Martin (Jay) Roberts   b. Oakland   c. 1889   d. Ancon, Panama   July 28, 1932

Lee S. Roberts   b. Oakland   November 12, 1884   d. San Francisco, CA   September 10, 1949

COLORADO

Max Edward Morath   b. Colorado Springs   October 1, 1926

Walter Harry Wayland   b. Pueblo   February 12, 1884   d. Girard, KS   March 13, 1980

CONNECTICUT

Philmore (Phil) Ohman   b. New Britain   October 7, 1896   d. Santa Monica, CA   August 8, 1954

George J. Trinkhaus   b. Bridgeport   April 13, 1878   d. Ridgewood, NJ   May 19, 1960

Herbert H. Whiting   b. Hartford   March 14, 1869   d. Sanford, ME   April 1, 1935

DISTRICT OF COLUMBIA

Ford T. Dabney   b. March 15, 1883   d. New York City   June 21, 1958

Theodore Morse   b. April 13, 1873   d. New York City   May 25, 1924

GEORGIA

Nellie Weldon Cocroft   b. Quitman   November 4, 1885   d. Jacksonville, FL   June 27, 1986

Malvin M. Franklin   b. Atlanta   August 24, 1889   d. New York City   July 9, 1981

Ferdinand Alexander Guttenberger, Jr.   b. Macon   November 29, 1888   d. Macon, GA   October 1, 1945

Strauss L. Lloyd   b. Montezuma   December 27, 1872   d. Inverness, FL   November 22, 1953

George W. Lowe   b. Atlanta   c. 1872-75   d. Columbia, KY   February 5, 1936

Thomas Million Turpin   b. Savannah   November 1873   d. St. Louis, MO   August 13, 1922

ILLINOIS

Milton Ager   b. Chicago   October 6, 1893   d. Los Angeles, CA   April 6, 1979

Victor Arden (see Lewis John Fuiks)

Marshall Moore Bartholomew   b. Belleville   March 3, 1885   d. New York City   1978

Edward D. Ballantine   b. Chicago   January 26, 1907

Axel Waldemar Fritchoff Christensen   b. Chicago   March 23, 1881   d. Los Angeles, CA   August 17, 1955

Edward Elzear (Zez) Confrey   b. Peru   April 3, 1895   d. Lakewood, NJ   November 22, 1971

Thomas J. Filas   b. Chicago   March 5, 1908

Lewis John Fuiks   b. Wenona   March 8, 1893   d. New York City   July 31, 1962

Herbert Ingraham   b. Aurora   January 7, 1883   d. Saranac Lake, NY   August 24, 1910

Arnold Johnson   b. Chicago   March 23, 1893   d. St. Petersburg, FL   July 15, 1975

Frank Henri Klickmann   b. Chicago   February 4, 1885   d. New York City   June 25, 1966

William Frederick (Bill) Krenz   b. Rock Island   February 23, 1899

Sol Paul Levy   b. Chicago   July 22, 1881   d. New York City   February 14, 1920

Artie Matthews   b. Braidwood   November 15, 1888   d. Cincinnati, OH   October 25, 1958

Lindsey McPhail   b. Chicago   November 9, 1895   d. Tupper Lake, NY   March 3, 1965

Glenn Rowell   b. Pontiac   November 2, 1899   d. Rapid City, SD   October 8, 1965

Thomas William (Tom) Shea   b. Mattoon   November 14, 1931   d. Raleigh, NC   March 12, 1982

Arthur L. Sizemore   b. Marion   February 5, 1891   d. Chicago, IL   September 24, 1954

Ted Snyder   b. Freeport   August 15, 1881   d. Woodland Hills, CA   July 16, 1965

Ray Stewart Soladay   b. Lena   February 23, 1892   d. Carlsbad, NM   May 12, 1960

Harry Sosnik   b. Chicago   July 13, 1906

Herbert Spencer   b. Bunker Hill   May 27, 1878   d. St. Louis, MO   August 26, 1944

Charles T. Straight   b. Chicago   January 16, 1891   d. Chicago, IL   September 21, 1940

Joe Sullivan   b. Chicago   November 5, 1906   d. San Francisco, CA   October 13, 1971

Egbert Anson Van Alstyne   b. Marengo   March 6, 1878   d. Chicago, IL   July 9, 1951

Frank C. Westphal   b. Chicago   June 15, 1889   d. Bridgeport, CT   November 23, 1948

Richard A. Whiting   b. Peoria   November 12, 1891   d. Beverly Hills, CA   February 10, 1938

Joseph M. Wilcockson   b. Braidwood   March 15, 1876   d. Hammond, IN   November 6, 1952

INDIANA

William Albright   b. Gary   October 20, 1944   d. Ann Arbor, MI   September 17, 1998

May Frances Aufderheide   b. Indianapolis   May 21, 1888   d. Pasadena, CA   September 1, 1972

King W. Baker   b. Warrick County   May 8, 1880   d. Rumsey, KY   April 18, 1963

Harry Bell   b. Somerville   September 15, 1885   d. Evansville, IN   April 14, 1965

Opal Boyar   b. Pine Village   1890   d. Lafayette, IN   1986

Jerre Ward Cammack   b. Marion   September 10, 1890   d. St. Louis, MO   January 20, 1963

Forest L. Cook   b. Warsaw   May 1, 1893   d. Huntington, IN   July 23, 1979

Cecil Duane Crabb   b. Centerville   May 6, 1890   d. Rice Lake, WI   April 27, 1953

Sam H. Ewing   b. Princeton   June 6, 1885   d. Columbus, OH   January 23, 1957

Albert Gumble   b. North Vernon   September 10, 1883   d. New York City   November 30, 1946

Moses Edwin Gumble   b. Mount Vernon   c. 1871   d. Elkhart, IN   September 28, 1947

Robert George Ingraham   b. Whiting   December 5, 1895   d. St. Louis, MO

Lloyd L. Johnson   b. Somerville   1884   d. Chicago, IL   c. 1957

E. Clinton Keithley   b. Greenville   November 15, 1880   d. Tampa, FL   April 7, 1955

John Nelson Lang   b. Marion   May 24, 1899   d. Indianapolis, IN   August 6, 1978

Glenn C. Leap   b. Indianapolis   May 16, 1890   d. Indianapolis, IN   January 18, 1956

Carey Morgan   b. Brownsburg   December 25, 1885   d. Pittsburgh, PA   January 6, 1960

Will B. Morrison   b. Seymour   October 12, 1874   d. Indianapolis, IN   December 18, 1937

Julia Lee Niebergall   b. Indianapolis   February 15, 1886   d. Indianapolis, IN   October 19, 1968

Paul Charles Pratt   b. New Salem   November 1, 1890   d. Indianapolis, IN   July 7, 1948

Richard Rabe   b. Indianapolis

Armond C. Rhodehamel   b. Indianapolis   March 4, 1890   d. Indianapolis, IN   1932

J. Russel Robinson   b. Indianapolis   July 8, 1892   d. Palmdale, CA   September 30, 1963

Fred Rose   b. Evansville   August 24, 1897   d. Nashville, TN   December 1, 1954

Isidore Seidel   b. Indianapolis   1890   d. Indianapolis, IN   1972

Etilmon J. Stark   b. Gosport   1868   d. Maplewood, MO   January 1962

Hubert Tanner   b. Plymouth   1889   d. Plymouth, IN   1965

Albert Von Tilzer   b. Indianapolis   March 29, 1878   d. Los Angeles, CA   October 1, 1956

Allister Wylie   b. Connersville   June 23, 1898   d. St. Louis, MO   November 28, 1962

Gladys Yelvington   b. Indianapolis   1891   d. Indianapolis, IN   1957

IOWA

Leon Bix Beiderbecke   b. Davenport   March 10, 1903   d. New York City   August 6, 1931

Fleta Jan Brown   b. Storm Lake   March 8, 1883   d. Hillsdale, NJ   September 2, 1938

Lee B. Grabbe   b. Davenport   1860   d. Glendale, CA   March 1911

Adaline Shepherd   b. Algona   August 19, 1885   d. Milwaukee, WI   March 12, 1950

Harold Taylor Weeks   b. Eagle Grove   March 28, 1893   d. Seattle, WA   January 7, 1967

KANSAS

Leslie C. (Les) Copeland   b. Wichita   June 4, 1887   d. San Francisco, CA   March 3, 1942

Charles Neil Daniels   b. Leavenworth   April 12, 1878   d. Los Angeles, CA   January 21, 1943

Waylande Gregory   b. Osborne   1905   d. Osborne, KS   1971

Charles Leslie Johnson   b. Kansas City   December 3, 1876   d. Kansas City, MO   December 28, 1950

George E. Rausch   b. Leavenworth   c. 1874

KENTUCKY

Louis Ferdinand Busch   b. Louisville   July 18, 1910   d. Camarillo, CA   September 18, 1979

Joe "Fingers" Carr (see Louis Ferdinand Busch)

Charles L. Cooke   b. Louisville   September 3, 1891   d. Wurtsboro, NY   December 25, 1958

Earle E. Edmonds   b. Covington   November 27, 1895   d. Covington, KY   June 16, 1960

Alfred Gasdorf   b. Newport   October 30, 1883   d. Los Angeles, CA   December 6, 1957

Phil M. Hacker   b. Louisville   1863   d. Memphis, TN   1933

Oscar F. Hanna   b. Lexington   1883   d. Lexington, KY   June 26, 1942

Fate Marable   b. Paducah   1890   d. St. Louis, MO   1947

Julian C. (Matty) Matlock   b. Paducah   April 27, 1907   d. Van Nuys, CA   June 14, 1978

Louis Mentel   b. Covington   August 14, 1880   d. Cincinnati, OH   April 4, 1955

Russell Smith   b. Versailles   June 12, 1890   d. Indianapolis, IN   July 17, 1969

Floyd H. Willis   b. Falmouth   1885   d. Covington, KY   November 19, 1959

LOUISIANA

Larry Buck (see Laurent Dubuclet)

Laurent Dubuclet   b. New Orleans   October 4, 1866   d. Chicago, IL   November 25, 1909

Dominick James (Nick) LaRocca   b. New Orleans   April 11, 1889   d. New Orleans, LA   February 22, 1961

Irwin Percy Leclere   b. New Orleans   February 21, 1891   d. New Orleans, LA   September 29, 1981

Ferdinand Joseph (Jelly Roll) Morton   b. New Orleans   October 20, 1890   d. Los Angeles, CA   July 10, 1941

Paul Sarabresole   b. New Orleans   May 1875   d. New Orleans, LA   October 3, 1911

Edwin H. See   b. Lake Charles   1892   d. Lake Charles, LA   1963

Alphonse (Al) Verges   b. New Orleans   1874   d. New Orleans, LA   July 25, 1924

Clarence Williams   b. Plaquemine   October 8, 1893   d. Jamaica, NY   November 6, 1965

MAINE

Walter Rolfe   b. Rumford Corners   December 18, 1880   d. Brighton, MA   January 18, 1944

MARYLAND

James Hubert (Eubie) Blake   b. Baltimore   February 7, 1883   d. Brooklyn, NY   February 12, 1983

Edward B. Claypoole   b. Baltimore   December 20, 1883   d. Baltimore, MD   January 16, 1952

Horace Kirkus Dugdale   b. Baltimore   November 24, 1890   d. Seaford, DE   December 4, 1980

Julius Lenzberg   b. Baltimore   January 3, 1878   d. Orlando, FL   April 24, 1956

MASSACHUSETTS

Thomas S. Allen   b. Natick   December 16, 1876   d. Boston, MA   October 23, 1919

Louis Alter   b. Haverhill   June 18, 1902   d. New York City   November 5, 1980

Harry B. Armstrong   b. Somerville   July 22, 1879   d. Bronx, NY   February 28, 1951

Nat D. Ayer   b. Boston   1887   d. Bath, England   1952

James Alexander Brennan   b. Boston   November 18, 1885   d. Middleboro, MA   August 24, 1956

J. Newell Chase   b. Roxbury   February 3, 1904   d. New York City   January 26, 1955

Joseph Michael Daly   b. Boston   February 7, 1883   d. New York City   June 16, 1968

Frank E. Hersom   b. Fair Haven   May 19, 1894   d. Jamaica, NY   October 26, 1941

Mayhew Lester Lake   b. Southville   October 25, 1879   d. Palisades, NJ   March 16, 1955

James Francis (Jimmy) McHugh   b. Boston   July 10, 1895   d. Beverly Hills, CA   May 23, 1969

John McLaughlin   b. Lynn   February 17, 1897

MICHIGAN

Roy Frederick Bargy   b. Newaygo   July 31, 1894   d. Vista, CA   January 16, 1974

George D. Barnard   b. Jackson   October 14, 1858   d. Maysville, KY   January 19, 1933

Harold Berg   b. Saginaw   May 3, 1900   d. Southfield, MI   July 24, 1973

Roy Johnson Carew   b. Grand Rapids   December 15, 1883   d. Washington, DC   August 4, 1967

Robert Russell (Ragtime Bob) Darch   b. Detroit   March 31, 1920

Sydney P. Harris   b. Detroit

Max Kortlander   b. Grand Rapids   September 1, 1890   d. New York City   October 11, 1961

Walter E. Miles   b. Grand Rapids   May 10, 1885   d. Ft. Lauderdale, FL   May 9, 1961

James Royce Shannon   b. Adrian   May 13, 1881   d. Pontiac, MI   May 19, 1946

George Lemworth (Lem) Trombley   b. Michigan   October 27, 1883   d. Sonoma, CA
December 30, 1963

Bob Zurke   b. Detroit   January 17, 1912   d. Los Angeles, CA   February 16, 1944

MINNESOTA

Frederick Theodore Swanson   b. Red Wing   August 28, 1870   d. St. Paul, MN   March 2,
1954

Harry H. Williams   b. Faribault   August 29, 1879   d. Oakland, CA   May 15, 1922

MISSOURI

Hubert Theodore Bauersachs   b. St. Louis   May 15, 1882   d. St. Louis, MO   February 7,
1964

Theron Catlin Bennett   b. Pierce City   July 9, 1879   d. Los Angeles, CA   April 6, 1937

John William (Blind) Boone   b. Miami   May 17, 1864   d. Warrensburg, MO   October 4,
1927

Clarence E. Brandon   b. St. Louis   September 26, 1887   d. St. Louis, MO   September 29,
1962

James Owen Fahy   b. Springfield   October 1887   d. Springfield, MO   October 8, 1911

Irene M. Giblin   b. St. Louis   August 12, 1888   d. St. Louis, MO   May 12, 1974

Walter Gustave Haenschen   b. St. Louis 1889

Scott Hayden   b. Sedalia   March 31, 1882   d. Chicago, IL   September 16, 1915

Edward Harry Kelly   b. Kansas City   July 11, 1879   d. Kansas City, MO   April 15, 1955

Lilburn Kingsbury   b. New Franklin   1884   d. Sedalia, MO   1983

Arthur Marshall   b. Saline County   November 20, 1881   d. Kansas City, MO   August 18,
1968

Edward J. Mellinger   b. St. Louis   November 26, 1890   d. St. Louis, MO   January 11, 1947

George A. Norton   b. St. Louis   April 16, 1880   d. Tucson, AZ   September 14, 1923

Willard Robison   b. Shelbina   September 18, 1894   d. New York City   June 24, 1968

William S. Rowland   b. Sedalia   1948

James Sylvester Scott   b. Neosho   February 12, 1885   d. Kansas City, KS   August 30, 1938

Lee Edgar (Jelly) Settle   b. New Franklin   July 20, 1882   d. New Franklin, MO   February
4, 1949

Wilbur Sweatman   b. Brunswick   February 7, 1882   d. New York City   March 9, 1961

Charles Hubbard (Charlie) Thompson   b. St. Louis   June 19, 1891   d. St. Louis, MO   June
13, 1964

Trebor Jay Tichenor   b. St. Louis   January 28, 1940

Calvin Lee Woolsey   b. Tinney's Point   December 26, 1884   d. Braymer, MO   November 12, 1946

NEW HAMPSHIRE

Ernie Golden   b. Manchester August 27, 1890

NEW JERSEY

Harry Carroll   b. Atlantic City   November 28, 1892   d. Mt. Carmel, PA   December 26, 1962

Anna Case (Mrs. Clarence Mackey)   b. Clinton   1889

James Price Johnson   b. New Brunswick   February 1, 1894   d. Jamaica, NY   November 17, 1955

Mel B. Kaufman   b. Newark   April 23, 1879   d. New York City   February 21, 1932

Joseph Francis Lamb   b. Montclair   December 6, 1887   d. Brooklyn, NY September 3, 1960

Harry Austin Tierney   b. Perth Amboy   May 21, 1890   d. New York City   March 22, 1965

NEW MEXICO

Ignacio (Nacio) Herb Brown   b. Deming   February 22, 1896   d. San Francisco, CA   Sept. 28, 1964

NEW YORK

Pauline Alpert   b. New York City   December 27, 1900   d. Bronx, NY   April 11, 1988

Felix Arndt   b. New York City   May 20, 1889   d. New York City   October 16, 1918

Harry Akst   b. New York City   August 15, 1894   d. Hollywood, CA   March 31, 1963

William Axt   b. New York City   April 19, 1888   d. Ukiah, CA   February 12, 1959

Frank Edgar Banta   b. New York City   September 8, 1897   d. Avon, NJ   December 27, 1968

Ted S. Barron   b. Flushing   December 14, 1879   d. Flushing, NY   November 28, 1943

Mike Bernard   b. New York City   March 17, 1881   d. New York City   June 27, 1936

Rube Bloom   b. New York City   April 24, 1902   d. New York City   March 30, 1976

Frederick Bryan   b. Brooklyn   September 13, 1889   d. Brooklyn, NY   August 16, 1929

George Linus Cobb   b. Mexico   November 4, 1885   d. Brookline, MA   December 25, 1942

Con Conrad   b. New York City   June 18, 1891   d. Van Nuys, CA   September 28, 1938

Silvio DeRienzo   b. New York City   October 6, 1909   d. New York City   October 2, 1966

Harry DaCosta   b. New York City   June 25, 1885   d. Hollywood, CA   June 23, 1964

Will Donaldson   b. Brooklyn   April 21, 1891   d. Hollywood, CA   December 16, 1954

Peter DeRose   b. New York City   March 10, 1900   d. New York City   April 23, 1953

Bob Emmerich   b. New York City   July 26, 1904

George Gershwin   b. Brooklyn   September 26, 1898   d. Beverly Hills, CA   July 11, 1937

Jacob (Jack) Glogau   b. New York City   December 31, 1886   d. Woodhaven, NY   October 30, 1953

Joe Glover   b. Westhampton Beach   February 6, 1903

Joe Gold   b. New York City   November 20, 1894   d. New York City   November 5, 1978

Bert F. Grant   b. New York City   July 12, 1878   d. New York City   May 10, 1951

Jesse Greer   b. New York City   August 26, 1896   d. Columbia, CT   October 3, 1970

Ferde Grofe   b. New York City   March 27, 1892   d. Santa Monica, CA   April 3, 1972

Silvio Hein   b. New York City   March 15, 1879   d. Saranac Lake, NY   December 19, 1928

Richard Roven (Dick) Hyman   b. New York City   March 8, 1927

David Alan Jasen   b. New York City   December 16, 1937

Harry Jentes   b. New York City   August 28, 1887   d. New York City   January 19, 1958

Joe Keden   b. Astoria   August 10, 1898

Robert A. King   b. New York City   September 20, 1862   d. New York City April 13, 1932

Vee Lawnhurst   b. New York City   November 24, 1905   d. New York City   May 14, 1992

Tom Lemonier   b. New York City   March 29, 1870   d. Chicago, IL   March 14, 1945

Al Lewis   b. New York City   April 18, 1901   d. New York City   April 4, 1967

Frank Hoyt Losey   b. Rochester   March 18, 1870   d. Erie, PA   May 3, 1931

Harold (Hal) Mooney   b. Brooklyn   February 4, 1911

Melville Morris   b. New York City   October 5, 1888   d. New York City   February 10, 1987

Will Morrissey   b. New York City   June 19, 1887   d. Santa Barbara, CA   December 17, 1957

Lewis Frank Muir   b. New York City   May 30, 1883   d. New York City   December 3, 1915

Al Piantadosi   b. New York City   July 18, 1884   d. Encino, CA   April 8, 1955

William C. Polla   b. New York City   August 12, 1876   d. New York City   November 4, 1939

Lew Pollack   b. New York City   June 16, 1895   d. Hollywood, CA   January 18, 1946

Muriel Pollock   b.Kingsbridge   January 21, 1895   d. Hollywood, CA   May 25, 1971

Harry Puck   b. Brooklyn   May 15, 1890   d. Metuchen, NJ   January 29, 1964

Ralph Rainger   b. New York City   October 7, 1901   d. Beverly Hills, CA   October 24, 1942

Milton J. Rettenberg   b. New York City   January 27, 1899   d. New York City   December 24, 1986

Justin Ringleben   b. New York City   June 28, 1876   d. Miami, FL   December 25, 1962

Henry Lew Roberts   b. New York City   December 25, 1880   d. Nashville, TN   September 26, 1919

Charles Rosoff   b. Brooklyn   May 1, 1898

Harry Ruby   b. New York City   January 27, 1895   d. Beverly Hills, CA   February 23, 1974

Sydney King Russell   b. New York City   November 29, 1898   d. Palm Beach, FL   November 28, 1976

Joe Schenck   b. Brooklyn   1892   d. Detroit, MI   June 28, 1930

William A. Schroeder   b. Brooklyn   November 10, 1888   d. Wilton, CT   April 20, 1960

Raymond Scott   b. New York City   September 10, 1909   d. North Hills, CA   February 8, 1994

Ted Shapiro   b. New York City   October 31, 1899   d. New York City   May 26, 1980

Frank Signorelli   b. New York City   May 24, 1901   d. Brooklyn, NY   December 9, 1975

Louis Silvers   b. New York City   September 6, 1889   d. Hollywood, CA   March 26, 1954

William Henry Joseph Bonaparte Berthloff (Willie the Lion) Smith   b. Goshen   November 25, 1897   d. New York City   April 18, 1973

Herbert Steiner   b. New York City   December 25, 1895   d. Forest Hills, NY   March 17, 1964

Albert C. (Al) Sweet   b. Dansville   July 7, 1876   d. Chicago, IL   May 12, 1945

Gus Van   b. Brooklyn   August 12, 1887   d. Miami Beach, FL   March 13, 1968

Warren Raymond Walker   b. Brooklyn   December 29, 1883   d. Brooklyn, NY   June 20, 1960

Thomas Wright (Fats) Waller   b. New York City   May 21, 1904   d. Kansas City, KS   December 15, 1943

Albert J. Weidt   b. Buffalo   February 15, 1866   d. Middletown, NJ   December 9, 1945

Pete Wendling   b. New York City   June 6, 1888   d. Maspeth, NY   April 8, 1974

Fred T. Whitehouse   b. New York City   June 14, 1895   d. New York City   June 6, 1954

William F. Wirges   b. Buffalo   June 26, 1894   d. East Norwich, NY   September 28, 1971

Jay Whidden   b. New York City   1886   d. 1968

OHIO

Ernest R. Ball   b. Cleveland   July 22, 1878   d. Santa Ana, CA   May 3, 1927

Al W. Brown   b. Cleveland   January 3, 1884   d. New York City   November 27, 1924

Edwin A. Burkart   b. Cincinnati   1893   d. Dunedin, FL   February 18, 1969

Ernie Burnett   b. Cincinnati   December 19, 1884   d. Saranac Lake, NY   September 11, 1959

Homer Denney   b. Norwood   1885   d. Springfield, OH   September 1975

James Henry Fillmore, Jr.   b. Cincinnati   February 3, 1881   d. Miami, FL   December 7, 1956

Richard Goosman   b. Cincinnati   January 31, 1882   d. Cincinnati, OH   March 1, 1941

Thomas (Tom) Griselle   b. Sandusky   January 10, 1891   d. Hollywood, CA   December 27, 1955

Harry P. Guy   b. Zanesville   July 17, 1870   d. Detroit, MI   September 16, 1950

Theodore Hahn, Jr.   b. Cincinnati   June 27, 1884   d. Dayton, OH   August 18, 1961

Fred Heltman   b. Ashland   May 3, 1887   d. Manistique, MI   August 2, 1960

Cliff Hess   b. Cincinnati   June 19, 1894   d. Texas   June 8, 1959

Clarence M. Jones   b. Wilmington   August 15, 1889   d. New York City   June 1, 1949

Isham E. Jones   b. Coalton   January 31, 1894   d. Hollywood, CA   October 19, 1956

Joe Jordan   b. Cincinnati   February 11, 1882   d. Tacoma, WA   September 9, 1971

Henry Lange   b. Toledo   July 20, 1895   d. Dayton, OH   June 10, 1985

Reuben Lawson   b. Cincinnati   c. 1889   d. Cincinnati, OH   April 14, 1968

Fred L. Neddermeyer   b. Columbus   July 4, 1866   d. Columbus, OH   August 9, 1924

Robert J. O'Brien   b. Cincinnati   c. 1882   d. Cincinnati, OH   June 3, 1948

Abe Olman   b. Cincinnati   December 20, 1888   d. Rancho Mirage, CA   January 4, 1984

William Frederick Peters   b. Sandusky   August 9, 1876   d. Englewood, NJ   December 1, 1938

Robert S. Roberts   b. Cincinnati   c. 1879   d. Cincinnati, OH   January 21, 1930

Archie W. Scheu   b. Cincinnati   1881

Walter Cleveland Simon   b. Cincinnati   October 27, 1884   d. New York City   March 5, 1958

Ralph Emerson (Terry) Waldo   b. Ironton   November 26, 1944

Edwin E. Wilson   b. Dayton

H. Clarence Woods   b. Blue Earth   June 19, 1888   d. Davenport, IA   September 30, 1956

John Stephen Zamecnik   b. Cleveland   May 14, 1872   d. Los Angeles, CA   June 13, 1953

PENNSYLVANIA

John E. Broderick   b. Sharon   November 30, 1901

Adam Carroll   b. Philadelphia   March 19, 1897   d. New York City   February 28, 1974

Ernie Erdman   b. Pittsburgh   October 23, 1879   d. Rockford, IL   November 1, 1946

Vinton Freedley   b. Philadelphia   1891   d. 1969

George Otto Frey   b. Honesdale   August 22, 1881   d. Philadelphia, PA   May 13, 1951

Sam Goold   b. Philadelphia   January 29, 1893   d. Philadelphia, PA   January 14, 1931

Fred Hager   b. Pennsylvania   December 31, 1874   d. Dunedin, FL   March 31, 1958

Dave Harris   b. Pittsburgh   October 20, 1889

Earl (Fatha) Hines   b. Duquesne   December 28, 1905   d. Oakland, CA   April 22, 1983

Guy Hall   b. Scranton   December 13, 1892   d. Harrisburg, PA   November 21, 1974

Billy James   b. Philadelphia   July 3, 1895   d. Philadelphia, PA   November 18, 1965

Henry Kleinkauf   b. Pennsylvania   May 1886   d. Wilkes-Barre, PA   August 5, 1942

Arthur Lange   b. Philadelphia   April 16, 1889   d. Washington, DC   December 7, 1956

Harry J. Lincoln   b. Shamokin   April 13, 1878   d. Philadelphia, PA   April 19, 1937

Frederick Allen (Kerry) Mills   b. Philadelphia   February 1, 1869   d. Hawthorn, CA   December 5, 1948

Charles Luckeyth (Luckey) Roberts   b. Philadelphia   August 7, 1892   d. New York City   February 5, 1968

Thomas A. Schmutzler   b. Philadelphia   1943

Arthur Schutt   b. Reading   November 21, 1902   d. San Francisco, CA   January 28, 1965

Harold D. Squires   b. Philadelphia   May 10, 1897   d. Brooklyn, NY   December 19, 1961

Will H. Vodery   b. Philadelphia   October 8, 1885   d. New York City   November 18, 1951

RHODE ISLAND

Frankie Carle   b. Providence   March 25, 1903

George Michael Cohan   b. Providence   July 3, 1878   d. New York City   November 5, 1942

Thomas Henry Lodge   b. Providence   February 9, 1884   d. West Palm Beach, FL   February 16, 1933

SOUTH CAROLINA

Joseph A. (Fud) Livingston   b. Charleston   April 10, 1906   d. New York City   March 25, 1957

SOUTH DAKOTA

Donald Bestor   b. Langford   September 23, 1889   d. Metamora, IL   January 13, 1970

George Botsford   b. Sioux Falls   February 24, 1874   d. New York City   February 11, 1949

TENNESSEE

Charles Hunter   b. Columbia   May 16, 1876   d. St. Louis, MO   January 23, 1906

TEXAS

Euday Louis Bowman   b. Ft. Worth   November 9, 1887   d. New York City   May 26, 1949

David Wendell DeFentresse Guion   b. Ballinger   December 15, 1892   d. Dallas, TX   October 17, 1981

Scott Joplin   b. Bowie County   November 24, 1868   d. New York City   April 1, 1917

Deane Kincaide   b. Houston   1911

Benjamin F. (Reb) Spikes   b. Dallas   October 31, 1888

John C. Spikes   b. Dallas July 22, 1882   d. Pasadena, CA   June 28, 1955

VIRGINIA

Larry T. Briers   b. Virginia   December 25, 1892   d. Columbus, OH   October 9, 1946

George W. Fairman   b. Front Royal   December 3, 1881   d. Miami, FL   October 16, 1962

Monroe H. Rosenfeld   b. Richmond   April 22, 1862   d. New York City   December 12, 1918

WASHINGTON

William Elden Bolcom   b. Seattle   May 26, 1938

J. Warren H. Camp   b. Seattle   1888   d. Seattle, WA   December 8, 1911

Alec M. Malin   b. Seattle   May 7, 1894   d. Seattle, WA   June 29, 1984

Thomas P. Quinn   b. Kelso   1925   d. Pomona, CA   February 3, 1999

WISCONSIN

Walter E. Blaufuss   b. Milwaukee   July 26, 1883   d. Chicago, IL   August 24, 1945

Charles B. Brown   b. Milwaukee   1871

Ethwell (Eddy) Hanson   b. New London   August 1, 1893

Alvin L. Marx   b. Ashland   1882   d. Superior, WI   June 1956

RAGTIME COMPOSERS BORN OUTSIDE OF THE U.S.

John Arpin   b. Port McNicholl, Ontario, Canada   December 3, 1936

Winifred Atwell   b. Trinidad   1914   d. Sydney, Australia   February 28, 1983

Bernard Barnes   b. Worcester, England   1894   d. Seattle, WA   1947

Saul Bluestein   b. Berditchief, Russia   1886   d. Memphis, TN   May 2, 1939

Castro Carazo   b. San Jose, Costa Rica   June 18, 1895   d. Baton Rouge, LA   December 28, 1981

Guido Salto Deiro   b. Canvonese, Italy   June 10, 1886   d. California   July 26, 1950

Lucien Denni   b. Nancy, France   December 23, 1886   d. Hermosa Beach, CA   August 20, 1947

Max Dreyfus   b. Kuppenheim, Germany   1874   d. New York City   1964

Willie Eckstein   b. Montreal, Canada   December 6, 1888   d. Montreal, Canada   September 23, 1963

Gus Edwards   b. Hohensaliza, Germany   August 18, 1879   d. Los Angeles, CA   November 7, 1945

William Fazioli   b. Frosolone, Italy   October 27, 1898   d. New York City   May 4, 1924

Dennis Haworth   b. England   September 1860

Paul Henneberg   b. Bobessberg, Germany   1863   d. New York City   December 15, 1929

Max Hoffman   b. Gnesen, Poland   December 8, 1873   d. Hollywood, CA   May 21, 1963

May Irwin   b. Whitby, Ontario, Canada   June 27, 1862   d. New York City   October 26, 1938

J. Bodewalt Lampe   b. Ribe, Denmark   November 8, 1869   d. New York City   May 26, 1929

(Little) Jack Little   b. London, England   May 28, 1900   d. Hollywood, CA   April 9, 1956

Peter Lundberg   b. Gothenburg, Sweden   February 9, 1942

Albert F. Marzian   b. Russia   September 9, 1875   d. Louisville, KY   June 29, 1947

Billy Mayerl   b. London, England   May 31, 1902   d. London, England   March 25, 1959

Otto Motzan   b. Hungary   October 12, 1880   d. New York City   January 15, 1937

Ernst Otto   b. Schoenwalde, Germany   October 25, 1865   d. Davenport, IA   April 2, 1939

Sam A. Perry   b. Russia   March 28, 1884   d. Los Angeles, CA   November 1, 1936

Erno Rapee   b. Budapest, Hungary   June 4, 1891   d. New York City   June 26, 1945

Charles J. Roberts   b. Kassa, Hungary   July 25, 1868   d. Albuquerque, NM   August 3, 1957

Donald A. Robertson   b. Scotland   1886   d. Seattle, WA   March 22, 1934

Vincent Rose   b. Palermo, Italy   June 13, 1880   d. Rockville Center, NY   May 20, 1944

Luis Carl Russell   b. Careening Cay, Panama   August 5, 1902   d. New York City   December 11, 1963

Jean Schwartz   b. Budapest, Hungary   November 4, 1878   d. Sherman Oaks, CA   November 30, 1956

Ray Sinatra   b. Gergenti, Sicily   November 1, 1904   d. Las Vegas, NV   November 1, 1980

Fred S. Stone   b. Chatham, Ontario, Canada   1873   d. Detroit, MI   1912

Harry Thomas   b. Bristol, England   March 24, 1890   d. Halifax, Nova Scotia   July 11, 1941

Sol Violinsky   b. Kiev, Russia   July 4, 1885   d. Binghamton, NY   May 5, 1963

Horace O. Wheeler   b. Germany   March 24, 1861   d. Kansas City, MO   May 21, 1940

Pseudonyms and Professional Names of Ragtime Composers

Victor Arden	Lewis John Fuiks
William Arthurs	William or M.C. Rowe
Joe Arzonia	George Fairman
Barney & Seymore	Theron C. Bennett
Glen Barton	Harley F. Brocht
Mike Bernard	Michael Barnett
Raymond Birch	Charles L. Johnson
Ted Browne	Fred Brownold
Larry Buck	Laurent Dubuclet
Walter Byron	Melvin Walter Weschler
Joe "Fingers" Carr	Louis F. Busch
Ribe Danmark	J. Bodewalt Lampe
Ethel Earnist	Charles L. Johnson
H.A. Fischler	Harry J. Lincoln
George E. Florence	Theron C. Bennett

Leo Gordon ——————George L. Cobb

J. Gaines ——————Dick Hyman

J.C. Halls——————Harry J. Lincoln

Robert A. King ——————Robert Keiser

Jean Ledies ——————Emil Seidel

Abe Losch——————Harry J. Lincoln

Bud Manchester ——————Etilmon J. Stark

Arthur Manlowe——————Abe Olman

Victor Maurice ——————B. Edward Hallis

Neil Moret ——————Charles N. Daniels

Victor Moulton——————Richard G. Grady

James Nonnahs ——————James Royce Shannon

Lawrence B. O'Connor——————Joseph Michael Daly

Joe Perry ——————Joseph Michael Peropota

W.C. Powell ——————William C. Polla

Ralph Rainger——————Ralph Reichenthal

Rednip——————Harold Pinder

Dolly Richmond ——————Percy Wenrich

Justin Ring ——————Justin Ringleben

Karl Schmidt——————Percy Wenrich

Raymond Scott ——————Harry Warnow

Cy Seymore——————William C. Polla

Walter Shannon ——————Walter Lipman

Herbert Steiner——————Sam Herman

Logan Thane——————Nat E. Solomons

Harry Thomas——————Reginald Thomas Broughton

Violinsky——————Sol Ginsberg

Waiman——————James Royce Shannon

Fannie B. Woods——————Charles L. Johnson

Ragtime Publication by State (and Canada)

ALABAMA

Florence
Sweety, Won't You Be Kind
to Me

Mobile
Ragtime Follies

Tuscaloosa
Happy Dixie Rag

ALASKA

Juneau
Flicker Red Rag

ARKANSAS

Little Rock
Craps
Mattie's Rags

Pine Bluff
Theatorium Rag

CALIFORNIA

Alameda
Bull Moose Rag

Berkeley
Too Much Raspberry

Fresno
Goin' Sum
LaHabra
Calico Rag

Lodi
New Standard Rag

Long Beach
Transformation Rag

Los Angeles
Alabama Hop
Arlene's Doilies
Chewin' the Rag
Copper King Rag
Dynamite Rag
Froggie Moore
Glad Rag
Golden Gate Rag
Raggety Rag
Shoe Tickler Rag
Silver Swan Rag
Southern Blossoms
Syncopated Echoes
That Dawggone Rag
Three Weeks Rag

Oakland
Entertainer's Rag

Pasadena
Portuguese Rag

San Diego
Cinder-Ella Rag
Peachtree Street Rag

San Francisco
Arabian Rag
Bobette
Crossed Hands
Dainty Doll
Dainty Miss
Doll Dance
Everybody Two Step
Glad Rags
Idawanna
Johnny-Jump-Ups
Jumping Jack
Kewpie
Lucky Dog
Meadow Lark Rag
Polar Bear Rag
Rag Doll
Ragtime Jingles
Rah Rah Boy!!!
San Francisco Pretty Girl
Rag
Spitfire Rag
Torpedo
Whoa! Nellie
World's Fair Rag

San Jose
Queen Sugar Beet Rag

San Pedro
That New Regeneration
Rag

COLORADO

Boulder
  May Bloom Rag

Cripple Creek
  Trey o' Hearts Rag

Denver
  "A" Natural
  Barber Pole Rag
  Black Hand Rag
  Everybody's Rag
  High Life Rag
  Old Carpet Rag
  Rocky Ford Melon Pickers
  Scotch Rye
  X-Ray Rag

CONNECTICUT

New Haven
  Capital City Rag
  Dixie Rag
  Publicity Rag
  Satisfaction

DISTRICT OF
COLUMBIA
  Baltimore Convention
    Rag
  Candy Kid
  Chocolate Sweets
  Cotton Leaf Rag
  Dat Cacklin' Rag
  Frog-I-More Rag
  Ginger Snap Rag
  Helter-Skelter Rag
  Jitney Bus Rag
  Measles Rag
  Meer-Sham Rag
  Naked Dance
  Pearl's Rag
  Pretty Peggy
  Ragweed Rag
  Rattle Snake Rag
  Rising Moon
  Rochester Rag

Some Wampus Cat Rag
South Dakota Rag
Southern Shuffle
Speedometer Rag
Tangolizing Rag
Technic Touch Rag
Tex Tangle Foot Rag
Texas Wiggle Rag
That Cherry Rag
That Jumping Rag
That Spooky Rag
That Tantalizing Rag
Thomas Brothers' Rag
Virginia Creeper Rag
Virginia Rag
Wide Awake Rag

FLORIDA

Inverness
  Orange Leaf Rag

Jacksonville
  Any Old Rag

GEORGIA

Atlanta
  Rathskeller Drag
  Queen of Rags

Eastman
  Georgia Ball

Macon
  Kalamity Kid
  Log Cabin Rag
  Shaka Foot

Thomasville
  Cotton States Rag
  Halifax Rag
  Pinywoods Rag

Valdosta
  Billy Possum Rag

IDAHO

Idaho Falls
  Black Crow Rag

ILLINOIS

Chicago
  Aeroplane Rag
  Alabama Shuffle
  Alabama Slide
  Angel Food
  Ashy Africa
  Banana Peel Rag
  Bear Tracks
  Beautiful Sensation Rag
  Black Bawl
  Black Devil Rag
  Black Feather
  Blarney Kisses
  Blue Blazes
  Blue Goose
  Blue Moon
  Blue Streak
  Broadway Rag
  Bubbles
  Buffalo Rag
  Bum Rag
  Calico Rag
  Canadian Capers
  Cannon Ball
  Cauldron Rag
  Chasing the Chickens
  Chasing the Fox
  Cherry Leaf Rag
  Chestnuts
  Chicago Breakdown
  Chicken Charlie
  Chicken Pranks
  Chippewa Rag
  Chocolate Creams Rag
  Chop Suey Rag
  Cincinnati Rag
  Clover Leaf Rag
  Comet Rag
  Coon Can
  Cracker Jack Rag

Crash!!!

Crazy Bone Rag

Crazy Horse Rag

Dakota Rag

Dancing Fingers

Darkies Spring Song

Delirium Tremens Rag

Diabolo Rag

Dimpley Smiles

Dixie Dimples

Dixie Kicks

Doll Rags

Domino Rag

Down Home Rag

Dusky Damsels Rag

Dynamite

Educational Rag

Eight O'Clock Rush Rag

Empire City Rag

Eugenia

Fiddlesticks

Floating Along

Florida Cracker

Fluffy Ruffles

Foolishness Rag

Frankfort Rag

Freckles

Frenzied Rag

Friar Tuck Rag

Fun Bob

Funny Folks

Ginger Snaps

Git Bizzy

Glad Cat Rag

Glad Rag

Glad Rags

Glen Oaks Rag

Gold Dust Twins
   Rag

Golden Smile

Good Bye Rag

Grandpa's Spells

Grasshopper Rag

Green Mill Rag

Hallowe'en Rag

Happy Go Lucky Rag

Happy Rag

Harriman Cake Walk

Hazlesplitter

Holy Moses Rag

Hot Ashes

Hot Off the Griddle

Hot Rag

Imperial Rag

Intermission Rag

Irmena Rag

J.J.J. Rag

Jack Rabbit Rag

Jagtime Johnson's Ragtime
   March

Jaxon Rag

Jay Roberts Rag

Jerusha Pepper

Joy Rag

Kansas City Stomp

Kehama Rag

Kentucky Rag

Keyboard Kapers

Kimberly Rag

King of Them All

King Porter Stomp

Knockout Drops

Lauterbach

Lawn Eyrie Rag

Lemons and Limes

Levee Rag

Live Wires Rag

Log Cabin Rag

Louisiana Rag

Made in Germany

Manilla Rag

Marilynn

Marita

Memphis Rag

Merry-Go-Round Rag

Midnight Rag

Midnight Trot

Minnesota Rag

Miss Molly

Modernesque

Modulations

Moustache Johnson

Muslin Rag

Mutilaton Rag

My Favorite Rag

Nat Johnson's Rag

National Colors Rag

Navy Blue Rag

New Russian Rag

Nobody's Business

Nonette Rag

Noodles

Octopus Rag

On the Bayou

Original Chicago Blues

Originola

Palm Leaf Rag

Panama Rag

Pansy Blossoms

Pathetic Rag

Pearls

Peek-A-Boo Rag

Pekin Rag

Percy

Piano Rag

Pianola Concert Rag

Pigeon Wing Rag

Pike Pikers Rag

Pin Cushion Rag

Pineywood Rag

Pink Poodle

Pork and Beans

Powder Rag

Press Club Rag

Progressive Rag

Rag Alley Dream

Rag Time Chimes

Rag-A-More

Ragged Edges

Ragged Jack

Ragovitch Rag

Ragtime Refreshments

Ragtime Ripples

Reinette Rag

Restless Rag

Rochelle
Rosewood Rag
Russian Rag
Safety Pin Catch
Saratoga Glide
Saskatoon Rag
Sassafras Rag
Sassafras Sam
Scizzor Bill
Shreveport Stomps
Silence and Fun
Silver King Rag
Simplicity Rag
Smiler Rag
Smiles and Chuckles
Snookums Rag
Society Rag
Some Stuff
Sophisticated Rhythm
Sorority Rag
Southern Snowballs
Sparkler Rag
Speckled Spider Rag
Sprint Splinter Rag
Squirrel Rag
St. Louis Tickle
Streamers Rag
Sunflower Tickle
Sure Fire Rag
Swamptown Shuffle
Swanee Ripples
Sweet and Tender
Sweet Bunch
Sweet Pickin's Rag
Sweet Pickles
Sweetie Dear
Sweetmeats
Sweetness
Sycamore
Tango
Teasing Rag
Teasing the Cat
Teasing the Klassics
Tennessee Rag
That Dahm Rag

That Dixie Dip
That Dixie Rag
That Moaning Saxophone
    Rag
That Peculiar Rag
That Pleasing Rag
That Potatoe Bug Rag
That Stop Time Rag
That Tuneful Rag
Tickled to Death
Tom-Boy
Torrid Dora
Tucker Trot
Turkish Trophies
Vivacity Rag
Webster Grove Rag
Wedding Bells Rag
Weird Rag
Wild-Fire Rag
Winter Garden Rag
Wireless Rag
Woolworth Rag
Woozy
Yankee Doodle Rag
Yvonette
Zephyr

Galesburg
  Rag Time Joke

Herrin
  Louisiana Rag

Modesto
  Opalescent Rag

Moline
  Grand Concert Rag
  Jungle Time
  Sky Rockets
  That Nekoma Rag

Peoria
  Dish Rag
  Symphony Rag

Peru
  Who Got the Lemon?

Prairie City
  That Dynamite Rag

Rockford
  Welsh Rarebit

St. Elmo
  Rag-Time Daud

Urbana
  University Rag

INDIANA
Bluffton
  Bluffton Carnival Rag

Fort Wayne
  India Rubber
  Jim Crow Rag
  Rambling Rags
  Thelma Rag

Gary
  Eleventh Street Rag

Hammond
  Pride of the Smoky Row

Huntington
  Scarlet Rag

Indianapolis
  American Rag
  Baseball Rag
  Blue Ribbon Rag
  Buzzer Rag
  Candle-Stick Rag
  Checker
  Colonial Glide
  Delightful Rag
  Dex
  Dingy's Serenade

Dusty Rag
Fox-Terrier Rag
Freckles
Honeymoon Rag
Hoosier Rag
Horseshoe Rag
Hummer Rag
Klassicle Rag
News Rag
Nightingale Rag
Novelty Rag
Orinoco
Piano Tuner's Walkaway
   Rag
Piffle Rag
Red Rambler Rag
Richmond Rag
Rocky Rags
Scarecrow Rag
Sour Grapes Rag
Sparkles
That Demon Rag
That Eccentric Rag
Thriller
Totally Different Rag
Trouble
Vanity Rag
Walhalla
Yellow Bridge

Kendallville
   That Captivating Rag

Lafayette
   Chili Con Carne
   Purdue Rag
   Purdue Spirit
   Teddy in the Jungle
   That Dizzy Rag

New Albany
   Bale o' Cotton

Petersburg
   Ragology

Plymouth
   Scraps from the Rag Bag

Princeton
   Gee Whiz
   Wizzle Dozzle

Richmond
   Solitaire Rag

IOWA
Cedar Rapids
   Princess Rag

Davenport
   Kinky
   Velma Chocolates

Des Moines
   Fuzzy Wuzzy
   Glide Away Rag
   Lucky Lou
   Nappy Lee
   Rag Time Fiend
   That Hateful Rag

Ft. Dodge
   Paramount Rag
   Famous Players Rag

Keokuk
   King of Rags

Manson
   Rexall Rag

Newton
   Wise Gazabo

Oelwein
   That American Rag

Oskaloosa
   Car-Barlick Acid Rag
   Mister Buzz Saw

Sioux City
   That Enticing Two Step

Sumner
   Fuzzy Ideas

KANSAS
Baxter Springs
   That Touchy Kid Rag
   Uncle Zeke's Medley Rag

Cherry Vale
   Sensible Rag

Girard
   Billy Possum

Kansas City
   Electric Rag!

Kiowa
   Felix Rag

Liberal
   Manilla Rag

Osborne
   Octave Rag

Pittsburg
   Kitty Wobble

Topeka
   Varsity Days

Troy
   Alfalfa Rag

Wichita
   Cabbage Leaf Rag
   Dat Johnson Rag
   Harem Skirt Rag
   Imp Rag
   Microbe
   Mop Rag

Popular Rag
Red Raven

KENTUCKY

Columbia
King Baggot's Rag

Covington
Alhambra Rag
Diplomat Rag
Hobble Rag
Kentucky Rag
Lagoon Rag
Powder Rag
Smiling Bill
Watermelon Mose

Lexington
Natural Gas Rag
Sympathetic Rag

Louisville
Aviation Rag
Bumble Bee Rag
Dixie Kisses
Fluffy Ruffles Rag
Kissing Bug Rag
Lion Tamer Rag
Little Bit o' Honey
Merry Widow Rag
Shovel Fish
Stop Rag

Mooleyville
Cotton Belt Rag

Morgantown
Budweiser Rag

Newport
Coney Island Tickle
Motor Boat Rag
Sic 'Em Prinz
Squiggilum Drag
That Queen City Rag

Rumsey
Twilight Whispers

LOUISIANA

Lake Charles
Snappy Rag
That Angell Rag

New Orleans
Barrel House Rag
Black Hand
Can You Beat It Rag
Chow Chow
Classy Rag
Dat's It
Delta Rag
Dixie Queen
Dixie Slow Drag
Dynamite Rag
Easy Money
Electric Rag!
Full Moon
Going Some
Happy Sammy
Holly and Mistletoe Rag
I'm Alabama Bound
Laughing Dick Rag
Mary Jane Rag
Mephisto Rag
Metropolitan Rag
Nervy George
New Orleans Buck
North Pole Rag
Peter Pan Rag
Roller-Skater's Rag
Roustabout Rag
Salome Rag
Something Doing Soon
Sponge Rag
Tee Na Nah
That Bull Frog Rag
That Crazy Rag
Thunderbolt Rag
Tom Cat Rag
Triangle Jazz Blues

What Is It?
Whoa! You Heifer
Wild Flower Rag
Yellow Rose Rag

Shreveport
Hutchinson Bro's Rag
That Hypnotic Rag

MAINE

Sanford
Dance of the Crocodiles
Rag

MASSACHUSETTS

Boston
Aero Rag
African Smile
Aggravation Rag
Alabama Rag
All of a Twist Rag
Bag of Rags
Baltimore Buck
Big Ben
Blacksmith Rag
Blue Grass Rag
Bone Head Blues
Bric-a-Brac Rag
Cannibal Rag
Chromatic Capers
Comet Rag
Cracked Ice
Cubistic Rag
Dixie Rag
Dust'Em Off
Feedin' the Kitty
Five Little Brown Jugs
Rag
Fussin' Around
Georgia Rainbow
Green Rag
Home Spun Rag
Honeymoon Rag
Hop Scotch
Hypnotic Rag
Inclination Fox-trot

Irish Confetti
Joy Boy
Klinkers
Lazy Luke
Meteor Rag
Nautical Nonsense
New York Rag
Persian Lamb Rag
Piano Salad
Piano Sauce
Piccalilli Rag
Pippins
Pitter-Patter Rag
Procrastination Rag
Pussy Foot
Rabbit Foot Rag
Radio Rag
Ragtime Patsy
Red Rag
Rose Leaf Rag
Rubber Plant Rag
Russian Pony Rag
Sandy River Rag
Say When
Scarecrow Rag
Scrambled Eggs
Screen Door Rag
Snuggle Pup
Soap Bubbles Rag
Stop It
Swell Affair
That Chinese Rag
That Hindu Rag
Town Talk
Turkish Towel Rag
Virginia Creeper
Water Wagon Blues
Wild Flower Rag

Cambridge
Auto Rag

Dorchester
That Sparkling Rag

Lowell
Charming Rag

Melrose
Great Morris Rag

Springfield
Heliotrope Rag

MICHIGAN
Battle Creek
Bunny Hug Rag
Good Bye Blues
Michigan Rag
That Everlasting Rag

Bay City
Oh You Tigers

Detroit
Ain't I Lucky
April Fool Rag
Aviator Rag
Black Beauty
Borneo Rag
Cazador
Chatterbox Rag
Chicken Chowder
Chow-Chow Rag
Cotton Time
Cum-Bac Rag
Daffydill Rag
Dixie Blossoms
Double M Rag
Down South
Georgia Rag
Giggler
Glad Rag
Goin' Some
Haytian Rag
Honey Rag
Invitation Rag
Jamaica Jinger
Mop Rag
Nervous Rag

Pearl of the Harem
Pop Corn Man
Razzle Dazzle
Royal Flush Rag
Sneaky Shuffles Rag
Snowball
Southern Roses
Sycamore Saplin'
Tattered Melody Rag
Texas Steer
That Dandy Rag
That Spooney Dance
That Tired Rag
Waiman Rag
Wiggle Rag

Flint
Boiled Owl

Grand Rapids
Black Cat Rag

Kalamazoo
Harem Scarem Rag
My Aeroplane Jane

Port Huron
Huron Glide

Saginaw
Virginia Rag

MINNESOTA
Baudette
Red Raven Rag

Duluth
Holy Smokes

Mankato
Oak Leaf Rag
Snappy Rag

Minneapolis
Fool 'Em Fingers

Fussy Flossie
Put 'En on the Brakes
Rag De Luxe
Shock Rag
Spatter Rag
Town Talk
Unnamed Rag
Watermelon

Pine Island
Wilson's Favorite Rag

St. Paul
Minnesota Street
Rag
Old Kentuck

MISSOURI
Braymer
Mashed Potatoes
Peroxide
Poison Rag

Campbell
Corn Cracker Rag

Carthage
Fascinator
On the Pike
Summer Breeze

Columbia
Blind Boone's Southern
Rag Medley #1
Blind Boone's Southern
Rag Medley #2
Great Scott Rag
Some Pumpkins

Joplin
Cabbage Rag
Claudia Rag

Kansas City
Affinity Rag
All the Money

Bachelor's Button
Beedle-Um-Bo
Black Smoke
Bug-House Rag
Candied Cherries
Cloud Kisser
Cold Feet Rag
Corn Shucks Rag
Cotton Patch
Derby Day Rag
Devil Rag
Dill Pickles Rag
Dixie Dimples
Eatin' Time Rag
Georgia Giggle Rag
Going Some
Hardwood Rag
Hen Cackle Rag
Lady Slippers Rag
Lovey-Dovey
Melody Rag
Mississippi Smilax
Missouri Maze
Opera Rags
Original Rags
Peaceful Henry
Peach Blossoms
Peanuts
Petticoat Lane
Pickled Beets Rag
Powder Rag
Rags to Burn
Red Devil Rag
Scandalous Thompson
Shamrock Rag
Sleepy Hollow Rag
Slivers
Sneeky Peet
Snipes
Splinters
Tar Babies
That Fascinating Rag
That Irresistible Rag
Tickler
Wounded Lion

Memphis
Lopez Rag

Sedalia
Favorite
Frivolous Rags
Maple Leaf Rag
Missouri Rag
Ra! Ra! Ra!
State Fair Cadonian
Stenotypic Rag
X.L. Rag

Springfield
All the Grapes
Three Hundred Green

St. Joseph
Alison Rag
Leona Rag
Lotus Club Rag
Lover's Lane Glide

St. Louis
African Pas'
Agitation Rag
Allen Glide
American Beauty
Apple Sass Rag
Arcadia Rag
Bandit King Rag
Billiken Rag
Black Cat Rag
Blue Jay Rag
Bohemia Rag
Bowery Buck
Breeze from Alabama
Broadway Rag
Broncho Buck
Brownie Rag
Burning Rags
Cactus Rag
Candy Rag
Captivatin' Rag
Carnation

Cascades
Cataract
Champagne Rag
Checkerboard Rag
Chic
Chromatic Rag
Cleopatra Rag
Climax Rag
Climbers
Clover Blossom Rag
Cole Smoak
Contentment Rag
Darktown Capers
Deuces Wild Rag
Domino Rag
Don't Jazz Me-Rag
Double Fudge
Easy Winners
Edward J. Mellinger Rag
Efficiency Rag
Elite Syncopations
Entertainer
Esther
Evergreen Rag
Felicity Rag
Fontella Rag
Fuss and Feathers
Gobler Rag
Good Gravy Rag
Grace and Beauty
Gum Shoe
Harlem Rag
Harlem Rag (arr. #2)
Havana Rag
Hilarity Rag
Honey Moon Rag
Hot House Rag
Humpy's Buck
Ishudworry
Jester Rag
Jinx Rag
Just a Li'l Rag
Just Missed
Kansas City Rag
Kentucky Rag

Key Stone Rag
Kismet Rag
Latonia Rag
Leola
Lily Rag
Mando Rag
Manhattan Rag
Melrose Rag
Minstrel Man
Missouri Rag
Modesty Rag
Moonshine Rag
Musical Zig Zags
My Rag
New Era Rag
Nitric-Acid Rag
Noisy Notes Rag
Nonpareil
On the Rural Route
One More Rag
One O' Them Things!
Ophelia Rag
Paramount Rag
Pastime Rag No. 1
Pastime Rag No. 2
Pastime Rag No. 3
Pastime Rag No. 4
Pastime Rag No. 5
Patricia Rag
Peace and Plenty
Peacherine Rag
Pegasus
Poison Ivy
Poor Jim
Princess Rag
Prosperity Rag
Quality
Rag La Joie
Rag Sentimental
Rag Time Nightingale
Ragtime Nightmare
Ragtime Oriole
Ragtime Riggles
Real Swing Rag
Reflection Rag

Reindeer
Robardina Rag
S. O. S.
Saint Louis Ripple Rag
Sandella Rag
Sand Paper Rag
Sapho Rag
Schultzmeier Rag
Scrub Rag
Shave 'Em Dry
Slivers
Something Doing
Son Set Rag
Southern Sneeze
Spring Time Rag
St. Louis Mule
Steamboat Rag
Strenuous Life
Stung Rag
Sunflower Slow Drag
Swipesy Cake Walk
Sympathetic Jasper
Talk of the Town
Tanglefoot
Tantalizer Rag
Ten Penny Rag
That Contagious Rag
That Corrugated Rag
That Easy Rag
That Hand Played Rag
That Irresistible Rag
That Rag
Tom and Jerry Rag
Tom Brown's Trilling Tune
Top Liner Rag
Topsey's Dream
Troubadour Rag
Twinkle Dimples Rag
Universal Rag
Victory Rag
Weeping Willow
Whirl Wind
Who Let the Cows Out

MONTANA

Billings
  That's It

Butte
  Meadow Lark Rag

NEBRASKA

Kearney
  Fern Leaf Rag

Lincoln
  Cerise
  Coldwater Rag
  Corn Tassle Rag

Omaha
  Dutch Mill Rag
  Happy Feelings Rag
  Ink Splotch Rag
  Kinky Head
  Service Rag

NEVADA

Ely
  That Bombshell Rag

Virginia City
  Opera House Rag

NEW JERSEY

Atlantic City
  Slippery Steps

Elizabeth
  Rag Bag Rag
  Uneeda Rag Time

Newark
  Calico Rag
  Metropolitan Rag

NEW YORK

Bellport
  Long Island Rag

Binghamton
  Riverside Rag

Brooklyn
  Cotton Pickers Carnival

Buffalo
  Buffalo Means Business
  Canned Corn Rag
  Comet Rag
  Daffy Dingies
  Desire Rag
  Happy Jack
  Hesitatin' Hez'
  Perpetual Rag
  Tooth Pick Rag

Kyserike
  Chicken Dance

New York
  African 400
  African Hunter
  African Reverie
  African Ripples
  Alabama Jigger
  Alabama Rag
  Alaskan Rag
  Alligator Bait
  American Dancers
  American Jubilee
  Anoma
  Apeda Rag
  Appetite Pete
  Apron Rag
  Arctic Sunset
  Arm Breaker
  At a Ragtime Reception
  Audacity
  Aunt Jemima's Birthday
  Axel Grease
  Back to Life
  Baltimore Blues
  Baltimore Todalo
  Bantam Step

Barbed Wire Rag
Barber Shop Rag
Barnyard Rag
Bell Hop Rag
Bing! Bing!
Bird-Brain Rag
Birds' Carnival
Black & White Rag
Black Canary
Black Diamond Rag
Black Key Kapers
Blame It on the Blues
Blue Grass Rag
Blue Note Blues
Bluin' the Black Keys
Bohemian Rag
Bolo Rag
Bon Ton
Bone Dry
Boogie Rag
Boomerang Rag
Booster
Bouncing on the Keys
Bounding Buck
Brain-Storm Rag
Brazilian Nut
Breakin' the Piano
Brittwood Rag
Broadway Rag
Broken Buttons
Brun Campbell Express
Buffalo Dish Rag
Bugle Call Rag
Bully Rag
Bumble Bee Rag
Bunny Hug Rag
Bunny-Boy
Burning the Keys
Business in Town
Caberavings
California Sunshine
Call 'Em Toodles
Calla Lilly Rag
Calliope Rag
Campus Rag

Canhanibalmo Rag
Carolina Fox Trot
Carolina Romp
Carolina Shout
Carr's Hop
Castle Doggy
Castle House Rag
Cat Grin Rag
Cat's Pajamas
Celestial Rag
Century Prize
Certain Party
Changes
Chanticleer Rag
Charleston Rag
Chasing the Fox
Checkerboard Rag
Chestnut Valley Rag
Chevy Chase
Chicago Tickle
Chicken Patty
Chicken's Rag
Chili Pepper
Chilly Billy Bee Rag
Chopiano
Chromatic Rag
Classic Rag
Classicanna
Coaxing the Ivories
Coaxing the Piano
Collars and Cuffs
College Rag
Colonial Rag
Columbia Rag
Coon Band Parade
Corn on the Cob
Coronation Rag
Cotton
Cottontail Rag
Country Club
Cozy Corner Rag
Cradle Rock
Crimson Rambler Rag
Cross Word Puzzle
Cubist

Cucumber Rag
Curl-I-Cues
Cute and Pretty
Cuttin' Up
Cyclone
Cyclone in Darktown
Dance of the Notes
Dancing Animal Crackers
Dancing Shadows
Dancing Tambourine
Dandelion
Darkey Todalo
Dat Lovin' Rag
Dave's Rag
Deiro Rag
Del Mar Rag
Desecration
Deuces Wild
Dicty's on Seventh Avenue
Dingle Pop Hop
Dischord Rag
Dixie Doodles
Dizzy Fingers
Dockstader Rag
Doctor Brown
Dog on the Piano
Dogzigity Rag
Doodle Bug
Dorothy
Down Town Rag
Dreamy Rag
Eccentric
Echo of Spring
Egyptian Rag
Elephant Rag
Erratic
Estelle
Ethiopia Rag
Euphonic Sounds
Evolution Rag
Excelsior Rag
Extr'ordinary Rag
Eye Opener
Fadettes Call
Fanatic Rag

Fancy Fingers
Fashionette
Father Knickerbocker
Feather Fingers
Festival Rag
Fiddler's Rag
Fidgety Fingers
Fig Leaf Rag
Fine Feathers
Finesse
Finger Breaker
Finger Buster
Finicky Fingers
Firefly Rag
Fishin' for Flats
Fizz Water
Flapperette
Fleur de Lis
Florida Rag
Fluffy Ruffles
Foolin' Around
Foot Warmer
Forty-Second Street Rag
Franco-American Rag
French Pastry Rag
Friday Night
Frisco Frazzle
Frisco Rag
Frog Legs Rag
Full of Tricks
Funny Bones
Garden of Eden
Gatling Gun Rag
Gay Birds
Gayety
Georgia Grind
Ghost of the Piano
Giddy Ditty
Ginger
Ginger Snaps
Gladiolus Rag
Gloria
Going South
Going to Pieces
Gold Bar Rag

Good and Plenty Rag
Good Years
Gravel Rag
Green Rag
Greenwich Witch
Grizzly Bear Rag
Gun-Cotton Rag
Gypsy Rag
Ham And!
Handful of Keys
Hanky Pank
Harlem Rag (arr. #3)
Harlequins' Grand March
Harpsichord Rag
Harry Fox Trot
Haunting Rag
Heavy on the Catsup
Heliotrope Bouquet
Hi-Yeller
Hifalutin Rag
High Hattin'
High Jinks
High Stepper Rag
Hippocampus Two-Step
Hit or Miss
Hobble Rag
Hobble Skirt Drag
Homespun Rag
Honey Lou-Lu Rag
Honeysuckle
Honeysuckle Rag
Hoosier Rag
Hot Chestnuts
Hot Chocolate Rag
Hot Cinders
Hot Fingers
Hot Hands
Hot Ivories
Hot Stuff
Hot Tamale Man! Rag
Humorestless
Humpty Dumpty
Hungarian Rag
Hurricane Rag
Hyacinth Rag

Hypnotizer Rag
Hysterics Rag
Icycles
Igloo Stomp
Imagination
In a Mist
In the Groove
In the Spotlight
Incandescent Rag
Innocence
Iridescence
Irresistible Rag
Ivory Chips
Jack Frost Rag
Jack in the Box
Jass Band Rag
Jay Walk
Jes' Dandy
Jingles
Juggling the Piano
Jumping Jack
Junk Man Rag
Kangaroo Hop
Kansas Appleknocker
    Rag
Kautious Kittens
Kee to Kee
Keep A-Movin'
Keep Busy
Keep Fingering
Keep Off the Grass
Keep Your Temper
Kentucky Beauty
Kerry Mills' Ragtime
    Dance
Ketchup Rag
Keyboard Klassic
Keyboard Konversation
Kinda Careless
Kinklets
Kitchen Tom
Kitten on the Keys
Klondike Rag
Krazy Kat
Lace Embroidery

Lakeside Whistle Rag
Last Rag
Laughing at the Ivories
Laurette
Leap Frog
Lemon Drops
Let's Go
Lily Queen
Lip-Stick
Little Jack's Rag
Little Rock Getaway
Little Sticks o' Licorice
London Rag
Lopez Speaking
Lopeziana
Lost Rag
Lotta Trix
Lovey-Dovey
Mad Fingers
Madagascar Mangle
Magnetic Rag
Magpie Rag
Mah Jong
Make Believe Rag
Manhattan Rag
Marathon Rag
Mardi Gras Rag
Marine Syncopations
Maurice Rag
Meddlesome
Medic Rag
Medical Rag
Meditation
Melancholy Charlie
Melody Man
Merry Minnow
Merry Widow Glad Rag
Merry-Go-Round Rag
Mew Mew Rag
Midnight Whirl Rag
Milkman's Rag
Minstrel Band Rag
Miserable Rag
Misery Blues
Mississippi Shivers

Missouri Romp
Modernistic
Moonlight Rag
Mosquito Bites
Mouse's Hoofs
Mousie in the Piano
Mud Cat Rag
Munki Doodle Dum
Musette
Music Box Rag
Mutt and Jeff Rag
My Pet
Nanette
Naughty Naurette
Nervous Nuckles
New Black Eagle Buck
New Hippodrome
New Orleans Rag
Nice and Easy
Nicest, Sweetest, Cutest, Rag
Nickel in the Slot
Nobody's Rag
Nonsense Rag
Noodlin'
Notoriety
Nuckels O'Tool Woulds't Ride Again
Off the Elbow
Oh You Angel
Oh You Turkey
Oh! Willie, Play That Thing
Oh! You Darkeys
Oh! You Devil
Old Crow Rag
Old Folks Rag
Old Home Rag
Old Professor
Old Tom-Cat on the Keys
Old Virginia Rag
Olga
On the Riviera
One Finger Joe
One for Amelia

Operatic Rag
Original Blues
Out of the South
Over and Under
Over the Bars
Over the Ice
Oyster Rag
Page Mr. Pianist
Palm Beach
Pan-Am Rag
Paragon Rag
Pastime Rag
Patsy
Patsy Lou
Peach
Peaches and Cream
Pear Blossoms
Peekaboo Peek
Perils of Pauline
Pettin' the Keys
Phantom Rag
Pianist Rag
Piano Capers
Piano Mania
Piano Marmalade
Piano Pan
Piano Phun
Piano Pranks
Piano Puzzle
Pianogram
Pianola
Pianola Rag
Pianophiends Rag
Piccalili Rag
Pine Apple Rag
Pinochole Rag
Pipe Dream
Pipe the Piper
Pippin
Playin' Possum
Poison Ivories
Poison Ivy
Poker Rag
Polyragmic
Poodle Rag

Poor Buttermilk
Poor Jimmy Green
Poor Katie Redd
Popularity
Porcupine Rag
Pork and Beans
Porto Rico Rag
Power House
Pozzo
Pretty Pol'
Pudnin Tame
Punch and Judy
Putting on the Dog
Pyramyths
Qwindo's Rag
Racing Down the Black and Whites
Rag A Muffin Rag
Rag Carpet
Rag Doll Carnival
Rag of Rags
Rag Time Chimes
Rag-a-Minor
Rag-a-Muffin
Rag-a-Tag Rag
Rag-ged
Rag-o-Rhythm
Ragamuffin
Ragged Thoughts
Raggedy-Ann Rag
Raggin' Rudi
Raggin' the Blues
Ragging the Scale
Raggy Fox Trot
Ragman's Exercise
Ragtime Betty
Ragtime Bobolink
Ragtime Dance
Ragtime Eyes
Ragtime Jim
Ragtime Razzmatazz
Ragtime Revelations
Ragtime Showers
Raindrops
Rambler

Ramblin' Rag
Rambling in Rhythm
Ramshackle Rag
Rapscallion Rag
Rattlesnake Rag
Ravioli Rag
Raymond's Rag
Red and Black Rag
Red Clover
Red Fox Trot
Red Onion Rag
Red Pepper
Red Peppers
Red Raven Rag
Red Slipper Rag
Reisenweber Rag
Remorse Blues
Rhapsody in Ragtime
Rhapsody Rag
Rhinewine Rag
Rhythmic Fantasy
Rialto Ripples
Riffin'
Rig-a-Jig
Rig-a-Jig Rag
Rigamarole
Rigamarole Rag
Rinaldo Rag
Rio de Janeiro
Rita
Rival Rag
Romantic Rag
Rooster Rag
Rotation Rag
Round Up Rag
Royal Purple
Rube Bennett's Raggedy
    Rag
Rubies and Pearls
Running Up and Down
Sailing Along Over the
    Keys
Sakes Alive
Salt and Pepper Rag
Saronoff Rag

Scale It Down
Scott Joplin's New Rag
Scoutin' Around
Scrambles
Sea Weeds Rag
Seabiscuits Rag
Search Light Rag
Sen-Sen Rag
Sensation Rag
Shadow Rag
Shimmie Shoes
Shoe String Rag
Shootin' the Agate
Shootin' the Chutes
Show Me Rag
Showboat Rag
Shy and Sly
Silhouette
Silver Rocket
Silver Tip
Skidding
Skipinova
Sleepy Lou
Slippery Elm Rag
Slippery Fingers
Slippery Place
Smart Alec
Smash Up Rag
Snappin' Turtle
Sneak Away
Snow Shoes
Snuffuns
Soap Suds
Soft Shoe Dancer
Soliloquy
Some Baby
Some Blues, For You All
Some Class Rag
Some Jazz
Soup and Fish Rag
Southern Beauties
Southern Charms
Southern Symphony
Spaghetti Rag
Sparkles

Sparks
Spinal Chords
Spitfire
Spitfire Rag
Spring Fever
Spring Holiday
St. Louis Rag
St. Vitus Dance
Stack 'Em Up
Steam Roller Rag
Step on It
Stepping on the Ivories
Stewed Chicken Rag
Stewed Prunes Rag
Stop Your Kiddin'
Stop-Trot Rag
Stoptime Rag
Stumbling (Paraphrase)
Such a Rag
Such Is Life
Sugar Cane Rag
Sumthin' Doin'
Sunbeams
Sunburst Rag
Sunflower Rag
Sunny South Rag
Sunset Rag
Supper Club
Susan's Rag
Sweet Nothings
Sweet Potatoes
Sweet Sixteenths
Swiss Cheese Rag
Symphonola
Syncopated Fox Trot
Syncopating the Scales
Take It Easy
Tangle Foot Rag
Tanglefoot Rag
Tango Rag
Tantalizing Tingles
Tar Baby
Temptation Rag
Tempus Ragorum
Tenth Interval Rag

Texas Fox Trot
That American Ragtime
  Dance
That Entertaining Rag
That Erratic Rag
That Ever Lovin' Rag
That Flying Rag
That Futuristic Rag
That Gigglin' Rag
That Harmonizing Rag
That Hungarian Rag
That Irresistible Rag
That Madrid Rag
That Natural Rag
That Nifty Rag
That Puzzlin' Rag
That Real Rag
That Runaway Rag
That Scandalous Rag
That Sentimental Rag
That Tango Rag
That Teasin' Rag
That Ticklin' Rag
That's a Plenty
Thirty-Eighth Street
  Rag
Thoroughbred Rag
Thunderbolt Rag
Tickle the Ivories
Tickled Pink
Tiddle-de-Winks
Tierney Rag
Tin Pan Rag
Tin Whistle Blues
Tipsy Topsy
Toad Stool Rag
Toddlin'
Toddling
Tokio Rag
Told at Twilight
Tomato Sauce
Tomfoolery
Toots
Toy Piano Rag
Toy Town Topics

Tricky Fingers
Tricky Trix
Trilby Rag
Trillium Rag
Troublesome Ivories
Try and Play It
Turkey Trot
Twinkle Toes
Twinkles
Two-Key Rag
U. of M. Harmony Rag
Uncle Sammy at the
  Piano
Uncle Tom's Cabin Rag
Up and Down in China
Up and Down the Keys
Upright and Grand
Variety Rag
Virginia Rag
Volcanic Rag
Wall Street Rag
Wash Rag
Watermelon Trust
What's Your Hurry?
Whipped Cream
Whippin' the Keys
White Seal Rag
Whitewash Man
Who's Who
Wig-Wag Rag
Wild Cat Blues
Wild Cherries
William's Wedding
Wippin' the Ivories
Wish Bone
Wyoming Prance
Yankee Land
Yellow Rose Rag
You Tell 'Em, Ivories
Yumuri
Zig Zag Rag
Zu-Zu Rag

Patchogue
  American Sunshine Rag

Rochester
  Foolishead
  Rochester Fair

Schuyleville
  Monumental Echos

Troy
  Dixie Rag
  Oh! You Rag
  Salted Peanuts

Walton
  Dixie Life Rag

NORTH DAKOTA
Hope
  Danger Rag

OHIO
Aberdeen
  Draggy Rags

Akron
  B & O Rag

Barberton
  Thunderbolt Rag

Bellefontaine
  Rapid Firing Rag

Canton
  At a Coffee Colored Party

Cincinnati
  Amazon Rag
  Any Old Rag
  Banjo Rag
  Barbecue Rag
  Black Diamond Rag
  Blue Moon Two Step
  Blue Streak Rag
  Broadway Rag
  Brush Creek Rag
  Buccaneer

Bully Rag
Bunch of Burr Heads
Bunch of Noise
Bundle of Rags
Butcher Rag
Caliope Rag
Candy
Cheese and Crackers
Chimes
Clover Leaf
Coney Island Dip
Coney Island Girl
Curiosity
Cyclone
Daffodils
Diamond Rag
Dimples and Smiles
Doll Rags
Gasoline Rag
Glad Rags
Growls
Ham Bones
Hard Boiled Rag
Hinges
Hot Cabbage
Hustling Rag
It's a Bird!
Jack Frost
Japanese Rag
Japanimo
Keek-Es-Man-Dah!
Lagoon Breeze
Lasses
Lemons
Levee Rag
Lightning
Louisiana Rag
Mississippi Rag
Molly Coddle Rag
Monkey Motion Rag
Monograms
More Noise Rag
Moving Rag
Nickelodeon Rag
No-Ze

North Pole Rag
Oh You Rag
Oh You Sally Rag
Pekin Rag
Polka Dots Rag
Pride of Bucktown
Queen of Coney Island
Queen Rag
Rag Picker's Rag
Raggy Rag
Ragtime Parade in
    Darktown
Ravlins
Red Onion Rag
Remington Rag
River
Scramble Rag
Scrub Rags
Sheath
Ski Do Rag
Sleepy Sidney
Smiling Sadie
Spots
Squirrel Food Rag
That Gravitating Rag
Toodles
Ventura Rag
Virginia Rag
Water Queen
Wild Grapes Rag
Winnie's Arrival
Yoestic Two Step
Zinzinnati

Cleveland
All of a Twist
Antiquary
Behave Yourself
Black & Blue Rag
Bombshell
Bud Rag
Chewin' the Rag
Chills and Fever
Clover Blossom Rag
Clover Club

Cyclone Rag
Daisy Rag
Dish Rag
Eskimo Shivers
Fluffy Ruffles Girls
    Rag
Fred Heltman's Rag
Gold Dust Rag
Harmony Rag
Hi-Jinx
Hollyhock
Horse Laugh
Jazz Master
Jazz Mistress
Jazzaristrix
Jim Jams
Justin-Tyme
Knice and Knifty
Knick Knocks
Loose Elbows
Loose Fingers
Marigold
Mephisto Rag
Movie Rag
Operatic Nightmare
Pennant Rag
Pianoflage
Pickanniny Rag
Polly
Puppets Suite
Rag-a-Muffin Rag
Rhapsody Rag
Ring-Tum-Diddie
Rufenreddy
Shine or Polish Rag
Sleepy Piano
Slipova
Sunflower Babe
Sunshine Capers
Swanee Rag
Tatters
Toboggan Rag
Virginia Creeper
Water Bug
Weaving Around Rag

Columbus
  Anniversary Rag
  Centennial Rag
  Favorite Rag
  In Colored Circles
  Jingo
  Pianophiend
  Silk Hose Rag

Edgerton
  Kaiser's Rag

Lima
  Tickle It

Lorain
  Ticklish Rag

Manchester
  Kinky Kinks

Marion
  Bugavue Rag
  Dainty Foot Glide

Medina
  Okisko Rag

Middleport
  Gossipers Rag

Mount Healthy
  Hot Air Rag

Piqua
  Rip Rag

Portsmouth
  Alhambra

Sidney
  Red Mouse Rag
  That Contagious Rag

West Milton
  That Hesitating Rag

OKLAHOMA
Enid
  Pirate Rag

Tahlequah
  Mutt and Jeff Rag

Tulsa
  Just Noise

OREGON
Portland
  That Postal Rag

PENNSYLVANIA
Corry
  Fire Cracker Rag
  Trouble Maker Rag
  Will o' the Wisp Rag

Erie
  Crab Apples
  Moose Rag

Glenside
  Oriental Blues

Hallstead
  Can You Do That?

Philadelphia
  Akron Rag
  Blue Ribbon Rag
  Break the Piano
  Carpet Rags
  Gunpowder Rag
  Hot Air Rag
  King of Rags
  Missouri Rag
  Race Horse Rag
  Steppin' on the Ivories
  Sunstroke Rag

Texas Rag
  That Tired Feelin'

Pittsburgh
  Wash Day Rag
Reading
  Imperial Rag

Scranton
  Buster Rag

Sharon
  Demon Rag
  Yiddish Rag

Wilkes-Barre
  Holly Rag
  Hurricane Rag
  Johnson Rag
  Tango Rag

Williamsport
  Apple Jack
  Bees Wax
  Bingo Rag
  Black Diamond Rag
  Black Wasp Rag
  Checkers
  Chili Sauce
  Fashion Rag
  Fuss and Feathers
  Golden Spider
  Halley's Comet
  Hickory Nuts Rag
  Hot Scotch Rag
  Ivory Kapers
  Jack Rabbit Rag
  Jolly Jingles Rag
  Nigger-Toe Rag
  Pepper Sauce
  Poverty Rag
  Rag Baby Rag
  Rag Bag Rag
  Rastus Rag
  Tanglefoot Rag
  Weeping Willow

RHODE ISLAND
Providence
  Benzine Rag

SOUTH DAKOTA
Aberdeen
  That Tiger Rag

Canova
  South Dakota Rag

Fulton
  Corn Palace

TENNESSEE
Cookeville
  Tennessee Rag

McMunnville
  Carmen Rag

Memphis
  Bean Soup Blues
  Bull Dog Rag
  Craps
  Cutter
  Dish Rag
  Encore Rag
  Fuzzy Wuzzy Rag
  Gallery Gods Delight
  Hobble Skirt Rag
  Mississippi Teaser
  Monkey Rag
  Possum Rag

Nashville
  Cotton Bolls
  Devilish Rag
  Domino Rag
  Glad Rag
  Just Ask Me
  Klu-Lukum Rag
  Mandy's Broadway Stroll
  Octagon Rag
  Possum and Taters
  Queen of Love

Queen Raglan
Real Rag
Snowball Babe
Teddy's Pardners
Tennessee Jubilee
Tennessee Tantalizer
That Dog Gone Rag
Tickled to Death
Whittling Remus
Why We Smile

TEXAS
Crockett
  Hard Knots

  Broncho Billy
  Cedar Crest Rag
  Flap Jacks Rag
  Imperial Rag
  Majestic Rag
  Motor Bus
  Niagara Rag
  Nothing Doin' Rag
  Quality Rag
  Ragged Terry
  Rats!!!
  Teddy Bear Rag
  Texas Rag
  That Gosh-Darned Two
    Step Rag
  That Texas Rag

Fort Worth
  Classy Rag
  Hightower Rag
  New Dixie Rag
  Slippery Elm Rag
  Twelfth Street Rag

Galveston
  Armadillo
  Cotton Belt Rag
  Fiddling George
  Fried Chicken Rag
  That Moving Picture
    Rag

Whoa! Maude
Turpentine Rag

Henrietta
  Rattler Rag

Houston
  Coffee Rag
  Red Ribbon Rag
  Regal Rag

Mercedes
  Border Blues Rag

Rotan
  Very Raggy

Sherman
  Bugs Rag

Stanford
  That Picture Show Rag

UTAH
Salt Lake City
  Comet Rag

VIRGINIA
East Redford
  Scroochin' Up Rag

WASHINGTON
Colville
  That Nobby Rag

Seattle
  Alaska Rag
  Bear Club Rag
  Can't Think of the Name
  Potlatch Tickle
  Rag with No Name
  Sunset

Spokane
  Bob's Chili Rag
  Yankee Girl

WEST VIRGINIA
Charleston
  White Rag

WISCONSIN
Chippewa Falls
  Black Crow

Janesville
  Ripples Rag

Milwaukee
  College Rag
  Domino Rag
  Dope
  Easy Money
  Fiddle Sticks
  Happy Lulu Rag
  Pickles and Peppers
  Silver Buckle Rag
  University Rag

Neenah
  Rattlesnake Rag
Superior
  Frigid Frolics

WYOMING
Russell
  Aunt Dinah's Head Rag

CANADA
Hamilton
  That Captivating Rag

Mississauga
  Mississauga Rag

Montreal
  Club Cabin
  Rag Tags Rag

  Raggity-Rag
  Some Rag

Tharold
  That Whistling Rag

Toronto
  Centennial Rag
  Fly Paper Rag
  Hurry a Little
  Prairie Queen
  Spasm Rag
  Storyville Sport

Vancouver
  Pacific Rag

Winnepeg
  Checker Rag
  Dansopation
  Silver Leaf Rag

A Checklist of 2,002 Published Rags

Title	Author	Date	Publisher	City
"A" Natural	Joe Mauro	December 28, 1908	H.A.Triggs	Denver, CO
Aero Rag	Bert F. Grant	April 30, 1910	O'Neil & Story	Boston, MA
Aeroplane Rag	Jack Glogau	January 25, 1913	Will Rossiter	Chicago, IL
Affinity Rag	Irene Cozad	September 19, 1910	J.W. Jenkins	Kansas City, MO
African 400	Charles J. Roberts	April 26, 1909	Carl Fischer	New York, NY
African Hunter	Edwin F. Kendall	1909	Seminary Music	New York, NY
African Pas'	Maurice Kirwin	December 29, 1902	John Stark & Son	St. Louis, MO
African Reverie	H.B. Newton	September 8, 1900	F.A. Mills	New York, NY
African Ripples	Thomas "Fats" Waller	April 20, 1931	Joe Davis	New York, NY
African Smile	Paul Eno	May 5, 1906	Walter Jacobs	Boston, MA
Aggravation Rag	George L. Cobb	March 1, 1910	Walter Jacobs	Boston, MA
Agitation Rag	Robert Hampton	January 10, 1915	Stark Music Company	St. Louis, MO
Ain't I Lucky	Bess Rudisell	April 18, 1905	Jerome H. Remick	Detroit, MI
Akron Rag	Melvin Champion	December 16, 1911	M.D. Swisher	Philadelphia, PA
Alabama Hop	Phil H. Kaufman	September 8, 1908	Self	Los Angeles, CA
Alabama Jigger	Ed Claypoole	January 28, 1913	Joseph W. Stern	New York, NY
Alabama Rag	Joseph F. Lamb	1964	Mills Music	New York, NY
Alabama Rag	Wynona Smith	1918	James S. White	Boston, MA
Alabama Shuffle	Roy Barton	February 4, 1910	Sunlight Music	Chicago, IL
Alabama Slide	Charles L. Johnson	July 21, 1915	Forster Music	Chicago, IL
Alaska Rag	Alec M. Malin	August 4, 1915	Echo Music Publishing Co	Seattle, WA
Alaskan Rag	Joseph F. Lamb	June 27, 1966	Oak Publishing	New York, NY
Alfalfa Rag	Frank W. Ryan	July 25, 1910	Self	Troy, KS
Alhambra	George A. Nageleisen	1912	Self	Portsmouth, OH
Alhambra Rag	Roy Steventon & C. Morris Haigh	March 14, 1910	Steventon & Haigh	Covington, KY
Alison Rag	Karl Edgar Johnson	April 14, 1916	Nomad Publishing	St. Joseph, MO
All of a Twist	Billy Mayerl	August 21, 1925	Sam Fox	Cleveland, OH

All of a Twist Rag	Frank E. Hersom	1920	Walter Jacobs	Boston, MA
All the Grapes	James Fahy	July 1, 1908	Self	Springfield, MO
All the Money	Raymond Birch	March 13, 1908	Charles L. Johnson	Kansas City, MO
Allen Glide	Louise Allen	1915	Syndicate Music	St. Louis, MO
Alligator Bait	Hal G. Nichols	January 27, 1912	F.A. Mills	New York, NY
Amazon Rag	Teddy Hahn	February 11, 1904	Miller–Arnold	Cincinnati, OH
American Beauty	Joseph F. Lamb	December 27, 1913	Stark Music Company	St. Louis, MO
American Dancers	Bob Alden	July 2, 1908	Jerome H. Remick	New York, NY
American Jubilee	Ed Claypoole	June 24, 1916	Broadway Music	New York, NY
American Rag	John N. Lang	September 6, 1917	Self	Indianapolis, IN
American Sunshine Rag	Louis Altman	March 27, 1917	Altman & Fuss	Patchogue, NY
Angel Food	Al F. Marzian	December 16, 1911	Forster Music	Chicago, IL
Anniversary Rag	Glyn Williams	December 7, 1915	Self	Columbus, OH
Anoma	Ford Dabney	December 14, 1910	Jerome H. Remick	New York, NY
Antiquary	Billy Mayerl	March 9, 1926	Sam Fox	Cleveland, OH
Any Old Rag	Bert Beyerstedt	1915	Self	Jacksonville, FL
Any Old Rag	Richard Goosman	June 2, 1909	Self	Cincinnati, OH
Apeda Rag	Dave Harris	March 12, 1913	Waterson, Berlin & Snyder	New York, NY
Appetite Pete	H.H. Kratz	December 13, 1909	F.B. Haviland	New York, NY
Apple Jack	Charles L. Johnson	April 7, 1909	Vandersloot Music	Williamsport, PA
Apple Sass Rag	Harry Belding	1914	Buck & Lowney	St. Louis, MO
April Fool Rag	Jean Schwartz	May 1, 1911	Jerome H. Remick	Detroit, MI
Apron Rag	George D. Lewis	July 15, 1911	Maurice Shapiro	New York, NY
Arabian Rag	George Gould	November 2, 1917	Sherman, Clay	San Francisco, CA
Arcadia Rag	Albert L. Klein	March 14, 1914	Self	St. Louis, MO
Arctic Sunset	Joseph F. Lamb	1964	Mills Music	New York, NY
Arlene's Doilies	Thomas P. Quinn	November 6, 1980	Self	Los Angeles, CA
Arm Breaker	Fred Rose	April 7, 1923	Jack Mills	New York, NY
Armadillo	Clarence F. Brown	May 29, 1911	Thomas Goggan & Brothers	Galveston, TX
Ashy Africa	Percy Wenrich	October 29, 1903	Buck & Carney	Chicago, IL
At a Coffee Colored Party	O.S. Wald	February 6, 1899	Canton MPC	Canton, OH
At a Ragtime Reception	Ben M. Jerome	March 21, 1900	Howley, Haviland	New York, NY

Audacity	Zez Confrey	October 17, 1936	Robbins Music	New York, NY
Aunt Dinah's Head Rag	W.R. Sawyer	February 27, 1912	Self	Russell, WY
Aunt Jemima's Birthday	Rube Bloom	May 15, 1931	Robbins Music	New York, NY
Auto Rag	T.H. Trenholm	June 2, 1905	Self	Cambridge, MA
Aviation Rag	Mark Janza	1910	Keithley–Marzian Company	Louisville, KY
Aviator Rag	Irene M. Giblin	December 15, 1910	Jerome H. Remick	Detroit, MI
Axel Grease	Axel Christensen	January 26, 1924	Jack Mills	New York, NY
B & O Rag	John L. Armsey	February 19, 1917	Self	Akron, OH
Bachelor's Button	W.C. Powell	May 3, 1909	J.W. Jenkins	Kansas City, MO
Back to Life	Charles Hunter	November 18, 1905	Charles K. Harris	New York, NY
Bag of Rags	W.R. McKanlass	January 22, 1912	Joseph M. Daly	Boston, MA
Bale o' Cotton	Mark Janza	December 18, 1914	A.F. Marzian	New Albany, IN
Baltimore Blues	Henry Lodge	June 20, 1917	Jerome H. Remick	New York, NY
Baltimore Buck	Harry Brown	October 13, 1905	Vinton Music	Boston, MA
Baltimore Convention Rag	Stephen Corbin	October 1, 1912	H. Kirkus Dugdale	Washington, DC
Baltimore Todalo	Eubie Blake	1975	Eubie Blake Music	New York, NY
Banana Peel Rag	Gus Winkler	January 24, 1913	Forster Music	Chicago, IL
Bandit King Rag	G.W. Haskins & J.A. Poston	November 20, 1914	Mellinger Music	St. Louis, MO
Banjo Rag	E.K. Bennett	April 13, 1912	Joseph Krolage Music	Cincinnati, OH
Bantam Step	Harry Jentes	February 21, 1916	Shapiro, Bernstein	New York, NY
Barbecue Rag	Mamie Thornton	1909	Emerson Music	Cincinnati, OH
Barbed Wire Rag	Herbert Spencer	March 14, 1910	Jerome H. Remick	New York, NY
Barber Pole Rag	Charles L. Johnson	April 3, 1911	Hal G. Nichols Company	Denver, CO
Barber Shop Rag	Bill Krenz	January 19, 1953	Mills Music	New York, NY
Barnyard Rag	Timothy Jones	December 15, 1913	John T. Hall	New York, NY
Barrel House Rag	Fate Marable & Clarence Williams	November 9, 1916	Williams & Piron	New Orleans, LA
Baseball Rag	Mata Wulff	1910	Self	Indianapolis, IN
Bean Soup Blues	Jess H. Valentine	April 19, 1918	Pace & Handy	Memphis, TN
Bear Club Rag	Joseph Hensberg	January 8, 1912	Empire Music	Seattle, WA
Bear Tracks	Edward C. Barroll	April 10, 1930	Rubank	Chicago, IL
Beautiful Sensation Rag	Lew J. Novy	October 9, 1916	National Music	Chicago, IL

Beedle–Um–Bo	Raymond Birch	December 17, 1908	Charles L. Johnson	Kansas City, MO
Bees Wax	Harry J. Lincoln	August 19, 1911	Vandersloot Music	Williamsport, PA
Behave Yourself	Roy Bargy	June 27, 1922	Sam Fox	Cleveland, OH
Bell Hop Rag	Frederick Bryan	December 30, 1914	Joseph W. Stern	New York, NY
Benzine Rag	Edward A. Denish	October 10, 1910	Harrison MPC	Providence, RI
Big Ben	Thomas S. Allen	1916	Walter Jacobs	Boston, MA
Big Sandy Rag	Verne Bestor			
Billie Ritchie Rag	Margaret E. Crump	1915	Self	
Billiken Rag	E.J. Stark	February 21, 1913	Stark Music Company	St. Louis, MO
Billy Possum	Walter H. Wayland	1909	Self	Girard, KS
Billy Possum Rag	B. Claude Davis	August 27, 1909	Self	Valdosta, GA
Bing! Bing!	Mel B. Kaufman	January 20, 1915	Plaza Music	New York, NY
Bingo Rag	F.H. Losey	March 28, 1910	Vandersloot Music	Williamsport, PA
Bird-Brain Rag	Joseph F. Lamb	1964	Mills Music	New York, NY
Birds' Carnival	Zez Confrey	October 7, 1935	Robbins Music	New York, NY
Black & Blue Rag	Hal G. Nichols	January 2, 1914	Sam Fox	Cleveland, OH
Black & White Rag	George Botsford	1908	Jerome H. Remick	New York, NY
Black Bawl	Harry C. Thompson	June 16, 1905	W.C. Polla	Chicago, IL
Black Beauty	Jean Schwartz	November 9, 1910	Jerome H. Remick	Detroit, MI
Black Canary	Harry A. Tierney	May 5, 1911	Ted Snyder Company	New York, NY
Black Cat Rag	Lina Mumford	July 5, 1901	Self	Grand Rapids, MI
Black Cat Rag	Frank Wooster & Ethyl B. Smith	September 7, 1905	Frank Wooster Company	St. Louis, MO
Black Crow	Max Schuldt, Jr.	1912	Self	Chippewa Falls, WI
Black Crow Rag	Tommy Moreland	April 24, 1914	Self	Idaho Falls, ID
Black Devil Rag	C.C. Muth	March 27, 1919	Self	Chicago, IL
Black Diamond Rag	Emmett E. Fawcett	December 26, 1908	Groene Music	Cincinnati, OH
Black Diamond Rag	Harry J. Lincoln	September 23, 1914	Vandersloot Music	Williamsport, PA
Black Diamond Rag	Henry Lodge	February 5, 1912	M. Witmark & Sons	New York, NY
Black Feather	Irene M. Giblin-O'Brien	November 13, 1908	Vinton Music	Chicago, IL
Black Hand	Robert Hoffman	February 24, 1908	John H. Keyser	New Orleans, LA
Black Hand Rag	George A. Norton	December 31, 1910	Self	Denver, CO
Black Key Kapers	Silvio DeRienzo	January 7, 1929	Alfred & Company	New York, NY
Black Smoke	Charles L. Johnson	1902	Carl Hoffman Music	Kansas City, MO
Black Wasp Rag	H.A. Fischler	February 21, 1911	Vandersloot Music	Williamsport, PA

Blacksmith Rag	Rednip	April 14, 1920	Ted Garton Music	Boston, MA
Blame It on the Blues	Charles L. Cooke	March 3, 1914	Jerome H. Remick	New York, NY
Blarney Kisses	Holmes Travis	1911	M.L. Carlson	Chicago, IL
Blind Boone's Southern Rag Medley #1	Blind Boone	October 22, 1908	Allen Music	Columbia, MO
Blind Boone's Southern Rag Medley #2	Blind Boone	November 1, 1909	Allen Music	Columbia, MO
Blue Blazes	Arthur L. Sizemore	July 8, 1909	Victor Kremer	Chicago, IL
Blue Goose	Raymond Birch	January 3, 1916	Forster Music	Chicago, IL
Blue Grass Rag	Joseph F. Lamb	1964	Mills Music	New York, NY
Blue Grass Rag	Charley Straight	November 11, 1918	Joe Morris	New York, NY
Blue Grass Rag	Ernest S. Williams	October 23, 1909	Self	Boston, MA
Blue Jay Rag	Frank Wooster	June 22, 1907	Self	St. Louis, MO
Blue Moon	Max Kortlander & Lee S. Roberts	May 9, 1918	Lee S. Roberts	Chicago, IL
Blue Moon Two Step	E.M. Cook	1906	H.A. Sturm	Cincinnati, OH
Blue Note Blues	Billy James	September 7, 1922	F.B. Haviland	New York, NY
Blue Ribbon Rag	May Aufderheide	October 3, 1910	J.H. Aufderheide	Indianapolis, IN
Blue Ribbon Rag	Irwin Dash	1911	Longbrake & Edwards	Philadelphia, PA
Blue Streak	Roy Bargy	1921	Forster Music	Chicago, IL
Blue Streak Rag	Birchard Wegenhardt	November 5, 1912	Self	Cincinnati, OH
Bluffton Carnival Rag	Verdi Karns	August 14, 1899	Self	Bluffton, IN
Bluin' the Black Keys	Arthur Schutt	February 24, 1926	Robbins–Engel	New York, NY
Bob's Chili Rag	Robert E. Cleary	November 11, 1921	Self	Spokane, WA
Bobette	Bernard Barnes	August 4, 1926	Weeks & Winge	San Francisco, CA
Bohemia Rag	Joseph F. Lamb	February 17, 1919	Stark Music Company	St. Louis, MO
Bohemian Rag	Gus Edwards & Louis Silvers	June 2, 1914	Jerome H. Remick	New York, NY
Boiled Owl	Margaret Wooden	April 28, 1911	Self	Flint, MI
Bolo Rag	Albert Gumble	November 11, 1908	Jerome H. Remick	New York, NY
Bombshell	Thomas R. Confare & Morris S. Silver	1909	Charles I. Davis	Cleveland, OH
Bon Ton	C. Luckeyth Roberts	May 7, 1915	G. Ricordi	New York, NY
Bone Dry	Sidney Landfield	November 15, 1918	Jerome H. Remick	New York, NY
Bone Head Blues	Leo Gordon	1917	Walter Jacobs	Boston, MA
Boogie Rag	Wilbur Sweatman	1917	Shapiro, Bernstein	New York, NY
Boomerang Rag	George Botsford	June 21, 1916	Jerome H. Remick	New York, NY

Booster	Mayhew L. Lake	December 12, 1913	Carl Fischer	New York, NY
Border Blues Rag	Guy A. Surber	October 6, 1916	Self	Mercedes, TX
Borneo Rag	Neil Moret	April 8, 1911	Jerome H. Remick	Detroit, MI
Bouncing on the Keys	Ed Claypoole	December 31, 1924	Jack Mills	New York, NY
Bounding Buck	Henry Lodge	March 1, 1918	M. Witmark & Sons	New York, NY
Bowery Buck	Tom Turpin	March 6, 1899	Robert DeYong	St. Louis, MO
Brain-Storm Rag	Bud Manchester	June 3, 1907	Stark Music Company	New York, NY
Brazilian Nut	Sol Wolerstein	May 5, 1915	Jerome H. Remick	New York, NY
Break the Piano	Billy James	March 27, 1918	Self	Philadelphia, PA
Breakin' the Piano	Billy James	May 20, 1922	Jack Mills	New York, NY
Breeze from Alabama	Scott Joplin	December 29, 1902	John Stark & Son	St. Louis, MO
Bric-a-Brac Rag	Maurice Porcelain	1906	Vinton Music	Boston, MA
Brittwood Rag	Eubie Blake	1975	Eubie Blake Music	New York, NY
Broadway Rag	Marcella A. Henry	October 1, 1917	Christensen School	Chicago, IL
Broadway Rag	Eva Nieman	June 28, 1910	Self	Cincinnati, OH
Broadway Rag	W.C. Powell	April 2, 1909	T.B. Harms	New York, NY
Broadway Rag	James Scott	January 3, 1922	Stark Music Company	St. Louis, MO
Broken Buttons	Harrison E. Baumbaugh	September 24, 1925	Jack Mills	New York, NY
Broncho Billy	Nell Wright Slaughter	October 7, 1914	Bush & Gerts	Dallas, TX
Broncho Buck	Edward C. Barroll	March 2, 1914	Mid-West Music	St. Louis, MO
Brownie Rag	Frank Wooster & Max Wilkens	November 15, 1905	Frank Wooster Company	St. Louis, MO
Brun Campbell Express	Tom Shea	June 27, 1966	Oak Publishing	New York, NY
Brush Creek Rag	Eleanora Beauchamp	1913	Geo. Jennings	Cincinnati, OH
Bubbles	M.M. Nash	September 27, 1911	Standard Music	Chicago, IL
Buccaneer	Phil Kussel	1911	United Music Publishing	Cincinnati, OH
Bud Rag	Budd L. Cross	July 22, 1909	Sam Fox	Cleveland, OH
Budweiser Rag	Grace Kuykendall	June 13, 1908	Self	Morgantown, KY
Buffalo Dish Rag	Bernisne G. Clements	September 23, 1910	F.B. Haviland	New York, NY
Buffalo Means Business	George L. Cobb	June 14, 1909	Louis C. Snyder	Buffalo, NY
Buffalo Rag	Tom Turpin	November 2, 1904	Will Rossiter	Chicago, IL
Bug-House Rag	Randolph C. Newton & Will E. Skidmore	1916	Skidmore Music Company	Kansas City, MO
Bugavue Rag	George W. Fairman	1902	William Dowler	Marion, OH

Bugle Call Rag	Eubie Blake & Carey Morgan	January 27, 1916	Joseph W. Stern	New York, NY
Bugs Rag	Nina B. Kohler	January 22, 1913	Self	Sherman, TX
Bull Dog Rag	Geraldine Dobyns	November 19, 1908	Anderson–Rienhardt Company	Memphis, TN
Bull Moose Rag	K.M. Gilham	November 12, 1912	Self	Alameda, CA
Bully Rag	James E.C. Kelly	February 10, 1911	Kelly, Geiger, & Becker	Cincinnati, OH
Bully Rag	J. Fred O'Connor	January 3, 1910	F.A. Mills	New York, NY
Bum Rag	J. Schiller	July 1, 1904	Pioneer Music	Chicago, IL
Bumble Bee Rag	E. Clinton Keithley	1909	Keith Music	Louisville, KY
Bumble Bee Rag	Harry A. Tierney	November 24, 1909	Ted Snyder Company	New York, NY
Bunch of Burr Heads	Percy Fullinwider	1903	W.H. Willis	Cincinnati, OH
Bunch of Noise	Louis Mentel	June 17, 1908	Mentel Brothers	Cincinnati, OH
Bundle of Rags	Robert S. Roberts	December 17, 1897	Phillip Kussel	Cincinnati, OH
Bunny Hug Rag	Kenneth V. Abendana	January 20, 1913	Globe Music	New York, NY
Bunny Hug Rag	George L. Cobb	August 4, 1913	Charles E. Roat Music	Battle Creek, MI
Bunny Hug Rag	Harry DeCosta	May 1, 1912	Waterson, Berlin & Snyder	New York, NY
Bunny-Boy	Eric C. Gatty	November 22, 1912	Joseph W. Stern	New York, NY
Burning Rags	Bess Rudisell	July 1, 1904	Samuel Simon	St. Louis, MO
Burning the Keys	Robert Marine	1928	Self	New York, NY
Business in Town	Donald Ashwander	June 27, 1966	Oak Publishing	New York, NY
Buster Rag	Bessie M. Powell	1915	Whitmore Publishing	Scranton, PA
Butcher Rag	Louis Mentel	November 22, 1912	Mentel Brothers	Cincinnati, OH
Buzzer Rag	May Aufderheide	September 4, 1909	J.H. Aufderheide	Indianapolis, IN
Cabbage Leaf Rag	Les Copeland	November 2, 1909	Marsh & Needles	Wichita, KS
Cabbage Rag	Bertha Stanfield	November 24, 1911	Spiker & McMillen	Joplin, MO
Caberavings	Richard A. Whiting	March 31, 1914	Jerome H. Remick	New York, NY
Cactus Rag	Lucian P. Gibson	May 10, 1916	Stark Music Company	St. Louis, MO
Calico Rag	Richard G. Behan	February 1, 1909	Self	Newark, NJ
Calico Rag	Lee B. Grabbe	November 16, 1905	Emmett & Johns	Chicago, IL
Calico Rag	Nat Johnson	October 19, 1914	Forster Music	Chicago, IL
Calico Rag	Les Jones	August 9, 1953	Self	LaHabra, CA
California Sunshine	Harry Jentes	November 29, 1913	Theron C. Bennett	New York, NY
Caliope Rag	Sylvester L. Hartlaub & Charles L. Hartlaub	June 30, 1911	Joseph Krolage Music	Cincinnati, OH

Call 'Em Toodles	Corrie Huddleston	April 19, 1921	Jack Mills	New York, NY
Calla Lilly Rag	Logan Thane	1907	Stark Music Company	New York, NY
Calliope Rag	James Scott	June 27, 1966	Oak Publishing	New York, NY
Campus Rag	Benjamin Richmond	April 27, 1911	Charles D. Gallagher	New York, NY
Can You Beat It Rag	Frederick Christeen	1911	Henry B. Kronlage	New Orleans, LA
Can You Do That?	G.E. Fuller	1900	Self	Hallstead, PA
Can't Think of the Name	Bernard B. Brin & Al Newman	1922	Melody Shop	Seattle, WA
Canadian Capers	Gus Chandler & Henry Cohen & Bert White	March 26, 1915	Roger Graham	Chicago, IL
Candied Cherries	Lucien Denni	October 26, 1911	J.W. Jenkins	Kansas City, MO
Candle–Stick Rag	Abe Olman	February 12, 1910	J.H. Aufderheide	Indianapolis, IN
Candy	Clarence Jones	1909	John Arnold	Cincinnati, OH
Candy Kid	Floyd Bartlett	1911	H. Kirkus Dugdale	Washington, DC
Candy Rag	Robert Bircher	October 4, 1909	Self	St. Louis, MO
Canhanibalmo Rag	Arthur Pryor	August 8, 1911	Carl Fischer	New York, NY
Canned Corn Rag	George L. Cobb	March 1, 1910	Bell Music	Buffalo, NY
Cannibal Rag	Ed Dangel	1911	Evans–Dangel Music	Boston, MA
Cannon Ball	Jos. C. Northup	April 17, 1905	Victor Kremer	Chicago, IL
Capital City Rag	Catherine W. O'Connor	June 17, 1905	Self	New Haven, CT
Captivatin'Rag	Harry Ellman & S. Lew Schwab	March 16, 1910	Wellworth Music	St. Louis, MO
Car-Barlick Acid Rag	Clarence C. Wiley	August 9, 1901	Self	Oskaloosa, IA
Carmen Rag	Severino Giovannoli	November 13, 1912	Self	McMunnville, TN
Carnation	Clyde D. Douglas	1903	John Stark & Son	St. Louis, MO
Carolina Fox Trot	Will H. Vodery	July 7, 1914	Joseph W. Stern	New York, NY
Carolina Romp	Will H. Vodery	July 14, 1913	Joseph W. Stern	New York, NY
Carolina Shout	James P. Johnson	October 16, 1925	Clarence Williams Music	New York, NY
Carpet Rags	Ray W. Conner	December 10, 1902	Joe Morris	Philadelphia, PA
Carr's Hop	Lou Busch	March 5, 1952	Chatsworth Music	New York, NY
Cascades	Scott Joplin	August 22, 1904	John Stark & Son	St. Louis, MO
Castle Doggy	Ford Dabney & James Reese Europe	1915	G. Ricordi	New York, NY
Castle House Rag	James R. Europe	March 9, 1914	Joseph W. Stern	New York, NY
Cat Grin Rag	Flora Bergman	November 8, 1910	Ted Snyder Company	New York, NY

Cat's Pajamas	Harry Jentes	January 10, 1923	Jack Mills	New York, NY
Cataract	Robert Hampton	July 27, 1914	Stark Music Company	St. Louis, MO
Cauldron Rag	Axel Christensen	April 26, 1909	Christensen School	Chicago, IL
Cazador	H.L. Berger	1906	Graul Publishing	Detroit, MI
Cedar Crest Rag	Meade Graham	March 14, 1924	Song Shop	Dallas, TX
Celestial Rag	Joe Glover	April 14, 1959	Melrose Music	New York, NY
Centennial Rag	John Arpin	April 1, 1966	BMI Canada Ltd.	Toronto, CN
Centennial Rag	Charles Roy Cox	1912	Buckeye Music	Columbus, OH
Century Prize	Arthur Marshall	June 27, 1966	Oak Publishing	New York, NY
Cerise	Jesse L. Williams	August 1, 1914	Self	Lincoln, NE
Certain Party	Tom Kelly	October 3, 1910	Maurice Shapiro	New York, NY
Champagne Rag	Joseph F. Lamb	September 15, 1910	Stark Music Company	St. Louis, MO
Changes	Ed Claypoole	November 23, 1922	Jack Mills	New York, NY
Chanticleer Rag	Albert Gumble	March 22, 1910	Jerome H. Remick	New York, NY
Charleston Rag	Eubie Blake	1975	Eubie Blake Music	New York, NY
Charming Rag	Alamanzer Leon Dupuis	May 1, 1913	Self	Lowell, MA
Chasing the Chickens	Abe Olman & Raymond Walker	June 29, 1917	Forster Music	Chicago, IL
Chasing the Fox	J. Louis Merkur	August 4, 1928	Jack Mills	New York, NY
Chasing the Fox	Percy Wenrich	June 5, 1922	Forster Music	Chicago, IL
Chatterbox Rag	George Botsford	October 4, 1910	Jerome H. Remick	Detroit, MI
Checker	Bulah Arens	1908	Carlin & Lennox	Indianapolis, IN
Checker Rag	Dan Goldsmith	November 18, 1911	Self	Winnepeg, CN
Checkerboard Rag	Elijah Jimerson	1914	Syndicate Music	St. Louis, MO
Checkerboard Rag	Harry A. Tierney	May 13, 1911	Ted Snyder Company	New York, NY
Checkers	Harry J. Lincoln	November 1, 1913	Vandersloot Music	Williamsport, PA
Cheese and Crackers	Homer Denney	September 15, 1909	Self	Cincinnati, OH
Cherry Leaf Rag	El Cota	September 20, 1909	Victor Kremer	Chicago, IL
Chestnut Valley Rag	Trebor J. Tichenor	June 27, 1966	Oak Publishing	New York, NY
Chestnuts	Percy Wenrich	November 7, 1906	Arnett–Delonais	Chicago, IL
Chevy Chase	Eubie Blake	October 28, 1914	Joseph W. Stern	New York, NY
Chewin' the Rag	E.C. Kammermayer	1900	Self	Los Angeles, CA
Chewin' the Rag	Fred Heltman	September 6, 1912	Popular Music Publishers	Cleveland, OH
Chic	A.C. Brockmeyer	September 15, 1918	Crescent Publishing Company	St. Louis, MO

Chicago Breakdown	"Jelly Roll" Morton	January 12, 1926	Melrose Brothers	Chicago, IL
Chicago Tickle	Harry A. Tierney	August 8, 1913	Charles T. French	New York, NY
Chicken Charlie	Ashley Ballou	February 9, 1905	W.C. Polla	Chicago, IL
Chicken Chowder	Irene M. Giblin	April 12, 1905	Jerome H. Remick	Detroit, MI
Chicken Dance	Herbert Cortess	July 17, 1913	Chauncey Van Demark	Kyserike, NY
Chicken Patty	Theodore Morse	April 24, 1908	F.B. Haviland	New York, NY
Chicken Pranks	Max Kortlander & Lee S. Roberts	1917	Self	Chicago, IL
Chicken's Rag	Rafael Balseiro	September 23, 1915	J. Fischer & Bro.	New York, NY
Chili Con Carne	Elmer B. Griffith	1911	Rinker Music	Lafayette, IN
Chili Pepper	Fred W. Longshaw	September 18, 1925	Perry Bradford Music	New York, NY
Chili Sauce	H.A. Fischler	September 24, 1910	Vandersloot Music	Williamsport, PA
Chills and Fever	Theron C. Bennett	August 27, 1912	Sam Fox	Cleveland, OH
Chilly Billy Bee Rag	Lewis F. Muir	January 5, 1910	J. Fred Helf	New York, NY
Chimes	Homer Denney	July 20, 1910	Joseph Krolage Music	Cincinnati, OH
Chippewa Rag	Myrtle Hoy	March 22, 1911	Windsor Music	Chicago, IL
Chocolate Creams Rag	Warren Camp	September 20, 1909	Victor Kremer	Chicago, IL
Chocolate Sweets	Walter G. Wilmarth	1902	E.F. Droop & Sons	Washington, DC
Chop Suey Rag	Edward Hayne	September 20, 1915	Self	Chicago, IL
Chopiano	Henry Lange	March 6, 1922	Jack Mills	New York, NY
Chow Chow	Robert Hoffman	1909	Crescent Music	New Orleans, LA
Chow-Chow Rag	Phil Schwartz	August 12, 1909	Jerome H. Remick	Detroit, MI
Chromatic Capers	George L. Cobb	June 12, 1925	Walter Jacobs	Boston, MA
Chromatic Rag	Will Held	March 10, 1916	Stark Music Company	St. Louis, MO
Chromatic Rag	Pete Wendling & Ed Gerhart	May 17, 1916	Waterson, Berlin & Snyder	New York, NY
Cincinnati Rag	W.C. Powell	June 21, 1909	Arnett–Delonais	Chicago, IL
Cinder-Ella Rag	Mabel L. Asher	May 24, 1910	Self	San Diego, CA
Classic Rag	Neil Moret	April 3, 1909	Jerome H. Remick	New York, NY
Classicanna	Henry Lange	May 4, 1923	Waterson, Berlin & Snyder	New York, NY
Classy Rag	Lillian M. Lawler	August 15, 1917	Self	New Orleans, LA
Classy Rag	Ethel S. Phillips	February 27, 1915	Self	Fort Worth, TX
Claudia Rag	Grace Shaw	1910	Gottfried & McMillan	Joplin, MO
Cleopatra Rag	Joseph F. Lamb	June 16, 1915	Stark Music Company	St. Louis, MO

Climax Rag	James Scott	March 5, 1914	Stark Music Company	St. Louis, MO
Climbers	Arthur L. Sizemore	July 27, 1911	Stark Music Company	St. Louis, MO
Cloud Kisser	Raymond Birch	January 3, 1911	Charles L. Johnson	Kansas City, MO
Clover Blossom Rag	Fred Heltman	July 30, 1910	Self	Cleveland, OH
Clover Blossom Rag	Bud Manchester	August 17, 1912	Stark Music Company	St. Louis, MO
Clover Club	Felix Arndt	May 9, 1918	Sam Fox	Cleveland, OH
Clover Leaf	John Lind	October 16, 1905	Self	Cincinnati, OH
Clover Leaf Rag	Cy Seymour	March 1, 1909	Albright Music	Chicago, IL
Club Cabin	S. Em. Duguay	1903	Le Passe-Temps	Montreal, CN
Coaxing the Ivories	Robert Marine	June 1, 1928	Self	New York, NY
Coaxing the Piano	Zez Confrey	March 6, 1922	Jack Mills	New York, NY
Coffee Rag	Lily Coffee	July 21, 1915	W.C. Munn Company	Houston, TX
Cold Feet Rag	Mamie Williams	1907	J.W. Jenkins	Kansas City, MO
Coldwater Rag	Mollie F. Cloud	August 7, 1913	G.L. Dearing	Lincoln, NE
Cole Smoak	Clarence H. St. John	December 28, 1906	John Stark & Son	St. Louis, MO
Collars and Cuffs	Clarence H. St. John	December 23, 1907	Stark Music Company	New York, NY
College Rag	William Hunter	December 17, 1910	Herald Square Music	New York, NY
College Rag	Ruth Knipperberg	July 22, 1910	Self	Milwaukee, WI
Colonial Glide	Paul Pratt	January 13, 1910	J.H. Aufderheide	Indianapolis, IN
Colonial Rag	Ernest R. Ball & Julius Lenzberg	October 3, 1914	M. Witmark & Sons	New York, NY
Columbia Rag	Armorell Cochran	November 8, 1913	Luckhardt & Belder	New York, NY
Columbia Rag	Irene M. Giblin	March 5, 1910	Jerome H. Remick	New York, NY
Comet Rag	Leslie C. Groff	1910	Self	Chicago, IL
Comet Rag	Jean J. Haas	1910	Bixby & Castle	Buffalo, NY
Comet Rag	Ed C. Mahoney	November 10, 1910	Joseph M. Daly	Boston, MA
Comet Rag	Alfred V. Peterson	April 22, 1910	Self	Salt Lake City, UT
Coney Island Dip	Addison J. Ressegue	July 10, 1901	Union Music Company	Cincinnati, OH
Coney Island Girl	Homer Denney	February 26, 1906	Self	Cincinnati, OH
Coney Island Tickle	Alfred Gasdorf	1906	Self	Newport, KY
Contentment Rag	Joseph F. Lamb	January 10, 1915	Stark Music Company	St. Louis, MO
Coon Band Parade	James R. Europe	October 14, 1905	Sol Bloom	New York, NY
Coon Can	Edward Derville	1901	Sol Bloom	Chicago, IL
Copper King Rag	Marguerite Ray	October 12, 1912	Hatch & Loveland	Los Angeles, CA

Corn Cracker Rag	Eugene S. Pyle	June 19, 1911	Self	Campbell, MO
Corn on the Cob	Cliff Hess	October 17, 1923	Jack Mills	New York, NY
Corn Palace	Ray Stewart Soladay	September 22, 1915	Advocate Printers	Fulton, SD
Corn Shucks Rag	Ed Kuhn	1908	J.W. Jenkins	Kansas City, MO
Corn Tassle Rag	E. Earle Marx	June 11, 1912	Self	Lincoln, NE
Coronation Rag	Winifred Atwell	April 22, 1953	Jefferson Music	New York, NY
Cotton	Albert VonTilzer	1907	York Music	New York, NY
Cotton Belt Rag	Irma V. Dawson	April 29, 1916	Thomas Goggan & Brothers	Galveston, TX
Cotton Belt Rag	J.H. O'Bryan	August 5, 1908	Self	Mooleyville, KY
Cotton Bolls	Charles Hunter	June 7, 1901	Frank G. Fite	Nashville, TN
Cotton Leaf Rag	Len Larimer	February 13, 1911	H. Kirkus Dugdale	Washington, DC
Cotton Patch	Charles A. Tyler	July 31, 1902	J.W. Jenkins	Kansas City, MO
Cotton Pickers Carnival	Maurice Taube	January 2, 1904	William R. Haskins Company	Brooklyn, NY
Cotton States Rag	Annie Ford McKnight	February 19, 1910	Cocroft Music	Thomasville, GA
Cotton Time	Charles N. Daniels	September 26, 1910	Jerome H. Remick	Detroit, MI
Cottontail Rag	Joseph F. Lamb	1964	Mills Music	New York, NY
Country Club	Scott Joplin	October 30, 1909	Seminary Music	New York, NY
Cozy Corner Rag	Carroll Stephens	April 28, 1911	F.B. Haviland	New York, NY
Crab Apples	Percy Wenrich	January 27, 1908	Brehm Brothers	Erie, PA
Cracked Ice	George L. Cobb	1918	Walter Jacobs	Boston, MA
Cracker Jack Rag	E.W. Francis	November 5, 1909	Victor Kremer	Chicago, IL
Cradle Rock	Abe Frankl & Phil Kornheiser	August 11, 1916	Leo Feist	New York, NY
Craps	L.Z. Phillips	1908	J. Goldsmith & Sons	Memphis, TN
Craps	Will E. Skidmore	May 21, 1910	Cosmopolitan Music	Little Rock, AR
Crash!!!	Gus Van & Joe Schenck	April 14, 1914	Will Rossiter	Chicago, IL
Crazy Bone Rag	Charles L. Johnson	March 29, 1913	Forster Music	Chicago, IL
Crazy Horse Rag	Roscoe Carter	August 18, 1909	Victor Kremer	Chicago, IL
Crazy Quilt	Lawrence L. Willey	March 8, 1910	Self	Manchester, NH
Crimson Rambler Rag	Harry A. Tierney	May 19, 1911	Ted Snyder Company	New York, NY
Cross Word Puzzle	Charles Olson	March 23, 1925	Jack Mills	New York, NY
Crossed Hands	Saul Sieff	November 24, 1925	Villa Moret	San Francisco, CA
Cubist	Tom Griselle	June 1, 1918	Artmusic	New York, NY

Cubistic Rag	George L. Cobb	October 14, 1927	Walter Jacobs	Boston, MA
Cucumber Rag	W.C. Powell	December 9, 1910	Joe Morris	New York, NY
Cum-Bac Rag	Charles L. Johnson	December 22, 1911	Jerome H. Remick	Detroit, MI
Curiosity	James E.C. Kelly	May 17, 1910	Ballard & Kelly	Cincinnati, OH
Curl-I-Cues	Walter E. Miles	August 10, 1945	Sam Fox	New York, NY
Cute and Pretty	Melville Morris	September 26, 1917	Jerome H. Remick	New York, NY
Cutter	Elma Ney McClure	1909	O.K. Houck	Memphis, TN
Cuttin' Up	Charles G. Haskell	December 31, 1906	Jerome H. Remick	New York, NY
Cyclone	Ferde Grofe	April 7, 1923	Jack Mills	New York, NY
Cyclone	Edward G. Rieman	July 21, 1908	Self	Cincinnati, OH
Cyclone in Darktown	George D. Barnard	December 30, 1910	Carl Fischer	New York, NY
Cyclone Rag	F. Brown	April 12, 1909	Fritz & Floyd	Cleveland, OH
Daffodils	James E.C. Kelly	January 5, 1912	Joseph Krolage Music	Cincinnati, OH
Daffy Dingies	Harry Raymond	January 16, 1901	Raymond & Wood	Buffalo, NY
Daffydill Rag	Waiman	December 29, 1911	Grinnell Bros.	Detroit, MI
Dainty Doll	Bernard Barnes	1934	Sherman, Clay	San Francisco, CA
Dainty Foot Glide	G.M. Tidd	February 16, 1915	Self	Marion, OH
Dainty Miss	Bernard Barnes	November 24, 1924	Sherman, Clay	San Francisco, CA
Daisy Rag	Fred Heltman	December 5, 1908	Sam Fox	Cleveland, OH
Dakota Rag	O.H. Andersen	June 7, 1899	S. Brainard's Sons	Chicago, IL
Dance of the Crocodiles Rag	H.H. Whiting	October 1, 1912	Self	Sanford, ME
Dance of the Notes	Phil Saltman	November 30, 1935	Robbins Music	New York, NY
Dancing Animal Crackers	Harry DeCosta & Herbert Steiner	April 22, 1929	Mills Music	New York, NY
Dancing Fingers	Earl Hines	November 16, 1935	Modern Standard	Chicago, IL
Dancing Shadows	Ernie Golden	September 29, 1927	Al Piantadosi	New York, NY
Dancing Tambourine	W.C. Polla	August 4, 1927	Harms, Inc.	New York, NY
Dandelion	Ted S. Barron	October 23, 1909	M. Witmark & Sons	New York, NY
Danger Rag	Vivian A. Tillotson	May 23, 1912	Self	Hope, ND
Dansopation	Martin K. Mortensen	November 26, 1923	Hearst Music	Winnipeg, CN
Darkies' Spring Song	Egbert Van Alstyne	1901	Will Rossiter	Chicago, IL
Darkey Todalo	Joe Jordan	November 15, 1910	Harry Von Tilzer Music	New York, NY
Darktown Capers	Walter Starck	December 15, 1897	Shattinger Music	St. Louis, MO
Dat Cacklin' Rag	Kenneth W. Bradshaw	September 26, 1911	H. Kirkus Dugdale	Washington, DC

Dat Johnson Rag	N. Clark Smith & C.E. Matchett	1910	Marsh & Needles	Wichita, KS
Dat Lovin'Rag	Bernard Adler	1908	F.B. Haviland	New York, NY
Dat's It	Sebastian Lutz	November 10, 1903	Hakenjos	New Orleans, LA
Dave's Rag	David A. Jasen	June 28, 1979	The Big Three	New York, NY
Deiro Rag	Guido Deiro	December 18, 1913	Jerome H. Remick	New York, NY
Del Mar Rag	Joe Sullivan	1945	Robbins Music	New York, NY
Delightful Rag	Lester Sill	January 19, 1914	Warner C. Williams	Indianapolis, IN
Delirium Tremens Rag	F. Henri Klickmann	January 20, 1913	Harold Rossiter	Chicago, IL
Delta Rag	Virginia A Birdsong	December 20, 1913	L. Grunewald Company	New Orleans, LA
Demon Rag	John E. Broderick	June 20, 1918	W.C. DeForest	Sharon, PA
Derby Day Rag	Leafy Colvin	May 26, 1909	Self	Kansas City, MO
Desecration	Felix Arndt	September 29, 1914	G. Ricordi	New York, NY
Desire Rag	Charles DeGeorge	1918	Buffalo Music	Buffalo, NY
Deuces Wild	Max Kortlander	November 17, 1923	Jack Mills	New York, NY
Deuces Wild Rag	Hubert Bauersachs	October 19, 1922	Self	St. Louis, MO
Devil Rag	Frank R. Powell	1907	Self	Kansas City, MO
Devilish Rag	Lew Roberts	April 27, 1908	Lew Roberts Music	Nashville, TN
Dex	Armond C. Rhodehamel	June 5, 1909	Self	Indianapolis, IN
Diabolo Rag	Dorothy I. Wahl	March 11, 1908	Victor Kremer	Chicago, IL
Diamond Rag	H.A. Cholmondeley	1908	Self	Cincinnati, OH
Dicty's on Seventh Avenue	Eubie Blake	1971	Edward B. Marks Music	New York, NY
Dill Pickles Rag	Charles L. Johnson	1906	Carl Hoffman Music	Kansas City, MO
Dimples and Smiles	Alfred H. Cooper	1913	Joseph Krolage Music	Cincinnati, OH
Dimpley Smiles	Harry C. Thompson	1915	Crest Music	Chicago, IL
Dingle Pop Hop	Harry A. Tierney	April 12, 1911	Ted Snyder Company	New York, NY
Dingy's Serenade	Roy Mullendore	December 10, 1898	Carlin & Lennox	Indianapolis, IN
Diplomat Rag	William H. Hickman	January 25, 1910	Self	Covington, KY
Dischord Rag	Annette Stone	February 1, 1915	Popular Music Publishers	New York, NY
Dish Rag	Saul Bluestein	1909	Self	Memphis, TN
Dish Rag	Floyd D. Godfrey	1909	Charles C. Adams & Company	Peoria, IL
Dish Rag	Richard Goosman	August 14, 1908	Charles I. Davis	Cleveland, OH
Dish Rag	John Nelson	1915	J.R. Hall	

Dixie Blossoms	Percy Wenrich	July 16, 1906	Jerome H. Remick	Detroit, MI
Dixie Dimples	Frank Loewenstein	August 5, 1911	Will Rossiter	Chicago, IL
Dixie Dimples	James Scott	1918	Will L. Livernash Music	Kansas City, MO
Dixie Doodles	Josef Ruben	September 9, 1913	Jerome H. Remick	New York, NY
Dixie Kicks	Percy Wenrich	September 14, 1908	McKinley Music	Chicago, IL
Dixie Kisses	E. Clinton Keithley	1909	Keith Music	Louisville, KY
Dixie Life Rag	Frank E. Brown	September 21, 1920	Self	Walton, NY
Dixie Queen	Robert Hoffman	1906	Cable Company	New Orleans, LA
Dixie Rag	Irene M. Giblin	February 8, 1913	Joseph M. Daly	Boston, MA
Dixie Rag	Al Lewis	July 21, 1908	Koninsky Music	Troy, NY
Dixie Rag	Gustav Roberti	October 14, 1922	Self	New Haven, CT
Dixie Slow Drag	Robert Hoffman	1903	Cable Company	New Orleans, LA
Dizzy Fingers	Zez Confrey	November 17, 1923	Jack Mills	New York, NY
Dockstader Rag	Les Copeland	November 29, 1912	Jerome H. Remick	New York, NY
Doctor Brown	Fred Irvin	October 27, 1914	Jerome H. Remick	New York, NY
Dog on the Piano	Ted Shapiro	September 5, 1924	Jack Mills	New York, NY
Dogzigity Rag	Billie Taylor	June 1, 1910	Ted Snyder Company	New York, NY
Doll Dance	Nacio Herb Brown	July 6, 1927	Sherman, Clay	San Francisco, CA
Doll Rags	Homer A. Hall	May 4, 1906	Victor Kremer	Chicago, IL
Doll Rags	Bernard Ungar	1909	Hits Publishing Company	Cincinnati, OH
Domino Rag	Clarence E. Brandon	July 30, 1913	Syndicate Music	St. Louis, MO
Domino Rag	Richard Glade	September 12, 1908	Self	Chicago, IL
Domino Rag	Reba Powers	March 28, 1908	Lew Roberts Music	Nashville, TN
Domino Rag	Harry L. Sack	May 10, 1907	Self	Milwaukee, WI
Don't Jazz Me-Rag	James Scott	September 18, 1921	Stark Music Company	St. Louis, MO
Doodle Bug	Cliff Hess	August 30, 1915	Waterson, Berlin & Snyder	New York, NY
Dope	W.C. Powell	April 28, 1909	Joseph Flanner	Milwaukee, WI
Dorothy	Frank Banta & Jimmy McHugh	May 7, 1929	Jack Mills	New York, NY
Double Fudge	Joe Jordan	December 20, 1902	Hunleth Music	St. Louis, MO
Double M Rag	Joe Morris & William Morris	March 25, 1914	William Morris Publishing Company	Detroit, MI
Down Home Rag	Wilbur Sweatman	September 18, 1911	Will Rossiter	Chicago, IL
Down South	C.A. Grimm	February 23, 1907	Jerome H. Remick	Detroit, MI

Down Town Rag	Frank Signorelli & George Carrozza	April 7, 1923	Jack Mills	New York, NY
Draggy Rags	D.P. Argo	August 29, 1908	Sterling Publishing Company	Aberdeen, OH
Dreamy Rag	Ethel M. McKray	August 16, 1912	Globe Music	New York, NY
Dusky Damsels Rag	F.W. Sanger	July 17, 1905	Pioneer Music	Chicago, IL
Dust'Em Off	George L. Cobb	1920	Walter Jacobs	Boston, MA
Dusty Rag	May Aufderheide	February 6, 1908	Duane Crabb Publishing Company	Indianapolis, IN
Dutch Mill Rag	A.J. Babich	1916	Dutch Mill Company	Omaha, NE
Dynamite	Paul Biese & F. Henri Klickmann	September 18, 1913	Will Rossiter	Chicago, IL
Dynamite Rag	J. Russel Robinson	October 1, 1910	Southern California Music	Los Angeles, CA
Dynamite Rag	Samuel J. Stokes	August 14, 1908	Self	New Orleans, LA
Easy Money	Will D. Moyer	October 11, 1915	William C. Stahl	Milwaukee, WI
Easy Money	A.H. Tournade	January 27, 1905	Hakenjos	New Orleans, LA
Easy Winners	Scott Joplin	October 10, 1901	Self	St. Louis, MO
Eatin' Time Rag	Irene Cozad	April 27, 1913	J.W. Jenkins	Kansas City, MO
Eccentric	J. Russel Robinson	October 17, 1923	Jack Mills	New York, NY
Echo of Spring	Willie the Lion Smith	April 4, 1935	Clarence Williams Music	New York, NY
Educational Rag	William L. Needham	February 26, 1914	Self	Chicago, IL
Edward J. Mellinger Rag	Edward J. Mellinger	1913	Stark Music Company	St. Louis, MO
Efficiency Rag	James Scott	January 10, 1917	Stark Music Company	St. Louis, MO
Egyptian Rag	Percy Wenrich	November 16, 1910	Jerome H. Remick	New York, NY
Eight O'Clock Rush Rag	Bess Rudisell	September 29, 1911	Sear-Wilson Music	Chicago, IL
Electric Rag!	Glennie C. Batson	April 11, 1914	L. Grunewald Company	New Orleans, LA
Electric Rag!	Mary Gilmore	February 23, 1914	W.M. Bodine	Kansas City, KS
Elephant Rag	Malvin M. Franklin	June 3, 1913	Jerome H. Remick	New York, NY
Eleventh Street Rag	Euday Bowman	July 15, 1918	Bowman & Ward	Gary, IN
Elite Syncopations	Scott Joplin	December 29, 1902	John Stark & Son	St. Louis, MO
Empire City Rag	Frank Broekhoven	January 14, 1911	Sunlight Music	Chicago, IL
Encore Rag	Tad Fischer	February 3, 1912	O.K. Houck	Memphis, TN
Entertainer	Scott Joplin	December 29, 1902	John Stark & Son	St. Louis, MO
Entertainer's Rag	Jay Roberts	September 30, 1910	Pacific Coast Music	Oakland, CA

Erratic	J. Russel Robinson	October 17, 1923	Jack Mills	New York, NY
Eskimo Shivers	Billy Mayerl	August 21, 1925	Sam Fox	Cleveland, OH
Estelle	Frankie Carle	November 15, 1930	Mills Music	New York, NY
Esther	David Reichstein	January 9, 1915	Mellinger Music	St. Louis, MO
Ethiopia Rag	Joseph F. Lamb	1909	Stark Music Company	New York, NY
Eugenia	Scott Joplin	February 26, 1906	Will Rossiter	Chicago, IL
Euphonic Sounds	Scott Joplin	October 30, 1909	Seminary Music	New York, NY
Evergreen Rag	James Scott	1915	Stark Music Company	St. Louis, MO
Everybody Two Step	Wallie Herzer	June 30, 1910	Self	San Francisco, CA
Everybody's Rag	Dan Goldsmith & Robert D. Sharp	November 9, 1909	Darrow & Sharp	Denver, CO
Evolution Rag	Thomas S. Allen	1979	The Big Three	New York, NY
Excelsior Rag	Joseph F. Lamb	1909	Stark Music Company	New York, NY
Extr'ordinary Rag	Otto Motzan	March 22, 1915	T.B. Harms	New York, NY
Eye Opener	Bob Zurke & Julian Matlock	April 10, 1939	Leo Feist	New York, NY
Fadettes Call	Grace Gooding	April 28, 1914	Jerome H. Remick	New York, NY
Famous Players Rag	Harry Baisden	September 27, 1915	Baisden & Poole	Ft. Dodge, IA
Fanatic Rag	Harry A. Tierney	February 15, 1911	Ted Snyder Company	New York, NY
Fancy Fingers	Burn Knowles	July 14, 1936	ABC Standard	New York, NY
Fascinator	James Scott	September 23, 1903	Dumars Music	Carthage, MO
Fashion Rag	Charles Cohen	January 17, 1912	Vandersloot Music	Williamsport, PA
Fashionette	Jack Glogau & Robert A. King	June 28, 1928	Shapiro, Bernstein	New York, NY
Father Knickerbocker	Edwin E. Wilson	August 19, 1907	Joseph W. Stern	New York, NY
Favorite	Scott Joplin	June 23, 1904	A.W. Perry & Sons	Sedalia, MO
Favorite Rag	Willard Bailey	1900	Puntenney & Eutsler	Columbus, OH
Feather Fingers	Claude Lapham	May 14, 1928	Alfred & Company	New York, NY
Feedin' the Kitty	George L. Cobb	1919	Walter Jacobs	Boston, MA
Felicity Rag	Scott Joplin & Scott Hayden	July 27, 1911	Stark Music Company	St. Louis, MO
Felix Rag	H.H. McSkimming	March 19, 1910	Self	Kiowa, KS
Fern Leaf Rag	Hobart E. Swan	April 5, 1906	Self	Kearney, NE
Festival Rag	David A. Jasen	June 28, 1979	The Big Three	New York, NY
Fiddle Sticks	Florence Wilson	April 12, 1910	Joseph Flanner	Milwaukee, WI
Fiddler's Rag	Trovato & A.C. Manning	November 6, 1911	Leo Feist	New York, NY

Fiddlesticks	Al B. Coney	June 17, 1912	Will Rossiter	Chicago, IL
Fiddling George	J.P. Doss	1905	Thomas Goggan & Brothers	Galveston, TX
Fidgety Fingers	Norman J. Elholm	February 27, 1923	Jack Mills	New York, NY
Fig Leaf Rag	Scott Joplin	February 24, 1908	Stark Music Company	New York, NY
Fig Leaf Rag	William R. Lawrence	1909	Self	New York, NY
Fine Feathers	Larry Briers	1923	Jack Mills	New York, NY
Finesse	Bernard Maltin & Ray Doll	April 11, 1929	Santly Bros.	New York, NY
Finger Breaker	"Jelly Roll" Morton	1975	Edwin H. Morris	New York, NY
Finger Buster	Willie the Lion Smith	October 15, 1934	Clarence Williams Music	New York, NY
Finicky Fingers	Lou Busch	March 5, 1952	Chatsworth Music	New York, NY
Fire Cracker Rag	Will Held	May 5, 1911	Charles H. Henderson	Corry, PA
Firefly Rag	Joseph F. Lamb	1964	Mills Music	New York, NY
Fishin' for Flats	Billy James	August 22, 1922	Jack Mills	New York, NY
Five Little Brown Jugs Rag	Lawrence B. O'Connor	April 30, 1909	Joseph M. Daly	Boston, MA
Fizz Water	Eubie Blake	October 28, 1914	Joseph W. Stern	New York, NY
Flap Jacks Rag	J. Bowie Gouger	December 20, 1916	Self	Dallas, TX
Flapperette	Jesse Greer	February 22, 1926	Jack Mills	New York, NY
Fleur de Lis	Harry A. Tierney	August 16, 1911	Joseph W. Stern	New York, NY
Flicker Red Rag	Robert R. Darch	December 30, 1953	Red-Dog Saloon	Juneau, AK
Floating Along	Henry Fredericks	August 8, 1914	McKinley Music	Chicago, IL
Florida Cracker	Ellis Brooks	February 22, 1898	S. Brainard's Sons	Chicago, IL
Florida Rag	George L. Lowry	September 25, 1905	Joseph W. Stern	New York, NY
Fluffy Ruffles	Jack Glogau	November 27, 1928	Bibo, Bloeden & Lang	New York, NY
Fluffy Ruffles	Frank C. Keithley	February 1, 1908	Monroe	Chicago, IL
Fluffy Ruffles	Joe Zimmerman	November 27, 1928	Bibo, Bloeden & Lang	New York, NY
Fluffy Ruffles Girls Rag	Marion I. Davis	February 19, 1908	Charles I. Davis	Cleveland, OH
Fluffy Ruffles Rag	Harry Cook	December 9, 1907	Self	Louisville, KY
Fly Paper Rag	A. Lorne Lee	April 15, 1909	A.H. Goetting	Toronto, CN
Fontella Rag	Ethyl B. Smith	August 5, 1907	Thiebes–Stierlin Music	St. Louis, MO
Fool 'Em Fingers	Odgard C. Stemland	1929	Self	Minneapolis, MN
Foolin' Around	Henry W. Ross	November 3, 1922	Jack Mills	New York, NY
Foolishead	Russell Griffen & Edith Miller	1911	Griffen Music Publishing	Rochester, NY

Foolishness Rag	Mort Weinstein	August 21, 1911	Harold Rossiter	Chicago, IL
Foot Warmer	Harry Puck	February 20, 1914	Kalmar & Puck	New York, NY
Forty-Second Street Rag	Les Copeland & Jack Smith	December 2, 1913	Waterson, Berlin & Snyder	New York, NY
Fox-Terrier Rag	John N. Lang	May 1, 1915	Self	Indianapolis, IN
Franco-American Rag	Jean Schwartz	October 13, 1909	Jerome H. Remick	New York, NY
Frankfort Rag	Maude M. Thurston	January 14, 1909	Self	Chicago, IL
Freckles	Larry Buck	November 25, 1905	W.C. Polla	Chicago, IL
Freckles	Fleta B. Davis	November 30, 1908	Self	Indianapolis, IN
Fred Heltman's Rag	Fred Heltman	February 16, 1918	Self	Cleveland, OH
French Pastry Rag	Les Copeland	September 1, 1914	Jerome H. Remick	New York, NY
Frenzied Rag	Joseph H. Miller	November 6, 1905	C. Melbourne	Chicago, IL
Friar Tuck Rag	Jop Lincott	1898	Self	Chicago, IL
Friday Night	Donald Ashwander	December 30, 1976	Edward B. Marks Music	New York, NY
Fried Chicken Rag	Ella Hudson Day	February 27, 1912	Thomas Goggan & Brothers	Galveston, TX
Frigid Frolics	A.L. Marx	June 5, 1905	Self	Superior, WI
Frisco Frazzle	Nat Johnson	June 27, 1912	M. Witmark & Sons	New York, NY
Frisco Rag	Harry Armstrong	November 6, 1909	M. Witmark & Sons	New York, NY
Frivolous Rags	Flora L. Noll	March 12, 1918	A.W. Perry's Sons	Sedalia, MO
Frog Legs Rag	James Scott	December 10, 1906	John Stark & Son	New York, NY
Frog-I-More Rag	"Jelly Roll" Morton	1946	R.J. Carew	Washington, DC
Froggie Moore	"Jelly Roll" Morton & Benjamin F. Spikes & John C. Spikes	April 16, 1923	Spikes Brothers	Los Angeles, CA
Full Moon	Roy G. Carew	January 13, 1909	Puderer Publishing Company	New Orleans, LA
Full of Tricks	Robert Marine	1928	Self	New York, NY
Fun Bob	Percy Wenrich	March 30, 1907	Arnett–Delonais	Chicago, IL
Funny Bones	Calvin Lee Woolsey	July 17, 1909	Jerome H. Remick	New York, NY
Funny Folks	W.C. Powell	February 25, 1904	W.C. Polla Company	Chicago, IL
Fuss and Feathers	J.C. Halls	1909	United States Music	Williamsport, PA
Fuss and Feathers	F.L. Moreland	August 22, 1904	John Stark & Son	St. Louis, MO
Fussin' Around	William C. Isel	1915	Walter Jacobs	Boston, MA
Fussy Flossie	Charles H. Hagedon	March 25, 1908	Wiegel	Minneapolis, MN
Fuzzy Ideas	C.E. Hoxworth	July 12, 1913	Self	Sumner, IA
Fuzzy Wuzzy	Frank C. Keithley	August 24, 1908	Keithley–Joy Music	Des Moines, IA

Fuzzy Wuzzy Rag	Al Morton	May 4, 1915	Pace & Handy	Memphis, TN
Gallery Gods Delight	Joseph H. Denck	1905	O.K. Houck	Memphis, TN
Garden of Eden	William Bolcom	May 24, 1971	Edward B. Marks Music	New York, NY
Gasoline Rag	Louis Mentel	July 23, 1906	Mentel Brothers	Cincinnati, OH
Gatling Gun Rag	Oreste Migliaccio	April 17, 1908	George Mitchell	New York, NY
Gay Birds	Ed Claypoole	December 1, 1924	Jack Mills	New York, NY
Gayety	Harry Sosnik	February 4, 1935	Robbins Music	New York, NY
Gee Whiz	Sam H. Ewing	September 23, 1908	Self	Princeton, IN
Georgia Ball	Burt H. Flanders	June 30, 1910	Sapp	Eastman, GA
Georgia Giggle Rag	Will L. Livernash	1918	Self	Kansas City, MO
Georgia Grind	Ford Dabney	March 12, 1915	Joseph W. Stern	New York, NY
Georgia Rag	Albert Gumble	December 15, 1910	Jerome H. Remick	Detroit, MI
Georgia Rainbow	Leo Gordon	1916	Walter Jacobs	Boston, MA
Ghost of the Piano	Arthur Schutt	March 5, 1923	Jack Mills	New York, NY
Giddy Ditty	Zez Confrey	October 24, 1935	Exclusive Publications	New York, NY
Giggler	Chauncey Haines	April 5, 1905	Jerome H. Remick	Detroit, MI
Ginger	Mrs. Wm. Neal McCoy	1908	Globe Music	New York, NY
Ginger Snap Rag	Horace K. Dugdale	August 3, 1907	H. Kirkus Dugdale & Corbitt	Washington, DC
Ginger Snaps	Rosario Bourdon	December 27, 1928	Harms, Inc.	New York, NY
Ginger Snaps	Egbert Van Alstyne	1904	Will Rossiter	Chicago, IL
Git Bizzy	Hardaway Frazer	October 31, 1905	Pioneer Music	Chicago, IL
Glad Cat Rag	Will Nash	1905	Pioneer Music	Chicago, Il
Glad Rag	Glen W. Caldwell	June 1, 1909	Self	Los Angeles, CA
Glad Rag	Ribe Danmark	May 18, 1910	Jerome H. Remick	Detroit, MI
Glad Rag	R.G. Grady	September 22, 1910	Gamble Hinged Music	Chicago, IL
Glad Rag	Lew Roberts	December 3, 1907	Lew Roberts Music	Nashville, TN
Glad Rags	Anna Hughes Carpenter	September 18, 1907	George Jaberg	Cincinnati, OH
Glad Rags	George Gould	October 27, 1911	H.W. Williams	San Francisco, CA
Glad Rags	W.E. Nuss	1911	Windsor Music	Chicago, IL
Glad Rags	Harry Williams	October 27, 1911	H.W. Williams	San Francisco, CA
Gladiolus Rag	Scott Joplin	September 24, 1907	Joseph W. Stern	New York, NY
Glen Oaks Rag	Axel Christensen	November 26, 1912	Christensen School	Chicago, IL
Glide Away Rag	Frank C. Keithley	July 5, 1910	Keithley–Joy Music	Des Moines, IA

Gloria	Fred Hager & Justin Ring	August 30, 1923	Robbins–Engel	New York, NY
Gobler Rag	Libbie Allen	August 30, 1913	Shattinger Music	St. Louis, MO
Goin' Some	James Nonnahs	January 5, 1910	Grinnell Bros.	Detroit, MI
Goin' Sum	J. Dechant	1908	Gearhart & Tilton	Fresno, CA
Going Some	Marcel Francis Dumas	April 2, 1909	Philip Werlein	New Orleans, LA
Going Some	Mabel Harrison		Carl Hoffman Music	Kansas City, MO
Going South	Palmer Jones & Will Riley	November 24, 1914	Jerome H. Remick	New York, NY
Going to Pieces	Karl Kaffer	October 20, 1915	Jerome H. Remick	New York, NY
Gold Bar Rag	Max Morath	October 20, 1964	Hollis Music	New York, NY
Gold Dust Rag	D.M. Headricks	1911	Charles I. Davis	Cleveland, OH
Gold Dust Twins Rag	Nat Johnson	June 20, 1913	Forster Music	Chicago, IL
Golden Gate Rag	F.B. Mueller & A. H. Zeller	October 2, 1913	Emitgar Company	Los Angeles, CA
Golden Smile	Garfield Wilson	May 22, 1912	Will Rossiter	Chicago, IL
Golden Spider	Charles L. Johnson	November 30, 1910	Vandersloot Music	Williamsport, PA
Good and Plenty Rag	Joseph F. Lamb	1964	Mills Music	New York, NY
Good Bye Blues	George L. Cobb	1916	Charles E. Roat Music	Battle Creek, MI
Good Bye Rag	Carleton L. Colby	May 17, 1920	Harold Rossiter	Chicago, IL
Good Gravy Rag	Harry Belding	January 18, 1913	Buck & Lowney	St. Louis, MO
Good Years	Teddie Beth Hardy	October 20, 1964	Hollis Music	New York, NY
Gossipers Rag	Norwood M. Grant	May 16, 1905	Self	Middleport, OH
Grace and Beauty	James Scott	November 12, 1909	Stark Music Company	St. Louis, MO
Grand Concert Rag	E. Philip Severin	February 11, 1918	Self	Moline, IL
Grandpa's Spells	"Jelly Roll" Morton	August 20, 1923	Melrose Brothers	Chicago, IL
Grasshopper Rag	Leon Eleizer	April 28, 1909	Victor Kremer	Chicago, IL
Gravel Rag	Charlotte Blake	December 22, 1908	Jerome H. Remick	New York, NY
Great Morris Rag	Marjorie Burgess	1974	Emerson Music Company	Melrose, MA
Great Scott Rag	James Scott	August 18, 1909	Allen Music	Columbia, MO
Green Mill Rag	Marcella A. Henry	1918	Christensen School	Chicago, IL
Green Rag	Evangeline Green	July 8, 1913	Shapiro Music	New York, NY
Green Rag	Jack Murfree	February 10, 1911	Murfree Music	Boston, MA
Greenwich Witch	Zez Confrey	August 4, 1921	Jack Mills	New York, NY
Grizzly Bear Rag	George Botsford	April 18, 1910	Ted Snyder Company	New York, NY
Growls	Alfred H. Cooper	July 21, 1911	Joseph Krolage Music	Cincinnati, OH

Gum Shoe	E.J. Stark	January 10, 1917	Stark Music Company	St. Louis, MO
Gun–Cotton Rag	Merle Von Hagen	June 7, 1916	Jerome H. Remick	New York, NY
Gunpowder Rag	Roy W. Spangler	February 10, 1910	Joe Morris	Philadelphia, PA
Gypsy Rag	Gypsy Countess Verona	November 24, 1916	T.B. Harms	New York, NY
Halifax Rag	H.D. Carter	March 15, 1910	Cocroft Music	Thomasville, GA
Halley's Comet	Harry J. Lincoln	June 11, 1910	Vandersloot Music	Williamsport, PA
Hallowe'en Rag	Arthur Manlowe	March 6, 1911	Will Rossiter	Chicago, IL
Ham And!	Arthur Marshall	February 24, 1908	Stark Music Company	New York, NY
Ham Bones	Homer Denney	January 30, 1912	Joseph Krolage Music	Cincinnati, OH
Handful of Keys	Thomas "Fats" Waller	December 29, 1930	Southern Music Publishing Company	New York, NY
Hanky Pank	Clifford Adams & Harry G. Robinson	May 4, 1914	M. Witmark & Sons	New York, NY
Happy Dixie Rag	Joe Scott	October 10, 1913	Self	Tuscaloosa, AL
Happy Feelings Rag	Dan Desdumes	May 10, 1912	Self	Omaha, NE
Happy Go Lucky Rag	John M. Fait	July 3, 1918	Pace & Handy	Chicago, IL
Happy Jack	Jack Lampe	1903	Lampe Music Company	Buffalo, NY
Happy Lulu Rag	Alfonso Hart	July 25, 1912	Self	Milwaukee, WI
Happy Rag	R.G. Grady	September 4, 1913	Ajax Music	Chicago, IL
Happy Sammy	Fred C. Schmidt	October 15, 1906	Cable Company	New Orleans, LA
Hard Boiled Rag	Louis Mentel	March 10, 1910	Mentel Brothers	Cincinnati, OH
Hard Knots	Vicory Barker Tunstall	April 23, 1906	Self	Crockett, TX
Hardwood Rag	Jack Sight	May 3, 1909	J.W. Jenkins	Kansas City, MO
Harem Scarem Rag	Lem Trombley	Self		Kalamazoo, MI
Harem Skirt Rag	Harold H. Hampson	1913	Marsh & Needles	Wichita, KS
Harlem Rag	Tom Turpin	December 17, 1897	Robert DeYong	St. Louis, MO
Harlem Rag (arr. #2)	Tom Turpin	March 6, 1899	Robert DeYong	St. Louis, MO
Harlem Rag (arr. #3)	Tom Turpin	1899	Joseph W. Stern	New York, NY
Harlequins' Grand March	Harold Dixon	October 7, 1927	Self	New York, NY
Harmony Rag	Hal G. Nichols	September 25, 1911	Sam Fox	Cleveland, OH
Harpsichord Rag	Buddy Weed	April 13, 1955	Tee Kaye Music	New York, NY
Harriman Cake Walk	Lee S. Roberts	September 17, 1915	Self	Chicago, IL
Harry Fox Trot	Lew Pollack	June 12, 1918	Maurice Richmond	New York, NY
Haunting Rag	Julius Lenzberg	December 4, 1911	M. Witmark & Sons	New York, NY

Havana Rag	Maurice Kirwin	August 22, 1904	John Stark & Son	St. Louis, MO
Haytian Rag	Ford Dabney	October 4, 1910	Jerome H. Remick	Detroit, MI
Hazlesplitter	Charles Pigg	August 11, 1906	Pioneer Music	Chicago, IL
Heavy on the Catsup	Lewis F. Muir	December 26, 1913	F.A. Mills	New York, NY
Heliotrope Bouquet	Louis Chauvin & Scott Joplin	December 23, 1907	Stark Music Company	New York, NY
Heliotrope Rag	Edmund Braham	1906	A.H. Goetting	Springfield, MA
Helter–Skelter Rag	Emma Bila	November 18, 1914	Marks–Goldsmith Company	Washington, DC
Hen Cackle Rag	Charles L. Johnson	January 31, 1912	J.W. Jenkins	Kansas City, MO
Hesitatin' Hez'	Willmont U. Webb	October 27, 1904	Self	Buffalo, NY
Hi-Jinx	Harold Berg & Fred A. Libby	April 8, 1929	Sam Fox	Cleveland, OH
Hi-Yeller	Sal Rugoff & Bernard Schmidt	1918	Richmond Music	New York, NY
Hickory Nuts Rag	Abe Losch	June 4, 1928	Vandersloot Music	Williamsport, PA
Hifalutin Rag	Henry Lodge	March 28, 1918	M. Witmark & Sons	New York, NY
High Hattin'	Zez Confrey	July 16, 1924	Jack Mills	New York, NY
High Jinks	Whidden & Conrad	1910	Leo Feist	New York, NY
High Life Rag	Harry Levinsohn & Robert D. Sharp	1913	Robert D. Sharp Music Company	Denver, CO
High Stepper Rag	Lew Pollack	January 25, 1917	Joe Morris	New York, NY
Hightower Rag	Winnifred Hightower	August 31, 1914	Self	Fort Worth, TX
Hilarity Rag	James Scott	September 15, 1910	Stark Music Company	St. Louis, MO
Hinges	Teddy Hahn	September 16, 1909	Symplex	Cincinnati, OH
Hippocampus Two-Step	Peter Lundberg	October 20, 1964	Hollis Music	New York, NY
Hit or Miss	Buck Wilson	November 17, 1923	Jack Mills	New York, NY
Hobble Rag	Luther B. Hayes	April 22, 1911	Hayes & Mardis	Covington, KY
Hobble Rag	Will Morrissey	April 7, 1911	F.B. Haviland	New York, NY
Hobble Skirt Drag	Sylvester E. George	December 21, 1910	Maurice Shapiro	New York, NY
Hobble Skirt Rag	R. Rembert Goldsby	December 22, 1910	E. Witzmann	Memphis, TN
Holly and Mistletoe Rag	Geraldine Dobyns	1909	Philip Werlein	New Orleans, LA
Holly Rag	Raymond Litzenberger	November 25, 1911	Self	Wilkes-Barre, PA
Hollyhock	Billy Mayerl	December 21, 1927	Sam Fox	Cleveland, OH
Holy Moses Rag	Cy Seymour	April 26, 1906	Arnett–Delonais	Chicago, IL
Holy Smokes	Franz Von Loew	1916	Universal Music	Duluth, MN

Home Spun Rag	Thomas S. Allen	February 14, 1913	Joseph M. Daly	Boston, MA
Homespun Rag	Austin S. Benson	June 2, 1910	Charles K. Harris	New York, NY
Honey Lou–Lu Rag	Charles Johnston	1915	P.J. Howley	New York, NY
Honey Moon Rag	James Scott	August 15, 1916	Stark Music Company	St. Louis, MO
Honey Rag	Egbert Van Alstyne	July 7, 1909	Jerome H. Remick	Detroit, MI
Honeymoon Rag	Lawrence B. O'Connor	July 5, 1910	Ernest S. Williams	Boston, MA
Honeymoon Rag	Abe Olman	November 23, 1908	W.B. Morrison	Indianapolis, IN
Honeysuckle	J. Louis Merkur	December 22, 1927	Jack Mills	New York, NY
Honeysuckle Rag	George Botsford	December 19, 1911	Jerome H. Remick	New York, NY
Hoosier Rag	Sophus Jergensen	October 21, 1905	Abby Music	Indianapolis, IN
Hoosier Rag	Julia Lee Niebergall	November 1, 1907	Jerome H. Remick	New York, NY
Hop Scotch	George L. Cobb	1921	Walter Jacobs	Boston, MA
Horse Laugh	Sam H. Ewing	1909	Self	Cleveland, OH
Horseshoe Rag	Julia Lee Niebergall	April 1, 1911	J.H. Aufderheide	Indianapolis, IN
Hot Air Rag	F.A. Walker	April 27, 1907	Self	Mount Healthy, OH
Hot Air Rag	Thomas V. White	December 24, 1900	M.D. Swisher	Philadelphia, PA
Hot Ashes	Earl K. Smith	October 28, 1909	Levan Music	Chicago, IL
Hot Cabbage	Homer Denney	July 31, 1908	Self	Cincinnati, OH
Hot Chestnuts	George J. Trinkhaus	December 16, 1910	Herald Square Music	New York, NY
Hot Chocolate Rag	Malvin M. Franklin & Arthur Lange	April 6, 1909	Joseph W. Stern	New York, NY
Hot Cinders	Joseph F. Lamb	1964	Mills Music	New York, NY
Hot Fingers	Joe Gold	October 15, 1925	Jack Mills	New York, NY
Hot Fingers	Robert Marine	June 1, 1928	Self	New York, NY
Hot Hands	Charley Straight	February 16, 1916	Jerome H. Remick	New York, NY
Hot House Rag	Paul Pratt	July 27, 1914	Stark Music Company	St. Louis, MO
Hot Ivories	Ray Sinatra	April 11, 1927	Bibo, Bloedon & Lang	New York, NY
Hot Off the Griddle	James White	December 31, 1915	Frank K. Root	Chicago, IL
Hot Rag	S.R. Lewis	March 19, 1900	S. Brainard's Sons	Chicago, IL
Hot Scotch Rag	H.A. Fischler	January 7, 1911	Vandersloot Music	Williamsport, PA
Hot Stuff	D.E. Maharb	August 7, 1911	Backman & Backman	New York, NY
Hot Tamale Man! Rag	Herbert Ingraham	March 5, 1909	Shapiro Music	New York, NY
Hummer Rag	J. Rollie Bibb	July 25, 1917	Warner C. Williams	Indianapolis, IN
Humorestless	Zez Confrey	March 12, 1925	Jack Mills	New York, NY

Humpty Dumpty	Charley Straight	January 13, 1914	M. Witmark & Sons	New York, NY
Humpy's Buck	Charles Humfeld	January 30, 1914	Self	St. Louis, MO
Hungarian Rag	Julius Lenzberg	June 26, 1913	Jerome H. Remick	New York, NY
Huron Glide	W.R. McKanlass	March 25, 1913	McKanlass & Marone	Port Huron, MI
Hurricane Rag	Joe Glover	April 14, 1959	Melrose Music	New York, NY
Hurricane Rag	Frederick G. Johnson	1910	Self	Wilkes-Barre, PA
Hurry a Little	Charles Cooper	1904	H.H. Sparks	Toronto, CN
Hustling Rag	Roy Steventon & Lloyd Kidwell	1914	Great Eastern	Cincinnati, OH
Hutchinson Bro's Rag	William H. Stockwell	August 7, 1911	Hutchinson Bros.	Shreveport, LA
Hyacinth Rag	George Botsford	December 11, 1911	Jerome H. Remick	New York, NY
Hypnotic Rag	Ed C. Mahoney	October 4, 1912	Joseph M. Daly	Boston, MA
Hypnotizer Rag	Clarence H. Graham	September 24, 1910	Maurice Shapiro	New York, NY
Hysterics Rag	Paul Biese & F. Henri Klickmann	December 23, 1914	Jerome H. Remick	New York, NY
I'm Alabama Bound	Robert Hoffman	September 28, 1909	Robert Ebberman	New Orleans, LA
Icycles	James E. Kelly	November 11, 1907	Jerome H. Remick	New York, NY
Idawanna	Newell Chase	May 2, 1929	Sherman, Clay	San Francisco, CA
Igloo Stomp	Bill Wirges	January 26, 1927	Alfred & Company	New York, NY
Imagination	Fud Livingston	October 6, 1927	Robbins Music	New York, NY
Imp Rag	Webb Long	June 21, 1910	Self	Wichita, KS
Imperial Rag	Walter M. Davis	March 15, 1910	Self	Chicago, IL
Imperial Rag	Joseph M. Eshelman	July 29, 1908	Self	Reading, PA
Imperial Rag	Billie Talbot	November 28, 1914	Bush & Gerts	Dallas, TX
In a Mist	Bix Beiderbecke	November 18, 1927	Robbins Music	New York, NY
In Colored Circles	Fred L. Neddermeyer	October 7, 1898	Self	Columbus, OH
In the Groove	Willie the Lion Smith	August 18, 1936	Mills Music	New York, NY
In the Spotlight	Jerry Jarnagin	September 5, 1924	Jack Mills	New York, NY
Incandescent Rag	George Botsford	October 21, 1913	Jerome H. Remick	New York, NY
Inclination Fox-trot	Frank A. Anderson	1916	Louis H. Ross	Boston, MA
India Rubber	Duke Baier	December 12, 1913	Baier & Slagle	Fort Wayne, IN
Ink Splotch Rag	Clifford Adams	1909	A. Hospe Company	Omaha, NE
Innocence	Harry A. Tierney	June 24, 1911	Ted Snyder Company	New York, NY
Intermission Rag	Charles Wellinger	January 6, 1916	Roger Graham	Chicago, IL
Invitation Rag	Les Copeland	December 20, 1911	Jerome H. Remick	Detroit, MI
Iridescence	Phil Saltman	July 12, 1938	Robbins Music	New York, NY

Irish Confetti	George L. Cobb	1918	Walter Jacobs	Boston, MA
Irmena Rag	Axel Christensen	March 9, 1908	Christensen School	Chicago, IL
Irresistible Rag	W.C. Powell	March 14, 1910	Church, Paxson	New York, NY
Ishudworry	Robert Milton Storer	April 22, 1914	Charles Edward Storer	St. Louis, MO
It's a Bird!	Cliff Hess	December 28, 1905	Groene Music	Cincinnati, OH
Ivory Chips	Phil Ohman	October 8, 1929	Robbins Music	New York, NY
Ivory Kapers	Giff Fahrmeyer	November 19, 1929	Vandersloot Music	Williamsport, PA
J.J.J. Rag	Joe Jordan	April 17, 1905	Pekin Publishing	Chicago, IL
Jack Frost	Archie W. Scheu	March 26, 1906	Self	Cincinnati, OH
Jack Frost Rag	William Haskins	November 14, 1928	Denton & Haskins	New York, NY
Jack in the Box	Zez Confrey	December 30, 1927	Jack Mills	New York, NY
Jack Rabbit Rag	H.J. Beckerman	1914	American Music	Chicago, IL
Jack Rabbit Rag	Donald Garcia	January 24, 1910	Vandersloot Music	Williamsport, PA
Jagtime Johnson's Ragtime March	Fred L. Ryder	June 14, 1901	McKinley Music	Chicago, IL
Jamaica Jinger	Egbert Van Alstyne	March 19, 1912	Jerome H. Remick	Detroit, MI
Japanese Rag	Mose Gumble	March 25, 1901	W. H. Willis	Cincinnati, OH
Japanimo	Arthur D. Porter	January 15, 1906	John Arnold	Cincinnati, OH
Jass Band Rag	Frank S. Butler	August 1, 1917	Self	New York, NY
Jaxon Rag	Edward G. Byers & Lucius C. Dunn	February 24, 1908	Victor Kremer	Chicago, IL
Jay Roberts Rag	Jay Roberts	December 16, 1911	Forster Music	Chicago, IL
Jay Walk	Zez Confrey	February 12, 1927	Jack Mills	New York, NY
Jazz Master	Billy Mayerl	August 4, 1925	Sam Fox	Cleveland, OH
Jazz Mistress	Billy Mayerl	September 25, 1925	Sam Fox	Cleveland, OH
Jazzaristrix	Billy Mayerl	November 4, 1925	Sam Fox	Cleveland, OH
Jerusha Pepper	Jay G. Coffman	March 26, 1908	Victor Kremer	Chicago, IL
Jes' Dandy	Joe Solman	March 5, 1923	Jack Mills	New York, NY
Jester Rag	W.R. McKanlass	1917	Buck & Lowney	St. Louis, MO
Jim Crow Rag	Lizzie Mowen	January 3, 1910	C.C. Powell	Fort Wayne, IN
Jim Jams	Roy Bargy	June 27, 1922	Sam Fox	Cleveland, OH
Jingles	James P. Johnson	July 1, 1926	Clarence Williams Music	New York, NY
Jingo	Edwin Gale	1907	W.H. Croner	Columbus, OH
Jinx Rag	Lucian P. Gibson & Jesse Dukes	December 7, 1911	Lucian P. Gibson	St. Louis, MO
Jitney Bus Rag	Grover Thompson	September 1, 1915	Marks–Goldsmith Company	Washington, DC

Johnny-Jump-Ups	Sydney S. Barker	February 20, 1905	Sherman, Clay	San Francisco, CA
Johnson Rag	Guy Hall & Henry Kleinkauf	February 28, 1917	Self	Wilkes-Barre, PA
Jolly Jingles Rag	F.H. Losey	September 24, 1913	Vandersloot Music	Williamsport, PA
Joy Boy	A.J. Weidt	1916	Walter Jacobs	Boston, MA
Joy Rag	Jay Roberts	December 15, 1911	Forster Music	Chicago, IL
Juggling the Piano	Sam A. Perry	December 1, 1924	Jack Mills	New York, NY
Jumping Jack	Rube Bloom & Bernie Seaman	July 3, 1928	ABC Standard	New York, NY
Jumping Jack	Chet Ferguson	1917	Daniels & Wilson	San Francisco, CA
Jungle Time	E. Philip Severin	February 23, 1905	Self	Moline, IL
Junk Man Rag	C. Luckeyth Roberts	May 26, 1913	Joseph W. Stern	New York, NY
Just a Li'l Rag	Urban A. Schick	November 20, 1915	Shattinger Music	St. Louis, MO
Just Ask Me	Charles Hunter	April 5, 1902	Frank G. Fite	Nashville, TN
Just Missed	Clarence W. Murphey	September 4, 1912	Self	St. Louis, MO
Just Noise	C.I. Stewart	June 4, 1906	Southwestern Music	Tulsa, OK
Justin-Tyme	Roy Bargy	June 27, 1922	Sam Fox	Cleveland, OH
Kaiser's Rag	Clare Mast	1915	Self	Edgerton, OH
Kalamity Kid	Ferd Guttenberger	1909	Self	Macon, GA
Kangaroo Hop	Melville Morris	November 24, 1915	Jerome H. Remick	New York, NY
Kansas Appleknocker Rag	Frank Frank	August 16, 1909	F.B. Haviland	New York, NY
Kansas City Rag	James Scott	January 2, 1907	Stark Music Company	St. Louis, MO
Kansas City Stomp	"Jelly Roll" Morton	August 20, 1923	Melrose Brothers	Chicago, IL
Kautious Kittens	Silvio DeRienzo	May 26, 1930	Alfred & Company	New York, NY
Kee to Kee	Ted Eastwood & Eugene Platzmann	September 28, 1917	Artmusic	New York, NY
Keek-Es-Man-Dah!	C. Bellstedt	1906	Ilsen & Company	Cincinnati, OH
Keep a-Movin'	Al Sweet	May 2, 1910	Ted Snyder Company	New York, NY
Keep Busy	Hardaway Fraser	July 2, 1912	Globe Music	New York, NY
Keep Fingering	Willie the Lion Smith	March 11, 1938	Mills Music	New York, NY
Keep Off the Grass	James P. Johnson	July 1, 1926	Clarence Williams Music	New York, NY
Keep Your Temper	Willie the Lion Smith	September 19, 1925	Clarence Williams Music	New York, NY
Kehama Rag	Emma A. Bouska	March 12, 1909	Victor Kremer	Chicago, IL
Kentucky Beauty	Albert Gumble & Monroe H. Rosenfeld	February 20, 1904	Joseph W. Stern	New York, NY

Kentucky Rag	Marcella A. Henry	July 1, 1917	Christensen School	Chicago, IL
Kentucky Rag	John H. Tenney	May 8, 1905	Joseph Placht & Son	St. Louis, MO
Kentucky Rag	Floyd Willis	September 30, 1908	Self	Covington, KY
Kerry Mills' Ragtime Dance	Kerry Mills	February 8, 1909	F.A. Mills	New York, NY
Ketchup Rag	Irene M. Giblin	March 5, 1910	Jerome H. Remick	New York, NY
Kewpie	Gene Rose	April 4, 1929	Sherman, Clay	San Francisco, CA
Key Stone Rag	Willie Anderson	1921	Stark Music Company	St. Louis, MO
Keyboard Kapers	Hunter L. Kahler	July 2, 1934	M.M. Cole	Chicago, IL
Keyboard Klassic	Robert Marine	June 1, 1928	Self	New York, NY
Keyboard Konversation	Vee Lawnhurst	April 9, 1923	Jack Mills	New York, NY
Kimberly Rag	H.H. Hoyt, Jr.	November 5, 1909	Victor Kremer	Chicago, IL
Kinda Careless	Zez Confrey	July 16, 1924	Jack Mills	New York, NY
King Baggot's Rag	G.W. Lowe	February 19, 1914	Self	Columbia, KY
King of Rags	Bob Haney	1900	Self	Keokuk, IA
King of Rags	Sherman Swisher	1908	Self	Philadelphia, PA
King of Them All	William Murray Simpson	November 20, 1909	McKinley Music	Chicago, IL
King Porter Stomp	"Jelly Roll" Morton	December 6, 1924	Melrose Brothers	Chicago, IL
Kinklets	Arthur Marshall	December 10, 1906	Stark Music Company	New York, NY
Kinky	Carrie E. Zeman	November 5, 1906	Andreas Music	Davenport, IA
Kinky Head	George E. Rausch	1910	Self	Omaha, NE
Kinky Kinks	Louis K. Carroll	1907	Self	Manchester, OH
Kismet Rag	Scott Joplin & Scott Hayden	February 21, 1913	Stark Music Company	St. Louis, MO
Kissing Bug Rag	Charles L. Johnson	1909	Keith Music	Louisville, KY
Kitchen Tom	Eubie Blake	1975	Eubie Blake Music	New York, NY
Kitten on the Keys	Zez Confrey	July 8, 1921	Jack Mills	New York, NY
Kitty Wobble	Waylande Gregory	1920	Self	Pittsburg, KS
Klassicle Rag	Cecil Duane Crabb	April 10, 1911	J.H. Aufderheide	Indianapolis, IN
Klinkers	Albert Stedman	1906	Empire Music	Boston, MA
Klondike Rag	George Botsford	January 23, 1908	William R. Haskins Company	New York, NY
Klu-Lukum Rag	Claude P. Christopher & Carl T. Williams	1909	Lew Roberts Music	Nashville, TN
Knice and Knifty	Roy Bargy & Charley Straight	February 7, 1922	Sam Fox	Cleveland, OH
Knick Knocks	Phil Schwartz	March 29, 1915	Sam Fox	Cleveland, OH

Knockout Drops	F. Henri Klickmann	December 8, 1910	Victor Kremer	Chicago, IL
Krazy Kat	Ben Ritchie	November 6, 1911	Self	New York, NY
Lace Embroidery	Bob Zurke	April 10, 1939	Leo Feist	New York, NY
Lady Slippers Rag	Raymond Birch	May 26, 1910	Charles L. Johnson	Kansas City, MO
Lagoon Breeze	Louis Mentel	September 28, 1903	Mentel Brothers	Cincinnati, OH
Lagoon Rag	Louis Mentel	August 5, 1907	Mentel Brothers	Covington, KY
Lakeside Whistle Rag	Carl H. Copenhaver	June 4, 1912	Frank Harding	New York, NY
Lasses	Lucy Thomas	December 28, 1905	Groene Music	Cincinnati, OH
Last Rag	William Bolcom	December 30, 1976	Edward B. Marks Music	New York, NY
Latonia Rag	Leon Donaldson	July 23, 1903	American Music	St. Louis, MO
Laughing at the Ivories	Theo Uden Masman	February 15, 1926	Jack Mills	New York, NY
Laughing Dick Rag	Riffe H. Smith	1908	Louis Grunewald	New Orleans, LA
Laurette	Frank Banta	March 4, 1929	Robbins Music	New York, NY
Lauterbach	Ernest A. Ittner	November 24, 1906	Victor Kremer	Chicago, IL
Lawn Eyrie Rag	Jesse Rehkopf	1905	Pioneer Music	Chicago, IL
Lazy Luke	George J. Philpot	December 10, 1904	Walter Jacobs	Boston, MA
Leap Frog	Edwin F. Kendall	July 2, 1908	Jerome H. Remick	New York, NY
Lemon Drops	Mike Bernard	December 31, 1910	Joe Morris	New York, NY
Lemons	Ollie McHugh	October 28, 1907	H.A. Sturm Music	Cincinnati, OH
Lemons and Limes	Cora Salisbury	November 1, 1909	Will Rossiter	Chicago, IL
Leola	Scott Joplin	1905	American Music	St. Louis, MO
Leona Rag	Leona Coker	April 19, 1906	Self	St. Joseph, MO
Let's Go	Charley Straight	December 30, 1915	Jerome H. Remick	New York, NY
Levee Rag	Fred E. Gates	December 7, 1914	Gates & Jacobson	Cincinnati, OH
Levee Rag	Charles E. Mullen	September 29, 1902	Will Rossiter	Chicago, IL
Lightning	Clarence Jones	December 26, 1908	Groene Music	Cincinnati, OH
Lily Queen	Arthur Marshall & Scott Joplin	November 8, 1907	Willis Woodward	New York, NY
Lily Rag	Charles Thompson	1914	Syndicate Music	St. Louis, MO
Lion Tamer Rag	Mark Janza	January 2, 1913	A.F. Marzian	Louisville, KY
Lip-Stick	Ted Murray & Charles Rosoff	February 4, 1928	Harms, Inc.	New York, NY
Little Bit o' Honey	E. Clinton Keithley	March 15, 1909	Keith Music	Louisville, KY
Little Jack's Rag	Arthur Marshall	October 29, 1976	Hawthorne Books	New York, NY
Little Rock Getaway	Joe Sullivan	April 1, 1938	Leo Feist	New York, NY
Little Sticks o' Licorice	Ray Ruddy	December 29, 1911	Jerome H. Remick	New York, NY

Live Wires Rag	Adaline Shepherd	November 16, 1910	Harold Rossiter	Chicago, IL
Log Cabin Rag	Ferd Guttenberger	1908	Self	Macon, GA
Log Cabin Rag	James R. Shannon	November 9, 1914	Forster Music	Chicago, IL
London Rag	David A. Jasen	June 28, 1979	The Big Three	New York, NY
Long Island Rag	Ida B. Robinson	February 13, 1912	Self	Bellport, NY
Loose Elbows	Billy Mayerl	March 9, 1926	Sam Fox	Cleveland, OH
Loose Fingers	Maurice E. Swerdlow	May 31, 1923	Sam Fox	Cleveland, OH
Lopez Rag	J.R. Lopez	August 31, 1918	Self	Memphis, MO
Lopez Speaking	Harry Jentes	August 27, 1926	Robbins–Engel	New York, NY
Lopeziana	Louis Alter	August 9, 1926	Robbins–Engel	New York, NY
Lost Rag	Herbert Ingraham	March 5, 1909	Shapiro Music	New York, NY
Lotta Trix	Robert Marine	June 1, 1928	Self	New York, NY
Lotus Club Rag	Ernie Burnett	September 24, 1919	Keystone Music	St. Joseph, MO
Louisiana Rag	Leon Block	February 6, 1911	Will Rossiter	Chicago, IL
Louisiana Rag	Theo. H. Northrup	October 20, 1897	Thompson Music	Chicago, IL
Louisiana Rag	Harry A. Tierney	May 3, 1913	Joseph Krolage Music	Cincinnati, OH
Louisiana Rag	Edward R. Wagner	May 5, 1908	Treece & Bowen	Herrin, IL
Lover's Lane Glide	Calvin Lee Woolsey	October 5, 1914	Self	St. Joseph, MO
Lovey–Dovey	George Botsford	May 19, 1910	Ted Snyder Company	New York, NY
Lovey–Dovey	Charles L. Johnson	1907	Charles L. Johnson	Kansas City, MO
Lucky Dog	Herbert Bryan Marple	January 15, 1917	Sherman, Clay	San Francisco, CA
Lucky Lou	Frank C. Keithley	1906	Keithley–Joy Music	Des Moines, IA
Lusitania Rag	Edward R. Wagner	May 5, 1908	Treece & Bowen	Herrin, IL
Mad Fingers	Billy James	April 24, 1930	Mills Music	New York, NY
Madagascar Mangle	Vinton Freedley	February 3, 1912	Jerome H. Remick	New York, NY
Made in Germany	Karl Schmidt	1906	Frank K. Root	Chicago, IL
Magnetic Rag	Scott Joplin	July 21, 1914	Self	New York, NY
Magpie Rag	Malvin M. Franklin	December 15, 1908	Joseph W. Stern	New York, NY
Mah Jong	Sid Reinherz	March 5, 1924	Jack Mills	New York, NY
Majestic Rag	Ben Rawls & Royal Neel	May 14, 1914	Bush & Gerts	Dallas, TX
Make Believe Rag	David A. Jasen	June 28, 1979	The Big Three	New York, NY
Mando Rag	Robert George Ingraham	July 10, 1914	Stark Music Company	St. Louis, MO
Mandy's Broadway Stroll	Thomas E. Broady	1898	Henry A. French	Nashville, TN

Manhattan Rag	Fred Brownold	December 28, 1901	John Stark & Son	St. Louis, MO
Manhattan Rag	Edwin F. Kendall	August 23, 1906	Joseph W. Stern	New York, NY
Manhattan Rag	Frank Signorelli & Deane Kincaide	July 3, 1963	Bregman, Vocco & Conn	New York, NY
Manilla Rag	Gregorio Domingo	March 14, 1916	Self	Liberal, KS
Manilla Rag	Zellah Edith Sanders	1898	Lyon & Healy	Chicago, IL
Maple Leaf Rag	Scott Joplin	September 18, 1899	John Stark & Son	Sedalia, MO
Marathon Rag	Whitney Combes	February 26, 1909	Nightingale Music	New York, NY
Mardi Gras Rag	George Lyons & Bob Yosco	February 24, 1914	George W. Meyer Music	New York, NY
Marigold	Billy Mayerl	June 18, 1928	Sam Fox	Cleveland, OH
Marilynn	Wheeler Wadsworth & Victor Arden	1919	Forster Music	Chicago, IL
Marine Syncopations	Robert Marine	June 1, 1928	Self	New York, NY
Marita	Bill Krenz	December 14, 1934	M.M. Cole	Chicago, IL
Mary Jane Rag	Robert Klock	1909	Philip Werlein	New Orleans, LA
Mashed Potatoes	Calvin Lee Woolsey	August 12, 1911	Self	Braymer, MO
Mattie's Rags	Mattie C. Thompson	April 22, 1916	Self	Little Rock, AR
Maurice Rag	William H. Penn	April 16, 1912	Self	New York, NY
May Bloom Rag	Ramond Henry Willis	March 4, 1904	Self	Boulder, CO
Meadow Lark Rag	Tom Pitts	1916	Charles N. Daniels Music	San Francisco, CA
Meadow Lark Rag	Jean Rameau	May 10, 1910	Self	Butte, MT
Measles Rag	Arthur H. Nokes	1913	H. Kirkus Dugdale	Washington, DC
Meddlesome	Clarence H. St. John	October 8, 1908	Stark Music Company	New York, NY
Medic Rag	Calvin Lee Woolsey	April 13, 1910	Jerome H. Remick	New York, NY
Medical Rag	Lucas & Phelps	1912	Broadway Music	New York, NY
Meditation	Lee Sims	1927	Robbins	New York, NY
Meer-Sham Rag	Cliff Irvin	January 30, 1914	H. Kirkus Dugdale	Washington, DC
Melancholy Charlie	Frank Crum	March 9, 1927	Robbins Music	New York, NY
Melody Man	Charles Gillen	December 28, 1910	Theodore Morse Music	New York, NY
Melody Rag	Raymond Birch	January 3, 1911	Charles L. Johnson	Kansas City, MO
Melrose Rag	Hubert Bauersachs	December 29, 1921	Self	St. Louis, MO
Memphis Rag	Percy Wenrich	September 14, 1908	McKinley Music	Chicago, IL
Mephisto Rag	S.C. Baumann			New Orleans, LA
Mephisto Rag	Anthony J. Stasny	August 20, 1908	Self	Cleveland, OH

Merry Minnow	Pauline Alpert	November 29, 1935	Mills Music	New York, NY
Merry Widow Glad Rag	Victor Maurice	1908	Metropolitan Music	New York, NY
Merry Widow Rag	E. Clinton Keithley	March 5, 1908	Keith Music	Louisville, KY
Merry-Go-Round Rag	Gus Edwards	November 11, 1908	Self	New York, NY
Merry-Go-Round Rag	Ralph Larsh	January 8, 1918	Self	Chicago, IL
Meteor Rag	Arthur C. Morse	1920	Walter Jacobs	Boston, MA
Metropolitan Rag	Anna Case	March 21, 1917	T.W. Allen	Newark, NJ
Metropolitan Rag	A.R. Langermann & F.C. Humsinger	July 30, 1912	Langermann & Humsinger	New Orleans, LA
Mew Mew Rag	H. Taylor Weeks	December 17, 1910	Ted Snyder Company	New York, NY
Michigan Rag	Adrian Carter	May 28, 1910	Self	Battle Creek, MI
Microbe	Webb Long	April 22, 1909	Marsh & Needles	Wichita, KS
Midnight Rag	Gus Winkler	June 17, 1912	Forster Music	Chicago, IL
Midnight Trot	George L. Cobb	April 5, 1916	Will Rossiter	Chicago, IL
Midnight Whirl Rag	Silvio Hein	January 26, 1914	T.B. Harms	New York, NY
Milkman's Rag	Shep Camp	April 28, 1913	F.B. Haviland	New York, NY
Minnesota Rag	Axel Christensen	July 10, 1913	Christensen School	Chicago, IL
Minnesota Street Rag	Fred Swanson	November 5, 1903	Self	St. Paul, MN
Minstrel Band Rag	Albert Gumble	April 30, 1909	Jerome H. Remick	New York, NY
Minstrel Man	J. Russel Robinson	July 27, 1911	Stark Music Company	St. Louis, MO
Miserable Rag	Malvin M. Franklin	June 19, 1915	Waterson, Berlin & Snyder	New York, NY
Misery Blues	Henry Lodge	May 1, 1918	M. Witmark & Sons	New York, NY
Miss Molly	Hirshfield & Levy	1903	Fred J. Hamill	Chicago, IL
Mississauga Rag	Austin E. Kitchen	December 6, 1974	Eldorado Music	Mississauga, CN
Mississippi Rag	Alfred Gasdorf	1914	Great Eastern	Cincinnati, OH
Mississippi Shivers	Zez Confrey	July 16, 1924	Jack Mills	New York, NY
Mississippi Smilax	H. Harry Landrum	1907	J.W. Jenkins	Kansas City, MO
Mississippi Teaser	Hugh Canon	February 27, 1911	O.K. Houck	Memphis, TN
Missouri Maze	Ulysses E. Cross	March 21, 1913	E.W. Berry Music	Kansas City, MO
Missouri Rag	Maie Fitzgerald	December 20, 1900	A.W. Perry & Sons	Sedalia, MO
Missouri Rag	W.C. Powell	November 8, 1907	Joe Morris	Philadelphia, PA
Missouri Rag	David Silverman & Arthur Ward	March 10, 1919	Weile Publishing	St. Louis, MO
Missouri Romp	Arthur Marshall	June 27, 1966	Oak Publishing	New York, NY
Mister Buzz Saw	Jean Kastowsky	March 17, 1916	C.L. Barnhouse	Oskaloosa, IA

Modernesque	Charles E. Wilkinson	April 10, 1930	Rubank	Chicago, IL
Modernistic	James P. Johnson	November 3, 1933	Clarence Williams Music	New York, NY
Modesty Rag	James Scott	September 15, 1920	Stark Music Company	St. Louis, MO
Modulations	Clarence Jones	April 17, 1923	Will Rossiter	Chicago, IL
Molly Coddle Rag	Julius De Van	1907	George H. Remington	Cincinnati, OH
Monkey Motion Rag	O.E. Keenan	July 17, 1911	W.H. Willis	Cincinnati, OH
Monkey Rag	Wheatley Davis	April 17, 1911	O.K. Houck	Memphis, TN
Monograms	Homer Denney	1911	Self	Cincinnati, OH
Monumental Echos	F.G. Howland	1900	Self	Schuyleville, NY
Moonlight Rag	Henry Lodge	May 5, 1913	M. Witmark & Sons	New York, NY
Moonshine Rag	Edward Hudson	May 10, 1916	Stark Music Company	St. Louis, MO
Moose Rag	Ted Johnson	March 7, 1910	Brehm Brothers	Erie, PA
Mop Rag	Merton T. Buckley	January 25, 1912	Self	Wichita, KS
Mop Rag	Helen S. Eaton	October 20, 1909	Jerome H. Remick	Detroit, MI
More Noise Rag	Louis Mentel	May 12, 1909	Mentel Brothers	Cincinnati, OH
Mosquito Bites	Edwin F. Kendall	July 13, 1907	Seminary Music	New York, NY
Motor Boat Rag	Henry W. Gaul	November 9, 1911	Tropwen Music	Newport, KY
Motor Bus	Annie Houston	1914	Bush & Gerts	Dallas, TX
Mouse's Hoofs	Zez Confrey	December 9, 1935	Exclusive Publications	New York, NY
Mousie in the Piano	Joe Keden	October 29, 1928	Al Piantadosi	New York, NY
Moustache Johnson	Dora Loucks Hillman	March 24, 1909	Webb Rockefeller Miller	Chicago, IL
Movie Rag	John S. Zamecnik	August 6, 1913	Sam Fox	Cleveland, OH
Moving Rag	Earl E. Edmonds	February 13, 1912	Joseph Krolage Music	Cincinnati, OH
Mud Cat Rag	Bill Krenz	November 24, 1953	Mills Music	New York, NY
Munki Doodle Dum	Chester A. Freeman	April 10, 1903	B.J. Tiemann	New York, NY
Musette	Ferde Grofe	July 25, 1928	Robbins Music	New York, NY
Music Box Rag	C. Luckeyth Roberts	October 23, 1914	Joseph W. Stern	New York, NY
Musical Zig Zags	O.J. Goehmer	July 24, 1905	Thiebes–Stierlin Music Company	St. Louis, MO
Muslin Rag	Mel B. Kaufman	December 16, 1918	Forster Music	Chicago, IL
Mutilaton Rag	Zema Randale	July 31, 1915	Cable Company	Chicago, IL
Mutt and Jeff Rag	Phillip E. Eubank	January 12, 1912	Self	Tahlequah, OK
Mutt and Jeff Rag	M.C. Rowe & William Arthurs	1911	Gotham–Attucks Music	New York, NY
My Aeroplane Jane	G L. Trombley	1911	Self	Kalamazoo, MI

My Favorite Rag	James White	September 20, 1915	Roger Graham	Chicago, IL
My Pet	Zez Confrey	March 11, 1921	Jack Mills	New York, NY
My Rag	Amerigo V. Bafunno	June 28, 1907	Bafunno Bros. Music	St. Louis, MO
Naked Dance	"Jelly Roll" Morton	1950	Tempo Music	Washington, DC
Nanette	Adam Carroll	July 14, 1927	Robbins Music	New York, NY
Nappy Lee	Joe Jordan	December 15, 1903	James E. Agnew	Des Moines, IA
Nat Johnson's Rag	Nat Johnson	December 16, 1911	Forster Music	Chicago, IL
National Colors Rag	Marcella A. Henry	June 1, 1917	Christensen School	Chicago, IL
Natural Gas Rag	Oscar F. Hanna	June 14, 1910	Self	Lexington, KY
Naughty Naurette	Lew Pollack	September 15, 1927	Jack Mills	New York, NY
Nautical Nonsense	George L. Cobb	1917	Walter Jacobs	Boston, MA
Navy Blue Rag	Leo Piersanti	1919	National Music	Chicago, IL
Nervous Nuckles	Norman J. Elholm	December 7, 1923	Jack Mills	New York, NY
Nervous Rag	Bernard E. Fay & Blackford	June 20, 1910	Jerome H. Remick	Detroit, MI
Nervy George	Viola Dominique	May 13, 1903	Self	New Orleans, LA
Neutrality Rag	W.F. Lewinski	1915		
New Black Eagle Buck	Max Morath	December 30, 1976	Edward B. Marks Music	New York, NY
New Dixie Rag	Thomas M. Byrne	December 24, 1910	Self	Fort Worth, TX
New Era Rag	James Scott	June 1, 1919	Stark Music Company	St. Louis, MO
New Hippodrome	Herman E. Schultz	September 1, 1914	Jerome H. Remick	New York, NY
New Orleans Buck	A.C. Bernard	1904	Hakenjos	New Orleans, LA
New Orleans Rag	Castro Carazo	1960	Mills	New York, NY
New Russian Rag	George L. Cobb	May 16, 1923	Will Rossiter	Chicago, IL
New Standard Rag	Elliot L. Adams	1974	Paragon Sheet Music	Lodi, CA
New York Rag	George C. Durgan	August 1, 1910	Union Music Company	Boston, MA
News Rag	Glenn C. Leap	1910	Swibar Publishing	Indianapolis, IN
Niagara Rag	Laverne Hanshaw	October 3, 1914	Bush & Gerts	Dallas, TX
Nice and Easy	Cliff McKay	October 17, 1916	Jerome H. Remick	New York, NY
Nicest, Sweetest, Cutest Rag	Herbert Ingraham	March 5, 1909	Shapiro Music	New York, NY
Nickel in the Slot	Zez Confrey	April 6, 1923	Leo Feist	New York, NY
Nickelodeon Rag	Ada M. Burnett	April 3, 1909	Alf E. Burnett & Company	Cincinnati, OH
Nigger-Toe Rag	H.A. Fischler	April 20, 1910	Vandersloot Music	Williamsport, PA

Nightingale Rag	Lester Sill	January 19, 1914	Warner C. Williams	Indianapolis, IN
Nitric-Acid Rag	Edward Hudson	January 3, 1922	Stark Music Company	St. Louis, MO
No-Ze	Homer Denney	February 7, 1905	Self	Cincinnati, OH
Nobody's Business	Axel Christensen	July 11, 1923	Forster Music	Chicago, IL
Nobody's Rag	David A. Jasen	June 28, 1979	The Big Three	New York, NY
Noisy Notes Rag	Ralph Wray	March 1, 1915	Mellinger Music	St. Louis, MO
Nonette Rag	Herbert Spencer	August 16, 1912	Will Rossiter	Chicago, IL
Nonpareil	Scott Joplin	1907	Stark Music Company	St. Louis, MO
Nonsense Rag	R.G. Grady	January 14, 1911	Joseph W. Stern	New York, NY
Noodles	Percy Wenrich	August 21, 1906	Arnett–Delonais	Chicago, IL
Noodlin'	Tom Griselle	May 30, 1923	Richmond–Robbins	New York, NY
North Pole Rag	John Lind	October 14, 1909	Self	Cincinnati, OH
North Pole Rag	Samuel J. Stokes	1909	Louis Grunewald	New Orleans, LA
Nothing Doin' Rag	Frances Willard Neal	November 4, 1914	Bush & Gerts	Dallas, TX
Notoriety	Kathryn L. Widmer	July 31, 1913	Jerome H. Remick	New York, NY
Novelty Rag	May Aufderheide	April 11, 1911	J.H. Aufderheide	Indianapolis, IN
Nuckels O'Tool Woulds't Ride Again	Claude Bolling	1970	Famous Music	New York, NY
Oak Leaf Rag	Arthur L. Sizemore	May 10, 1911	Self	Mankato, MN
Octagon Rag	Horace Dowell	January 5, 1903	Alcorn & Hutsell	Nashville, TN
Octave Rag	Frank Weeks	March 20, 1917	Self	Osborne, KS
Octopus Rag	John Oliver Erlan	January 14, 1907	Darrow & Quadland	Chicago, IL
Off the Elbow	Joe Keden	September 5, 1929	Al Piantadosi	New York, NY
Oh You Angel	Ford Dabney	January 4, 1911	Maurice Shapiro	New York, NY
Oh You Rag	Josephine Becker	1909	Emerson Music	Cincinnati, OH
Oh You Sally Rag	Clarence Jones	April 29, 1911	John Arnold	Cincinnati, OH
Oh You Tigers	Anna deVarennes	1909	Self	Bay City, MI
Oh You Turkey	Henry Lodge	January 20, 1914	Waterson, Berlin & Snyder	New York, NY
Oh! Willie, Play That Thing	Bill Krenz	May 23, 1952	Mills Music	New York, NY
Oh! You Darkeys	Henry Lange	May 4, 1923	Waterson, Berlin & Snyder	New York, NY
Oh! You Devil	Ford Dabney	July 2, 1909	Maurice Shapiro	New York, NY
Oh! You Rag	Sydney Chapman	April 16, 1910	Koninsky Music	Troy, NY
Okisko Rag	Harry S.G. Stoudt	September 18, 1915	Self	Medina, OH
Old Carpet Rag	Jennie Aaron	February 2, 1911	Tolbert R. Ingram Music	Denver, CO

Old Crow Rag	George Botsford	April 13, 1909	Jerome H. Remick	New York, NY
Old Folks Rag	Wilbur Sweatman	April 14, 1914	Joseph W. Stern	New York, NY
Old Home Rag	Joseph F. Lamb	1964	Mills Music	New York, NY
Old Kentuck	Frank Schmuhl	October 3, 1898	W.J. Dyer & Bro.	St. Paul, MN
Old Professor	Dick Hyman	April 18, 1955	Hollis Music	New York, NY
Old Tom-Cat on the Keys	Bob Zurke	November 4, 1940	Leo Feist	New York, NY
Old Virginia Rag	Clyde Douglass	December 19, 1907	W.C. Parker	New York, NY
Olga	Chas. F. Gall	July 14, 1913	Joseph W. Stern	New York, NY
On the Bayou	Theo. H. Northrup	September 2, 1898	American Musical Assn.	Chicago, IL
On the Pike	James Scott	April 13, 1904	Dumars Music	Carthage, MO
On the Riviera	Alfred J. Doyle	June 24, 1911	Ted Snyder Company	New York, NY
On the Rural Route	Paul Pratt	May 10, 1917	Stark Music Company	St. Louis, MO
One Finger Joe	Rube Bloom	May 15, 1931	Robbins Music	New York, NY
One for Amelia	Max Morath	October 20, 1964	Hollis Music	New York, NY
One More Rag	Minnie Berger	1909	Stark Music Company	St. Louis, MO
One o' Them Things!	James Chapman & Leroy Smith	1904	Joseph Placht & Son	St. Louis, MO
Opalescent Rag	Opal A. Allyn	Self		Modesto, IL
Opera House Rag	Robert R. Darch	August 19, 1960	The Ragtime Music	Virginia City, NV
Opera Rags	E. Chouteau Legg	May 13, 1903	J.W. Jenkins	Kansas City, MO
Operatic Nightmare	Felix Arndt	August 2, 1916	Sam Fox	Cleveland, OH
Operatic Rag	Julius Lenzberg	October 27, 1914	Jerome H. Remick	New York, NY
Ophelia Rag	James Scott	June 6, 1910	Stark Music Company	St. Louis, MO
Orange Leaf Rag	Strauss L. Lloyd	February 5, 1908	Self	Inverness, FL
Oriental Blues	Jack Newlon	May 25, 1933	Self	Glenside, PA
Original Blues	Ted S. Barron	May 11, 1914	Metropolitan Music	New York, NY
Original Chicago Blues	James White	March 8, 1915	Frank K. Root	Chicago, IL
Original Rags	Scott Joplin	March 15, 1899	Carl Hoffman Music	Kansas City, MO
Originola	Hunter L. Kahler	July 2, 1934	M.M. Cole	Chicago, IL
Orinoco	Cecil Duane Crabb	March 5, 1909	J.H. Aufderheide	Indianapolis, IN
Ottawa Rag	George E. Lynn	1913	Northern Music	
Out of the South	Willard Robison	April 21, 1926	Robbins–Engel	New York, NY
Over and Under	Arnold Johnson	April 7, 1923	Jack Mills	New York, NY
Over the Bars	James P. Johnson	February 15, 1939	Clarence Williams Music	New York, NY

Over the Ice	Bill Wirges	January 26, 1927	Alfred & Company	New York, NY
Oyster Rag	Tom Lyle	May 9, 1910	Jerome H. Remick	New York, NY
Pacific Rag	James Watson	June 2, 1913	Self	Vancouver, CN
Page Mr. Pianist	Henry Lange	April 7, 1923	Jack Mills	New York, NY
Palm Beach	C. Luckeyth Roberts	October 23, 1914	Joseph W. Stern	New York, NY
Palm Leaf Rag	Scott Joplin	November 14, 1903	Victor Kremer	Chicago, IL
Pan-Am Rag	Tom Turpin	1966	Oak Publishing	New York, NY
Panama Rag	Cy Seymour	August 15, 1904	Albright Music	Chicago, IL
Pansy Blossoms	Charles L. Johnson	June 28, 1909	American Music	Chicago, IL
Paragon Rag	Scott Joplin	October 30, 1909	Seminary Music	New York, NY
Paramount Rag	Harry Baisden	June 26, 1915	Self	Fort Dodge, IA
Paramount Rag	James Scott	November 24, 1917	Stark Music Company	St. Louis, MO
Pastime Rag	Henry Lodge	April 28, 1913	M. Witmark & Sons	New York, NY
Pastime Rag No. 1	Artie Matthews	August 15, 1913	Stark Music Company	St. Louis, MO
Pastime Rag No. 2	Artie Matthews	1913	Stark Music Company	St. Louis, MO
Pastime Rag No. 3	Artie Matthews	1916	Stark Music Company	St. Louis, MO
Pastime Rag No. 4	Artie Matthews	September 15, 1920	Stark Music Company	St. Louis, MO
Pastime Rag No. 5	Artie Matthews	1918	Stark Music Company	St. Louis, MO
Pathetic Rag	Axel Christensen	1913	Christensen School	Chicago, IL
Patricia Rag	Joseph F. Lamb	November 19, 1916	Stark Music Company	St. Louis, MO
Patsy	Sam A. Perry	November 12, 1925	Robbins Music	New York, NY
Patsy Lou	Muriel Pollock	August 19, 1935	Joe Davis	New York, NY
Peace and Plenty	James Scott	December 1, 1919	Stark Music Company	St. Louis, MO
Peaceful Henry	E. Harry Kelly	1901	Carl Hoffman Music	Kansas City, MO
Peach	Arthur Marshall	December 7, 1908	Stark Music Company	New York, NY
Peach Blossoms	Maude Gilmore	1910	Charles L. Johnson	Kansas City, MO
Peacherine Rag	Scott Joplin	March 18, 1901	John Stark & Son	St. Louis, MO
Peaches and Cream	Percy Wenrich	November 27, 1905	Jerome H. Remick	New York, NY
Peachtree Street Rag	John Chagy	1977	Kjos West	San Diego, CA
Peanuts	Ethel Earnist	July 20, 1911	Charles L. Johnson	Kansas City, MO
Pear Blossoms	Scott Hayden	1966	Oak Publishing	New York, NY
Pearl of the Harem	Harry P. Guy	April 19, 1901	Willard Bryant	Detroit, MI
Pearl's Rag	William E. Pearl & W.H. Bell	January 10, 1914	H. Kirkus Dugdale	Washington, DC
Pearls	"Jelly Roll" Morton	August 20, 1923	Melrose Brothers	Chicago, IL

Peek-A-Boo Rag	Charles L. Johnson	September 28, 1914	Forster Music	Chicago, IL
Peek-A-Boo Rag	Warren & Edwards	1905	Newton	Chicago, IL
Peekaboo Peek	Gussie Goodfried	1911	F.A. Mills	New York, NY
Pegasus	James Scott	September 15, 1920	Stark Music Company	St. Louis, MO
Pekin Rag	Joe Jordan	September 24, 1904	Jordan & Motts Pekin Pub	Chicago, IL
Pekin Rag	Harry W. Martin	1910	Emerson Music	Cincinnati, OH
Pennant Rag	Percy Wenrich	September 12, 1913	Charles I. Davis	Cleveland, OH
Pepper Sauce	H.A. Fischler	September 24, 1910	Vandersloot Music	Williamsport, PA
Percy	Archie W. Scheu	1909	Self	Chicago, IL
Perils of Pauline	Pauline Alpert	June 22, 1927	Jack Mills	New York, NY
Peroxide	Calvin Lee Woolsey	May 3, 1910	Self	Braymer, MO
Perpetual Rag	B.W. Castle	May 15, 1908	Bixby & Castle	Buffalo, NY
Persian Lamb Rag	Percy Wenrich	June 15, 1908	Walter Jacobs	Boston, MA
Peter Pan Rag	Leonie Ecuyer	1906	Self	New Orleans, LA
Petticoat Lane	Euday Bowman	August 14, 1915	J.W. Jenkins	Kansas City, MO
Pettin' the Keys	Allister Wylie	January 31, 1924	Richmond–Robbins	New York, NY
Phantom Rag	Sol Violinsky & Al W. Brown	June 9, 1911	J. Fred Helf	New York, NY
Pianist Rag	Frank Schwarz	1917	Winn School of Popular Music	New York, NY
Piano Capers	Allister Wylie	January 31, 1924	Richmond-Robbins	New York, NY
Piano Mania	William Fazioli	May 26, 1922	Jack Mills	New York, NY
Piano Marmalade	Willie the Lion Smith	June 8, 1937	Mills Music	New York, NY
Piano Pan	Phil Ohman	October 10, 1922	Richmond–Robbins	New York, NY
Piano Phun	Louis Alter	November 14, 1925	Robbins–Engel	New York, NY
Piano Pranks	Silvio DeRienzo	April 3, 1929	Alfred & Company	New York, NY
Piano Puzzle	Ralph Reichenthal	February 26, 1923	Jack Mills	New York, NY
Piano Rag	Russell J. Frank	May 5, 1913	Forster Music	Chicago, IL
Piano Salad	George L. Cobb	January 19, 1923	Walter Jacobs	Boston, MA
Piano Sauce	George L. Cobb	August 13, 1927	Hub Music	Boston, MA
Piano Tuner's Walkaway Rag	Orion Wilson & Rabe	1915	Wilson & Rabe	Indianapolis, IN
Pianoflage	Roy Bargy	June 27, 1922	Sam Fox	Cleveland, OH
Pianogram	Ralph Rainger	October 8, 1929	Robbins Music	New York, NY
Pianola	Frank Westphal	August 2, 1923	Jack Mills	New York, NY
Pianola Concert Rag	Otto Welcome	September 1, 1922	American Standard	Chicago, IL

Pianola Rag	Bill Krenz	December 29, 1953	Mills Music	New York, NY
Pianophiend	Reuben J. Haskin	August 26, 1914	Buckeye Music	Columbus, OH
Pianophiends Rag	George Botsford	May 17, 1909	William R. Haskins Company	New York, NY
Piccalili Rag	Herbert Ingraham	March 5, 1909	Shapiro Music	New York, NY
Piccalilli Rag	George A. Reeg, Jr.	1912	Daly Music	Boston, MA
Pickanniny Rag	Irene M. Giblin	January 2, 1909	Sam Fox	Cleveland, OH
Pickled Beets Rag	Ed Kuhn	January 1, 1910	J.W. Jenkins	Kansas City, MO
Pickles and Peppers	Adaline Shepherd	November 7, 1906	Joseph Flanner	Milwaukee, WI
Piffle Rag	Gladys Yelvington	April 8, 1911	J.H. Aufderheide	Indianapolis, IN
Pigeon Wing Rag	Charles L. Johnson	July 26, 1909	Will Rossiter	Chicago, IL
Pike Pikers Rag	Ida G. Bierman	August 4, 1904	W.C. Polla	Chicago, IL
Pin Cushion Rag	R.G. Grady	October 28, 1909	Levan Music	Chicago, IL
Pine Apple Rag	Scott Joplin	October 12, 1908	Seminary Music	New York, NY
Pineywood Rag	Adam Minsel	August 18, 1909	Victor Kremer	Chicago, IL
Pink Poodle	Charles L. Johnson	May 6, 1914	Forster Music	Chicago, IL
Pinuchole Rag	Seymour Furth	February 11, 1911	Joe Morris	New York, NY
Pinywoods Rag	Nellie Weldon Cocroft	October 16, 1909	Cocroft Music	Thomasville, GA
Pipe Dream	Mose Gumble	March 3, 1902	Shapiro, Bernstein	New York, NY
Pipe the Piper	Joe Keden	July 12, 1937	ABC Standard	New York, NY
Pippin	Arthur Marshall	December 7, 1908	Stark Music Company	New York, NY
Pippins	Ed C. Mahoney	October 16, 1909	Colonial Music	Boston, MA
Pirate Rag	E.A. Windell	January 14, 1905	Self	Enid, OK
Pitter-Patter Rag	Jos. M. Daly	April 1, 1910	Joseph M. Daly	Boston, MA
Playin' Possum	J. Mahlon Duganne	January 18, 1909	Joseph W. Stern	New York, NY
Poison Ivories	Harry Akst & Walter Haenschen	July 23, 1923	Richmond-Robbins	New York, NY
Poison Ivy	Arthur John Drees	March 27, 1919	Self	St. Louis, MO
Poison Ivy	Herbert Ingraham	March 9, 1908	Maurice Shapiro	New York, NY
Poison Rag	Calvin Lee Woolsey	May 3, 1910	Self	Braymer, MO
Poker Rag	Charlotte Blake	June 3, 1909	Jerome H. Remick	New York, NY
Polar Bear Rag	George P. Howard	December 1, 1910	Wilson Music	San Francisco, CA
Polka Dots Rag	Reuben Lawson	1907	Self	Cincinnati, OH
Polly	John S. Zamecnik	February 25, 1929	Sam Fox	Cleveland, OH
Polyragmic	Max Morath	October 20, 1964	Hollis Music	New York, NY
Poodle Rag	Bill Krenz	August 12, 1954	Mills Music	New York, NY

Poor Buttermilk	Zez Confrey	August 5, 1921	Jack Mills	New York, NY
Poor Jim	James Chapman	August 17, 1903	Joseph Placht & Son	St. Louis, MO
Poor Jimmy Green	Eubie Blake	1975	Eubie Blake Music	New York, NY
Poor Katie Redd	Eubie Blake	1975	Eubie Blake Music	New York, NY
Pop Corn Man	Jean Schwartz	December 15, 1910	Jerome H. Remick	Detroit, MI
Popular Rag	Webb Long	July 30, 1912	Martin & Adams Music	Wichita, KS
Popularity	George M. Cohan	August 27, 1906	F.A. Mills	New York, NY
Porcupine Rag	Charles L. Johnson	September 15, 1909	M. Witmark & Sons	New York, NY
Pork and Beans	Theron C. Bennett	January 26, 1909	Victor Kremer	Chicago, IL
Pork and Beans	C. Luckeyth Roberts	June 24, 1913	Joseph W. Stern	New York, NY
Porto Rico Rag	Ford Dabney	December 14, 1910	Maurice Shapiro	New York, NY
Portuguese Rag	Mike L. Baird	May 28, 1972	Dottie Bee Music	Pasadena, CA
Possum Rag	Geraldine Dobyns	June 11, 1907	O.K. Houck	Memphis, TN
Possum and Taters	Charles Hunter	April 20, 1900	Henry A. French	Nashville, TN
Potlatch Tickle	Donald A. Robertson	July 17, 1911	Empire Music	Seattle, WA
Poverty Rag	Harry J. Lincoln	October 27, 1909	Vandersloot Music	Williamsport, PA
Powder Rag	Raymond Birch	August 20, 1908	Charles L. Johnson	Kansas City, MO
Powder Rag	Roy Steventon & Lloyd Kidwell	1906	Steventon & Kidwell	Covington, KY
Powder Rag	Jones Yow	April 13, 1906	Will Rossiter	Chicago, IL
Power House	Raymond Scott	August 4, 1937	Circle Music	New York, NY
Pozzo	Vincent Rose	November 8, 1916	Jerome H. Remick	New York, NY
Prairie Queen	Tom Shea	June 28, 1963	Ragtime Society	Toronto, CN
Press Club Rag	Axel Christensen	November 22, 1912	Christensen School	Chicago, IL
Pretty Peggy	John Queen Slye	May 17, 1905	Self	Washington, DC
Pretty Pol'	Little Jack Little	October 3, 1927	ABC Standard	New York, NY
Pride of Bucktown	Robert S. Roberts	1897	Phillip Kussel	Cincinnati, OH
Pride of the Smoky Row	J.M. Wilcockson	February 5, 1911	Self	Hammond, IN
Princess Rag	James Scott	1911	Stark Music Company	St. Louis, MO
Princess Rag	Gayle von Kamacke Wood	1915	Self	Cedar Rapids, IA
Procrastination Rag	George L. Cobb	June 29, 1927	Walter Jacobs	Boston, MA
Progressive Rag	Tobe Brown	July 3, 1913	Christensen School	Chicago, IL
Prosperity Rag	James Scott	March 10, 1916	Stark Music Company	St. Louis, MO
Publicity Rag	Henry P. Menges	December 18, 1911	Charles H. Loomis	New Haven, CT

Pudnin Tame	Theron C. Bennett	March 25, 1909	Jerome H. Remick	New York, NY
Punch and Judy	Paul Vincent	July 9, 1928	Triangle Music	New York, NY
Puppets Suite	Billy Mayerl	June 1, 1927	Sam Fox	Cleveland, OH
Purdue Rag	Opal Boyer	February 9, 1914	Self	Lafayette, IN
Purdue Spirit	Edward J. Freeberg	May 14, 1909	Rinker Music	Lafayette, IN
Pussy Foot	Robert Hoffman	1914	Walter Jacobs	Boston, MA
Put 'En on the Brakes	Charles Olson	October 3, 1927	Self	Minneapolis, MN
Putting on the Dog	Ted Shapiro	October 17, 1923	Jack Mills	New York, NY
Pyramyths	Jess Sutton	March 5, 1923	Jack Mills	New York, NY
Quality	James Scott	July 27, 1911	Stark Music Company	St. Louis, MO
Quality Rag	Ella Hudson Day	March 2, 1909	J.P. Nuckolls	Dallas, TX
Queen of Coney Island	Alfred Gasdorf	1904	Self	Cincinnati, OH
Queen of Love	Charles Hunter	June 21, 1901	Henry A. French	Nashville, TN
Queen of Rags	Walter Dunn	1909	Self	Atlanta, GA
Queen Rag	Floyd Willis	June 16, 1911	Joseph Krolage Music	Cincinnati, OH
Queen Raglan	A.E. Henrich	June 13, 1902	Henry A. French	Nashville, TN
Queen Sugar Beet Rag	M.M. Moore	1912	Self	San Jose, CA
Qwindo's Rag	David A. Jasen	June 28, 1979	The Big Three	New York, NY
Ra! Ra! Ra!	Floyd Reuter	December 5, 1910	Kauffman Music	Sedalia, MO
Rabbit Foot Rag	Al Harriman	November 30, 1910	Self	Boston, MA
Race Horse Rag	Mike Bernard	September 11, 1911	Joe Morris	Philadelphia, PA
Racing Down the Black and Whites	Adam Carroll	April 3, 1926	Harms, Inc.	New York, NY
Radio Rag	Lillian W. Shackford	October 10, 1927	C.I. Hicks Music	Boston, MA
Rag a Muffin Rag	Arthur Lange	1909	Mignon Ziegfeld	New York, NY
Rag Alley Dream	Mattie Harl Burgess	1902	Will Rossiter	Chicago, IL
Rag Baby Mine	George Botsford	March 28, 1913	Jerome H. Remick	New York, NY
Rag Baby Rag	F.H. Losey	October 27, 1909	Vandersloot Music	Williamsport, PA
Rag Bag Rag	Harry J. Lincoln	May 17, 1909	Vandersloot Music	Williamsport, PA
Rag Bag Rag	H.S. Taylor	September 4, 1909	Self	Elizabeth, NJ
Rag Carpet	Sol Levy	February 5, 1912	M. Witmark & Sons	New York, NY
Rag De Luxe	Elmer Olson & Scott Cowles	November 20, 1913	Van Publishing	Minneapolis, MN
Rag Doll	Nacio Herb Brown	March 20, 1928	Sherman, Clay	San Francisco, CA
Rag Doll Carnival	Zez Confrey	August 10, 1945	Mills Music	New York, NY
Rag La Joie	Jerry Cammack	1918	Stark Music Company	St. Louis, MO

Rag of Rags	William E. Macquinn	January 25, 1915	Chappell & Company	New York, NY
Rag Picker's Rag	Robert J. O'Brien	October 19, 1901	Union Music Company	Cincinnati, OH
Rag Sentimental	James Scott	1918	Stark Music Company	St. Louis, MO
Rag Tags Rag	Harry Thomas	May 10, 1909	Delmar Music	Montreal, CN
Rag Time Chimes	Egbert Van Alstyne	October 16, 1900	Will Rossiter	Chicago, IL
Rag Time Chimes	Percy Wenrich	July 26, 1911	Jerome H. Remick	New York, NY
Rag Time Fiend	Scotty McClure	December 30, 1914	Self	Des Moines, IA
Rag Time Joke	Andy L. Burke	December 7, 1905	Self	Galesburg, IL
Rag Time Nightmare	Tom Turpin	April 13, 1900	Robert DeYong	St. Louis, MO
Rag with No Name	Warren Camp	May 23, 1911	Self	Seattle, WA
Rag-a-Minor	Julius Lenzberg	October 8, 1917	T.B. Harms	New York, NY
Rag-a-More	George Nolton	May 19, 1924	Master Music	Chicago, IL
Rag-a-Muffin	William F. Peters	May 26, 1913	M. Witmark & Sons	New York, NY
Rag-a-Muffin Rag	Will T. Pierson	October 3, 1913	Sam Fox	Cleveland, OH
Rag-a-Tag Rag	Al W. Brown	February 16, 1910	Leo Feist	New York, NY
Rag-Ged	Joe Perry	April 23, 1930	Self	New York, NY
Rag-o-Rhythm	Harry Jentes	May 17, 1924	Self	New York, NY
Rag-Time Daud	Dawn Renfro	January 2, 1906	Self	St. Elmo, IL
Ragamuffin	Jesse Greer	January 18, 1929	Spier & Coslow	New York, NY
Ragged Edges	Otto Frey	February 28, 1911	Victor Kremer	Chicago, IL
Ragged Jack	Jack Bradshaw	September 15, 1909	Victor Kremer	Chicago, IL
Ragged Terry	Margaret Agnew White	1913	Bush & Gerts	Dallas, TX
Ragged Thoughts	J.Louis von der Mehden	August 10, 1906	Carl Fischer	New York, NY
Raggedy-Ann Rag	Lou Busch	March 5, 1952	Chatsworth Music	New York, NY
Raggety Rag	Meryle Payne	October 19, 1910	Fordi Music	Los Angeles, CA
Raggin' Rudi	William Bolcom	August 22, 1974	Edward B. Marks Music	New York, NY
Raggin' the Blues	Bill Krenz & Allan Clark	April 24, 1953	Mills Music	New York, NY
Ragging the Scale	Ed Claypoole	April 2, 1915	Broadway Music	New York, NY
Raggity-Rag	J.B. Lafreniere	1907	Delmar Music	Montreal, CN
Raggy Fox Trot	Laurence E. Goffin	October 20, 1915	Jerome H. Remick	New York, NY
Raggy Rag	Floyd Willis	1909	W.H. Willis	Cincinnati, OH
Ragman's Exercise	Harold D. Squires	April 3, 1922	Jack Mills	New York, NY

Ragology	Forest L. Traylor	March 25, 1912	Self	Petersburg, IN
Ragovitch Rag	Walter Lipman	July 22, 1910	Self	Chicago, IL
Rags to Burn	Frank X. McFadden	November 28, 1899	J.W. Jenkins	Kansas City, MO
Ragtime Betty	James Scott	October 5, 1909	Stark Music Company	New York, NY
Ragtime Bobolink	Joseph F. Lamb	1964	Mills Music	New York, NY
Ragtime Dance	Scott Joplin	December 21, 1906	Stark Music Company	New York, NY
Ragtime Eyes	W.C. Powell	1907	P.J. Howley	New York, NY
Ragtime Follies	May Olive Arnold	October 31, 1910	Self	Mobile, AL
Ragtime Jim	A. Fred Phillips	November 21, 1912	Jerome H. Remick	New York, NY
Ragtime Jingles	Al J. Markgraf	March 15, 1916	Self	San Francisco, CA
Ragtime Nightingale	Joseph F. Lamb	June 10, 1915	Stark Music Company	St. Louis, MO
Ragtime Oriole	James Scott	December 10, 1911	Stark Music Company	St. Louis, MO
Ragtime Parade in Darktown	William A. Calhoun	1899	Groene Music	Cincinnati, OH
Ragtime Patsy	O. Wellington Snell	September 12, 1903	Self	Boston, MA
Ragtime Razzmatazz	J. Gaines	September 2, 1958	Record Songs	New York, NY
Ragtime Refreshments	William L. Needham	1903	Golden Rule Music	Chicago, IL
Ragtime Revelations	J. Gaines	September 2, 1958	Record Songs	New York, NY
Ragtime Riggles	Isidor Heidenreich	1902	Hunleth Music	St. Louis, MO
Ragtime Ripples	Percy Wenrich	September 14, 1908	McKinley Music	Chicago, IL
Ragtime Showers	Kathryn Athol Morton	May 3, 1902	Richard A. Saalfield	New York, NY
Ragweed Rag	Harry Bussler	June 26, 1911	H. Kirkus Dugdale	Washington, DC
Rah Rah Boy!!!	Wallie Herzer	November 18, 1908	Herzer & Brown	San Francisco, CA
Raindrops	Bill Wirges	June 12, 1928	Self	New York, NY
Rambler	Walter G. Haenschen & Arthur F. Beyer	1906	Stark Music Company	New York, NY
Ramblin' Rag	Bill Krenz	July 11, 1952	Mills Music	New York, NY
Rambling in Rhythm	Arthur Schutt	November 5, 1927	Jack Mills	New York, NY
Rambling Rags	L.J. Meyerholtz	1908	C.C. Powell	Fort Wayne, IN
Ramshackle Rag	Ted Snyder	March 10, 1911	Ted Snyder Company	New York, NY
Rapid Firing Rag	C. Kenneth Yoder	November 13, 1915	Self	Bellefontaine, OH
Rapscallion Rag	Lou Busch	March 5, 1952	Chatsworth Music	New York, NY
Rastus Rag	H.A. Fischler	September 21, 1909	Vandersloot Music	Williamsport, PA
Rathskeller Drag	Walter L. Dunn	December 31, 1910	Self	Atlanta, GA
Rats!!!	M. Kendree Miller	October 1, 1914	Bush & Gerts	Dallas, TX
Rattle Snake Rag	Clyde W. Headley	December 19, 1910	H. Kirkus Dugdale	Washington, DC

Rattler Rag	Susie Wells	December 7, 1912	Self	Henrietta, TX
Rattlesnake Rag	Lou Busch & Eddie Hansen	December 29, 1952	Chatsworth Music	New York, NY
Rattlesnake Rag	Ethwell Hanson	April 9, 1917	Self	Neenah, WI
Ravioli Rag	Frank Lucanese & Charles Lucotti	July 21, 1914	Jerome H. Remick	New York, NY
Ravlins	Floyd Willis	May 20, 1910	W.H. Willis	Cincinnati, OH
Raymond's Rag	David A. Jasen	June 28, 1979	The Big Three	New York, NY
Razzle Dazzle	Lilburn Kingsbury & Alma Smith	July 6, 1905		Detroit, MI
Razzle Dazzle	Nellie M. Stokes	October 20, 1909	Jerome H. Remick	Detroit, MI
Real Rag	Lawrence W. Blair	November 22, 1912	Lew Roberts Music	Nashville, TN
Real Swing Rag	Oswald Thumser	1908	Bafunno Bros. Music	St. Louis, MO
Red and Black Rag	Robert Reynolds	1909	Emerson Music	New York, NY
Red Clover	Max Kortlander	October 17, 1923	Jack Mills	New York, NY
Red Devil Rag	Lucien Denni	September 19, 1910	J.W. Jenkins	Kansas City, MO
Red Fox Trot	Albert Gumble	August 23, 1917	Jerome H. Remick	New York, NY
Red Mouse Rag	Wilbur Piper	August 15, 1910	H.R. McClure Company	Sidney, OH
Red Onion Rag	Abe Olman	January 17, 1912	George W. Meyer Music	New York, NY
Red Onion Rag	Roy Steventon & Lloyd Kidwell	November 11, 1911	Associated Music	Cincinnati, OH
Red Pepper	Henry Lodge	December 19, 1910	M. Witmark & Sons	New York, NY
Red Peppers	F.P. Aukens	1910	F.B. Haviland	New York, NY
Red Rag	Jack Murfree	December 1, 1910	Murfree Music	Boston, MA
Red Rambler Rag	Julia Lee Niebergall	July 16, 1912	J.H. Aufderheide	Indianapolis, IN
Red Raven	Carl E. Olson	August 30, 1910	Olson–Edwards Music	Wichita, KS
Red Raven Rag	Harry Kimpton	March 16, 1908	Self	Baudette, MN
Red Raven Rag	Charley Straight	December 30, 1915	Jerome H. Remick	New York, NY
Red Ribbon Rag	Z.M. Van Tress	February 1, 1915	Self	Houston, TX
Red Slipper Rag	Glenn Rowell	January 6, 1965	Bregman, Vocco & Conn	New York, NY
Reflection Rag	Scott Joplin	December 4, 1917	Stark Music Company	St. Louis, MO
Regal Rag	Lily Coffee	January 24, 1916	Self	Houston, TX
Reindeer	Joseph F. Lamb	1915	Stark Music Company	St. Louis, MO
Reinette Rag	David Reichstein	June 14, 1913	Christensen School	Chicago, IL
Reisenweber Rag	Dominic J. LaRocca	June 4, 1918	Leo Feist	New York, NY

Remington Rag	Martie Stoltz	1909	Groene Music	Cincinnati, OH
Remorse Blues	Henry Lodge	July 30, 1917	Jerome H. Remick	New York, NY
Restless Rag	Sarah E. Cook	August 5, 1908	Victor Kremer	Chicago, IL
Rexall Rag	J. Meredith Daniel	November 24, 1914	Self	Manson, IA
Rhapsody in Ragtime	Eubie Blake	1975	Eubie Blake Music	New York, NY
Rhapsody Rag	Budd L. Cross	January 28, 1911	Sam Fox	Cleveland, OH
Rhapsody Rag	Harry Jentes	January 17, 1911	Maurice Shapiro	New York, NY
Rhinewine Rag	Paul Henneberg	June 12, 1912	Carl Fischer	New York, NY
Rhythmic Fantasy	Phil Saltman	February 9, 1929	Denton & Haskins	New York, NY
Rialto Ripples	George Gershwin & Will Donaldson	June 6, 1917	Jerome H. Remick	New York, NY
Richmond Rag	May Aufderheide	December 12, 1908	J.H. Aufderheide	Indianapolis, IN
Riffin'	Willie the Lion Smith	March 21, 1938	Mills Music	New York, NY
Rig-a-Jig	Nat D. Ayer	August 2, 1912	Jerome H. Remick	New York, NY
Rig-a-Jig Rag	William Schroeder	February 20, 1917	M. Witmark & Sons	New York, NY
Rigamarole	Harold Mooney	January 30, 1935	Luz Brothers	New York, NY
Rigamarole Rag	Edwin F. Kendall	1910	Jerome H. Remick	New York, NY
Rinaldo Rag	Rinaldo	June 17, 1909	Ted Snyder Company	New York, NY
Ring-Tum-Diddie	Fred Heltman	January 13, 1912	Popular Music Publishers	Cleveland, OH
Rio De Janeiro	Willard Robison	September 14, 1926	Robbins-Engel	New York, NY
Rip Rag	Miriam Todd	1911	P.F. Sarver	Piqua, OH
Ripples Rag	Camilla Thiele	June 24, 1912	Peerless Music	Janesville, WI
Rising Moon	M. Mae Serviss	January 15, 1912	H. Kirkus Dugdale	Washington, DC
Rita	J. Russel Robinson & Bernie Cummins	May 20, 1929	Vincent Youmans Music	New York, NY
Rival Rag	Ada LaVerne Rogers	September 1, 1910	Eaton Music	New York, NY
River	Edwin A. Burkart	February 18, 1911	Arno Music	Cincinnati, OH
Riverside Rag	Charles Cohen	August 8, 1910	Self	Binghamton, NY
Robardina Rag	E. Warren Furry	September 6, 1902	Balmer & Weber Music	St. Louis, MO
Rochelle	Bill Krenz	December 15, 1934	M.M. Cole	Chicago, IL
Rochester Fair	Lawrence Leon Wiley	July 17, 1914	Self	Rochester, NY
Rochester Rag	J.C. Mills	December 1, 1912	H. Kirkus Dugdale	Washington, DC
Rocky Ford Melon Pickers	A. Garfield Wilson	November 6, 1902	Pepin & Triggs	Denver, CO
Rocky Rags	Isidore Seidel	April 26, 1911	Self	Indianapolis, IN

Roller-Skater's Rag	Sam Gompers	1906	Self	New Orleans, LA
Romantic Rag	Kathy Craig	December 30, 1976	Edward B. Marks Music	New York, NY
Rooster Rag	Muriel Pollock	February 26, 1917	Joseph W. Stern	New York, NY
Rose Leaf Rag	Scott Joplin	November 15, 1907	Joseph M. Daly	Boston, MA
Rosewood Rag	Peter M. Heaton	March 22, 1909	Victor Kremer	Chicago, IL
Rotation Rag	Al Sweet	September 19, 1911	Shapiro Music	New York, NY
Rough House Rag	W.E. Smith	1905		
Round Up Rag	Con Conrad & Weedon	October 17, 1911	F.A. Mills	New York, NY
Round Up Rag	Jerome Shay	August 4, 1909	Fred Fischer Music	New York, NY
Roustabout Rag	Paul Sarebresole	1897	Louis Grunewald	New Orleans, LA
Royal Flush Rag	George Botsford	March 27, 1911	Jerome H. Remick	Detroit, MI
Royal Purple	Errol Croom	November 20, 1913	P.J. Howley	New York, NY
Rubber Plant Rag	George L. Cobb	June 14, 1909	Walter Jacobs	Boston, MA
Rube Bennett's Raggedy Rag	Rube Bennett	February 27, 1914	Waterson, Berlin & Snyder	New York, NY
Rubies and Pearls	Harry A. Tierney	June 24, 1911	Ted Snyder Company	New York, NY
Rufenreddy	Roy Bargy & Charley Straight	November 14, 1921	Sam Fox	Cleveland, OH
Running Up and Down	Henry Cohen	March 5, 1928	Bibo, Bloedon & Lang	New York, NY
Russian Pony Rag	Don Ramsay	August 27, 1909	Walter Jacobs	Boston, MA
Russian Rag	George L. Cobb	April 27, 1918	Will Rossiter	Chicago, IL
S. O. S.	Kenneth W. Bradshaw & Joe McGrade	1919	Stark Music Company	St. Louis, MO
Safety Pin Catch	Lewis Fuiks	December 8, 1909	Thompson Music	Chicago, IL
Sailing Along Over the Keys	Silvio DeRienzo	March 5, 1928	Bibo, Bloedon & Lang	New York, NY
Saint Louis Ripple Rag	Paul Burmeister	July 1, 1912	Self	St. Louis, MO
Sakes Alive	Stephen Howard	May 2, 1903	M. Witmark & Sons	New York, NY
Salome Rag	Samuel J. Stokes	March 22, 1909	Self	New Orleans, LA
Salt and Pepper Rag	Herbert Ingraham	March 5, 1909	Shapiro Music	New York, NY
Salted Peanuts	Sydney Chapman	September 27, 1911	Koninsky Music	Troy, NY
San Francisco Pretty Girl Rag	Walter Shannon	November 17, 1910	San Francisco Music	San Francisco, CA
Sand Paper Rag	Harry Ellman & S. Lew Schwab	January 12, 1910	Stark Music Company	St. Louis, MO
Sandella Rag	Edward Hudson	September 18, 1921	Stark Music Company	St. Louis, MO

Sandy River Rag	Thomas S. Allen	1915	Walter Jacobs	Boston, MA
Sapho Rag	J. Russel Robinson	October 5, 1909	Stark Music Company	St. Louis, MO
Saratoga Glide	Harry L. Newman	1909	Sunlight Music	Chicago, IL
Saronoff Rag	Silvio Hein	May 15, 1913	T.B. Harms	New York, NY
Saskatoon Rag	Phil Goldberg	March 15, 1915	Roger Graham	Chicago, IL
Sassafras Rag	J. Levy	May 22, 1905	Arnett-Delonais	Chicago, IL
Sassafras Sam	George Grace	September 14, 1908	McKinley Music	Chicago, IL
Satisfaction	Percy B. Keenan	1908	Charles B. Loomis Music	New Haven, CT
Say When	George L. Cobb	1919	Walter Jacobs	Boston, MA
Scale It Down	Walker O'Neil	September 5, 1924	Jack Mills	New York, NY
Scandalous Thompson	Charles L. Johnson	May 27, 1899	J.W. Jenkins	Kansas City, MO
Scarecrow Rag	Frank Baer	1911	Evans–Dangel Music	Boston, MA
Scarecrow Rag	Will B. Morrison	April 15, 1911	J.H. Aufderheide	Indianapolis, IN
Scarlet Rag	Forest L. Cook	April 3, 1911	Self	Huntington, IN
Schultzmeier Rag	B.R. Whitlow	March 5, 1914	Stark Music Company	St. Louis, MO
Scizzor Bill	Logan Sizemore	June 5, 1909	Victor Kremer	Chicago, IL
Scotch Rye	E.W. Anderson	1909	Tolbert R. Ingram Music	Denver, CO
Scott Joplin's New Rag	Scott Joplin	May 1, 1912	Joseph W. Stern	New York, NY
Scoutin' Around	James P. Johnson	September 18, 1925	Perry Bradford Music	New York, NY
Scramble Rag	Louis Mentel	June 30, 1911	Mentel Brothers	Cincinnati, OH
Scrambled Eggs	James A. Brennan	February 16, 1914	O.E. Story	Boston, MA
Scrambles	Sid Reinherz	April 30, 1928	Robbins Music	New York, NY
Scraps From the Rag Bag	Hubert Tanner	1906	Self	Plymouth, IN
Screen Door Rag	Marjorie Burgess	1973	Self	Boston, MA
Scroochin' Up Rag	Lena Martin	August 11, 1911	Self	East Redford, VA
Scrub Rag	Alfred W. Brinkmeyer	April 30, 1910	Self	St. Louis, MO
Scrub Rags	Arthur W. Mueller	1904	Arnold Publishing Company	Cincinnati, OH
Sea Weeds Rag	Abe Olman	December 9, 1910	Joe Morris	New York, NY
Seabiscuits Rag	William Bolcom	May 24, 1971	Edward B. Marks Music	New York, NY
Search Light Rag	Scott Joplin	August 12, 1907	Joseph W. Stern	New York, NY
Sen-Sen Rag	Russell B. Harker	May 5, 1910	Jerome H. Remick	New York, NY
Sensation Rag	Joseph F. Lamb	October 8, 1908	Stark Music Company	New York, NY
Sensible Rag	Ed Avey	1914	Self	Cherry Vale, KS

Service Rag	Adolph Hansen	June 12, 1919	Self	Omaha, NE
Shadow Rag	William Brunsvold	December 16, 1910	F.B. Haviland	New York, NY
Shaka Foot	Ferd Guttenberger	September 12, 1933	Self	Macon, GA
Shamrock Rag	Euday Bowman	March 14, 1916	J.W. Jenkins	Kansas City, MO
Shave 'Em Dry	Sam Wishnuff	May 10, 1917	Stark Music Company	St. Louis, MO
Sheath	William E. Weigel	December 8, 1908	John Arnold	Cincinnati, OH
Shimmie Shoes	Max Kortlander	October 17, 1923	Jack Mills	New York, NY
Shine or Polish Rag	Fred Heltman	April 24, 1914	Fred Heltman Company	Cleveland, OH
Shock Rag	Elmer Olson	1911	A.W. Pinger	Minneapolis, MN
Shoe String Rag	David A. Jasen	June 28, 1979	The Big Three	New York, NY
Shoe Tickler Rag	Wilbur Campbell	April 11, 1911	Southern California Music	Los Angeles, CA
Shootin' the Agate	Thomas A. Schmutzler	December 30, 1976	Edward B. Marks Music	New York, NY
Shootin' the Chutes	Larry Briers	March 5, 1924	Jack Mills	New York, NY
Shovel Fish	Harry Cook	October 4, 1907	Herman Straus & Sons	Louisville, KY
Show Me Rag	Trebor J. Tichenor	December 30, 1976	Edward B. Marks Music	New York, NY
Showboat Rag	Bill Krenz & Thomas J. Filas	November 24, 1953	Mills Music	New York, NY
Shreveport Stomps	"Jelly Roll" Morton	April 1, 1925	Melrose Brothers	Chicago, IL
Shy and Sly	C. Luckeyth Roberts	May 7, 1915	G. Ricordi	New York, NY
Sic 'Em Prinz	Alfred Gasdorf	1905	Self	Newport, KY
Silence and Fun	Charles E. Mullen	December 22, 1904	Will Rossiter	Chicago, IL
Silhouette	Rube Bloom	May 9, 1927	Triangle Music	New York, NY
Silk Hose Rag	Omar L. Sims	December 15, 1916	Buckeye Music	Columbus, OH
Silver Buckle Rag	Joseph Sikorra	February 24, 1910	Joseph Flanner	Milwaukee, WI
Silver King Rag	Charles L. Johnson	April 5, 1909	Thompson Music	Chicago, IL
Silver Leaf Rag	Dan Goldsmith	October 17, 1911	Imperial Music	Winnepeg, CN
Silver Rocket	Arthur Marshall	June 27, 1966	Oak Publishing	New York, NY
Silver Swan Rag	Scott Joplin	1971	Maple Leaf Club	Los Angeles, CA
Silver Tip	Frederick Owens Hanks	May 12, 1914	Jerome H. Remick	New York, NY
Simplicity Rag	Eugene Ellsworth	April 15, 1912	Standard Music	Chicago, IL
Ski Do Rag	Alfred Gasdorf	March 19, 1906	Ilsen & Company	Cincinnati, OH
Skidding	Ed Claypoole	April 7, 1923	Jack Mills	New York, NY

Skipinova	Glen Barton	May 20, 1926	Jack Mills	New York, NY
Sky Rockets	E. Philip Severin	June 10, 1911	Self	Moline, IL
Sleepy Hollow Rag	Clarence Woods	1918	Will L. Livernash Music	Kansas City, MO
Sleepy Lou	Irene M. Giblin	November 15, 1906	Jerome H. Remick	New York, NY
Sleepy Piano	Billy Mayerl	July 15, 1926	Sam Fox	Cleveland, OH
Sleepy Sidney	Archie W. Scheu	August 22, 1907	Self	Cincinnati, OH
Slipova	Roy Bargy	November 14, 1921	Sam Fox	Cleveland, OH
Slippery Elm Rag	Herbert Ingraham	March 5, 1909	Shapiro Music	New York, NY
Slippery Elm Rag	Clarence Woods	1912	Self	Fort Worth, TX
Slippery Fingers	Henry Steele	January 8, 1927	Jack Mills	New York, NY
Slippery Place	P.M. Hacker	July 26, 1911	Jerome H. Remick	New York, NY
Slippery Steps	Bert Leach	April 15, 1915	Traler-Elliot Company	Atlantic City, NJ
Slivers	Harry Cook	March 18, 1909	Central Music	St. Louis, MO
Slivers	Maude Gilmore	1909	Charles L. Johnson	Kansas City, MO
Smart Alec	Zez Confrey	December 27, 1933	Mills Music	New York, NY
Smash Up Rag	Gwendolyn Stevenson	December 2, 1914	Jerome H. Remick	New York, NY
Smiler Rag	Percy Wenrich	January 2, 1907	Arnett-Delonais	Chicago, IL
Smiles and Chuckles	F. Henri Klickmann	October 8, 1917	Frank K. Root	Chicago, IL
Smiling Bill	Jack Schuesler	1911	Self	Covington, KY
Smiling Sadie	Archie W. Scheu	April 20, 1905	Self	Cincinnati, OH
Snappin' Turtle	Charles L. Cooke	October 27, 1913	Jerome H. Remick	New York, NY
Snappy Rag	Harry J. Palmer	1914	Self	Mankato, MN
Snappy Rag	Edwin H. See	October 28, 1913	Regent Music	Lake Charles, LA
Sneak Away	Willie the Lion Smith	August 21, 1937	Mills Music	New York, NY
Sneaky Shuffles Rag	Henry Lodge	October 4, 1910	Jerome H. Remick	Detroit, MI
Sneeky Peet	Charles L. Johnson	January 10, 1907	J.W. Jenkins	Kansas City, MO
Snipes	Mamie Williams	November 1, 1909	Carl Hoffman Music	Kansas City, MO
Snookums Rag	Charles L. Johnson	February 9, 1918	Forster Music	Chicago, IL
Snow Shoes	Bill Wirges	January 26, 1927	Alfred & Company	New York, NY
Snowball	Nellie M. Stokes	February 23, 1907	Jerome H. Remick	Detroit, MI
Snowball Babe	C. Roland Flick	1900	Frank G. Fite	Nashville, TN
Snuffuns	Harold Dixon	October 31, 1927	Self	New York, NY
Snuggle Pup	George L. Cobb	March 4, 1929	Walter Jacobs	Boston, MA
Soap Bubbles Rag	Charles F. Myers	1907	Vinton Music Publishing Company	Boston, MA

Soap Suds	Irene M. Giblin	March 1, 1906	Jerome H. Remick	New York, NY
Society Rag	Nat Johnson	June 27, 1912	Forster Music	Chicago, IL
Soft Shoe Dancer	Dent Mowrey	1933	Carl Fischer	New York, NY
Soliloquy	Rube Bloom	June 21, 1926	Triangle Music	New York, NY
Solitaire Rag	Clara Campbell Igelman	1909	Wilson Music	Richmond, IN
Some Baby	Julius Lenzberg	December 29, 1913	Jerome H. Remick	New York, NY
Some Blues, For You All	Theron C. Bennett	January 8, 1916	Joe Morris	New York, NY
Some Class Rag	S.E. Roberts	May 9, 1912	Shapiro Music	New York, NY
Some Jazz	S.J. Stocco	1919	Jerome H. Remick	New York, NY
Some Pumpkins	Ed Kuhn	1908	W.B. Allen Music	Columbia, MO
Some Rag	Willie Eckstein	January 10, 1911	Delmar Music	Montreal, CN
Some Stuff	Lindsay McPhail	February 24, 1923	Self	Chicago, IL
Some Wampus Cat Rag	James Wickiser	November 14, 1913	H. Kirkus Dugdale	Washington, DC
Something Doing	Scott Joplin & Scott Hayden	February 24, 1903	Val A. Reis Music	St. Louis, MO
Something Doing Soon	Regina Morphy Voitier	February 23, 1905	Philip Werlein	New Orleans, LA
Son Set Rag	Ted Browne	December 7, 1915	Buck & Lowney	St. Louis, MO
Sophisticated Rhythm	Bill Krenz	January 22, 1935	M.M. Cole	Chicago, IL
Sorority Rag	Margaret Bartlett	March 22, 1909	Thompson Music	Chicago, IL
Soup and Fish Rag	Harry Jentes & Pete Wendling	December 11, 1913	George W. Meyer Music	New York, NY
Sour Grapes Rag	Will B. Morrison	November 11, 1912	Self	Indianapolis, IN
South Dakota Rag	Dee Cort Keith Hammitt	January 22, 1913	H. Kirkus Dugdale	Washington, DC
South Dakota Rag	Joseph Liljenberg	February 2, 1902	Self	Canova, SD
Southern Beauties	Charles L. Johnson	October 12, 1907	Jerome H. Remick	New York, NY
Southern Blossoms	Harold G. Mitchell	January 20, 1905	Self	Los Angeles, CA
Southern Charms	Rube Bloom	May 15, 1931	Robbins Music	New York, NY
Southern Roses	Joe Bren	August 22, 1904	Shapiro, Remick	Detroit, MI
Southern Shuffle	T. Palmer Stephens	February 19, 1912	H. Kirkus Dugdale	Washington, DC
Southern Sneeze	Harry A. Slee	March 26, 1906	Joseph Placht & Brother	St. Louis, MO
Southern Snowballs	LaRue E. Black	December 30, 1907	Vinton Music	Chicago, IL
Southern Symphony	Percy Wenrich	April 13, 1910	Jerome H. Remick	New York, NY
Spaghetti Rag	George Lyons & Bob Yosco	April 11, 1910	Maurice Shapiro	New York, NY

Sparkler Rag	Horace Smith Wilson	November 12, 1908	Victor Kremer	Chicago, IL
Sparkles	Charles B. Ennis	1909	W.B. Morrison	Indianapolis, IN
Sparkles	Phil Ohman	June 12, 1935	Robbins Music	New York, NY
Sparks	Theo Uden Masman	1928	Marks Music	New York, NY
Spasm Rag	Tom Shea	March 21, 1963	Ragtime Society	Toronto, CN
Spatter Rag	Elmer Olson	1912	A.W. Pinger	Minneapolis, MN
Speckled Spider Rag	Harry French	April 6, 1910	Victor Kremer	Chicago, IL
Speedometer Rag	William B. Dale	November 7, 1912	H. Kirkus Dugdale	Washington, DC
Spinal Chords	Silvio DeRienzo	March 5, 1928	Bibo, Bloedon & Lang	New York, NY
Spitfire	Roy Allen	1910	F.B. Haviland	New York, NY
Spitfire Rag	E. Grazia Nardini	January 19, 1914	Self	San Francisco, CA
Spitfire Rag	Elsie Grace Rafael	May 20, 1909	Weller–Hartman Music	New York, NY
Splinters	Maude Gilmore	May 21, 1909	Charles L. Johnson	Kansas City, MO
Sponge Rag	Walter C. Simon	1911	Self	New Orleans, LA
Spots	Edward A. Blake	October 8, 1909	W.H. Willis	Cincinnati, OH
Spring Fever	Rube Bloom	June 21, 1926	Triangle Music	New York, NY
Spring Holiday	Rube Bloom	May 15, 1931	Robbins Music	New York, NY
Spring Time Rag	Paul Pratt	January 4, 1916	Stark Music Company	St. Louis, MO
Sprint Splinter Rag	Dena Merle Lantz	June 4, 1908	Victor Kremer	Chicago, IL
Squiggilum Drag	Harry Gasdorf	1911	Gasdorf Music	Newport, KY
Squirrel Food Rag	R.G. Grady	1916	Olympic Music	Cincinnati, OH
Squirrel Rag	Paul Biese & F. Henri Klickmann	October 9, 1913	Will Rossiter	Chicago, IL
St. Louis Mule	Jean Ledies	1914	Wolf–Camp	St. Louis, MO
St. Louis Rag	Tom Turpin	November 2, 1903	Sol Bloom	New York, NY
St. Louis Tickle	Barney & Seymore	August 20, 1904	Victor Kremer	Chicago, IL
St. Vitus Dance	Herbert Ingraham	March 5, 1909	Shapiro Music	New York, NY
Stack 'Em Up	H. Leo Levy & Luis C. Russell	August 25, 1927	Joe Davis	New York, NY
State Fair Cadonian	Horace C. Rudisell	1910	Kauffman Music Company	Sedalia, MO
Steam Roller Rag	Mary E.B. Redus	1912	Shapiro Music	New York, NY
Steamboat Rag	Ernie Burnett	1914	Syndicate Music	St. Louis, MO
Stenotypic Rag	Ben Kilmer, Jr.	May 15, 1915	A.W. Perry & Sons	Sedalia, MO
Step On It	Silvio DeRienzo	July 2, 1927	Alfred & Company	New York, NY
Steppin' on the Ivories	Wallace A. Johnson	October 15, 1924	T. Presser	Philadelphia, PA

Stepping on the Ivories	John McLaughlin	August 4, 1927	M. Witmark & Sons	New York, NY
Stewed Chicken Rag	Glenn C. Leap	April 22, 1912	Self	New York, NY
Stewed Prunes Rag	Oscar Lorraine	November 16, 1910	Jerome H. Remick	New York, NY
Stop It	George L. Cobb	1919	Walter Jacobs	Boston, MA
Stop Rag	C.A. Reccius	April 14, 1913	A.F. Marzian	Louisville, KY
Stop Your Kiddin'	Ferde Grofe & Jimmy McHugh	November 24, 1922	Jack Mills	New York, NY
Stop-Trot Rag	Cass. Freeborn	March 3, 1914	M. Witmark & Sons	New York, NY
Stoptime Rag	Scott Joplin	June 4, 1910	Joseph W. Stern	New York, NY
Storyville Sport	Tom Shea	1966	Ragtime Society	Toronto, CN
Streamers Rag	E. Earle Marx	August 18, 1909	Victor Kremer	Chicago, IL
Strenuous Life	Scott Joplin	1902	John Stark & Son	St. Louis, MO
Stumbling (Paraphrase)	Zez Confrey	July 1, 1922	Leo Feist	New York, NY
Stung Rag	Albert A. Stoll	1909	J. Placht & Brother	St. Louis, MO
Such a Rag	Carl H. Copenhaver	February 27, 1913	Frank Harding	New York, NY
Such Is Life	Charles L. Cooke	December 30, 1915	Jerome H. Remick	New York, NY
Sugar Cane Rag	Scott Joplin	April 21, 1908	Seminary Music	New York, NY
Summer Breeze	James Scott	March 14, 1903	Dumars Music	Carthage, MO
Sumthin Doin	Florence M. Wood	April 1, 1904	Automatic Perforating Company	New York, NY
Sunbeams	Bill Wirges	May 31, 1929	Self	New York, NY
Sunburst Rag	James Scott	1909	Stark Music Company	New York, NY
Sunflower Babe	Fred Heltman	February 20, 1909	Self	Cleveland, OH
Sunflower Rag	Percy Wenrich	July 26, 1911	Jerome H. Remick	New York, NY
Sunflower Slow Drag	Scott Joplin & Scott Hayden	March 18, 1901	John Stark & Son	St. Louis, MO
Sunflower Tickle	Dolly Richmond	September 14, 1908	McKinley Music	Chicago, IL
Sunny South Rag	Clyde Spence	October 16, 1907	Globe Music	New York, NY
Sunset	Allen P. Dougherty & Max Mayer	February 9, 1907	North-Western Music	Seattle, WA
Sunset Rag	Frederick Bryan	October 21, 1914	Joseph W. Stern	New York, NY
Sunshine Capers	Roy Bargy	February 7, 1922	Sam Fox	Cleveland, OH
Sunstroke Rag	M.W. Myers	October 2, 1911	Joe Morris	Philadelphia, PA
Supper Club	Harry Carroll	March 14, 1917	Jerome H. Remick	New York, NY
Sure Fire Rag	Henry Lodge	March 15, 1910	Victor Kremer	Chicago, IL
Susan's Rag	David A. Jasen	June 28, 1979	The Big Three	New York, NY

Swamptown Shuffle	Harry W. Jones	1902	Medbery Music	Chicago, IL
Swanee Rag	Charles L. Johnson	March 18, 1912	Sam Fox	Cleveland, OH
Swanee Ripples	Walter E. Blaufuss	December 27, 1912	Frank Clark Music	Chicago, IL
Sweet and Tender	Roy Bargy	April 17, 1923	Will Rossiter	Chicago, IL
Sweet Bunch	Morley Caldwell	September 15, 1904	Pioneer Music	Chicago, IL
Sweet Nothings	Milton J. Rettenberg	September 28, 1928	Ager, Yellen & Bornstein	New York, NY
Sweet Pickin's Rag	Charley Straight	April 30, 1918	Forster Music	Chicago, IL
Sweet Pickles	George E. Florence	October 23, 1907	Victor Kremer	Chicago, IL
Sweet Potatoes	Justin Ringleben	November 20, 1906	Seminary Music	New York, NY
Sweet Sixteenths	William Albright	December 30, 1976	Edward B. Marks Music	New York, NY
Sweetie Dear	Joe Jordan	November 26, 1906	Jordan & Cook	Chicago, IL
Sweetmeats	Percy Wenrich	February 18, 1907	Arnett–Delonais	Chicago, IL
Sweetness	Fannie B. Woods	June 14, 1912	Forster Music	Chicago, IL
Sweety, Won't You Be Kind to Me	D.W. Batsell	August 14, 1913	Self	Florence, AL
Swell Affair	Bert Potter	August 27, 1904	George M. Krey	Boston, MA
Swipesy Cake Walk	Scott Joplin & Arthur Marshall	July 21, 1900	John Stark & Son	St. Louis, MO
Swiss Cheese Rag	A.E. Bohrer	December 1, 1913	Self	New York, NY
Sycamore	Scott Joplin	July 18, 1904	Will Rossiter	Chicago, IL
Sycamore Saplin'	Theron C. Bennett	April 9, 1910	Jerome H. Remick	Detroit, MI
Sympathetic Jasper	E.L. Catlin	1905	John Stark & Son	St. Louis, MO
Sympathetic Rag	Arthur M. Siebrecht	June 2, 1911	Self	Lexington, KY
Symphonola	Henry Lange	March 6, 1922	Jack Mills	New York, NY
Symphony Rag	J.A. Cotter	May 3, 1913	Cotter's Theatrical & Musical	Peoria, IL
Syncopated Echoes	Elmer Olson	December 8, 1920	W.A. Quincke	Los Angeles, CA
Syncopated Fox Trot	E.S. Teall	December 15, 1915	Joseph W. Sturtevant	New York, NY
Syncopating the Scales	Arthur Schutt	November 3, 1922	Jack Mills	New York, NY
Take It Easy	Axel Christensen	February 9, 1924	Jack Mills	New York, NY
Talk of the Town	Elijah Jimerson & M. Cranston	1919	Syndicate Music	St. Louis, MO
Tangle Foot Rag	Fleta Jan Brown	December 14, 1906	Joseph W. Stern	New York, NY
Tanglefoot	E.A. Storman	1899	Self	St. Louis, MO
Tanglefoot Rag	John F. James	May 5, 1910	Jerome H. Remick	New York, NY
Tanglefoot Rag	F.H. Losey	May 21, 1910	Vandersloot Music	Williamsport, PA

Tango	Joe Jordan	January 16, 1913	Will Rossiter	Chicago, IL
Tango Rag	L.T. Dunlap	August 21, 1913	Owl Music	Wilkes-Barre, PA
Tango Rag	Abe Olman	January 6, 1914	Joe Morris	New York, NY
Tangolizing Rag	Ray Collins	October 15, 1914	H. Kirkus Dugdale	Washington, DC
Tantalizer Rag	Frank S. Butler	April 10, 1916	Mellinger Music	St. Louis, MO
Tantalizing Tingles	Mike Bernard & Solly Ginsberg	February 18, 1913	Waterson, Berlin & Snyder	New York, NY
Tar Babies	Charles L. Johnson	January 3, 1911	Charles L. Johnson	Kansas City, MO
Tar Baby	Gertrude Cady	May 19, 1904	H.L. Walker	New York, NY
Tattered Melody Rag	Hilda Ossusky	December 15, 1910	Jerome H. Remick	Detroit, MI
Tatters	Charles Cohen	October 2, 1906	Sam Fox	Cleveland, OH
Teasing Rag	Paul Pratt	1912	Charles A. Meyers	Chicago, IL
Teasing the Cat	Charles L. Johnson	August 19, 1916	Forster Music	Chicago, IL
Teasing the Klassics	Axel Christensen	June 25, 1923	Forster Music	Chicago, IL
Technic Touch Rag	Harold B. Knox	November 4, 1913	H. Kirkus Dugdale	Washington, DC
Teddy Bear Rag	Hattie Goben	October 18, 1907	Self	Dallas, TX
Teddy in the Jungle	Edward J. Freeberg	February 8, 1910	Rinker Music	Lafayette, IN
Teddy's Pardners	Horace Dowell	1903	Frank G. Fite	Nashville, TN
Tee Na Nah	Harry Weston	May 30, 1910	L. Grunewald Company	New Orleans, LA
Temptation Rag	Henry Lodge	September 9, 1909	M. Witmark & Sons	New York, NY
Tempus Ragorum	Marshall M. Bartholomew	February 21, 1906	Self	New York, NY
Ten Penny Rag	Clarence E. Brandon & Billy Smythe	December 6, 1911	Brandon & Smythe	St. Louis, MO
Tennessee Jubilee	Thomas E. Broady	1899	Henry A. French	Nashville, TN
Tennessee Rag	Severino Giovannoli	July 26, 1912	Self	Cookeville, TN
Tennessee Rag	George McDade & Henry Watterson	October 26, 1908	Victor Kremer	Chicago, IL
Tennessee Tantalizer	Charles Hunter	November 19, 1900	H.A. French	Nashville, TN
Tenth Interval Rag	Harry Ruby	January 2, 1924	Stark & Cowan	New York, NY
Tex Tangle Foot Rag	F.J. Boyer	October 1, 1912	H. Kirkus Dugdale	Washington, DC
Texas Fox Trot	David Guion	August 16, 1915	M. Witmark & Sons	New York, NY
Texas Rag	Callis W. Jackson	June 5, 1905	Self	Dallas, TX
Texas Rag	Frank Orth	November 6, 1909	Mack & Orth	Philadelphia, PA
Texas Steer	George Botsford	October 15, 1909	Jerome H. Remick	Detroit, MI
Texas Wiggle Rag	Ermon Smith	April 8, 1914	H. Kirkus Dugdale	Washington, DC
That American Rag	L. Vertugno & W.H. Kuney	November 26, 1912	Oelwein Music	Oelwein, IA

That American Ragtime Dance	David A. Jasen	June 28, 1979	The Big Three	New York, NY
That Angell Rag	Henry P. Schaefer	November 21, 1914	Regent Music	Lake Charles, LA
That Bombshell Rag	Jean Rameau	February 21, 1912	Self	Ely, NV
That Bull Frog Rag	George W. Thomas	July 27, 1917	Williams & Piron	New Orleans, LA
That Captivating Rag	Ruth Orndorff	February 23, 1912	Self	Kendallville, IN
That Captivating Rag	Charles Wellinger	September 8, 1914	Self	Hamilton, CN
That Cherry Rag	Edna Chappell Tiff	January 30, 1914	H. Kirkus Dugdale	Washington, DC
That Chinese Rag	Albert Stedman	1910	G.W. Setchell	Boston, MA
That Contagious Rag	Edward J. Mellinger	February 21, 1913	Stark Music Company	St. Louis, MO
That Contagious Rag	Wilbur Piper	1911	Self	Sidney, OH
That Corrugated Rag	Edward J. Mellinger	July 27, 1911	Stark Music Company	St. Louis, MO
That Crazy Rag	Frank Broekhoven	December 1, 1911	Self	New Orleans, LA
That Dahm Rag	Phil J. Dahm	April 13, 1912	Self	Chicago, IL
That Dandy Rag	W.L. Rand	October 3, 1912	Jerome H. Remick	Detroit, MI
That Dawggone Rag	Maurice K. Smith	March 18, 1914	W.A. Quincke	Los Angeles, CA
That Demon Rag	Russell Smith	January 27, 1911	I. Seidel Music	Indianapolis, IN
That Dixie Dip	Dippy Dip	October 14, 1912	Frank K. Root	Chicago, IL
That Dixie Rag	Victor Moulton	August 27, 1912	McKinley Music	Chicago, IL
That Dizzy Rag	Earl S. Rogers	May 15, 1916	Harmony Music	Lafayette, IN
That Dog Gone Rag	W.H. Petway	1911	Self	Nashville, TN
That Dynamite Rag	Guy Arter	June 14, 1915	Self	Prairie City, IL
That Easy Rag	Edward J. Mellinger	October 9, 1914	Mellinger Music	St. Louis, MO
That Eccentric Rag	J. Russel Robinson	January 22, 1912	I. Seidel Music	Indianapolis, IN
That Entertaining Rag	Arthur Wellesley	January 3, 1912	George W. Meyer Music	New York, NY
That Enticing Two Step	Blanch M. Tice	March 1, 1913	Self	Sioux City, IA
That Erratic Rag	J. Russel Robinson	1940	Self	New York, NY
That Ever Lovin' Rag	Walter Byron	March 28, 1952	Johnstone–Montei	New York, NY
That Everlasting Rag	Will Held	April 25, 1911	Charles E. Roat Music	Battle Creek, MI
That Fascinating Rag	Walter Rolfe	September 27, 1911	J.W. Jenkins	Kansas City, MO
That Flying Rag	Arthur Pryor	August 8, 1911	Carl Fischer	New York, NY
That Futuristic Rag	Rube Bloom	April 9, 1923	Jack Mills	New York, NY
That Gigglin' Rag	Howard M. Githens	August 1, 1912	Clarice Manning Company	New York, NY
That Gosh-Darned Two Step Rag	M. Kendree Miller	March 17, 1913	Bush & Gerts	Dallas, TX

That Gravitating Rag	Carl Eckerle	February 10, 1914	Self	Cincinnati, OH
That Hand Played Rag	David Silverman & Arthur Ward	1914	Silverman & Ward	St. Louis, MO
That Harmonizing Rag	James J. DeZego	January 28, 1914	Harmony Music	New York, NY
That Hateful Rag	Bertha Allen	July 21, 1925	Self	Des Moines, IA
That Hesitating Rag	Roy Hatfield	April 19, 1910	Self	West Milton, OH
That Hindu Rag	George L. Cobb	October 15, 1910	Walter Jacobs	Boston, MA
That Hungarian Rag	Arthur H. Gutman	October 29, 1910	Joe Morris	New York, NY
That Hypnotic Rag	Leon M. Block	February 24, 1913	Cahn & Block	Shreveport, LA
That Irresistible Rag	S. Charles Lavin	August 6, 1910	Ted Snyder Company	New York, NY
That Irresistible Rag	Fay Parker	1913	Syndicate Music	St. Louis, MO
That Irresistible Rag	Lucy B. Phillips	1912	Charles L. Johnson	Kansas City, MO
That Jumping Rag	Irma Hult	April 8, 1914	H. Kirkus Dugdale	Washington, DC
That Madrid Rag	Julius Lenzberg	May 31, 1911	Ted Snyder Company	New York, NY
That Moaning Saxophone Rag	Harry Cook & Tom Brown	September 18, 1913	Will Rossiter	Chicago, IL
That Moving Picture Rag	Willard A. Thomas	June 12, 1913	Thomas Goggan & Brothers	Galveston, TX
That Natural Rag	Ettore Bernardo Fisichelli	November 2, 1911	Ted Snyder Company	New York, NY
That Nekoma Rag	Floyd V. Swanson	March 9, 1914	Self	Moline, IL
That New Regeneration Rag	Lester Stewart Holland	October 11, 1915	Self	San Pedro, CA
That Nifty Rag	S.E. Roberts	1911	George F. Briegel	New York, NY
That Nobby Rag	Louis Fontaine	April 1, 1913	Self	Colville, WA
That Peculiar Rag	F.M. Fagan	September 12, 1910	Aubrey Stauffer	Chicago, IL
That Picture Show Rag	Horace Rosamond	October 31, 1913	Self	Stanford, TX
That Pleasing Rag	J. Fred O'Connor	November 29, 1911	Harold Rossiter	Chicago, IL
That Postal Rag	E.L. McKenzie	September 22, 1910	Self	Portland, OR
That Potatoe Bug Rag	Axel Christensen	December 1, 1916	Christensen School	Chicago, IL
That Puzzlin' Rag	Chris Smith	1912	F.B. Haviland	New York, NY
That Queen City Rag	O.B. Kramer	1916	Connett Sheet Music	Newport, KY
That Rag	Ted Browne	April 6, 1907	Thiebes–Stierlin Music	St. Louis, MO
That Real Rag	J.W. Mooney	1914	Mooney & Spears	New York, NY
That Runaway Rag	Vincent Baluta	April 23, 1914	Samuel H. Speck	New York, NY
That Scandalous Rag	Edwin F. Kendall	November 22, 1912	John Franklin Music	New York, NY

That Sentimental Rag	Mabel Tilton	May 6, 1913	Leo Feist	New York, NY
That Sparkling Rag	Frank A. Goulart	September 25, 1911	Self	Dorchester, MA
That Spooky Rag	Will J. Elener	April 20, 1912	H. Kirkus Dugdale	Washington, DC
That Spooney Dance	Jean Schwartz	July 6, 1910	Jerome H. Remick	Detroit, MI
That Stop Time Rag	Ernie Erdman	October 1, 1912	Tell Taylor	Chicago, IL
That Tango Rag	C. Roy Larson	March 16, 1914	Charles H. Henderson	New York, NY
That Tantalizing Rag	Thelma Kay	January 22, 1913	H. Kirkus Dugdale	Washington, DC
That Teasin' Rag	Joe Jordan	December 24, 1909	Joseph W. Stern	New York, NY
That Texas Rag	Nell Wright Watson	1914	Bush & Gerts	Dallas, TX
That Ticklin' Rag	Mike Bernard	July 27, 1910	Charles K. Harris	New York, NY
That Tiger Rag	W.J. Rawson, Jr.	October 6, 1911	Self	Aberdeen, SD
That Tired Feelin'	Joe Arzonia	1906	Joe Morris	Philadelphia, PA
That Tired Rag	Charlotte Blake	February 11, 1911	Jerome H. Remick	Detroit, MI
That Touchy Kid Rag	Bertha Stanfield	1912	Self	Baxter Springs, KS
That Tuneful Rag	Buel B. Risinger	January 14, 1911	Sunlight Music	Chicago, IL
That Whistling Rag	Joseph M. Foley	May 18, 1912	Self	Tharold, CN
That's a Plenty	Lew Pollack	February 25, 1914	Joe Morris	New York, NY
That's It	Charles C. Miller	December 23, 1912	Self	Billings, MT
Theatorium Rag	Leon M. Block	March 5, 1909	Self	Pine Bluff, AR
Thelma Rag	W.M. Reiff	1905	C.C. Powell	Fort Wayne, IN
Thirty-Eighth Street Rag	Les Copeland	January 17, 1913	Waterson, Berlin & Snyder	New York, NY
Thomas Brothers' Rag	Maurice B. Thomas	June 20, 1906	Sanders & Stayman	Washington, DC
Thoroughbred Rag	Joseph F. Lamb	1964	Mills Music	New York, NY
Three Hundred Green	A.E. Jeffers	June 16, 1913	Self	Springfield, MO
Three Weeks Rag	Harold G. Mitchell	May 22, 1908	Southern California Music	Los Angeles, CA
Thriller	May Aufderheide	September 4, 1909	J.H. Aufderheide	Indianapolis, IN
Thunderbolt Rag	Frank S. Butler	1913	Gotham–Attucks Music	New York, NY
Thunderbolt Rag	Samuel J. Stokes	August 19, 1910	Self	New Orleans, LA
Thunderbolt Rag	Fred T. Whitehouse	August 23, 1909	Self	Barberton, OH
Tickle It	Thomas Buster Page	August 10, 1912	Self	Lima, OH
Tickle the Ivories	Wallie Herzer	January 25, 1913	Jerome H. Remick	New York, NY
Tickled Pink	William S. Rowland	December 30, 1976	Edward B. Marks Music	New York, NY
Tickled to Death	Charles Hunter	May 11, 1901	Frank G. Fite	Nashville, TN

Tickled to Death	Ralph Larsh	1936	Ralph Larsh	Chicago, IL
Tickler	Frances Cox	1908	Charles L. Johnson	Kansas City, MO
Ticklish Rag	J.P. Traxler	January 6, 1905	Self	Lorain, OH
Tiddle-de-Winks	Melville Morris	September 16, 1916	Jerome H. Remick	New York, NY
Tierney Rag	Harry A. Tierney	August 8, 1913	Charles T. French	New York, NY
Tin Pan Rag	Lou Busch	March 5, 1952	Chatsworth Music	New York, NY
Tin Whistle Blues	Frank Capie	September 4, 1918	Jerome H. Remick & Company	New York, NY
Tipsy Topsy	Joe Keden	January 18, 1927	Jack Mills	New York, NY
Toad Stool Rag	Joseph F. Lamb	1964	Mills Music	New York, NY
Toboggan Rag	John F. Barth	August 27, 1912	Sam Fox	Cleveland, OH
Toddlin'	James P. Johnson	September 18, 1925	Perry Bradford Music	New York, NY
Toddling	William Axst & Erno Rapee	April 30, 1923	Richmond-Robbins	New York, NY
Tokio Rag	Henry Lodge	May 27, 1912	M. Witmark & Sons	New York, NY
Told at Twilight	Ed Kneisel	September 24, 1925	Jack Mills	New York, NY
Tom and Jerry Rag	Jerry Cammack	1913	St. Louis Publishing Company	St. Louis, MO
Tom Brown's Trilling Tune	Charles L. Cooke	December 20, 1916	Buck & Lowney	St. Louis, MO
Tom Cat Rag	Harry Weston	1912	Music Shop	New Orleans, LA
Tom-Boy	W. F. Bradford	February 18, 1907	Arnett–Delonais	Chicago, IL
Tomato Sauce	Fred W. Longshaw	September 18, 1925	Perry Bradford Music	New York, NY
Tomfoolery	Tom Griselle	August 30, 1923	Robbins Music	New York, NY
Too Much Raspberry	Sydney King Russell	September 6, 1916	Self	Berkeley, CA
Toodles	Clarence C. Jones	June 2, 1916	Joseph Krolage Music	Cincinnati, OH
Tooth Pick Rag	Gladys Andrews	August 25, 1912	Bixby Bros.	Buffalo, NY
Toots	Felix Arndt	November 27, 1915	G. Ricordi	New York, NY
Top Liner Rag	Joseph F. Lamb	January 4, 1916	Stark Music Company	St. Louis, MO
Topsey's Dream	Henry Williams	May 11, 1903	Shattinger Music	St. Louis, MO
Torpedo	George Oscar Young	June 5, 1917	Daniels & Wilson	San Francisco, CA
Torrid Dora	George L. Cobb	December 28, 1921	Will Rossiter	Chicago, IL
Totally Different Rag	May Aufderheide	July 16, 1910	J.H. Aufderheide	Indianapolis, IN
Town Talk	Elmer Olson	November 27, 1917	E.F. Bickhart's Song Shop	Minneapolis, MN
Town Talk	Rube Richardson & James S. White	1910	James S. White	Boston, MA
Toy Piano Rag	Bill Krenz & Eddie Ballantine	December 23, 1954	Mills Music	New York, NY

Toy Town Topics	Harold Dixon	October 7, 1927	Self	New York, NY
Transformation Rag	Babe Taylor	February 15, 1915	Howard L. Dodge	Long Beach, CA
Trey o' Hearts Rag	A.E. Holch	December 22, 1915	Self	Cripple Creek, CO
Triangle Jazz Blues	Irwin P. Leclere	February 21, 1917	Triangle Music	New Orleans, LA
Tricky Fingers	Eubie Blake	1971	Edward B. Marks Music	New York, NY
Tricky Trix	Harry Jentes	June 13, 1923	Jack Mills	New York, NY
Trilby Rag	Carey Morgan	May 11, 1915	Joseph W. Stern	New York, NY
Trillium Rag	Tom Shea	October 20, 1964	Hollis Music	New York, NY
Troubadour Rag	James Scott	February 7, 1919	Stark Music Company	St. Louis, MO
Trouble	C. Duane Crabb & Will B. Morrison	November 23, 1908	Morrison & Crabb	Indianapolis, IN
Trouble Maker Rag	Claude Messenger	August 2, 1910	Charles H. Henderson	Corry, PA
Troublesome Ivories	Eubie Blake	1971	Edward B. Marks Music	New York, NY
Try and Play It	Phil Ohman	August 5, 1922	Richmond-Robbins	New York, NY
Tucker Trot	Jules Buffano	January 4, 1921	Will Rossiter	Chicago, IL
Turkey Trot	Ribe Danmark	July 2, 1912	Jerome H. Remick	New York, NY
Turkish Towel Rag	Thomas S. Allen	January 16, 1912	Walter Jacobs	Boston, MA
Turkish Trophies	Sara B. Egan	May 31, 1907	Will Rossiter	Chicago, IL
Turpentine Rag	Jessie Murphy	November 10, 1905	Self	Greenville, TX
Twelfth Street Rag	Euday Bowman	August 31, 1914	Euday Bowman	Fort Worth, TX
Twilight Whispers	King W. Baker	June 16, 1919	Self	Rumsey, KY
Twinkle Dimples Rag	Edward C. Barroll & Hattie Leonara Smith	March 2, 1914	Mid-West Music	St. Louis, MO
Twinkle Toes	Harold Potter	1927	Jack Mills	New York, NY
Twinkles	Harry Jentes	June 1, 1925	Robbins–Engel	New York, NY
Two-Key Rag	Joe Hollander	April 19, 1916	H. Lesser & Brother	New York, NY
U. of M. Harmony Rag	Frank Stori	1914	Samuel H. Speck	New York, NY
Uncle Sammy at the Piano	Clarence Gaskill	February 26, 1923	Jack Mills	New York, NY
Uncle Tom's Cabin Rag	Harry A. Tierney	March 14, 1911	Joseph W. Stern	New York, NY
Uncle Zeke's Medley Rag	Bertha Stanfield	1912	Self	Baxter Springs, KS
Uneeda Rag Time	Bayard W. Craig	May 25, 1900	Self	Elizabeth, NJ
Universal Rag	Frank Wooster	1905	John Stark & Son	St. Louis, MO
University Rag	Claude V. Frisinger	August 28, 1911	Self	Urbana, IL

University Rag	Ruth Knippenburg	1912	Pollworth Music Publishing Company	Milwaukee, WI
Unnamed Rag	Frank Pallma	1917	Self	Minneapolis, MN
Up and Down in China	Willard Robison	September 14, 1926	Robbins-Engel	New York, NY
Up and Down the Keys	Phil Ohman	September 30, 1922	Richmond-Robbins	New York, NY
Upright and Grand	Frank Banta & PeterDeRose	September 1, 1923	Richmond–Robbins	New York, NY
Vanity Rag	Paul Pratt	April 17, 1909	J.H. Aufderheide	Indianapolis, IN
Variety Rag	Harry A. Tierney	July 1, 1912	George W. Meyer Music	New York, NY
Varsity Days	Frank W. Ryan	September 30, 1907	Self	Topeka, KS
Velma Chocolates	Ernst Otto	August 7, 1909	Self	Davenport, IA
Ventura Rag	Louis Mentel	March 12, 1907	Mentel Brothers	Cincinnati, OH
Very Raggy	Mrs. Merrill Morgan	June 10, 1907	Self	Rotan, TX
Victory Rag	James Scott	1921	Stark Music Company	St. Louis, MO
Virginia Creeper	Mae Davis	December 21, 1907	Walter Jacobs	Boston, MA
Virginia Creeper	Billy Mayerl	October 12, 1925	Sam Fox	Cleveland, OH
Virginia Creeper Rag	Chas. H. Roth	1909	Roth & Redding	Washington, DC
Virginia Rag	Bryant Gallagher	December 7, 1916	Mentel Brothers	Cincinnati, OH
Virginia Rag	Sydney P. Harris	July 22, 1907	Self	New York, NY
Virginia Rag	Isham E. Jones	November 11, 1913	Jones Brothers	Saginaw, MI
Virginia Rag	Harriet Reynolds Marchant	February 19, 1912	H. Kirkus Dugdale	Washington, DC
Vivacity Rag	Frank C. Keithley	February 5, 1910	New York & Chicago Music	Chicago, IL
Volcanic Rag	Leah Monks Robb	1911	Gotham–Attucks Music	New York, NY
Waiman Rag	James R. Shannon	June 27, 1910	Grinnell Bros.	Detroit, MI
Walhalla	Paul Pratt	January 13, 1910	J.H. Aufderheide	Indianapolis, IN
Wall Street Rag	Scott Joplin	February 23, 1909	Seminary Music	New York, NY
Wash Day Rag	Charles Goeddel	October 14, 1911	Panella & Murray Music	Pittsburgh, PA
Wash Rag	F.H. Losey	November 16, 1910	Carl Fischer	New York, NY
Water Bug	Walter E. Miles	November 9, 1925	Sam Fox	Cleveland, OH
Water Queen	Homer Denney	June 8, 1906	Denney & Flanigan	Cincinnati, OH
Water Wagon Blues	George L. Cobb	1919	Walter Jacobs	Boston, MA
Watermelon	Harry S. Krossin	1909	Self	Minneapolis, MN

Watermelon Mose	Floyd Willis	November 9, 1907	Self	Covington, KY
Watermelon Trust	Harry C. Thompson	May 25, 1906	Barron & Thompson	New York, NY
Weaving Around Rag	Lawrence A. Mitchel	January 20, 1913	Sam Fox	Cleveland, OH
Webster Grove Rag	Axel Christensen	March 31, 1915	Christensen School	Chicago, IL
Wedding Bells Rag	Al B. Coney	December 10, 1910	Will Rossiter	Chicago, IL
Weeping Willow	H.A. Fischler	January 16, 1911	Vandersloot Music	Williamsport, PA
Weeping Willow	Scott Joplin	June 6, 1903	Val A. Reis Music	St. Louis, MO
Weird Rag	Phil Schwartz	September 18, 1911	Will Rossiter	Chicago, IL
Welsh Rarebit	Maude E. Palmiter	1907	R.V. Gould	Rockford, IL
What Is It?	Oswald E. Planchard	1906	Cable Company	New Orleans, LA
What's Your Hurry?	Effie Kamman	January 19, 1923	Jerome H. Remick	New York, NY
Whipped Cream	Percy Wenrich	January 18, 1913	Wenrich–Howard	New York, NY
Whippin' the Keys	Sam Goold	1923	Stark & Cowan	New York, NY
Whirl Wind	J. Russel Robinson	December 11, 1911	Stark Music Company	St. Louis, MO
White Rag	Ella White	February 9, 1911	W.A. Cantrell	Charleston, WV
White Seal Rag	Kittie M. Hamel	October 21, 1907	Jerome H. Remick	New York, NY
Whitewash Man	Jean Schwartz	September 8, 1908	Cohan & Harris	New York, NY
Whittling Remus	Thomas E. Broady	April 20, 1900	Henry A. French	Nashville, TN
Who Got the Lemon?	Marcella A. Henry	June 26, 1909	Self	Peru, IL
Who Let the Cows Out	Charles Humfeld	March 10, 1910	Howard & Browne Music	St. Louis, MO
Who's Who	Melville Morris	June 6, 1917	Jerome H. Remick	New York, NY
Whoa! Maude	Will H. Etter	July 29, 1905	Thomas Goggan & Brothers	Galveston, TX
Whoa! Nellie	George Gould	1915	Charles N. Daniels Music	San Francisco, CA
Whoa! You Heifer	Al Verges	October 13, 1904	Hakenjos	New Orleans, LA
Why We Smile	Charles Hunter	September 28, 1903	Frank G. Fite	Nashville, TN
Wide Awake Rag	Jessie Spaenhower	November 3, 1915	Marks–Goldsmith Company	Washington, DC
Wig-Wag Rag	Harry C. Thompson	November 9, 1911	Leo Feist	New York, NY
Wiggle Rag	George Botsford	October 15, 1909	Jerome H. Remick	Detroit, MI
Wild Cat Blues	Thomas "Fats" Waller & Clarence Williams	September 24, 1923	Clarence Williams Music	New York, NY
Wild Cherries	Ted Snyder	September 23, 1908	Ted Snyder Company	New York, NY
Wild Flower Rag	Clarence Williams	August 21, 1916	Williams & Piron Music	New Orleans, LA

Wild Flower Rag	Carlotta Williamson	August 27, 1910	Colonial Music	Boston, MA
Wild Grapes Rag	Clarence Jones	1910	Emerson Music	Cincinnati, OH
Wild-Fire Rag	Holmes Travis	April 5, 1911	M.L. Carlson	Chicago, IL
Will o' the Wisp Rag	Richard Haasz	April 3, 1911	Charles H. Henderson	Corry, PA
William's Wedding	Harry A. Tierney	June 23, 1911	Ted Snyder Company	New York, NY
Wilson's Favorite Rag	Otto L. Stock, Jr.	July 11, 1913	Self	Pine Island, MN
Winnie's Arrival	Edna Ralya	1905	W.H. Willis	Cincinnati, OH
Winter Garden Rag	Abe Olman	December 5, 1912	Will Rossiter	Chicago, IL
Wippin' the Ivories	Henry Lange	May 4, 1923	Waterson, Berlin & Snyder	New York, NY
Wireless Rag	Adaline Shepherd	August 21, 1909	Standard Music	Chicago, IL
Wise Gazabo	Frank C. Keithley	1905	Keithley–Carl Publishing	Newton, IA
Wish Bone	Charlotte Blake	March 6, 1909	Jerome H. Remick	New York, NY
Wizzle Dozzle	Harry Bell & Lloyd L. Johnson	April 25, 1910	Bell & Johnson	Princeton, IN
Woolworth Rag	F. Henri Klickmann	May 7, 1913	Ajax Music	Chicago, IL
Woozy	A.E. Groves	December 14, 1903	Arnett-Delonais	Chicago, IL
World's Fair Rag	Harvey M. Babcock	May 13, 1912	Self	San Francisco, CA
Wounded Lion	Karl C. Robertson	1911	Self	Kansas City, MO
Wyoming Prance	Kerry Mills	November 14, 1910	F.A. Mills	New York, NY
X-Ray Rag	O. Lee Shoemaker	May 18, 1914	Self	Denver, CO
X.L. Rag	L. Edgar Settle	December 21, 1903	A.W. Perry & Sons	Sedalia, MO
Yankee Doodle Rag	Garfield Wilson	June 15, 1911	Will Rossiter	Chicago, IL
Yankee Girl	Harry L. Stone	December 24, 1919	Self	Spokane, WA
Yankee Land	Max Hoffman	August 31, 1904	Rogers Bros. Music	New York, NY
Yellow Bridge	Frankie Gooch McCool	December 29, 1899	Self	Indianapolis, IN
Yellow Rose Rag	Will H. Etter	September 1, 1904	L. Grunewald Company	New Orleans, LA
Yellow Rose Rag	Terry Waldo	December 30, 1976	Edward B. Marks Music	New York, NY
Yiddish Rag	A. Traxler	August 15, 1902	Self	Sharon, PA
Yoestic Two Step	Harry N. Koverman	1904	W.H. Willis	Cincinnati, OH
You Tell 'Em, Ivories	Zez Confrey	August 5, 1921	Jack Mills	New York, NY
Yumuri	Jos. LaCalle	April 25, 1903	Joseph W. Stern	New York, NY
Yvonette	Bill Krenz	February 1, 1935	M.M. Cole	Chicago, IL

Zephyr	Bill Krenz	February 12, 1935	M.M. Cole	Chicago, IL
Zig Zag Rag	H. Anderson	November 21, 1910	Charles K. Harris	New York, NY
Zig Zag Rag	Bob Emmerich	1926	Triangle Music	New York, NY
Zinzinnati	Nancy Bierbaum	1907	Self	Cincinnati, OH
Zu-Zu Rag	Max E. Fischler	August 30, 1916	John Franklin Music	New York, NY

Chapter Sources

Chapter 1

"An Interview with Arthur Marshall!!" *Rag Times* (September 1987).

Edward A. Berlin. *King of Ragtime: Scott Joplin and His Era.* New York: Oxford University Press, 1994.

"Blind Missouri Musician Wins International Fame," *Sedalia Capital* (December 4, 1959).

Dorothy Daniels Birk. *The World Came to St. Louis.* St. Louis: Bethany Press, 1979.

Nan Bostick. "Meet 'Uncle Charlie.'" *Rag Times* (September 1998).

S. Brunson Campbell. "The Ragtime Kid (An Autobiography)." *Jazz Report* (No. 6).

——— and R. J. Carew. "Sedalia, Missouri, Cradle of Ragtime." *Record Changer* (May and June 1945).

Russ Cassidy. "Centennial Recollections with Joseph Lamb." *Rag Times* (November 1987).

"Charles Johnson Dies." *Kansas City Times* (December 30, 1950).

James Milford Crabb. "A History of Music in Kansas City (1900–1965)." Doctoral dissertation prepared for the faculty of the University of Missouri at Kansas City, 1967.

"Did You Know Ragtime Music Was Born in Sedalia?" *Sedalia Democrat* (June 29, 1947).

Richard A. Egan, Jr. *Brun Campbell: The Music of the Ragtime Kid.* St. Louis: Morgan Publishing, 1993.

Gene Jones. *Tom Turpin: His Life and Music.* Savannah, Georgia: Tom Turpin Festival Press, 1995.

William H. Kinney. "James Scott and the Culture of Classic Ragtime." *American Music* (Summer 1991).

Ernst C. Krohn. *Music Publishing in St. Louis* (completed and edited by J. Bunker Clark). Warren, Mich.: Harmonie Park Press, 1988.

Landon Laird. "The '12th Street Rag' Story." *Kansas City Times* (October 23, 1942).

"Missouri Was the Birthplace of Ragtime." *St. Louis Post-Dispatch* (January 18, 1961).

"More About Bowman." *Rag Times* (November 1983).

Peter A. Munstedt. "Kansas City Music Publishing: The First Fifty Years." *American Music* (Winter 1991).

"Music Concern Increases Capital." *Kansas City Post* (August 2, 1908).

Terry Parrish. "The Paul Pratt Story." *Rag Times* (January 1984).

Dennis Pash. "E. Harry Kelly." *Rag Times* (March 1976).

———. "No Ragtime for Pryor." *Rag Times* (November 1979).

Perry's Musical Magazine. Sedalia, Missouri: A.W. Perry & Sons (May 1915).

J. B. Price. "Ragtime Has Played Integral Role in History of Joplin." *Joplin Globe* (June 24, 1973).

Patricia Rice. "Blind Boone: Link to Ragtime Origins." *Rag Times* (March 1978).

J. Russel Robinson. "Dixieland Piano." *Down Beat* (August 1947).

Kevin Sanders. "Doc Brown, Cakewalker." *Rag Times* (September 1986).

Philip A. Stewart. *The Music of Charles Leslie Johnson.* Paola, Kansas: Philip A. Stewart, 1993.

"Struggle to Keep Music Press Running." *Sedalia Democrat* (October 24, 1965).

The WPA Guide to 1930s Missouri. Lawrence, Kansas: University of Kansas Press, 1986.

Trebor Jay Tichenor. "John Stillwell Stark, Piano Ragtime Publisher. *BMR Journal* (Fall 1989).

———. Telephone interviews with Gene Jones, August 1998.

Marvin L. VanGilder. "The Childhood of Clarence Woods." *Rag Times* (March 1978).

———. "H. Clarence Woods." *The Ragtimer* (September–October 1976).

———. "James Scott." *Rag Times* (May 1977).

Dick Zimmerman. "C.L. Woolsey, the Ragtime Doctor." *Rag Times* (May 1976).

———. *Gems of Texas Ragtime.* Grass Valley, California: American Ragtime Co., 1996.

Chapter 2

"Alvin Marx and 'Frigid Frolics.'" *Rag Times* (January 1986).

Bruce and Tom Arneson. "The Roy Bargy Story." *Rag Times* (September 1972).

Herbert Asbury. *Gem of the Prairie.* New York: Alfred A. Knopf, 1940.

Paul E. Bierley. *Hallelujah Trombone!* Columbus, Ohio: Integrity Press, 1982.

David J. Bodenhamer and Robert G. Barrows, eds. *The Encyclopedia of Indianapolis.* Bloomington, Indiana: University of Indiana Press, 1994.

Q. David Bowers. *Put Another Nickel In.* New York: Bonanza Books, 1966.

Chester A. Bradley. "Origin of 'Missouri Waltz' Traced Through Maze of Conflicting Accounts." *Kansas City Star* (March 1949).

Robert L. Brubaker. *Making Music Chicago Style.* Chicago: Chicago Historical Society, 1985.

Christensen's Ragtime Review. Chicago: 1914–1918.

Ann Crooks. "Ragtime's Coming Back." *Lake Superior Port Cities Magazine* (July–August 1986).

Wendell P. Dabney. *Cincinnati's Colored Citizens.* Cincinnati: Dabney Publishing Co., 1926.

Emmett Dedmon. *Fabulous Chicago.* New York: Atheneum, 1983.

Stephen Kent Goodman. "Fred Jewell, the Forgotten Ragtime of Indiana's March King." *Rag Times* (November 1991).

———. "T. Fred Henry, Iowa's Greatest Bandmaster." *Rag Times* (May 1993).

———. Telephone interviews with David A. Jasen, July 1998.

John Edward Hasse. *Cincinnati Ragtime.* Cincinnati, Ohio: John Edward Hasse, 1983.

———. and Frank J. Gillis. *Indiana Ragtime.* Indianapolis, Indiana: Indiana Historical Society, 1981.

"Homer Denney." *Rag Times* (July 1982).

Rick Kennedy. "Clarence M. Jones." *78 Quarterly* (Vol. 1 No. 9, 1995).

Carolyn A. Lindeman. *Women Composers of Ragtime.* Bryn Mawr, Pennsylvania: Theodore Presser Co., 1985.

Karen Linn. *That Half-Barbaric Twang: The Banjo in American Popular Culture.* Urbana, Illinois: University of Illinois Press, 1991.

W. R. Meyers. "Remembering Alvin Marx—A Letter Home." *The Lake Superior Ragtimer* (December 1994).

"Milwaukee Girl Author of Campaign Lyric." *American Musician and Art Journal* (October 23, 1908).

Terry Parrish. "The Paul Pratt Story," Parts 1 and 2. *Rag Times* (January and March 1984).

Frank Powers. "Ragtime Antecedents in Cincinnati." *Rag Times* (May 1978).

David Reffkin. Telephone interviews with David A. Jasen, July 1998.

Harvey N. Roehl. *Keys to a Musical Past.* Vestal, N.Y.: Vestal Press, 1968.

"Sad Passage: Steamboat Calliope Musician, Mr. Fix-It, Homer Denney Dies." *Cincinnati Enquirer* (September 23, 1975).

Tom Shea. "Bart Howard." *The Ragtimer* (Vol. 6 No. 3, 1967).

———. "Finney's Orchestra." *The Ragtime Society* (July–August 1965).

Theodore Winton Thorson. "A History of Music Publishing in Chicago." Doctoral dissertation submitted to the Graduate School of Northwestern University. Evanston, Illinois. 1961.

"Two-Piano Ragtime: How Did It Really Sound?" *Rag Times* (March 1998).

Dick Zimmerman. "Cecil Duane Crabb." *Rag Times* (September 1995).

———. Telephone interviews with David A. Jasen, July 1998.

Chapter 3

Elliott Adams. "N. Weldon Cocroft: Ragtime Pioneer." *Rag Times* (May 1994).

Roy J. Carew. "New Orleans Recollections." *The Record Changer* (June 1943).

"F. A. Guttenberger Shot for Burglar." Macon, Georgia: *Daily Telegraph* (November 1912).

Pops Foster. *Pops Foster: The Autobiography of a New Orleans Jazzman.* Berkeley, California: University of California Press, 1973.

David Lee Joyner. "Southern Ragtime and Its Transition to Published Blues." Doctoral dissertation presented to the faculty of the Graduate School at Memphis State University, 1986.

Jacques Kelly. "Baltimore's Other Ragtime Composer." *The* (Baltimore) *News-American* (September 9, 1974).

"Prof. Guttenberger Dies from Apoplexy." Macon, Georgia: *Daily Telegraph* (September 1, 1905).

Louis Panzeri. *Louisiana Composers.* New Orleans, Louisiana: Dinstahl Printing and Publishing, 1972.

Al Rose. "Robert Hoffman." *Rag Times* (September 1975).

———, Vaughn L. Glasgow and Diana Rose. *Played with Immense Success: A Social History of Louisiana (1840–1940) as Shown in Its Published Sheet Music.* Notes on the exhibition of the same title. New Orleans, Louisiana: Louisiana State Museum, 1978.

Charles Reagan Wilson and William Ferris, eds. *Encyclopedia of Southern Culture.* Chapel Hill, North Carolina: University of North Carolina Press, 1989.

Chapter 4

Herbert Asbury. *The Barbary Coast.* New York: Alfred A. Knopf, 1933.

Ted Dealey. *Diaper Days of Dallas.* Dallas, Texas: SMU Press, 1966.

"Ed Little Dies." *Variety* (October 18, 1932).

Roy Hemming. *The Melody Lingers On: The Great Songwriters and Their Movie Musicals.* New York: Newmarket Press, 1986.

Thomas J. Noel. *The City and the Saloon: Denver 1858–1916.* Lincoln, Nebraska: University of Nebraska Press, 1982.

"Prominent Young Couple Wed—Stephenson–Soladay." *Fulton* (South Dakota) *Advocate* (November 26, 1914).

Merle Irene Smith. *Seattle Had a Tin Pan Alley, Too!* Seattle, Washington: Merle Irene Smith, 1989.

The Story of Sherman, Clay (2nd edition). San Francisco, California: Sherman, Clay & Company, 1952.

Bruce Vermazen. "The Jay Roberts Story." *Rag Times* (January 1988).

———. "The Jay Roberts Story Continued." *Rag Times* (November 1991).

Evelyn Wells. *Champagne Days of San Francisco.* New York: Doubleday, 1939.

Workers of the Writers' Program of the WPA in the State of Texas. *Texas: A Guide to the Lone Star State.* New York: Hastings House, 1940.

Chapter 5

George L. Cobb. "Just Between You and Me." *Melody* column excerpts. *Rag Times* (November 1988).

Douglas Gilbert. *American Vaudeville.* New York: Whittlesey House, 1940.

"H. Kirkus Dugdale and Associates Arrested." *The Music Trades* (October 11, 1913).

Robert H. Larson, Richard J. Morris, and John F. Piper, Jr. *Williamsport.* Woodland Hills, California: Windsor Publications, 1984.

Melody. Boston: Walter Jacobs Co., 1918-1934.

Al Palmer. "One Ambition Unfulfilled, Billy Eckstein Dies." *The* (Montreal) *Gazette* (September 24, 1963).

"The Musical Building: A Little Story of a Big Success." Washington, DC: The H. Kirkus Dugdale Co., 1913.

The Tuneful Yankee. Boston: Walter Jacobs Co., 1917.

Dick Zimmerman. "The Incredible Billy Eckstein." *Rag Times* (March 1968).

———. "The Saga of 'Johnson Rag.'" *Rag Times* (September 1997).

Chapter 6

Laurence Bergreen. *As Thousands Cheer.* New York: Viking, 1990.

Edward A. Berlin. "A Different Perspective on Tin Pan Alley." *CBMR Digest* (Spring 1991).

Lawrence W. Brown. "An Awful Lot of Music in Detroit." *Among Friends* (Winter 1958–59).

Ann Charters. "The Acknowledged Rag-Time Champion of the U.S." *Ragtime Review* (October 1962).

Leonard Feist. "The Early History of Music Publishing." *ASCAP in Action* (Fall 1980).

Mary Henderson. *The City and the Theatre.* Clifton, New Jersey: James T. White and Co., 1973.

"Jack Mills Dies." *Rag Times* (May 1979).

Edward B. Marks. *They All Sang.* New York: Viking Press, 1934.

"Rag-Time Piano Players." *Police Gazette* (January 20, 1900).

"Ted Snyder Talks About the Old Days." Reprint of a 1923 interview in *Metronome Orchestra Monthly. Rag Times* (September 1976).

"The Origin of Ragtime! Harney and Haynes." *The Billboard* (September 3, 1910).

Isidore Witmark and Isaac Goldberg. *From Ragtime to Swingtime.* New York: Lee Furman, Inc., 1939.

Dick Zimmerman. "Henry Lodge: The Providence Years." *Rag Times* (March 1994).

———. "The Henry Lodge Story." *Rag Times* (January 1976).

Select Bibliography

American Musician and Art Journal. New York: 1906–1914.

ASCAP Biographical Dictionary. New York: American Society of Composers, Authors, and Publishers, 1966.

Blesh, Rudi, and Harriet Janis. *They All Played Ragtime,* 4th edition. New York: Oak Publications, 1971.

Bordman, Gerald. *American Musical Theatre.* New York: Oxford University Press: 1978.

Claghorn, Charles Eugene. *Biographical Dictionary of American Music.* West Nyack, N.Y.: Parker Publishing Company, 1973.

Dichter, Harry, and Elliott Shapiro. *Handbook of Early American Sheet Music 1768–1889.* New York: Dover Publications, 1977.

Hasse, John Edward, ed. *Ragtime: Its History, Composers and Music.* New York: Schirmer Books, 1985.

Jablonski, Edward. *The Encyclopedia of American Music.* Garden City, N.Y.: Doubleday, 1981.

Jackson, Richard, ed. *Popular Songs of Nineteenth-Century America.* New York: Dover Publications, 1976.

Jasen, David A. *Recorded Ragtime 1897–1958.* Hamden, Connecticut: Archon Books, 1973.

———. *Tin Pan Alley.* New York: Donald I. Fine, 1988.

——— and Gene Jones. *Spreadin' Rhythm Around: Black Popular Songwriters, 1880–1930.* New York: Schirmer Books, 1998.

——— and Trebor Jay Tichenor. *Rags and Ragtime: A Musical History.* New York: Seabury Press, 1978.

Linton, Calvin D., ed. *The American Almanac.* Nashville, Tennessee: Thomas Nelson, Inc., 1977.

Music Trade Review. New York: 1899–1933.

Nergal, Ory Mazar, editor-in-chief. *The Encyclopedia of American Cities.* New York: E.P. Dutton, 1980.

Rag Times. Los Angeles and Grass Valley, California: 1967–1999.

Rust, Brian. *Jazz Records, 1897–1942.* 2 vols. New Rochelle, N.Y.: Arlington House, 1978.

Tichenor, Trebor Jay, ed. *Ragtime Rarities.* New York: Dover Publications, 1975.

———, ed. *Ragtime Rediscoveries.* New York: Dover Publications, 1979.

Waldo, Terry. *This Is Ragtime.* New York: DaCapo Press, 1991.

Whitburn, Joel. *Pop Memories, 1890-1954.* Menomonee Falls, Wisconsin: Record Research, 1986.

Index of Music Titles

General Index

ABOUT THE AUTHORS

David A. Jasen is an internationally recognized authority on ragtime, early jazz, and popular song. He is the author of numerous books, including *Tin Pan Alley, Recorded Ragtime, 1897–1958, Spreadin' Rhythm Around: Black Popular Songwriters, 1880–1930* (with Gene Jones), and *Rags and Ragtime: A Musical History* (with Trebor J. Tichenor). He has edited several collections of ragtime-era sheet music and produced numerous CD reissues of early pop song and ragtime recordings. He is Professor of Communications at the C.W. Post Campus of Long Island University.

Gene Jones, from Olla, Louisiana, is an actor and music historian. He has written monographs on Tom Turpin and the Original Dixieland Jazz Band, along with *Spreadin' Rhythm Around* with David A. Jasen. He is also the author of the ragtime revue, *Fables in Slang*, based on the writing of George Ade. He has appeared in Broadway and off-Broadway shows, and his voice is heard in several of Ken Burns's epic documentaries, including *The Civil War, The West*, and *Lewis and Clark*.

Gene Jones

David A. Jasen